# Hegel After Derrida

Hegel occupies a unique position within the development of Derrida's thought, for Hegel is both the antithesis of deconstruction and its very point of departure. Derida has stressed from his earliest work to his book-length study of Hegel, *Glas*, that we must come to terms with Hegel's work. For one of the fundamental tasks of deconstruction is to settle accounts with Hegel and his legacy.

This tension has been an essential but crucially overlooked feature of Derrida's work and is addressed for the first time in this fascinating collection. *Hegel After Derrida* presents eleven outstanding essays by some of the key commentators on continental philosophy today and approaches the Hegel–Derrida question from three vantage points. Part One presents readings of Hegel that pursue lines of thought opened up by Derrida. Part Two investigates the implications of Derrida's work on Hegel for our understanding of Marx and Freud. Part Three, a central feature of the book, is devoted to the contemporary significance of *Glas*, Derrida's full-length study of Hegel.

*Hegel After Derrida* provides a much-needed investigation not only of the importance of Hegel and the importance of Derrida's work on Hegel but also of the very foundations of postmodern and deconstructionist thought. It will be essential reading for all those engaged with the work of Derrida and Hegel as well as anyone seeking to explore some of the basic but neglected aspects of deconstruction.

**Contributors**: Stuart Barnett, Robert Bernasconi, Simon Critchley, Suzanne Gearhart, Werner Hamacher, Heinz Kimmerle, Jean-Luc Nancy, John H. Smith, Henry Sussman, Kevin Thompson, Andrzej Warminski.

**Stuart Barnett** is Associate Professor of English at Central Connecticut State University.

# Warwick Studies in European Philosophy

Edited by Andrew Benjamin
*Professor in Philosophy, University of Warwick*

This series presents the best and most original work being done within the European philosophical tradition. The books included in the series seek not merely to reflect what is taking place within European philosophy, rather they will contribute to the growth and development of that plural tradition. Work written in the English language as well as translations into English are to be included, engaging the tradition at all levels – whether by introductions that show the contemporary philosophical force of certain works, or in collections that explore an important thinker or topic, as well as in significant contributions that call for their own critical evaluation.

# Hegel After Derrida

*Edited by Stuart Barnett*

London and New York

First published 1998
by Routledge
11 New Fetter Lane, London EC4P 4EE

Simultaneously published in the USA and Canada
by Routledge
29 West 35th Street, New York, NY 10001

Typeset in Perpetua by J&L Composition Ltd, Filey, North Yorkshire

Printed and bound in Great Britain by
T.J. International Ltd, Padstow, Cornwall

*British Library Cataloguing in Publication Data*
A catalogue record for this book is available from the British Library

*Library of Congress Cataloging in Publication Data*
Hegel after Derrida/edited by Stuart Barnett
p. cm. (Warwick studies in European philosophy)
Includes bibliographical references.
1. Derrida, Jacques, *Glas.* 2. Hegel, Georg Wilhelm Friedrich,
1770–1831 I. Barnett, Stuart II. Series.
B2948.D463H44 1998
193–dc21 97–24518
CIP

ISBN 0–415–17104–0 (hbk)
ISBN 0–415–17105–9 (pbk)

# Contents

*List of contributors*                                                    vii

*Acknowledgements*                                                        ix

Introduction: Hegel Before Derrida                                          1

**Part I**
**Hegel After Derrida**                                                    **39**

1 Hegel at the Court of the Ashanti
  Robert Bernasconi                                                        41

2 Of Spirit(s) and Will(s)
  John H. Smith                                                            64

3 The Surprise of the Event
  Jean-Luc Nancy                                                          91

4 (The End of Art with the Mask)
  Werner Hamacher                                                         105

5 Eating My God
  Stuart Barnett                                                          131

**Part II**
**After Hegel After Derrida**                                             **145**

6 The Remnants of Philosophy: Psychoanalysis After *Glas*
  Suzanne Gearhart                                                        147

# Contents

7  Hegel/Marx: Consciousness and Life
Andrzej Warminski                                                    171

**Part III**
**Reading** *Glas*                                                   **195**

8  A Commentary Upon Derrida's Reading of Hegel in *Glas*
Simon Critchley                                                      197

9  On Derrida's Hegel Interpretation
Heinz Kimmerle                                                       227

10  Hegelian Dialectic and the Quasi-Transcendental in *Glas*
Kevin Thompson                                                      239

11  Hegel, *Glas*, and the Broader Modernity
Henry Sussman                                                       260

*Notes*                                                             293
*Select Bibliography*                                               346
*Index*                                                             351

# Contributors

**Stuart Barnett** is Associate Professor of English at Central Connecticut State University and is the author of several articles on literature and critical theory. He is currently editing and translating a volume by Friedrich Schlegel.

**Robert Bernasconi** is Moss Professor of Philosophy at Memphis State University. He is the author of *The Question of Language in Heidegger's History of Being* and *The Provocation of Levinas: Rethinking the Other Levinas and Heidegger*. He is also the editor, together with David Wood, of *Derrida and Différance*.

**Simon Critchley** is Professor of Philosophy at Essex University and is the author of *The Ethics of Deconstruction* in addition to numerous articles on philosophy.

**Suzanne Gearhart**, Professor of French at UC Irvine, is the author of *The Open Boundary of History in Fiction: A Critical Approach to the French Enlightenment* and *The Interrupted Dialectic: Philosophy, Psychoanalysis, and Their Tragic Other* in addition to numerous articles on literature and critical theory.

**Werner Hamacher** is Professor of German and the Humanities Center, Johns Hopkins University. He is the author of *Premises* and *Pleroma* in addition to numerous articles on philosophy and literary theory.

**Jean-Luc Nancy**, Professor of Philosophy at the Université de Strasbourg, is the author of numerous books and articles on philosophy. Titles that have appeared in English translation include *The Literary Absolute*, *The Birth to Presence*, *The Inoperative Community*, and *The Experience of Freedom*.

**Heinz Kimmerle**, Professor of Philosophy at the University of Rotterdam, has written numerous books and articles on topics ranging from hermeneutics to African philosophy. He has also written *Derrida zur Einführung*.

**John H. Smith** is Professor of German at the University of California at Irvine. He is the author of *The Spirit and Its Letter: Traces of Rhetoric in Hegel's Philosophy of 'Bildung,'* as well as numerous articles on literature and philosophy.

**Henry Sussman** is Professor of Comparative Literature at SUNY Buffalo. In addition to numerous articles on literature and critical theory, he is the author of *The Hegelian Aftermath*, *High Resolution: Critical Theory and the Problem of Literacy*, *Psyche and Text: The Sublime and the Grandiose in Literature, Psychopathology, and Culture*, and *Afterimages of Modernity: Structure and Indifference in Twentieth-Century Literature*.

**Kevin Thompson** is a Research Fellow at Florida Atlantic University. He has just completed a dissertation on contemporary continental philosophy.

**Andrzej Warminski** is Professor of Comparative Literature at the University of California at Irvine and is the author of *Readings in Interpretation: Hegel, Heidegger, Hölderlin* in addition to numerous articles on literature and philosophy.

# Acknowledgments

Rodolphe Gasché and Henry Sussman graciously provided insight and encouragement during the conceptualization of this project. Central Connecticut State University generously supported my work with grants and release time. Many people assisted this undertaking in ways they may not even be aware of: Benjamin Bennett, David Blitz, Peter Burgard, Lynn Festa, Eva Geulen, Werner Hamacher, Geoffrey Hartman, Jonathan Hess, Carol Jacobs, Loftus Jestin, Joan Packer, Marie-Claire Rohinsky, Sylvia Schmitz-Burgard, and Liliane Weissberg. I thank them all. I would also like to thank Andrew Benjamin, who is truly an editor's editor, Tony Bruce, Sarah Brown, and Dennis Hodgson at Routledge, who guided this volume through the *Aufhebungen* of the publication process, the indifatigable inter-library loan office of the Burritt library, the friendly and helpful staff at the Avon library, where much of the work on this volume was done, and the contributors, who made this project what it is and who kindly and patiently put up with me. Finally, I would like to thank my personal instructors in *die sittliche Substanz als unmittelbarer Geist*, my wife Patricia and my children Nicholas and Katherine.

Simon Critchley's essay first appeared in a special issue of the *Bulletin of the Hegel Society of Great Britain* (No. 18, 1988). It is reprinted here – with some alterations – by permission of the author.

Heinz Kimmerle's essay first appeared as 'Über Derridas Hegeldeutung' in *Philosophie und Poesie: Otto Pöggeler zum 60. Geburtstag*, Annemarie Gethmann-Siefert (ed) (Stuttgart: Fromman-Holzboog Verlag, 1988). It is has been translated by permission of the author and the publisher.

Jean-Luc Nancy's essay first appeared in *Être singulier pluriel* (Paris: Galilée, 1996). It is translated and published with the permission of Stanford University

Press. This essay will appear in a forthcoming Stanford University Press edition of the entire work, translated into English by Robert Richardson and Ann O'Byrne.

Andrzej Warminki's essay first appeared in *Yale French Studies*. It is published here by permission of the author and Yale University Press.

# Introduction

## Hegel Before Derrida

### *Stuart Barnett*

We will never be finished with the reading or rereading of Hegel, and, in a certain way, I do nothing other than attempt to explain myself on this point.

Jacques Derrida

The ultimate task facing a volume such as this one is the demonstration of the validity of what is implied in its very title. To begin this task, one must consider what, in fact, is contained in the phrase 'Hegel after Derrida.' First of all, it implies that the work of Jacques Derrida is something of an event in the understanding of Hegel, an event that constitutes a possible turning point in our relation to Hegel. It also implies that Derrida gestures towards a future that awaits both Hegel and us. The essays contained in this volume attempt to perform the beginning of the future that awaits Hegel in the wake of the intervention of Derrida. The true scope and nature of this future is, to a great extent, yet to be determined. What can and must be discussed at this point, however, is what lends the notion of Hegel after Derrida its critical focus.

This is necessary because the ultimate contention of this volume is that the relation between Derrida and Hegel is not simply one more topic in a range of narratives of philosophical affiliation. Both philosophers have inspired numerous studies of affiliation. Yet when one considers that Hegel – according to a general critical consensus – defines the modernity that our postmodern era seeks to escape, then the investigation of the relation between Derrida and Hegel acquires a certain significance. For our age can justifiably be character-ized as the desperate attempt to be a post-Hegelian culture. Our culture seeks to come 'after Hegel.' It is in contrast to this desire that the notion of 'Hegel after Derrida' acquires its polemical force. For the notion entails more than

1

simply setting forth the nature of Derrida's reading of Hegel. The true claim in the notion is that our culture has not succeeded in coming 'after Hegel.' Hegel, instead, persists as a philosophical and cultural force. It is this insight that organizes Derrida's work on Hegel. Derrida examines what remains of Hegel. Rather than employing Hegel as a straw man in order to announce a culture that has transcended Hegel, Derrida submits to what remains of Hegel in order to lend clarity to the force and subtlety as well as the illogic of speculative idealism. It is this procedure of deconstruction that functions to clear a path towards the closure of what Henry Sussman has aptly termed the 'Hegelian aftermath.' To truly overcome Hegel, then, it is necessary to begin to understand the extent to which we still stand before Hegel.

There will, apparently, be no end to Hegel. It is ironic and fitting that the philosopher who thought through so carefully the problems of historical culmination, transformation, and closure should himself become the primary index of an epoch in thinking that refuses to come to closure. Whether one argues for modernity as an uncompleted project or against modernity as having already collapsed into postmodernism, Hegel seems to be an implicit and explicit battlefield on which the possibility of the closure of modernity is fought out. Indeed, those who would argue that postmodernism is the final renunciation of all that is Hegelian do agree nonetheless that Hegel defines that modernity which is to be overcome. Accordingly, Hegel is seen as the architect of the dream of an absolute metanarrative of the historical unfolding of an always unitary reason. In all the clamor to proclaim postmodernism, however, one cannot avoid the suspicion that the simplification of Hegel that it entails is a necessary and enabling misreading. It is a misreading necessitated, moreover, by the fact that all that postmodernism proclaims has been carefully mapped out by Hegel. For Hegel is not only the philosopher of the unity of reason, he is also the thinker of difference, pluralism, relativism, and contingency. Thus to simply embrace these topics as if they in themselves would guarantee the closure of modernity and the end of Hegel is a gesture of naive optimism. One cannot help recalling the often-cited yet seldom-heeded suspicion that Michel Foucault voiced in a speech he delivered, interestingly enough, when he assumed Jean Hyppolite's chair at the Collège de France:

> But to truly escape Hegel involves an exact appreciation of the price we
> have to pay to detach ourselves from him. It assumes that we are aware of
> the extent to which Hegel, insidiously perhaps, is close to us; it implies a

knowledge, in that which permits us to think against Hegel, of that which remains Hegelian. We have to determine the extent to which our anti-Hegelianism is possibly one of his tricks directed against us, at the end of which he stands, motionless, waiting for us.[1]

Foucault clarifies the essential predicament of the postmodernist: to be anti-Hegelian is to be profoundly Hegelian. This is not only because Hegel thought through the role of the negative, but also because his philosophy absolutely requires the work of the negative. Hegelianism requires a philosophy of the finite and the contingent. Postmodern thought to a certain extent realizes this and has struggled to elaborate a conception of the negative that would not stand in the service of dialectics. Yet postmodern thought remains caught in the awkward predicament of being able to challenge Hegel only with tools that have been provided by Hegel. More troublingly, it perhaps articulates the thought of the negative that speculative thought presupposes. Thus, in our struggle to denounce and transcend, we only become all the more thoroughly Hegelian.

Nonetheless, it is those who would term themselves postmodernists who claim to be free of Hegel. Symptomatic of this desire is the presence of Hegel in that canonical postmodern text, *The Postmodern Condition*. At first glance, it might seem that Hegel has little to do with the postmodern science and knowledge that Lyotard outlines in this book. He is, in fact, seldom mentioned by name. Upon examination, however, one realizes that the often-used term 'speculative thought' is meant to stand for Hegel, with speculative thought defining that from which postmodernity seeks to liberate itself. In *Postmodernism Explained* Lyotard clarifies:

> The 'metanarratives' I was concerned with in *The Postmodern Condition* are those that have marked modernity: the progressive emancipation of reason and freedom, the progressive or catastrophic emancipation of labor (source of alienated value in capitalism), the enrichment of all humanity through the progress of capitalist technoscience, and even – if we include Christianity itself in modernity (in opposition to the classicism of antiquity) – the salvation of creatures through the conversion of souls to the Christian narrative of martyred love. Hegel's philosophy totalizes all of these narratives and, in this sense, is itself a distillation of speculative modernity.[2]

Lyotard understands speculative thought to be the final, enduring attempt to secure the position of philosophy as the queen of the sciences and thus of all forms of knowledge. Lyotard explains this defining ambition of modernity:

> Philosophy must restore unity to learning, which has been scattered into separate sciences in laboratories and in pre-university education; it can only achieve this in a language game that links the sciences together as moments in the becoming of spirit, in other words, which link them in a rational narration, or rather metanarration. Hegel's *Encyclopedia* (1817–27) attempts to realize this project of totalization.[3]

The impossible position of what Lyotard terms the speculative language game is that it delegitimizes scientific knowledge as it seeks to establish a metanarrative that would preserve its truth. Speculative language games strip other fields of knowledge of the right to make truth-claims, since truth is produced as other language games are translated into the metanarrative of speculative thought. As Lyotard explains:

> It [the speculative apparatus] shows that knowledge is only worthy of that name to the extent that it reduplicates itself ('lifts itself up,' *hebt sich auf*; is sublated) by citing its own statements in a second-level discourse (autonomy) that functions to legitimate them. This is as much to say that, in its immediacy, denotative discourse bearing on a certain referent . . . does not really know what it thinks it knows.[4]

This suzerainty must necessarily come to an end with postmodernism, for the language games of science not only no longer require legitimation through a speculative metanarrative, they also no longer serve as the means of legitimation for any other language game.

What is also at issue for Lyotard is idealism's attack on denotative discourse – not that he himself would claim that language can make purely present the object of thought. Yet Lyotard, like most postmodernists, seeks to secure a space for an other to the system of speculative idealism. It is this ambition that is definitive of postmodern thought, and that makes Kant, not Hegel, the avatar of postmodernism.[5] Kant is seen to demarcate the limits of knowledge and thus to define the other as ultimately non-appropriable to thought. Yet can an escape from such an avowedly all-encompassing system as Hegel's be so effortlessly achieved? Within its own logic is the knowledge that postmodernism is the attempt to think a limit from *within* speculative thought.

What is evident in Lyotard's treatment of Hegel is that certain aspects are exaggerated and employed to define modernity negatively so that what persists of Hegel is not as apparent. For Hegel taught philosophers to examine all fields of knowledge as quasi-autonomous language games. It is true that Hegel was ultimately more concerned with the role each language game played in the unfolding of spirit. It is also true that Hegel saw it as the task of philosophy to synthesize the various language games of knowledge. Yet Hegel emphasized the cultural and historical specificity of language games; he also devoted a good deal of his thought to dissecting the internal logic of various language games. Moving well beyond the disguised state-of-nature meditations of Rousseau, Hegel introjected cultural and historical difference into the very idea of reason. Hegel's solution to the troubling fact of historical and cultural difference is the narrative of the evolutionary articulation of the Absolute. The problem – accounting for the difference made manifest in different cultures, time periods, and modes of representation – seems to remain with philosophy whether one accepts his solution or not. It is only too clear, then, that Lyotard accepts to a great extent Hegel's understanding of philosophy.

Lyotard, moreover, can only make his case by making use of a profoundly Hegelian argument. For Lyotard claims that speculative idealism was an historical response to the growing power of scientific disciplines. The various sciences, however, continued to evolve, growing more independent and less in need of a legitimating discourse such as speculative idealism. The emergence of postmodernism is thus part of the very evolution of knowledge. Moreover, Lyotard writes supposedly after the maturation and death of a certain field of knowledge – namely, philosophy. Yet what would be more logical, after Hegel had announced the death of art and religion, than to announce the death of philosophy? Indeed, was it not Hegel who presented the history of philosophy as the death of philosophy? Postmodernism becomes, like the Hegel it denounces, a thinking of the post mortem. And it is precisely in its function as coroner that it maintains its own authority. Far from enacting a rupture with the past, then, postmodernism is the unconscious but logical culmination of speculative idealism.

To fully appreciate the significance of Derrida's work on Hegel it is necessary to indulge in some intellectual history. This is because a volume such as this one is necessarily an undertaking in mediation. Given that the relation of Derrida and deconstruction to the work of Hegel is being presented here to an Anglo-American audience, it is not too amiss to suggest that what is being broached here borders on a *mise en abîme* of theory. Several languages, several histories, and several traditions are being traversed here. To begin with, it must be admitted that the status of Hegel in Anglo-American philosophy remains tenuous. The attention granted Hegel often assumes what Russell proclaimed about Hegel: 'Even if (as I myself believe) almost all Hegel's doctrine's are false, he still retains an importance which is not merely historical, as the best representative of a certain kind of philosophy which, in others, is less coherent and less comprehensive.'[6] The assumption clearly is that, much as in pathological studies, extreme cases are required to understand a disease. Prominent philosophers such as Karl Popper added to this blame for both fascism and communism.[7] Thus, while it can admittedly boast of producing some of the finest Hegel scholars in the world, Anglo-American philosophy as a whole remains suspicious of Hegel.[8] Indeed, it would probably be fair to suggest that the conceptual tools, if not the very vocabulary, necessary to understand and grapple with Hegel are simply not present within analytic philosophy.[9] Hegel, in fact, seems more like the very embodiment of everything that ordinary language philosophy – a school whose influence within the analytic tradition is perhaps greater than suspected – sought to dispel and dismantle.[10]

Joseph Findlay, one of the important philosophers to work towards an acceptance of Hegel in the Anglo-American tradition, underscored his precarious status in a speech of 1959:

> I wish this evening to defend the proposition that Hegel is an extremely important philosopher, well deserving the closest of contemporary study, and not at all belonging to what some have called the 'paleontology' of philosophical thought. To defend this proposition in the present climate of opinion still requires a certain expenditure of energy and personal authority, though much less than it did a little while ago. . . . In Anglo-Saxon countries a Hegel-renaissance has been made more difficult by the comparative recency of a period in which Hegel's prestige was immense, though his doctrine and method were very imperfectly understood.[11]

Findlay accurately points out that the demise of the reputation of Hegel in the Anglo-American tradition is linked to the relatively recent influence and prestige he enjoyed in that same tradition. More is at stake in this matter, however, than the rancor that sustains a succeeding school of thought. For analytic philosophy – which for the most part still defines professional philosophy in this tradition – finds its very origin in its struggle to distinguish itself from idealism.[12]

English philosophy at the turn of century was thoroughly Hegelian. Idealism, as promulgated by such influential philosophers as McTaggert and Bradley, dominated British philosophy. Indeed, both Russell and Moore, who are arguably the founders of the analytic tradition, began their philosophical careers as idealists. However, they soon began to attack what they perceived to be the very foundation of Hegelianism in order to clear the way for philosophy proper. Moore announced his departure from idealism in 'The Refutation of Idealism' and other early essays.[13] Russell's turn became apparent with the publication of *The Principles of Mathematics*. The key issue for both Moore and Russell was the problem of external relations.[14] Moore and Russell sought to dismantle the 'dogma' of British Hegelianism that all relations – being components of a thoroughgoing monism – are of the order of subject–predicate relations.[15] What may strike the casual observer as a dry issue in logic is actually a crucial issue, which lent shape to the development of Anglo-American philosophy. The insistence on external relations allowed Russell and Moore to counter both the rationalist and Kantian strains of the idealist understanding of relations – which assert that relations are either part of the predicates of a single substance or purely mental.

For Russell, the refutation of the doctrine of internal relations paved the way for logical atomism. It enabled Russell to claim that relations (which are neither intrinsic nor necessary) may obtain between two entities. Meaningful statements can be made about the relations between terms that do not reduce these relations to predicates of those terms. This, in turn, refutes the (British) Hegelian position that all terms are bound up with the totality of which they form a part and that all valid knowledge must address this totality, not an isolated term. The validity of external relations permits truthful statements to be made about isolated terms. In this manner Russell was able to claim that he had dismantled the foundation of idealism – monism. Yet it is worth considering whether the insistence that monism is the defining characteristic of idealism is, in fact, disguising a hidden affinity. Indeed, when one examines Russell's understanding of the relation between knowledge and the empirical there seems to be more than a passing resemblance between idealism and logical atomism. For Russell submits the empirical to a radical Cartesian doubt. The result is a decidedly Kantian position, which admits that objects in the world are ultimately unknowable. At the same time, Russell does not want to argue that all we are left with then is the mind.[16] Accordingly, sense-data become Johnson's stone for him. Yet, while sense-data are not mental, they offer no secure basis for knowledge. Knowledge can only be based on description. Russell discusses this decidedly Kantian dilemma in *The Problems of Philosophy*:

My knowledge of the table as a physical object . . . is not direct knowl-edge. Such as it is, it is obtained through acquaintance with the sense-data that make up the appearance of the table. We have seen that it is possible, without absurdity, to doubt whether there is a table at all, whereas it is not possible to doubt the sense-data. My knowledge of the table is of the kind which we call 'knowledge by description.' The table is 'the physical object which causes such-and-such sense-data.' This *describes* the table by means of sense-data. In order to know anything at all about the table, we must know truths connecting it with things with which we have acquaintance: we must know that 'such-and-such sense-data are caused by a physical object.' There is no state of mind in which we are directly aware of the table; all our knowledge of the table is really knowledge of *truths*, and the actual thing which is the table is not, strictly speaking, known to us at all. We know a description, and we know that there is just one object to which this description applies, though the object itself is not directly known to us. In such a case, we say that our knowledge of the object is knowledge by description.[17]

The theory of descriptions maintained the independence of propositions and thus of truth from the empirical. Yet the theory of descriptions was not to sever knowledge from the empirical altogether. Indeed, knowledge was to be (in the final instance) about the empirical. Thus Russell sought ultimately to argue for the isomorphic relation between the structure of an ideal language and the structure of reality. One can see variants of this compromise throughout analytic philosophy, from Wittgenstein's picture theory of meaning to Quine's notion of semantic ascent. What Russell bequeathed to analytic philosophy was in actuality a variant of idealism that claimed to be anchored in empirical reality.[18]

The curious fate of empiricism within the analytic tradition – supposedly the motivation for the rejection of idealism – indicates in negative the persistence of idealism. Logically enough, the 'dogmas' of empiricism soon came under attack themselves. Yet one could justifiably argue that the analytic tradition has employed idealist strategies to put a halt to the threat of both empiricism and Hegelianism. The suspicion remains that distinctly idealist strategies were behind the successes of analytic philosophy. What was suppressed in the denial of the secret affinity with idealism was the subtle and nuanced sensitivity of idealism for the empirical. While reason in speculative thought was to pass over into the pure realm of the concept, it was to a great extent culturally and historically specific. For Hegel understood that, while reason was always unitary, it nonetheless was articulated in a range of languages. Reason was at work in a variety of quasi-autonomous spheres such as architecture, world religions, family structures, philosophical movements, etc. And once one considers Hegel's insistence that reason necessarily articulates itself in an historical and always contingent manner – that, in other words, reason must oppose, contradict itself in a necessarily fleeting and historically specific and limited manner – then Hegel begins to appear as perhaps more of a philosopher of external relations than either Russell or Moore. Other than anecdotal stories from everyday life that were used to bolster some aspect of a theory of meaning, analytic philosophy actually had very little to say about the nuts-and-bolts empirical world it fought so hard to preserve and protect. Even ordinary language philosophy became so enamored with its supposedly therapeutic role in philosophy that it never really got around to dealing with the wealth and variety of 'ordinary language.' In short, not only were the successes of the analytic tradition secretly dependent upon idealism, but the attainment of its highest ambitions remain dependent upon acknowledging and embracing this secret relation.[19]

It was inevitable that these tensions would lead to the re-emergence of idealism in Anglo-American philosophy. They would lead, moreover, to the re-emergence of issues associated with Hegel.[20] Aspects of Kantian and neo-Kantian idealism were in and of themselves not particularly disturbing to the analytic tradition.[21] Indeed, as Hans Sluga demonstrated in the case of Frege, they formed part of the background and heritage of the analytic tradition. It is specifically Hegel – if not in name, then in terms of the issues he articulated – who re-emerges as a troubling figure in the analytic tradition. What re-emerges is Hegel's understanding of history, cultural transformation, and the self-negation of reason. As a result, what had remained ahistorical and part of a pure logic has gradually acquired historical and cultural specificity. It should also be remembered that part of what motivated the reaction against Kant for Hegel and his generation was precisely the tenuous status of the empirical, the fact that the *Ding-an-sich* would be forever unknown. Hegel's reaction was to write the history of the Absolute as it articulated itself in the natural world and human history. While the ontological dimensions of Hegel's procedure still make philosophers uncomfortable, one of the central elements of his strategy remains of crucial importance. Hegel revealed that it is the task of philosophy to write the history of the empirical. For the empirical, both natural and especially human, has distinct contours – ruptures, closures, and transformations. Indeed, historical understanding can only follow the realization that what was considered an element of an immutable subjectivity, of ontology itself, is in fact part of a mutable empiricism. It is this insight that slowly comes to haunt the uneasy compromises that analytic philosophy has made.

The unsettling and yet thoroughly logical culmination of the analytic tradition – as well as that other significant line of post-Wittgensteinian thought, logical positivism – is represented in the work of Paul Feyerabend and Richard Rorty. They are the unsettling culmination of their traditions because they bring to the surface its Hegelian background. It was the work of Thomas Kuhn that paved the way for both philosophers. Kuhn did a thoroughly Hegelian examination of that supposedly most empirical branch of knowledge, science. It was the merit of Kuhn, then, to drive the point home for many philosophers of science and analytic philosophers that no field of knowledge is immune from the vicissitudes and transformations of history. In fact, Kuhn argued, all knowledge is riddled through with historicity. Knowledge – and, more importantly, the development of knowledge – was necessarily dependent upon the self-contradictory nature of reason, which could manifest itself only through utter epistemological failure. Far from being a simple positivistic growth of knowledge that gradually eliminated error, reason was and is always fragmented, partial. The truth of reason, such as it is, reveals itself in the course of history as a series of crises and self-negations. This thoroughly Hegelian reading of that field of knowledge felt to be most securely anchored in the empirical began to open up analytic philosophy to questions of history and culture.

Continuing Kuhn's work in the philosophy of science, Feyerabend pushed logical positivism into what Mary Hesse has rightly termed post-empiricism.[22] What is remarkable is the extent to which Feyerabend's strategy is Hegelian. He argues against the simple facticity of empirical objects and events. He argues not simply for the contamination of science by the subjectivity of individual researchers (as any post-Heisenberg physicist might), but for the cultural construction of the conditions that allow empirical evidence to become empirical evidence. Feyerabend, moreover, is interested in what regulates the transitions between paradigms of scientific research, what causes, in other words, the breakdown of normal science. For the shifts in paradigms indicate the transition from one form of reason to another – both of which are incommensurable with each other. What particularly interests Feyerabend is the notion that each form of reason will *necessarily* produce contradictions within its own system that inevitably lead to its dissolution. In this he subscribes to the Hegelian notion that the truth of reason lies not in any particular moment but in its self-contradictory historical unfolding. Like Hegel, moreover, Feyerabend embraces that anarchic and pitiless core at the heart of dialectics that lays waste to all systems of thought.

It is worth noting, moreover, that Feyerabend does not argue for permanent revolution in the philosophy of science for the sake of sheer relativism. Feyerabend's consistent conviction is that methodological anarchism will promote the growth of knowledge. As he phrases it: 'Is it not more realistic to assume that fundamental changes, entailing incommensurability, are still possible, and that they should be encouraged lest we remain forever excluded from what might be a higher stage of knowledge and of consciousness?'[23] Beneath the talk of revolution and relativism is the belief that there is a progression and growth of knowledge. Thus, like Hegel, Feyerabend sees that reason can only manifest itself through a gradual and self-contradicting unfolding through history. While reason is always flawed, partial, limited, and destined to be displaced by another guise of reason, it nonetheless carries along with it the accomplishments of earlier forms of thought. Feyerabend – despite having nothing to say about Hegel – thereby expresses a profoundly Hegelian depiction of the growth and transformation of scientific knowledge.[24] As such he gives expression to much that was suppressed in the analytic and positivist tradition.

Perhaps the paradoxical situation of analytic philosophy is seen most clearly in the work of Richard Rorty. While Rorty can easily be seen as an alarming case of apostasy within the analytic tradition, is it more accurate to see him as bringing back to the fore its Hegelian background. Like Feyerabend, Rorty is interested in the cultural contours of language games, in what Wittgenstein would term the *Lebensform* that any language game is inextricably part of. He has confronted the idealism implicit within the analytic tradition and has come to see that any Kantian resolution is inadequate. Rorty has, in fact, embraced a Hegelian solution to the paradoxes of the analytic tradition. Like few others, moreover, Rorty understands that Hegel is the architect of postmodernism. As Rorty observes: 'Reason cunningly employed Hegel, contrary to his own intentions, to write the charter of our modern literary culture. . . . It is as if Hegel knew all about this culture before its birth.'[25] Rorty perceives Hegel to have outlined the ironist culture, with its awareness of the contingency of vocabularies:

Hegel left Kant's ideal of philosophy-as-science in shambles, but he did, as I have said, create a new literary genre, a genre which exhibited the relativity of significance to choice of vocabulary, the bewildering variety of vocabularies from which we can choose, and the intrinsic instability of each. Hegel made unforgettably clear the deep self-certainty given by each achievement of a vocabulary, each new genre, each new style, each new dialectical synthesis – the sense that now, at last, for the first time, we have grasped things as they truly are. He also made unforgettably clear why such certainty lasts but a moment. He showed how the passion which sweeps through each generation serves the cunning of reason, providing the impulse which drives that generation to self-immolation and transformation. He writes in that tone of belatedness and irony which is characteristic of the literary culture of the present day.[26]

Hegel's shadow is actually longer than Rorty would have us believe, but his understanding of Hegel is remarkable in that he sees that postmodernism is predicated upon Hegel. Unlike other thinkers who might be characterized as postmodern, Rorty also sees that his own philosophy is itself an extension of Hegel. By transferring the Kuhnian notion of abnormal science to what he terms 'the literary,' Rorty focuses on those moments in a culture where contradiction comes to the fore – when a culture becomes aware of the contingency of its own vocabulary. This then is what throws that culture into a spasm of self-doubt and inaugurates a renewed self-description. It takes only a slight shift in vocabulary to see this pragmatist vision of an ironist culture as what Hegel discussed as the historical evolution of spirit.

Thus, while analytic philosophy as a whole remains suspicious of Hegel, there are signs that it is beginning to recall its own repressed origins. What remains problematic with Feyerabend and to a certain extent Rorty is that the implications of Hegel have not been sufficiently interrogated. As a result, there seems to be little hope of escaping the rule of Hegel. Instead, one must accept Hegel's version of the transience of all forms of knowledge and culture. What remains as a task for philosophy is making this state of affairs clear to all – a task fairly close to the one Hegel set himself. This is the opposite sin of Lyotard and the postmodernists, who claim to have already transcended Hegel and to be living in a post-Hegelian culture. Both responses to Hegel, however, are ultimately inadequate in that they fail to interrogate what it is that enables the Hegelian system to function and persist despite – or rather because of – that which would seem to be its own negation. In one version, Hegel becomes a straw man that is all too easily dispatched. In the other version, in what may be a bizarre variant of the Helsinki syndrome, Hegel is embraced as the only and inescapable way of doing philosophy. It is the unique achievement of Derrida to have begun the necessary task of confronting Hegel. In order to grasp the significance of what Derrida has achieved, however, it is necessary to explore the archeology of his work, that is, the career of the French Hegel.

The story of the French reception of Hegel has been told often, yet in this context it warrants some consideration.[27] French interest in Hegel was a sudden and relatively recent event. Up until the 1930s, little serious work on Hegel had been done in France. This was due to some extent to the lack of translations of Hegelian texts. Yet, as many critics have noted, there was a whole complex of reasons why Hegel was simply not up for discussion. At the most simple level was the antipathy towards all things German. As Alexandre Koyré noted: 'The war, among other disastrous results, led to a violent reaction against German thought, German art, and German civilization in general.'[28] Georges Canguilhem pointed out, moreover, that this antipathy also focused explicitly on Hegel: 'Almost everyone saw in Hegel the spiritual father of Germanism and Pangermanism. All of the German thinkers, from Hegel onwards, were victims of a nationalist prejudice, born of circumstances — which one could hold Hegel responsible for — such as the war of 1870 and the victory of Prussia.'[29] In addition to these reasons, academic French philosophy was dominated by a Cartesian rationalism whose concerns focused on Kant and the philosophy of mathematics. It thus could not find much use for a philosopher who was perceived to equate logic with temporal existence.

What little work that was done on Hegel was done at the fringes of the academy. Jean Wahl published in 1929 what was later to be seen as an important study — *Le malheur de la conscience dans le philosophie de Hegel*. Yet at the time it was an isolated work seemingly unrelated to the philosophical concerns of the times. Academic philosophy in France seemed to be pursuing what Mikel Dufrenne termed a 'conspiracy of silence' with regard to Hegel.[30] The other significant critic working on Hegel at this time was Alexandre Koyré.[31] While Koyré did not produce an extended study of Hegel, he prepared the way for a reception of Hegel through careful articles that contained generous translated excerpts of Hegel. Yet the status of Hegelian studies in France remained such that Koyré could report with some evident embarrassment in 1930 at the first Hegel Congress: 'I am somewhat afraid that, after the reports of my German, English, and Italian colleagues, which are so rich in facts and names, my report on the state of Hegelian studies in France will seem very meager and poor to you by comparison.'[32] Very soon after this — as Koyré himself admits in a postscript to the published version of this lecture — the status of Hegel changed dramatically. The first immediate sign was the flurry of translations that began to appear. Gibelin's *Leçons sur la Philosophie de l'Histoire* appeared in 1937; Lefèbvre's *Morceaux choisis* appeared in 1939; Hyppolite's *Phénoménologie* appeared in 1939 and 1941; Kann's *Principes de la Philosophie du droit* appeared in 1940; and Jankélévitch's *Esthétique* appeared in 1944. Many more translations followed after the war. What is remarkable (and this is substantiated by the critical commentary that soon follows the translations) is that Hegel was no longer associated with the reactionary and militaristic political developments in Germany. On the contrary, Hegel was seen to speak directly to the political situation of France. Work on Hegel flourished despite — or, perhaps more accurately, precisely *because* of — the war. As Mikel Dufrenne suggested: 'By means of a phenomenon that was quite Hegelian, Hegel has been *acknowledged* by us under the instigation of concrete history and in the context of political events. . . . History presses upon us from all sides and we *interrogate* Hegel.'[33] Hyppolite phrased it even more pointedly: 'After the last war (during which we experienced invasion, defeat, resistance) French thought, and, of course, philosophical thought, has not ceased refining its position on the *historical situation* of man.'[34] By the end of the war, then, the stage was set for a fully fledged Hegel renaissance. Indeed, by 1948 already Georges Canguilhem could report: 'Contemporary philosophical thought is dominated by Hegelianism.'[35] The transformation of the status of Hegel in French thought — and thus by extension French thought itself — was all in all relatively sudden and sweeping.[36]

While Wahl and Koyré laid the groundwork for a reassessment, the remarkable turnaround in the fortunes of Hegel was due above all else to the work of Alexandre Kojève and Jean Hyppolite. Before their intervention, interest in Hegel was sporadic and remained at the fringes of intellectual debate. Hyppolite produced the first French translation of Hegel's *Phenomenology*. And in 1947 he published his magisterial exegesis of the *Phenomenology*, *Genesis and Structure of Hegel's* Phenomenology. Eschewing slogans, Hyppolite brought scholarly patience to the study of Hegel. He resisted the seemingly universal temptation to produce a strong reading of Hegel that would bring him into line with another philosophical tradition. Hyppolite sought instead to carefully outline and explicate the intricacies of this notoriously tortuous book. Indeed, he was so faithful to the text that one early reviewer, Henri Niel, complained that it was impossible to determine what Hyppolite's own ideas were.[37] The mere fact that Hyppolite was focusing on the *Phenomenology*, however, played into the reading of Hegel offered by Kojève. For this reason, one suspects, Hyppolite turned later to Hegel's *Logic* and the question of the Absolute in *Logique et existence*. He turned, in other words, to an aspect of Hegel pointedly ignored by Kojève. The effect of this was to position man and the issue of self-consciousness as a moment in the unfolding of the Absolute. The merit of Hyppolite's work, and the source of its subtle and long-lasting impact, was the insistence on understanding the interconnectedness of Hegel's work. He made it more difficult to arbitrarily pick and choose elements in Hegel that seemed appealing. Thus while Kojève clearly had a greater immediate impact, Hyppolite taught French scholars to read Hegel with patience and to seek to understand Hegel in his full complexity. One can see this patience and rigor in two scholars he did in fact teach, Foucault and Derrida.

All in all, however, it was undeniably Kojève who defined the French reception of Hegel.[38] At the invitation of Koyré, Kojève delivered lectures on Hegel from 1933 to 1939 at the École Pratique des Hautes Études. Since Koyré had focused for the most part on the early Hegel, particularly the recently published writings on Christianity, Kojève, logically enough, picked up the story by addressing the *Phenomenology*. Kojève's lectures soon attracted attention because they were not only patient and brilliant explications of a central philosophical text that had remained inaccessible to the French but also an ongoing meditation on the philosophical and political situation of the early twentieth century. As a result, Kojève soon attracted a remarkable audience that included Bataille, Lacan, Aron, Queneau, Merleau-Ponty, Weil, and Levinas.[39] In an appropriately Hegelian fashion, the notes from these lectures were eventually published by Queneau in 1947 as *Introduction à la lecture de Hegel*.[40]

In these lectures Kojève presented a willfully strong reading of Hegel. Perhaps the most controversial aspect of Kojève's interpretation was his insistence on an anthropological foundation to Hegel's thought. Dismissing issues of theology, indeed, of ontology itself, Kojève focused on the notions of self-consciousness and history. Kojève paid little heed to what was clearly a central tenet of the *Phenomenology* — that it is the Absolute that articulates itself, as subject, through nature and human history. For Kojève, Hegel's philosophy is fundamentally a theory of the historical evolution of consciousness.

The centerpiece of Kojève's reading is the master/slave dialectic. Given the impact that this aspect in particular had, it is necessary to consider it briefly. Indeed, far more people associate the mere notion of the master/slave dialectic with Kojève (if not simply Hegel) than actually understand its significance for Kojève's reading. As stated, the constant assumption of Kojève is that Hegel's philosophy is an anthropology. Accordingly, Kojève seeks to establish how Hegel defines humans as beings that develop through time. Kojève argues that, for Hegel, the essential characteristic that guides the development of humans is desire: 'The very being of man, the self-conscious being, therefore, implies and presupposes Desire' (p. 4).

The difficulty with desire is that it does not strictly define man *per se*. For desire does not distinguish humans from other living beings. This is most evident in the desire for food. This desire is negating and leads to the destruction and ingestion of the object. This desire and action remains primitive according to Kojève because it will never lead to self-consciousness: 'The I created by the active satisfaction of such a Desire will have the same nature as the things toward which that Desire is directed: it will be a 'thingish' I, a merely living I, an animal I' (p. 4). This primitive form of desire only negates a given being; it does not transform consciousness. Inasmuch as humanity is defined by this form of desire it is not any different from the animal world. For the consciousness this form of desire produces remains unreflective. By contrast, human desire must and should be directed towards something that is not given. True desire is an absence, a lack, a nothingness that defines itself in relation to something that is not present. In this way, humans advance to self-consciousness. The non-being that humans should desire is desire. Thus humans do not desire a given being or object; rather, they desire the desire of others: 'Such a Desire can only be a human Desire, and human reality, as distinguished from animal reality, is created only by action that satisfies such Desires: human history is the history of desired Desires' (p. 6). The desire for desire, and the resultant appropriation of non-being, constitutes the human. Indeed, only through the quest for mediated desire does the human come into being at all. Moreover, since mediated desire can occur only in a collective, the advent of self-consciousness is synonymous with both history and social being.

In the pursuit of desired desire, there must be a confrontation with the other for recognition. This struggle is a struggle to the death. One of the combatants is willing to sacrifice existence itself in order to obtain the desired desire of the other. The other combatant, however, is not willing to sacrifice existence and, as a result, becomes a slave:

He must give up his desire and satisfy the desire of the other: he must 'recognize' the other without being 'recognized' by him. Now, to 'recognize' him thus is 'to recognize' him as his Master and to recognize himself and to be recognized as the Master's Slave. (p. 8)

This recognition provides the mediation necessary for self-consciousness to be articulated. While seemingly satisfactory to the master, this relation cannot remain as it is. For there is something profoundly insufficient about this master/slave relation. The medium of the articulation of the self-consciousness of the master – the slave – remains little more than a thing: 'He is, therefore, 'recognized' by a thing' (p. 19). The self-consciousness of the master remains flawed and partial. As Kojève notes, 'The master is not truly man; he is only a stage.'[41]

The slave, on the other hand, maintains a more direct relation to the natural world. The essence of that relation is labor. By means of labor, the slave represses desire. The slave does not negate given being; rather, he transforms it: 'He trans-forms things and trans-forms himself at the same time: he forms things and the World by transforming himself, by educating himself' (25).[42] By transforming the very world of both the master and the slave, the slave brings an end to the master/slave relation.[43] Labor allows the slave to transcend himself as slave and bring consciousness (as well as the increasingly alienated self-consciousness of the master) out of the impasse of the master/slave relation. Thus the transformation – and not the destruction – of the world brings the slave to a new stage of consciousness, one that in fact liberates all of humanity and brings an end to history itself. Furthermore, Kojève makes clear that the master/slave dialectic does not refer solely to a hypothetical primal scene of social existence. Rather, it functions in a trans-individual manner to propel history itself: '(This dialectic does not merely concern individual relations. But just as well: Rome and the barbarians, the nobility and the third-estate, etc . . .)'[44] The struggle for recognition thereby lends shape to history itself.

With this reading of the master/slave relation, Kojève was able to transform Hegel from an apologist for Prussian militarism to a Marxist phenomenologist. For his emphasis on the master/slave relation served to outline the constitution and genesis of consciousness in such a way that it was linked to the process of history. This was an entirely new perspective for those working in a phenomenological tradition still essentially defined by a Cartesian understanding of subjectivity. It was also a new perspective for those working in a Marxist tradition defined by a crude materialism that had no role for consciousness. Thus Kojève did not merely rehabilitate the reputation of Hegel; he transformed Hegel into the philosopher who had the solution to the philosophical problems of the twentieth century.

Perhaps the secret of Kojève's success in rehabilitating Hegel for contemporary philosophy was his polyvalent reading of Hegel, which made him compatible with a variety of philosophical impulses. His reading, for instance, made Hegel the logical terrain upon which to weld together phenomenology and Marxism. There is yet another layer to Kojève's reading, however, that helps to explain the persistence of the Kojèvian reading up to the present day. The central notion to this aspect is that of discourse. Kojève uses the notion of discourse to lend a material cast to Hegel's notion of spirit: 'Hegel's Spirit is not therefore truly a "divine" Spirit (because there are no *mortal* gods): It is *human* in the sense that it is a discourse that is immanent to the natural World and that has for its "support" a natural being limited in its existence by time and space.'[45] As Kojève succinctly puts it: 'Spirit is the Real revealed by Discourse.'[46] Spirit is not the emanation and self-articulation of the Absolute. Rather, for Kojève the evolution of spirit becomes the anthropogenetic self-articulation of discourse. The task of philosophy, in turn, is the elucidation of the character of discourse, of the fact that discourse has achieved an autonomous existence: 'it is precisely the reality of discourse that is the miracle that philosophy must explain.'[47]

In addition to recasting spirit as discourse, Kojève presents the constitutive element of discourse – the sign – in a decidedly modern light. Kojève argues that signs are the ideal vehicle for spirit because of their independence from their referents. What later critics were to call the arbitrariness of the sign is for Kojève a necessary precondition of absolute spirit. The arbitrariness of the sign enables the transformation of nature into sign and thus into a malleable component of discourse. The sign is thus the medium of transformation by means of which nature becomes a world of culture and technology:

> this power that thought has to separate and recombine things is in effect 'absolute,' because no real force of connection or repulsion is sufficiently powerful to oppose it. And that power is not at all fictitious or 'ideal.' For it is in separating and in recombining things in and through his discursive thought that man forms his technical projects, which, once realized through work, really transform the aspect of the natural [and] given World by creating therein a World of culture. (p. 126)

This understanding of spirit is less humanist than it might appear at first glance. In fact, it is in this reading of spirit that Kojève veers from his anthropological assessment of Hegel. For discourse becomes the condition of possibility of man as such. As Kojève notes, the 'birth of Discourse (= Man) in the heart of Being (= Nature)' (pp. 116–17). Discourse, which transforms nature, gives birth to the human – for humans exist only as spirit. Humans thereby become subject to the power of discourse, which is the power to negate given being. For this reason, Kojève states: 'Man is not only *mortal*; he is *death* incarnate; he *is* his own death' (p. 151). Discourse is the ongoing mediated suicide of humanity. Humans are merely a vehicle for discourse and are accordingly negated and *aufgehoben* by discourse. The goal of spirit – the end of history, the end of discourse – entails the end of humanity. Kojève's reading might therefore be more accurately described as an anthropo-thanotological reading of Hegel. Admittedly, this aspect of Kojève's reading was not drawn out and fully explored until much later. Yet it was this aspect of Kojève's reading that ensured its truly long-term impact.

What was initially attractive about Kojève's reading was his detranscendentalization of speculative idealism. The discomforting notions of the Absolute and spirit were transformed into more concrete material notions. While clearly a distortion of Hegelian philosophy, such a strong reading is doubtless what made a resurgence of interest in Hegel possible. Kojève's distortion of Hegel actually made Hegel a figure with relevance. Thus Kojève was continuing what Croce had insisted upon – distinguishing what was living from what was dead in Hegel. Kojève thereby forged a Hegel that had much to say to contemporary thought. Kojève emphasized that consciousness had a necessary temporal dimension that was not abstract but was coterminous with social history itself. The connection between phenomenology and social being, and the necessity for social struggle to achieve the development and completion of humanity, radically altered the status of Hegel. This was the Hegel behind Lukács's *History and Class Consciousness*; this was the Hegel that Lenin had exhorted his followers to read. As a result, Hegel quickly became the answer to the central dilemma that faced many French intellectuals of the time: how to find a way out of the impasse between an academic philosophy enthralled with the thoroughly abstract subject of Cartesian rationalism and a theory of society and history in the grips of the determinism of orthodox Stalinist Marxism.[48]

What must be made clear is that the issues that have been raised here in the context of the French reception of Hegel are not confined to the realm of intellectual history. The impact of Kojève was decisive and long-lasting.[49] It was also not merely restricted to the introduction of the work of Hegel into French intellectual life. The impact of the Hegelianism fostered by Kojève also manifested itself in a preoccupation with certain issues, with a certain style and method of inquiry. In this sense, this impact was to have far-reaching consequences. Indeed, we still live in the thrall of this brand of Hegelianism. In fact, most of the work of Anglo-American literary and cultural criticism can be explained by relating it to this Hegelianism. In order to substantiate such an apparently extravagant claim – which is, however, perhaps the ultimate motivation for this volume – it will be necessary to review the essential features of this French Hegelianism. It will also be necessary to establish its relation to contemporary criticism.

Early French Hegelianism found its origins in the need for a link between a philosophy of the subject and history. A tradition so defined by Cartesian rationalism naturally found it difficult to broach the question of history, let alone that of the social being of man. Thus, unlike the earlier British Hegelians, who were drawn to the *Logic* and the *Encyclopedia*, the French were instinctively drawn to *The Phenomenology of Spirit*. For what offered itself here was a careful exposition of the transition from consciousness to self-consciousness, which made clear that the development of self-consciousness was dependent upon others, upon the social. This is the reason for the fascination with the master/ slave relation. This relatively brief moment in the *Phenomenology* is the precise point where isolated self-consciousness must first acknowledge the existence of another consciousness. This in itself would be enough to explain its fascination. Hegel also describes how, because of the need for recognition, the encounter of self-consciousness with the other requires that one submit, that one render recognition in return for the right to live. Hegel thereby links the unfolding of self-consciousness to the very origins and genesis of the social. Hegel also made social and political struggle and evolution intrinsic to philosophy itself. These issues spoke directly to a generation that was attempting to link a philosophy of the subject with a social theory. For this reason, Hegel became the primary means by which Marxism and phenomenology were to be brought into articulation with one another. Hegel had made possible the advent of historicity within rationalism.

In addition to phenomenology and Marxism, Hegel was adopted to a certain extent by existentialism. In hindsight, it is ironic that existentialism was equated – particularly in the American critical understanding – with French Hegelianism. The Hegelian notion of the master/slave relation did indeed seem to sum up the necessarily conflictual relation of the existential subject with the other. Yet Sartre's *Being and Nothingness* was more the attempt of Cartesian rationalism to defend itself in the face of the dissolution of the individual subject into historical and social being. In short, the imagery of the master/slave relation was employed by Sartre to counter the argument of the *Phenomenology*.[50] Self-consciousness confronting another consciousness was not to lead  –

20

as in Hegel – to the articulation of *Sittlichkeit* as the medium of spirit, but to the affirmation of the isolation and freedom of the individual subject. Sartre did indeed appropriate much imagery from Hegel that involved the combative confrontation with the other. Thus it easily appeared that Sartre was arguing, as Hegel had done, that the transition from consciousness to self-consciousness was to found history itself, when, in fact, he was arguing just the opposite. Sartre was arguing against allowing the transition between consciousness and self-consciousness to function as a transition. Self-consciousness could only be consciousness of the self; it could not form the bridge to the social being of man. As a result, there could be no society and no history – only masters. Indeed, as Hyppolite commented: 'One suspected that Sartre, despite granting an important place to the historical situation, is at bottom a moralist who does not believe in *history* (as a totality yet to be achieved).'[51]

One could argue that the sense one can get from the *Encyclopedia* – that all of humanity and all of its practices form one coherent, signifying system – came eventually to confront existentialism's insistence upon the inviolability of the isolated and autonomous subject. That sense manifested itself in structuralism, which essentially was a variant of Hegelianism, a Hegelianism that pitted the philosophy of spirit against the phenomenology of spirit. Structuralism emphasized that the master functioned in and as discourse and was therefore more cunning than had been assumed. For the master was part of – indeed *was* – the social, world culture, and world spirit. As such, the master was everywhere, demanding submission. Some, like Genette, were content to elaborate how the master functioned. Others, like Barthes, sought to reintroduce desire in order to prevent the triumph of the master. In general, structuralism took up Kojève's suggestion that spirit was, in fact, discourse. It understood that discourse, much as spirit, encompassed all realms of human endeavor and that it was the task of criticism to account for its variety. Structuralism thereby reintroduced a more systematic and encyclopedic Hegelianism.

Hegel's importance was challenged in the wake of the upheaval following the events of May 1968. Nietzsche was pitted against Hegel in order to question the genetic and evolutionary assumptions of Hegelianism about history and society. Yet, as Vincent Descombes suggests, it was Hegel – as interpreted by Kojève – who made this anti-Hegelianism possible. For Hegel had focused on 'an account of universal history in which bloody strife – and not "reason" – is responsible for the progress of events towards the happy conclusion.'[52] It was thus Hegel who pointed out 'the unreasonable origins of reason.'[53] Hence within Kojève's Hegel were the very seeds for this wave of anti-Hegelianism. In

21

the final analysis, perhaps one version of Hegel was confronting another in the philosophical sea change of the late 1960s.

After 1968, French philosophy devoted itself to the exploration of discourse and language. Inasmuch as Hegel was equated with a humanist neo-Marxism, the relentless emphasis on language and discourse was perceived to be a renouncing of Hegel altogether. The fact that this emphasis was thoroughly anti-humanist underscored this sense of renunciation. Yet it is not difficult to argue that French philosophy sought thereby to return to Kojève's insight that discourse was arbitrary not only in its distance from any referent but also in the manner in which it can refashion and recombine its constituent elements. French philosophy was also perhaps recalling Kojève's insight that discourse was a mediated suicide – a suicide that implicated the very idea of man. Accordingly, many documents – such as Barthes' announcement of the death of the author and Foucault's evocative ending to *The Order of Things* – that seemed to announce (particularly in the American critical understanding) a new era in philosophy and criticism can be read as a continuation of the work that Kojève began. Thus what many took to be the most profound of reactions against Hegelianism, a reaction that announced the death of man and the ubiquity of a discourse that was either arbitrary or the means of resisting the master/slave relation, was, in fact, one more variant of Hegelianism.

Despite the emphasis on language and discourse, the terms of the interaction of the master and slave – which still seems to form the primal scene of French philosophical thought – dictated the means by which anti-Hegelianism could be conceptualized. A key element in this scenario was the force of desire. For desire is what initially draws consciousnesses into proximity with one another in the master/slave relation. Bataille and later Deleuze (among others) seized upon this notion to entertain the possibility of a world with only masters, in which desire is relentlessly pursued. Such thinkers were unwilling to accord so much power, such inevitability, to the master/slave dialectic. What was focused on instead was the realization that dialectics could not proceed without the participation of the slave. Thus desire and difference were celebrated as forces that would prevent the dialectic – in all its guises – from establishing itself. Yet, as Jean-Luc Nancy has reminded us, desire remains inevitably bound up with dialectics, which always seeks the appropriative recognition of the self in the other.[54] The slave, in short, is necessarily a part of desire. As is so often the case with anti-Hegelianism, what was pursued unwittingly here was the affirmation of one aspect of Hegel in the hopes that it would counter Hegelianism *in toto*.

How, then, does one relate this invisible yet rampant Hegelianism to the contemporary American critical scene? To address this final issue one must turn to the work of Michel Foucault. For if the contemporary American critical scene could be said to be under the spell of one philosopher it would be Foucault. Under the guidance of Foucault, the human and the culture that it is a moment of – in all its discursive and non-discursive practices, no matter how seemingly mundane – become a signifying system in which the stakes are always power. In particular, Foucault emphasized the Kojèvian notion of the master/slave dialectic. Indeed, it would not be too much of an exaggeration to suggest that the crux of Foucault's thought is to be found in Kojève's reading of Hegel. Running throughout Foucault's work is a fascination with the drama of self-consciousness. From the story of Pinel's use of a mirror to treat mad inmates who believed they were the king of France to the relentless controlling gaze of the Panopticon, to the ever-expanding discourse on the care and regulation of the self in all matters sexual, Foucault has spun an apparently historical narrative to present the philosophical drama of Kojève's master and slave. As Kojève presented it, the struggle of the master and slave is the confrontation of two consciousnesses, only one of which can achieve self-consciousness through the submission of the other. This is a primordial power struggle that precedes any established structure of power. The essence of this Kojèvian power struggle is that one consciousness recognizes the other as master and – just as important – recognizes itself as slave. It is this moment of self-recognition – and thus auto-constitution – of the slave that forms the primary focus of Foucault's work. Foucault sifts for different historical instances of the inauguration of consciousness as a vehicle of power. Indeed, all of Foucault's work can be read as a history of the consciousness of the slave. He presents narratives of historical moments in which consciousness was a means of enforcing and maintaining subjection. Despite his own warning, then, Foucault would seem to be travelling down a road mapped out by Hegel (and paved by Kojève).[55]

Unlike many of his contemporaries, however, Foucault does not tout the notion of desire as the means for the slave to liberate itself. Indeed, the very notion of liberation seems to be curiously absent in Foucault's thought. Thus, despite the solution Foucault seems to offer out of the impasse between deconstruction and a humanist Neo-Marxism, many critics remain troubled by Foucault's refusal to offer any suggestions as to how one might effect political change. As a result, Foucault has passed on an intractable dilemma to his followers: the price of fascinating and compelling analyses of power seems to be a commitment to a notion of power that is stripped ultimately of any historical or political specificity. Despite curious attempts to crossbreed Foucault with someone like Habermas – which allow one to make vague claims about the bourgeois public sphere and the rise of the middle class – the decisive political and discursive shifts that are pinpointed soon reveal themselves to be repeated in other political settings and other historical moments. The reason is clear. What Foucault was examining was what he believed to be a fundamental aspect of consciousness. Power for Foucault was an inextricable part of consciousness itself. History provided the material with which to present a philosophical – indeed, Hegelian – argument.

The explanation for this paradox lies, once again, in the French reception of Hegel. For, in addition to the notion of discourse as the disclosure and reworking of Being as well as the means of man's birth and death, Kojève also drew attention to the role of the wise man in the *Phenomenology*. Kojève's reading of the wise man does much to explain Foucault's position. For the wise man comes at the end of history, when discourse has effectively transformed nature and reconstituted humanity as spirit. The task that remains for the wise man is to make this transformation apparent in and as discourse. 'The wise man thinks all that is thinkable, and at the moment when the wise man lives, all that is *thinkable* is already effectively realized.'[56] As a result, the wise man brings to an end the dialectic of the master and slave. He does this by negating desire itself:

> At the moment when the wise man and, consequently, science, appears, the opposition in question is therefore already sublated. In other words, Man no longer has Desire; he is perfectly and definitively *satisfied* by that which *is*; he therefore does not *act*, no longer transforms the world, and in consequence no longer changes himself. In short, he has become . . . wise, very wise.[57]

The wise man realizes the end of history, which is the unfolding of the struggle between masters and slaves. Thus the wise man does not liberate slaves *per se*; he brings an end to the dialectic that makes slaves possible. Foucault's work can thus perhaps only be understood finally as the work of a wise man. He does not undertake action or urge others to action. His action, like that of the wise man's, is an action of discourse. As Kojève explains:

> He lives and acts; but only lives by means of Science, and he only acts for Science. And since he lives and acts as a real man, the product of his active

existence, that is to say Science or the Concept, has itself an empirical existence, a Dasein: if the wise man is a man of flesh and bone, Science is a discourse (logos) effectively pronounced or a book ('Bible'). This book is produced by the wise man.[58]

The production of this discourse should make man as well as desire part of history. This is a liberation, of sorts, the liberation of discourse. For consciousness has always been assumed to be a fact of given being. It has, instead, always been produced as the result of the struggle for recognition, which in turn is part of the unfolding of spirit. To make this servile consciousness historical – an explicitly produced effect of discourse – is to put an end to it. This end, this point of wisdom, comprises the goal that Foucault seeks to make a reality by means of his works. Thus much in Foucault that is often taken as a rhetorical flourish is to be taken literally. Foucault is quite correct, for instance, when he explains that his study of sexuality was 'a philosophical exercise. The object was to learn to what extent the effort to think one's own history can free thought from what it silently thinks, and so enable it to think differently.'[59] It is time for the slave to become wise. Foucault thereby presents a brilliant instance of the extent of the unwitting Hegelianism of contemporary philosophy and criticism.

For its part, American critical thought, when not celebrating the supposed transcendence of Hegelianism in postmodernism, remains caught in the Foucauldian predicament of endlessly rehearsing Kojève's master/slave dialectic. Accordingly, consciousness is always a slave consciousness and is always inaugurated by the master. The only real task left to this criticism is rehearsing this scenario in different arenas and in different modes of representation. This task is virtually endless, however, for this notion of power, much like spirit, is at work everywhere. Given that it must renounce all the teleological ambitions of Marxism, this mode of criticism also seems to renounce the possibility of political change that it nonetheless implicitly and consistently demands.

Wherever the emphasis lies, then, the current critical temper seems caught in a Hegelian labyrinth. It is a Hegelianism, moreover, that need never mention the name Hegel. As Paul de Man reminds us: 'Few thinkers have so many disciples who never read a word of their master's writings.'[60]

It is thus not too far-fetched to suggest that one could easily recast the story of post-war French philosophy (and recent American literary theory and criticism) as the story of Hegelianism by other means. Although one cannot make an argument such as the one just outlined in anything but a Hegelian manner, it is necessary to put it forth because we still inhabit a Hegelianism of sorts. To truly think the end of Hegel it will be necessary to remain Hegelian to a degree. Most of the confident attempts to transcend Hegelianism have been, in point of fact, brilliant continuations of Hegelianism. As a result, speculative thought remains for the most part unchallenged. To truly confront Hegel, therefore, it will be necessary to account fully for our failure to transcend Hegel. It will be necessary to inhabit Hegel, our Hegel.

It is Derrida who has sought to confront this silent Hegelianism of our age. From the early essays such as 'The Pit and the Pyramid' and 'A Hegelianism Without Reserve' to the extended study *Glas* and the recent writings on the political, Hegel has provided a constant point of reference for the articulation of deconstruction. It is clear, moreover, that Hegel is not just one more philosopher in the range of philosophical and literary figures that Derrida treats in his work. Rather, one could argue that it is *the* task of deconstruction to come to terms with Hegel. For Hegel's work, Derrida argues, occupies a unique and strangely ambivalent position in the history of Western philosophy. It is both the culmination of the Western philosophical tradition and the beginning of its dissolution. As such, Hegel's work forms both the horizon and limit of deconstruction as well as its very condition of possibility.

This productive ambivalence is in evidence throughout Derrida's treatment of Hegel's philosophy. On the one hand, for instance, Derrida portrays Hegel as the very consummation of the Western philosophical tradition that begins with the Greeks. As Derrida writes of Hegel in *Of Grammatology*: 'He undoubtedly *summed up* the entire philosophy of the logos. He determined ontology as absolute logic; he assembled all the delimitations of philosophy as presence; he assigned to presence the eschatology of parousia, of the self-proximity of infinite subjectivity.'[61] Hegel, in other words, announces the advent of the closure of metaphysics itself. For in Hegel, onto-theology finally achieves systematicity in the unfolding of an absolute subjectivity. As such, Hegel defines what forms the ultimate task of deconstruction: the imperative to disrupt the virtual self-realization of onto-theology in speculative idealism. The means of this self-realization – the *Aufhebung* – comprises the decisive site of investigation for deconstruction. For this reason, Derrida underscores in the interview with Jean-Louis Houdebine and Guy Sarpetta in *Positions* that the key 'concept' of *différance* was deployed in order to make a strategic intervention in Hegelian thought. 'If there were a definition of *différance*,' Derrida states, 'it would be precisely the limit, the interruption, the destruction of the Hegelian *relève wherever* it operates. What is at stake here is enormous.'[62] This is an essential point to bear in mind given the confused designation of Derrida as a 'post-structuralist.' The *Aufhebung* – as the elision of the material means of significa-tion – reasserts itself in the claim of structuralism to be the unfolding of the cultural logic of an absolute subjectivity. Thus Derrida's early work does not position itself *vis-à-vis* structuralism *per se* but addresses that which enables the persistence of the Hegelian dialectic in our century.

On the other hand, it is clear that Hegel also announces for Derrida the possibility of deconstruction. As Derrida phrases it in *Of Grammatology*, Hegel is the last philosopher of the book and the first philosopher of writing. Hegel is not only the most complete manifestation of that which deconstruction seeks to undo. Hegel also opens up the possibility of the task of thinking difference. It is for this reason that Derrida argues that Hegel occupies such a unique position in the history of Western metaphysics. As Derrida argues: 'All that Hegel thought within this horizon, all, that is, except eschatology, may be reread as a meditation on writing. Hegel is *also* the thinker of irreducible *différance*.'[63] This aspect of Hegel is no doubt most fully addressed in *Glas*. Here Derrida focuses on Hegel's early writings on Christianity and ethics. Hegel's consideration of the finitization of the divine are of particular interest because he had not yet articulated his mature system. Hence this unique period in Hegel's develop-ment is one in which he perhaps most carefully confronted the problem of finitude. *Glas* in turn examines what in Hegel resists the Hegelian dialectic. Derrida thereby expands upon what he had announced in *Positions*: 'In effect I believe that Hegel's text is necessarily fissured: that it is something more and other than the circular closure of its representation.'[64] This fissuring of the Hegelian text – which *Glas* performs – is what truly opens up the possibility of deconstruction. Paradoxically, then, Hegel's text, in its performance of the thinking of difference, comprises the enabling condition of the strategies of deconstruction.

Despite the clear centrality of Hegel to the work of Derrida, this issue has remained relatively unexplored. The relative critical silence that *Glas* has met is symptomatic of this. While many would no doubt agree with Geoffrey Hart-man that *Glas* is a masterpiece of criticism, few have actually ventured to broach this text.[65] All too often, the attention that has been granted *Glas* has focused on the seemingly arbitrary nature of its typography. The fact that such an extended study of Hegel could meet with a pronounced critical silence is both significant and telling. It reveals a persisting inability to grasp the full philosophical complexity of Derrida's work.[66] The urge to put Derrida 'to use' in such critical discourses as New Historicism and Cultural Studies only underscores the resistance to the truly philosophical nature of deconstruction. None-theless, it is only when we begin to come to terms with the true philosophical dimensions of deconstruction – and thus with its engagement with Hegel – that we will begin to confront the Hegelianism of our thought.

The essays contained in this volume present a beginning attempt to read our repressed Hegelian genealogy. They can be grouped according to three basic and necessary responses. The first is a return to the texts of Hegel to pursue a path Derrida has opened up. The second is a consideration of the impact this already transformed Hegel had and will have upon our culture. The third is a meditation on *Glas*, Derrida's most extensive treatment of Hegel. These three responses, accordingly, divide the volume into three distinct parts.

Part I of this volume, 'Hegel After Derrida,' responds to the implications of Derrida's work for the study of Hegel. The essays in this section reread Hegel in the light of the strategies and issues suggested by Derrida. Two distinct insights emerge from these investigations. One is that we remain implicated in a Hegelianism to a greater extent than might be anticipated. The other is that there is nonetheless a Hegel yet to be examined by us. The task these essays set for us – which has barely begun to be undertaken – is the interrogation of a Hegel that remains very much with us and yet unknown to us. Each in its own way testifies to the fact that we are far from done with Hegel.

In 'Hegel at the Court of the Ashanti,' Robert Bernasconi pursues a course suggested by Derrida in *Glas* and such political writings as *The Other Heading*. He examines Hegel's use and appropriation of Africa, particularly in the *Lectures on the Philosophy of History*. While seemingly marginal to the project of spec-ulative idealism, the presence of Africa in Hegel is, in fact, an index of the relation between the West and its colonial other. Hegel is thereby implicated – and, as Bernasconi reminds us, we too are implicated here – in a history (and a future) of exploitation. For Hegel Africans supposedly exist at the most primitive level of consciousness – immediate sensuousness, which is why Africa lies outside history and outside the very concept of justice. Indeed, it is only by encountering the West and, specifically, enduring slavery to the West, that Africa enters into the dialectical process of consciousness and thus world history. According to the logic of the unfolding of world spirit, it is both necessary and just that Africa be subjected to slavery and colonization. In his assessment of this complex issue, Bernasconi does not permit us to enjoy a simplistic and self-congratulatory dismissal of such politically incorrect views. Rather, Bernasconi seeks to document, with an eye to the question of justice, how Hegel used and abused a certain 'knowledge' of Africa. Accordingly, Africa – as a textual entity – is drawn into the realm of justice. Hegel is very much on trial in this essay. And, as prosecutor, Bernasconi shows us how reading, coupled with a philological scrupulousness, can be a form of ethics, a way of unravelling a history whose future we might not be condemned to.

In 'Of Spirit(s) and Will(s),' John H. Smith argues that the concept of the will serves to indicate the unthought remains of Hegel within Derrida's work. Will remains unthought within deconstruction because it has been mistakenly conflated with spirit. Far from being considered a distinct concept, will is collapsed into the metaphysics of subjectivity. The result, Smith argues, is a disavowal of a concept necessary for political thought. This issue is of particular importance because it lies at the root of deconstruction's problematic relation to politics. To address this issue, Smith undertakes an exercise in hermeneutics to uncover the nuanced reading that Hegel, in fact, gave to the concept of the will. For this reason Smith investigates the family in Hegel, which is the originary constellation of will in Hegel's system. Of particular interest to Smith are the transitions from the family to civil society to the state – the transition, in other words, from individual will to polity. Smith argues that this transition is most concretely thought out in the exploration of wills and testaments in the family. For it is in the will of the patriarch of the family that order (of spirit) and arbitrariness (of individual will) are fused together. This impossible fusion extends beyond spirit or any of its deconstructions. Will is thereby not drawn into the purity of absolute interiority but is instead laid out in all its intricacy, in all its finite plurality. Within Hegel is a thinking of will(s) that is not yet subject to spirit or a metaphysics of subjectivity. As Smith demonstrates, not only is there much to examine in Hegel after Derrida, but there is also much to examine in Derrida after Hegel. The cross-interrogation that Smith stages between Hegel and Derrida unsettles Hegelian thought and deconstruction. Smith suggests that this unsettling may yet make a politics for deconstruction possible.

In both a direct and an oblique way, Jean-Luc Nancy has for some time been considering the relation between Hegel and Derrida. Indeed, one of his earliest publications, *La rémarque speculative* – a book-length study of Hegel – emerged out of a seminar conducted by Derrida. What has interested Nancy from the outset is the bifurcated nature of both Hegel's texts and his status in the history of philosophy. Nancy has argued for the necessity of simultaneously thinking with and against Hegel. Perhaps more than in his other writings, 'The Surprise of the Event' – written in the challenging, evocative, and intensely literary style of his more recent essays – shows us the extent to which we can think against Hegel within Hegel. Nancy focuses on Hegel's *Science of Logic* in order to undertake a thinking of the event, for it is, in fact, in Hegel that the event is first thought. What interests Nancy is the distinction that Hegel makes between the cognition of truth and the 'event' of truth – its narrative presentation. It is this distinction that opens up the possibility of a thinking of the event – of the happening of truth. Hegel thus sets philosophy the task of comprehending not simply the truth, but the taking-place of the truth, the event of the truth. We must follow Hegel – pitting a canonical Hegel against the thought of Hegel – in thinking of the event as not distinct but as the primordial arrival of truth, of the coming-to-presence of the present. Yet Hegel – and this, Nancy argues, is what defines philosophical modernity – mainly seeks to overcome the event. As such, he does not think the surprise of the event. Beyond just event, one must think the surprise of the event, the leap of nothingness into Being. What must be thought, Nancy argues, is not the fact of Being, but that Being happens, that *there is* Being at all – indeed, simply *that there is*. Thought then is this surprise, which *is* nothing. Nancy thus presents a reading of Hegel – which perhaps is itself an event – that discloses not only the role of the event in Hegel, but also the role of Hegel in a thinking of the event.

Werner Hamacher, in '(The End of Art with the Mask),' interrogates Hegel's notorious pronouncement about the end of art. The stakes in such an assertion are enormous. For, as Hamacher points out, art is tantamount to the self-expression of substance itself and hence of the social world and the divine. Thus the end of art entails the end of substance, society, and God. In his examination, Hamacher focuses on the movement from epic to tragedy to comedy in the *Phenomenology* as well as the *Lectures on Aesthetics*. In tragedy, Hamacher argues, self-consciousness comes into conflict with unknown laws. These unknown laws are embodied as gods, as masks of an abstract substantiality. Tragedy thereby stages the impossibility of consciousness to know itself. The function of comedy is to play with these masks. Comedy becomes the means by which the subject plays with itself as other in that it plays with itself as the appearance of abstract substantiality – as, in short, a mask. In comedy there are no substantial forms, only a desubstantialization that deforms everything that could be its object. The subject eventually triumphs, however, over substance, retaining masks as trophies of this victory. Yet this victory is Pyrrhic, for the self has triumphed only over its own substance. Accordingly, the subject, in playing with masks, plays with its own death mask. Despite Hegel's pronouncement, however, this process cannot come to an end. The end of art does not stop ending. We, in turn, must think this end, this end without completion. This end(ing) of art (and thus of substance itself) is finite and incomplete and ongoing – its movement describes the path of thinking itself.

In 'Eating My God,' I examine Hegel's 'The Spirit of Christianity and its Fate,' an essay that forms a major focus of *Glas*. At issue in this essay – if one can in fact call it that – is the very idea of reading: for how does one read an essay that actually consists of fragments? The tension between part and whole, fragment and corpus, is addressed within this text(s)'s consideration of the problem of representing the divine. For Jesus is a representation, an embodiment of the divine. Yet to draw the infinite into the realm of finitude is to subject it to limitation. For this reason, Hegel argues that the spirit of Christianity necessitates the annihilation of the material sign of the divine, which is what the death of Jesus accomplishes. The most perfect example of this resolution for Hegel is provided by the Last Supper, for it is here that Jesus represents himself as the bread and wine of the meal, which the disciples are then invited to consume. The sign of the divine thus achieves signification without leaving any material trace of itself. This is the mechanism of the *Aufhebung* in nuce. Yet in the context of 'The Spirit of Christianity' it is made clear that the *Aufhebung* is dependent upon the ongoing destruction of the very materiality of the sign. The bread and wine of the Last Supper thus present a solution to the representation of the divine, to the becoming-subject of the Absolute, that is itself impossible – and yet that becomes the very foundation for Hegelian thought.

Part II of this volume, 'After Hegel After Derrida,' continues the discussion begun in Part I. Given the enormous role that Hegel plays in our philosophy and culture, it is only logical that the emergence of a different Hegel as a result of the work of Derrida will require extensive realignments in our culture. Thus the essays in this section explore the implications for our understanding of Freud and Marx. It is clear that this is only the beginning of a complex and enormous undertaking. Nonetheless, this undertaking is absolutely necessary, for Derrida's work presents not merely a rereading of Hegel but an indication of the ultimate impact that an as yet unexamined Hegel might have on our own decidedly Hegelian culture.

In 'The Remnants of Philosophy: Psychoanalysis After *Glas*,' Suzanne Gearhart intertwines Derrida's reading of Hegel with his reading of Freud to explore the implications of deconstruction for the psychoanalytic understanding of gender. Following up reflections by Sarah Kofman on this topic, Gearhart undertakes an examination of Derrida's critique of phallocentrism. Gearhart begins with an intriguing question: why does Hegel have a place at all in *Glas*? For if the target is phallocentrism, why should Hegel feature so prominently? The answer, Gearhart suggests, is that Hegel, in his analysis of the family and the concept of the *Aufhebung*, offers us a reworking of the concept of repression. For repression – which is linked with penile envy, castration fear, and the very origins of the constitution of gender in psycho-analysis – is tantamount to the *Aufhebung* itself. Derrida's Hegel makes clear, moreover, that repression is not linked to some precise event or activity in time but is instead a process that has always already begun. Rigorously thought, then, Derrida's Hegel presents an interpretation of repression that transforms it into a post-Freudian concept. Drawing from this insight, Gearhart proceeds to present a rereading of the role of Antigone in Hegel and Derrida. At first glance, Hegel's Antigone would seem to be far removed from Freud and Derrida since she supposedly stands outside desire. Yet what Antigone demonstrates, Gearhart argues, is that the overcoming of desire is bound up with desire. For Antigone ultimately serves the larger articulation of *Sittlichkeit*. She is therefore a figure of the process of repression/idealiza-tion. Thus Gearhart warns us that privileging Antigone entails accepting fetishism as a model of desire. This acceptance, in turn, entails acknowl-edging castration as the foundation of psychic experience. As a result, the opposition between Antigone and Oedipus never confronts 'that there is' at all as a primal scene but simply accepts it as 'given.' The investigations of gender and sexuality must take into account repression, the fact that the process of repression/idealization has always already begun. Thus, the task of post-Freudian and post-Hegelian thought is to rethink the feminine in terms of a repression that knows no discrete origin or final closure.

Andrzej Warminski reads the relation between Hegel and Marx as the attempt to read the relation between consciousness and life. Contrary to what has often been assumed about this relation, Warminski argues in 'Hegel/Marx: Consciousness and Life' that Marx does not simply perform an inversion of the relation between these two terms. Materialism, in other words, cannot simply be the chiasmic inversion of idealism. For this would result in merely a more naive, pre-critical idealism. Instead, materialism understands life to over-determine consciousness in a way that consciousness cannot master. Accordingly, consciousness is not the other of life; it is not the determinate negation of life. Consciousness transforms life into a figure for consciousness. The only authoritative ground for this transformation, however, is the system of consciousness itself. At the same time, consciousness can only come to be because of this trope, which turns life into a phenomenal figure for consciousness. The relation between consciousness and life is thereby rewritten in the materialist reading to be the arbitrary act of a linguistic imposition of meaning. As a result, self-consciousness as such is impossible. Thus Hegel, as Warminski suggests, is closer to Marx than most Marxists. What emerges then is a completely unfamiliar Hegel, a Hegel who would be divided against himself. Indeed, the Hegelian text becomes thereby heterogeneous to itself. Marx's reading discloses this heterogeneity; it also makes apparent that materialism — if the term is to mean anything — must be founded on the scrupulous labor of reading. As Warminski suggests, it is only in this manner that the texts of Hegel, Marx, and Derrida can be put to work, can be made to happen for an uncertain future.

The ultimate ambition of Part III, 'Reading *Glas*,' is, simply, to make further readings of *Glas* possible. Despite the range of scholarship on Derrida, *Glas* remains a shockingly unexamined text, better known as an example of concrete poetry than as a philosophical text. Yet, given the suspicions of Hegel scholars and the lack of a thorough familiarity with Hegel on the part of literary critics, this situation is perhaps not surprising. To a great extent, the essays collected in Part III present the 'argument' of *Glas*. As Simon Critchley has argued, it is necessary to explicate *Glas* in order to open it up as a text for others. The essays of Critchley and Heinz Kimmerle, accordingly, clarify *Glas*'s relation to Hegel's and Derrida's other work. This is, in a sense, the *conditio sine qua non* of any meditation of 'Hegel after Derrida.' Kevin Thompson's essay complements those of Critchley and Kimmerle in that it focuses on the issue of the quasi-transcendental in *Glas* — a key 'concept' that indicates the almost absolute proximity of deconstruction and speculative thought. Finally, Henry Sussman positions *Glas* in the larger context of Western modernity, reminding us that part of the task of reading *Glas* is unraveling the larger cultural implications of this complex text. Taken together, then, these four essays offer a good casebook for understanding *Glas*.

In 'A Commentary Upon Derrida's Reading of Hegel in *Glas*,' Simon Critchley offers us a sustained analysis of the Hegel column of *Glas* as well as a meditation on the relation between ethics and deconstruction. *Glas*, Critchley argues, is not a self-indulgent exercise in textual free play; it is a rigorous and detailed examination of Hegel, a 'devotional labor of reading.' Critchley undertakes a similarly systematic reading of Derrida, one that traces Derrida's own systematic reading of Hegel. Accordingly, Critchley focuses on one of the major 'threads' in *Glas*, the role of the family in Hegel. For the family is a crucial transitional hinge in the *Philosophy of Right* and the Hegelian system as a whole. In addition to being the first moment in the articulation of *Sittlichkeit*, the family regulates the transition from religion to philosophy in the elaboration of absolute spirit, while rendering the system problematic. The family constitutes, in short, a rupture in and of the system. The figure in the family that embodies this enabling rupture is the sister; more specifically, it is Antigone who embodies this impossible hinge. Antigone is thus a quasi-transcendental condition of possibility and impossibility for speculative thought, marking a place within Hegel where an ethics is discernible that cannot be reduced to dialectics or cognition. She gestures towards an ethics of singularity that would not be based on the dialectical recognition of the other, which, in fact, is nothing less than self-recognition. Indeed, Critchley argues that an ethics of the singular is the perpetual horizon of Derrida's reading of Hegel. He follows this issue into Derrida's discussion of the gift and holocaust. For the non-metaphysical donation of the gift exceeds Hegelian dialectics and opens it to the ethical. Critchley thereby demonstrates that the question of ethics — which is increasingly brought to bear on deconstruction — must confront Hegel and, more precisely, must confront Derrida's reading of Hegel.

Heinz Kimmerle addresses Derrida's reading of Bataille and Hegel in his essay 'On Derrida's Hegel Interpretation.' After outlining some preliminary issues in Derrida's reading of Bataille, Kimmerle turns to examine the remains of absolute knowledge, which resist internalization into the holocaust of speculative thought in which everything must be consumed. Derrida's merit, Kimmerle argues, is to demonstrate that everything is not consumed in this holocaust — there is always a remainder that is extrinsic to and yet utterly necessary for the system. The remains that interest Kimmerle are those that have resisted the attempt of absolute knowledge to incorporate nature, its own other. Hegel thinks of this relation to nature in terms of labor, in terms of reworking and appropriating objectivity. It is in the realm of the family, Kimmerle argues, that this relation comes to a point of crisis. As the family is to serve as the conduit for the full articulation of *Sittlichkeit* into the community, femininity — which constitutes nature in the realm of the family — becomes the enemy of the community. Femininity is nature, the otherness of exteriority, that must be *aufgehoben* in order for *Sittlichkeit* — and hence the social — to come into being. This, then, accounts for the tragic role of the sister in Hegel's description of the family. Once the resistance of the feminine is overcome, the true work of the speculative can continue in the relation between the father and son: a relation that comprises the foundation of the Hegelian community. Kimmerle argues, however, that there will always be a remainder to the work of spirit upon nature. The figure of the feminine – which in Hegel is represented by Antigone – comprises an exemplary instance of what remains in the wake of the holocaust of absolute knowledge.

'Hegelian Dialectic and the Quasi-Transcendental in *Glas*,' Kevin Thompson's examination of the role of Hegel in Derrida, makes clear that Hegel is not simply a topic within deconstruction, but that which makes deconstruction possible. Derrida's work, Thompson argues, does not inhabit a privileged space beyond speculative thought. Indeed, Derrida's work is perhaps not thinkable outside of speculative thought. At the same time, perhaps speculative thought cannot be truly understood without deconstruction. For deconstruction, as Thompson suggests, is intrinsic to the dialectic. This is because Hegel presents us with a rigorous thinking, a negativity that is neither abstract nor determinate. This constitutes, in turn, the quasi-transcendental structure of the remains within which the Hegelian dialectic is both inscribed and displaced. Following Derrida's example in *Glas*, Thompson focuses on the family in Hegel – which is both a finite moment in Hegel's system and a figure of its totality. In his essay, the relation between the brother and sister is taken as a key instance of this quasi-transcendental structure. For it is in this relation that singularity remains distinct. Nonetheless, this thinking of singularity undergoes the teleological constriction that dialectics enforces. Hence what is natural difference in the theater of the family becomes an ethical opposition. As such, speculative thought recovers itself – recovers itself from the thought of difference and hence the suspension of the dialectic itself – and moves on to the articulation of spirit. Thompson succeeds in mapping out the space of the point of almost absolute proximity between deconstruction and speculative thought. As Thompson also shows us, it is in that 'almost' that the difference between Hegel and Derrida – if not difference itself – lies.

Henry Sussman, in 'Hegel, *Glas*, and the Broader Modernity,' undertakes to situate *Glas* within the context of what he terms the larger Modernity – that is, Modernity considered not simply as an early twentieth-century cultural movement but as a project that the West has pursued since at least the eighteenth century. Derrida's intervention in the texts of Hegel, Sussman argues, is far from an exercise in esoterica of interest only to specialists. Rather, *Glas* speaks both to the larger Modernity and the cultural moment we currently occupy. Under the guidance of postmodernism and multiculturalism, critical thought claims to have prepared the West to confront and pass over into its own conceptual and political other. *Glas*, however, does not relate itself to a supposed externality. Instead, it burrows into the heart of the West itself in order to bring the West in relation to its own internalized and repressed other. *Glas* thereby intuits a plane of cultural articulation – a purely linguistic articulation – that is autonomous from the metaphysics of the subject. At the same time, Derrida makes clear that this derangement is not imposed upon this philosophical system; rather, it is already installed within it. Thus the search for the other does not need to posit an exteriority to the West – which is, in fact, always a positing of the West – because the other inhabits its innermost structures. Sussman suggests then that the larger Modernity is precisely this search for an other too easily forgotten, an other that the West has repressed and yet is utterly dependent upon. *Glas*, accordingly, is the making concrete of an architecture of derangement between the institutionalization of Modernity and its own ongoing deconstruction. Sussman's essay is a valuable complement to the essays of Critchley, Kimmerle, and Thompson in that it reminds us of the larger role *Glas* does, can, and should play in our culture.

This volume must necessarily go against the grain of contemporary critical thought. As has already been suggested, the contemporary critical scene is utterly inimical to what is seen to be hopelessly abstract – '*sauve qui peut*,' as Hegel said – philosophical thought.[67] Unless, of course, that thought can be shown to be disguising an oppressive ideological agenda. Most, moreover, seem eager to toll the death knell of deconstruction. Perhaps this is just as well. For, as Andrzej Warminski suggests in his essay, deconstruction in a sense never took place. Yet in the project of deconstruction – particularly in the confrontation between Derrida and Hegel – there is (still) being articulated what our contemporary situation silently presupposes. For, despite the effort to be a culture that comes after Hegel, ours is still a Hegelian culture. If anything, Hegel will still come after us. For we have yet to begin to read Derrida's reading of Hegel. This task, which has just begun to be undertaken, may be the only means of eventually dismantling the Hegelian edifice.

It is not the place of an introduction to set forth what only the volume as a whole can articulate. It is impossible not to recall here that both Hegel and Derrida have meditated on the impossibility of the very idea of an introduction. For the introduction belies the incompleteness the system (as text) denies.[68] This introduction in particular, with its thoroughly Hegelian evolutionary history of thought, negates its own supposed objective. It cannot be the introduction it claims to be. At best it is a Hegelian prelude to the introduction that will follow. This volume as a whole, then, will have been an introduction to an engagement that is yet to be enacted. Not just an *Einleitung*, this volume is also a *Vorrede*. It is prefatory, but it is also *vor der Rede* in the sense of Kafka's 'Vor dem Gesetz.' It awaits, perhaps in vain, but nonetheless with infinite patience, for a reading of the speculative.

# Part I

# HEGEL AFTER DERRIDA

# 1

# Hegel at the Court of the Ashanti

*Robert Bernasconi*

Hegel called world history a court of judgement (*Gericht*), a world court (*Weltgericht*),[1] and in his *Lectures on the Philosophy of World History* he took Africans before that court and found them to be barbaric, cannibalistic, preoccupied with fetishes, without history, and without any consciousness of freedom.[2] Most importantly for him, they lack any 'integral ingredient of culture (*Bildung*)' (VPW 214; LPW 174). Faced with this diatribe, commentators are largely divided between those who regard Hegel's discussion of Africa as unworthy of philosophical consideration and best forgotten and those who, once having quoted it, seem uncertain as to what more can be said about a text that is so extreme. Both approaches evade the question as to the place of this discussion within both Hegel's philosophy and the early nineteenth-century discourse about Africa. It is perhaps possible to argue that by excluding Africa from the dialectic of world history, Hegel had in some sense located his own remarks about Africa outside the scope of the system. It would therefore be the decision behind this exclusion that would have to be examined, rather than the specific details of an account whose unphilosophical character had been conceded by Hegel himself. By contrast, I want to engage with the specifics of Hegel's account. Far from excluding Africa, Hegel devoted a great deal of attention to it. If, as he said, Africa has no 'historical interest of its own' (VPW 214; LPW 174), why did Hegel insist on exploring it?

In this paper, after rehearsing some of the more familiar objections to Hegel's verdict against Africa, I turn the tables and put Hegel on trial. More specifically, given that much of Hegel's account is directed against the Ashanti, I will use what is known about them and especially what Hegel either did know or should have known, to take him before the court of the Ashanti, where his

41

use of evidence can be interrogated. The results of this examination render all the more pressing the need to give an account of how Hegel applied his system of justice to Africa, which I attempt to do in the second part of the paper. In the third part, I return to the interpretation of Hegel's statement about Africa as unhistorical and, having restored it to its context in Hegel's system, show its consequences.[3]

## I

An extensive literature criticizing Hegel's discussion of Africa has arisen in recent years, but that does not mean that he has not had defenders. One need only recall a note in Duncan Forbes's Introduction to *Hegel's Lectures on The Philosophy of World History*, which appeared in 1975. Forbes wrote:

> It is also fashionable to display one's broadmindedness by criticizing Hegel for being arrogantly Europo-centric or Western-orientated. The latest example is W. H. Walsh in *Hegel's Political Philosophy*. . . . But isn't Hegel's perspective broadly the right one? Or at least should one not wait until world history has shown its hand a bit more clearly?[4]

Leaving aside the huge gap that separates those two questions, it is worth recalling that in the essay to which Forbes referred, Walsh was anything but extreme in his criticism. Walsh described Hegel's treatment of Africa as 'to put it mildly, not very sympathetic' and added that 'the picture he offers of Negro society in Africa is far from attractive.'[5] Walsh exonerated Hegel from the charge of being a racist and, ignoring the discussion at the beginning of the Encyclopaedia account of the *Philosophy of Spirit*, insisted that Hegel has 'no tendency to divide mankind into superior and inferior races.'[6] The most that Walsh was prepared to say was that Hegel's account of history was 'the success story of modern European man' and that 'a less kind way of putting it' would be to say that Hegel 'arrogantly assumes the superiority of white Anglo-Saxon protestants.' The importance of his use of the term 'Anglo-Saxon,' which Walsh applied to what Hegel would call *germanisch*, is to suggest precisely what Forbes confirms: that Hegel's viewpoint is not totally alien or past. However, the problem goes further than that would suggest. Even if, when reading these pages of Hegel, one wants to divorce oneself from the conclusions and attitudes expressed there, one cannot do so simply by a declaration. It is not just a question of turning Walsh's studious understatement into something more appropriate to what is at stake. Each reader has to see how far he or she is implicated in the discussion. If a certain Eurocentrism is at stake here, then one needs to be aware of how pervasive that Eurocentrism still is.[7]

That the issues are a great deal more complicated than European commentators have hitherto recognized is apparent as soon as one turns to African and African-American critics of Hegel. Most European commentators have tended to accept with little more than raised eyebrows Hegel's division of Africa into 'European Africa,' the coastal region to the north of the Sahara desert, the region of the Nile 'which is closely connected with Asia,' and 'Africa proper (*das eigentliche Afrika*),' which lies to the south of the Sahara (VPW 213; LPW 173). Walsh's word is that it seems 'odd' that Egypt belongs to the history of the Persian Empire, rather than to the history of Africa.[8] It is hardly surprising that critiques written from an African point of view question this way of dividing Africa.[9] Even though the invention of Africa as a unity is perhaps at least as problematic as other parallel constructions, Africa was certainly a great deal less divided into separate parts than Europeans were inclined to believe. This view was sustained by the fact that Europeans found parts of Africa impenetrable, but even if it had been true that there was no longer any contact between the different parts of Africa (VPW 213; LPW 173), and Hegel knew from the spread of Mohammedanism that it was not (VPW 217; LPW 177), he was almost certainly familiar with the thesis that ancient Egypt had had intimate connections with other parts of Africa.

Hegel's self-serving exclusion of what would otherwise have been clear counter-examples to his discussion of Africa is certainly of importance in any assessment of his work, as well as in any history of the European understanding of Africa. However, a study of Hegel's use of his sources is even more revealing. The following questions need to be posed. First, what sources did Hegel use and how faithfully does his account reflect them? This would serve to address the question as to whether there is any evidence of distortion, perhaps even systematic distortion, in Hegel's presentation of Africa.[10] One must also ask, of course, whether there were other important sources that Hegel might reasonably have used and that he failed to use. This is not only a question about whether Hegel's account reflected the best knowledge of the day but also a question of the principle of selection, both of his sources and his chief objects of interest. Second, what information is now available to us that might allow us to correct the version presented by both Hegel and his contemporaries? The question of the reliability of Hegel's account is important because, given the widespread ignorance about African history, there must always be a question about the extent to which the story Hegel and his contemporaries told about

Africa still remains intact. In other words, there must always be a reflexive moment in which the reader of Hegel, as of the travel diaries on which Hegel based his account, must ask him- or herself about the extent that he or she remains captive to this account, not only in maintaining a certain image of Africa, but also in retaining a conceptuality about Europe and about history that is more closely tied to that image than one is aware until the question is asked.

There has not yet been a systematic study of Hegel's use of his sources. One commentator, Shlomo Avinieri, in the course of claiming that Hegel was one of the first European thinkers to incorporate the Asian world into the schema of Europe and so emancipate the non-European world from 'its historiosophical marginality,' noted that 'there are also a few passages about Africa, which bear witness to Hegel's astonishingly wide range of reading, but these are of a very rudimentary nature.'[11] If Avinieri's remark about Asia fails to do justice to the extent to which the project of Universal History had already prior to Hegel ceased to be a history of salvation and had become a record of what was known about the world, albeit told unashamedly from a European point of view, then surely his assessment of the extent of Hegel's reading about Africa is also exaggerated. The travel diaries of missionaries, explorers, and government officials had become a source of popular entertainment among the educated public. Although it is not entirely clear how much Hegel read about Africa, my own ongoing and highly provisional investigations suggest that it was much less than Avinieri thought, and far from astonishing by the standards of his day. Hegel was fulsome in his praise of the volume on Africa written by his colleague at the University of Berlin, Karl Ritter, but it seems to have been a source only for the initial geographical division of Africa, and not for the details that follow (VPW 212–3; LPW 173).[12] Hegel clearly relied heavily on Giovanni Antonio Cavazzi's *Istorica descrizione de' tre regni Congo, Matamba, Angola* from the seventeenth century.[13] There can also be little doubt that Hegel read T. E. Bowdich's *Mission from Cape Coast Castle to Ashantee*, probably in English.[14] Discussion of fetishism was sufficiently widespread and uniform for it to be unclear what Hegel's sources were on this subject. So far as I know there is no clear evidence that Hegel read either the main theoretical discussion of fetishism, Charles de Brosses's *Du Culte des Dieux Fétiches* or Bosman's *Description of the Coast of Guinea*, which was one of de Brosses's own main sources.[15] It is sometimes suggested that Hegel consulted Tuckey's *Narrative of an Expedition to Explore the River Zaire*, because he tried to obtain it from the Berlin Royal Library, but it is not clear if he succeeded, and if he read it at all it made little impact on his account.[16] The story that the King of Eyio (sic) learns that his reign is at an end when he is presented with three parrot's eggs and told that he is in need of rest (GPW 230; LPW 187) came from Archibald Dalzel's *The History of Dahomey*.[17] Hegel repeated from James Bruce's famous account of his attempt to find the source of the Nile the account of the people of Senaar, where there is a special officer among whose duties is to execute the king when the council decrees that it is to the advantage of the state to do so (VPW 210; LPW 187), but Hegel seems to have taken little else from this book.[18] Hegel also knew Herodotus' account of Africa, from which he quoted the remark that everyone in Africa is a sorcerer (VPW 220; LPW 179).[19] It is quite possible that there are other sources of Hegel's discussions. There were at that time numerous compilation volumes summarizing travellers' reports, as well as extensive reviews of the travel literature.[20] It is even possible that some of the information came to Hegel by word of mouth, a possibility made all the more likely because of the enthusiasm for this kind of information in Europe at that time. Nevertheless, it seems that, discounting the discussion of fetishism, the books by Ritter, Cavazzi, Bowdich, and Dalzel cover virtually all of the ground dealt with by Hegel in both the *Philosophy of History* and the *Philosophy of Religion*.[21] The only difficulty is that, although these are the likely sources of Hegel's account of Africa, in many cases they fail to support his descriptions.

From this distance, it is not always easy to tell precisely how reliable Hegel's sources were.[22] Hegel was certainly justified in criticizing the travel literature of his day for tantalizing readers by appearing 'incredible' and lacking 'a determinate image or principle' (VPW 217; LPW 176), but the manner in which he himself used that literature opens him to the charge of sensationalism as well. The accusation is sustained by the evidence of major and widespread distortion in his use of his sources.[23] I shall here focus on Hegel's use of Bowdich's *Mission*, which was his main source for his knowledge of the Ashanti. The first part of Bowdich's book is an account of how he took over the leadership of the mission and conducted the negotiations; the second part is more of a description and includes the diary of Hutchison, who is mistakenly referred to in Hegel's text (VPW 232 and 271; LPW 188 and 220) and by all subsequent commentators as Hutchinson.[24] Although there were a number of controversies surrounding the mission at the time, the most serious emerged only later when it came to light that the copy of the treaty that Bowdich negotiated with the Ashanti was different from that which he deposited on his return.[25] It turns out that Hegel himself was no more reliable a copyist than Bowdich. To begin with a relatively straightforward example, whereas Bowdich recorded that 'The King is heir to the gold of every subject from the highest to the lowest,'[26] Hegel reported that 'Among the Ashanti, the king inherits all the property left by his deceased subjects' (VPW 229; LPW 187).[27] More seriously, Hegel took from Hutchison the detail that the king of the Ashanti washed the bones of his dead mother. But whereas Hegel said that the bones were washed in human blood, Hutchison specified rum and water.[28] The problem is even more acute in other cases where there was a predisposition on the part of travellers to tell of practices that would feed the curiosity and prejudices of the reading public at home.[29] The desire of travellers to find tales of exotic behaviour were, once communicated to the local population, all too likely to be satisfied. This is particularly the case with the accusation of cannibalism.

> The observation of Thomas Winterbottom in 1803 on cannibalism is relevant here: That this horrid practice does not exist in the neighbourhood of Sierra Leone; nor for many hundred leagues along the coast to the northward and southward of that place, may be asserted with the utmost confidence; nor is there any tradition among the natives which can prove that it ever was the custom: on the contrary, they appear struck with horror when they are questioned individually on the subject; though at the same time they make no scruple of accusing other nations at a distance, and whom they barely know by name, of cannibalism.[30]

Bowdich accused the Ashanti of cannibalism only with reference to ceremonies that took place after a battle. Those who had never killed an enemy ate a portion of a mixture, one of the constituents of which was hearts taken from the enemy.[31] Whether Bowdich had seen this taking place is also unlikely, as most of the remarks made in association with the practice are third hand. In any case, Hegel embellished the story to the point where Ashanti chiefs were said to have 'torn their enemies' hearts from their bodies and eaten them while they were still warm and bleeding' (VPW 271; LPW 220). Nor did Bowdich provide Hegel with the story that at the end of public festivals hosted by the king of the Ashanti, 'a human being is torn to pieces; his flesh is cast to the multitude and greedily eaten by all who can lay hands on it' (VPW 271; LPW 220). If there is a basis for this story, and without an exhaustive list of every book that Hegel read about Africa one cannot be sure that there is none, my research suggests that it does not refer to the Ashanti. The point is important because these are not just anecdotes. They provide the basis on which Hegel rejected the idea of instinct and respect as a universal human characteristic (VPW 224; LPW 182–3).

If Bowdich, unlike Hegel, failed to satisfy those of his readers who wanted to be told that Africans were cannibals, he was more obliging when it came to stories of the ritual slaughters that accompanied funeral services.

> The kings, caboceers, and the higher class, are believed to dwell with the superior Deity after death, enjoying an eternal renewal of the state and luxury they possessed on earth. It is with this impression, that they kill a certain number of both sexes at the funeral customs, to accompany the deceased, to announce his distinction, and to administer to his pleasures.[32]

Later in the book, Bowdich described the process whereby on the death of an important person the slaves would run from the house to avoid being sacrificed, but apart from noting that one or two slaves would be sacrificed at the door, he gave no indication of the large numbers suggested by Hegel.[33] There is little here to justify Hegel's description, clearly given in the context of a discussion of the Ashanti, which reads:

> And it is much the same at funerals, where everything bears the mark of frenzy and dementedness. The slaves of the deceased man are slaughtered and it is decreed that their heads belong to the fetish and their bodies to the relatives who duly devour them.
>
> (VPW 232; LPW 189)

Similar problems arise when one turns to Hegel's account of the Dahomey. Indeed, Hegel allowed features drawn from the Ashanti to slip into his account of the Dahomey. His description of the funeral of the king of Dahomey seems to derive at least in part from Bowdich's description of the events surrounding the death of the Ashanti king. Hegel wrote:

> When the king dies in Dahomey, a general tumult breaks loose in his palace, whose dimensions are enormous; all utensils are destroyed, and universal carnage begins. The wives of the king prepare for death (and, as already mentioned, there are 3333 of them); they look upon their death as necessary, adorn themselves in preparation for it, and order their slaves to kill them. All the bonds of society are loosed in the town and throughout the kingdom; murder and theft break out everywhere, and private revenge is given free rein. On one such occasion, 500 women died in the palace in the space of six minutes.
>
> (VPW 232–3; LPW 189)

The reference to the number of wives suggests that it was the Ashanti that were meant. Hegel was following Bowdich in giving their number as 3333. Hegel had already attributed this number of the wives to the king of Dahomey a few pages earlier as part of an attempt to explain polygamy as a source of wealth because children could be sold as slaves (VPW 227; LPW 185). Hegel got this idea, it seems, from a single case reported by Cavazzi (VPW 221; LPW 185).[34] Clearly, however, this was not the case for the king, even on Bowdich's explanation:

> The laws of Ashantee allow the King 3333 wives, which number is carefully kept up, to enable him to present women to those who distinguish themselves, but never exceeded, being in their eyes a mystical one. . . . Many, probably, the King has never seen.[35]

Rattray, writing in the 1920s, explained that, in giving the number as 3333, Bowdich 'was misled in accepting as a fact a statement often heard but never intended to be taken literally, this number being ascribed to him purely from a desire to flatter.'[36]

When one turns to the account of the funeral arrangements themselves, there are similar problems whether the Ashanti or the Dahomey were meant. Although neither Bowdich nor Hutchison had seen the funeral of an Ashanti king, Bowdich went ahead and described how at the death of a king all the customs surrounding the deaths of any of his subjects had to be repeated by their families, including the human sacrifices.[37] Relatives of the king, 'affecting temporary insanity,' would kill people indiscriminately. 'The King's Ocras [who are the king's captains and not his wives] . . . are all murdered on his tomb, to the number of a hundred or more, and women in abundance.'[38] Dalzel, in his *The History of Dahomey*, described how at the death of the king, 'the wives of the deceased begin, with breaking and destroying the furniture of the house, the gold and silver ornaments and utensils . . . and then murder one another.'[39] However, it was said that 285 of the king's wives were killed on this occasion. There is nothing about the slaughter of 500 wives in six minutes in this text, although the book ends with the claim of five hundred slaughtered over three months in 1791 in connection with the king's coronation.[40] European settlers later in the century suggested that 'the natives' greatly exaggerated the numbers when reporting them to outsiders.[41] It is true that even if some Africans already exaggerated the numbers before giving them to the European travellers, who further exaggerated them before recording them in books read by Hegel, who himself indulged in systematic exaggeration for his own purposes, still this should not distract attention from the fact that the practices that were being described cannot be excused. But why did Hegel feel compelled to multiply the numbers?

Hegel's most graphic account of 'a terrible bloodbath' was drawn from Hutchison's account as included in Bowdich's *Mission from Cape Coast Castle*. Hegel acknowledged that no great numbers were murdered on this occasion as the warning had gone out in advance (VPW 232; LPW 188). However, although Hutchison described the king's executioners traversing the streets to place in irons anyone they found, the alleged human sacrifices seemed to be a matter of various people of rank being summoned to the palace over a period of time, seventeen days on this occasion, because the king suspected them of some offence, on which occasion they would be accused and summarily punished.[42]

> If they are thought desperate characters, a knife is thrust through their mouth to keep them from swearing the death of any other, when they are charged with their crime, real or supposed, and put to death or torture.[43]

Hegel only partially acknowledged the judicial function of these executions: 'On such occasions, the king has all whom he regards as suspect killed, and the deed then takes on the character of a sacred act' (VPW 232; LPW 189). He made no effort to attempt to locate the sacrifices within the social practices of the Ashanti using the information that was available to him.

Later visitors from Europe painted a more complex picture. Freeman reported how Kwaku Dua explained to him in 1842 that 'If I were to abolish human sacrifices, I should deprive myself of one of the most effectual means of keeping the people in subjection.'[44] Seven years later, Kwaku Dua explained to a missionary named Hillard, to the latter's general agreement, that this was indeed part of a legal process designed to prevent crime. Hillard could not help but remember that sheep-stealing had until recently been a capital crime in England.[45] The reply of Kwaku Dua to Governor Winniet of the Gold Coast, when the latter expressed the concern of the British Government over human sacrifices, is especially telling. Having complained that the number of human sacrifices had been greatly exaggerated, he added:

> I remember that when I was a little boy, I heard that the English came to the coast of Africa with their ships for cargoes of slaves for the purpose of taking them to their own country and eating them; but I have long since known that the report was false, and so it will be proved, in reference to many reports which have gone forth against me.[46]

Kwaku Dua's expectation that the Ashanti would eventually be vindicated of the charge of human sacrifice has not yet been fulfilled, but there have been instances when the record was corrected much later. For example, 'the most inhuman spectacle' and 'horrid barbarity' of human 'sacrifice' that Bowdich described as part of his account of the mission's entry into the capital for the first time, an event which no doubt coloured Bowdich's whole experience of the Ashanti, was in fact not a case of sacrifice at all.[47] An examination of the diary of Frederick James, the original leader of the mission, shows that he made further inquiries and discovered that the victim was a native of Annamaboe who had shot an Ashanti man and who had been apprehended after 'strict enquiry.'[48] Unfortunately, by the time James had made this discovery, he was no longer on speaking terms with Bowdich, who would soon take over as leader, so that Bowdich's false impression went unchallenged and became part of the historical record. Nevertheless, the error arose out of a tradition of associating Africans with human sacrifice. It should not be forgotten when reading these descriptions that belief in the existence of human sacrifices had been as important to European justifications of slavery as was the story that all the slaves had been prisoners captured in wars.[49]

Hegel did not select his sources simply because he shared the fascination of his contemporaries for the 'frightful details' they provided. It is true that by focusing on the Ashanti and the Dahomey, Hegel had turned his attention to those African peoples who had at that time a reputation as the most blood-thirsty. However, even within those limits Hegel would have been forced to modify his position had he relied on Benezet[50] instead of Dalzel. Both Dalzel and Norris, who was one of Dalzel's main sources, wrote their books in an attempt to further the pro-slavery cause, whereas Benezet wrote from an anti-slavery position. But Hegel was not simply illustrating extremes. His descriptions were in the service of an account of the universal spirit and shape of the African character (VPW 217; LPW 176). In his Berlin lectures on the *Philosophy of Spirit*, as part of an account of the division between races, Hegel offered what amounts to a summary of the portrait of Africans that emerges from the *Lectures on the Philosophy of World History*.[51] First, Blacks (*die Neger*) are a childish people in their naivety (*Unbefangenheit*). Second, they allow themselves to be sold without reflection as to whether or not this is right; they feel no impulse (*Trieb*) towards freedom.[52] Third, this childishness is reflected in their religion. They sense the higher, but do not retain it. They transfer the higher to a stone, thereby making it into a fetish, although they will throw it away if it fails them. Fourth, although good-natured and harmless when in a calm condition, they commit frightful atrocities when suddenly aroused. Fifth, although capable of

50

education (*Bildung*), as evidenced by their grateful adoption of Christianity on occasion and their appreciation of freedom when acquired, they have no propensity (*Trieb*) for culture (*Kultur*): their spirit is dormant and makes no progress. However, all these features that are set out in the *Encyclopaedia* lectures in mere summary fashion are presented in the *Lectures on the Philosophy of World History* with more attention to the structures of the specificity of the mode of self-consciousness of spirit in Africa (VPW 217; LPW 176) and with the support of the descriptions I have just examined. There was no shortage of gruesome tales of Africa available to Hegel, but he seems to have been unwilling to confine himself to these. Whether it was necessary for Hegel to distort and exaggerate those descriptions to sustain his interpretation of the African character or whether these changes were absolutely gratuitous can be answered, if at all, only by examining the work he made them do in the context of the larger argument.

## II

Hegel's discussion of Africa may not be an integral part of his account of the course of world history, which, like the sun, travels from East to West (VPW 243; LPH 197), but that does not mean that, in discussing Africa in the way he did, he was breaking with the plan of the *Lectures*. Hegel may not have regarded Africa as 'a historical part of the world (*Weltteil*)' (VPW 234; LPW 190), but he had no wish to deny that it was indeed a part of the world. Although Africa does not belong within the division of world history along with the Oriental, the Greek, the Roman, and the Germanic, it does occupy a place in the threefold division of the old world, conceived geographically. Africa conforms to the principle of the upland, a principle Hegel designates as the incapacity for culture (*Unbildsamkeit*) (VPW 212; LPW 172). One can say therefore that, although Africa was excluded from the dialectic of history, it was included in the systematic presentation of geography, in the broad sense of the term established by Kant in his *Physical Geography*, where there was already a discussion of the different peoples of the world, including an account of Africa drawn from travel diaries.

Whereas world history presents the idea of spirit as it shows itself in actuality as a series of world historical peoples, each with their own principle, Hegel needed to examine the influence of natural factors on this process. The urgency for doing so is all the more obvious if one recalls the studies of history and of national character of the eighteenth century, where climate had frequently been presented as of special importance. It is within this context that the idea of a people tied to sensuousness (*Sinnlichkeit*) and immediacy proved valuable for systematic purposes. Hegel judged that 'man' is sensuous insofar as 'he' is both unfree and natural (VPW 188; LPW 153). This is how Hegel subsequently identified Africans (VPW 212 and 218; LPW 172 and 177). In this way, Hegel's account of Africa served as a null-point or base-point to anchor what followed.

Nevertheless, there was for Hegel a serious problem of presentation, which, in terms of the system, had already been encountered in the transition from the philosophy of nature to the philosophy of subjective spirit. It is the problem of the relation of nature and spirit.[53] Hegel, of course, did not conceive their relation as the basis for a determinism that would leave no room for human freedom. Nevertheless, if their relation is also not to be a dualism in which spirit has an abstract form independent of nature, nature must be a determining factor. Thus Hegel did grant that in the case of climatic extremes, nature is determinative: 'Neither the torrid nor the cold region can provide a basis for human freedom or for world-historical peoples' (VPW 189; LPW 154). Sensuousness had for Hegel two aspects, the subjective and the external or geographic (VPW 188; LPW 153), but it is only where natural conditions are not extreme that the connection with nature is such that spiritual freedom is possible.

> The frost which grips the inhabitants of Lapland and the fiery heat of Africa are forces of too powerful a nature for man to resist, or for spirit to achieve free movement and to reach that degree of richness which is the precondition and source for a fully developed mastery of reality (*für eine gebildete Wirklichkeitsgestaltung*).
>
> (VPW 190–1; LPW 155)

Hence only the temperate zone can furnish the theatre for the drama of world history (VPW 191; LPW 155). Africans have remained locked in sensuousness (*Sinnlichkeit*), and it has been impossible for them to develop (VPW 212; LPW 172).

To make his case, Hegel attempted to show that Africans had not yet arrived at the intuition of fixed objectivity (*die feste Objektivität*) (VPW 217; LPW 177) by examining, first their religion and then their relationships with each other. Hegel's claim was not just that Africans lacked what 'we' call religion and the state, but also that one could not find among them a conception of God, the eternal, right, nature, or even of natural things (VPW 217; LPW 177). In consequence, Africans could be said to be in the condition of immediacy or unconsciousness. This is the basis on which Hegel characterized them as dominated by passion, savage, barbaric, and hence, most importantly for his discussion of history, at the first level (*Stufe*) (VPW 218; LPW 177).

Starting in 1824, Hegel in his *Lectures on the Philosophy of Religion* situated African religion within his discussion of the religion of magic. The Eskimos were said to be on the lowest rung of spiritual consciousness. It was with the religion of the Mongols, the Africans and the Chinese that 'the spiritual is beginning to assume an objective shape for consciousness' (VPR II 179; LPR II 274). In the *Lectures on the Philosophy of History*, Hegel singled out the African. To establish the claim that Africans lack a sense of something higher than man, Hegel focused first on the antithesis between man and nature within what passes for African religion. Africans feared nature and so sought to gain power over it through magic. It is also in this context that Hegel introduced the observation that death does not come from natural causes, but from sorcery. To counter this sorcery, one appeals to more sorcery (VPW 220–1; LPW 179).[54] This led Hegel to his second observation about African religion, which concerned fetishism.

The centrepoint of Hegel's treatment of African religion in both the *Lectures on the Philosophy of World History* and the *Lectures on the Philosophy of Religion* is his treatment of fetishism. The idea of the fetish was widespread in European accounts of Africa and, although the word was of Portuguese origin, it had apparently come to be widely used by Africans themselves in their efforts to explain their practices to Europeans.[55] The term 'fetishism' is first found in 1756 in de Brosses's *Histoire des navigations aux Terres Australes*[56] and was explicated further by him four years later in *Du Culte des Dieux Fétiches*. De Brosses's main sources for his knowledge of African fetishes were Bosman's *A New and Accurate Description of the Coast of Guinea* and Labat's *Voyage du Chevalier des Marchais en Guinée* (1730), but the significance of his study was its transformation of these accounts into a general theory. De Brosses posited 'a general religion spread far and wide over all the earth' from which only the Jews were excepted.[57] He insisted on 'the constant uniformity of savage man.'[58] This meant that one could learn about what was once practised at one place by identifying the corresponding stage somewhere else.[59] Furthermore, de Brosses had already argued in his book on the Australasian continent that through discipline and the promise of a gentler life all peoples could be educated.[60] De Brosses's account of the uniformity of primitive religion was an important prerequisite for developing a universal philosophy of history in which all peoples followed a single trajectory. The possible future of so-called savage peoples not only could be anticipated by observing the histories of other peoples who had already made the transition from fetishism to various degrees of civilization; one could also contribute to bringing it about through the civilizing mission of colonialism.[61]

Hegel's treatment of African fetishes is best approached by observing its modification of de Brosses's theory. The fetish was always described as 'the first object' encountered to emphasize the arbitrary nature of the choice (VPH 222; LPH 180). This was an aspect insisted upon by Bosman and after him by de Brosses.[62] Hegel also emphasized that if the fetish failed, its owner would discard it and select another (VPW 222; LPW 181). This supported his thesis that Africans retained power over what they imagined held power over them: 'The substance always remains in the power of the subject' (VPW 223; LPW 182). However, the substitution of one fetish for another played a further more important function in Hegel's account, which is apparent in the *Lectures on the Philosophy of Religion*, where he declared: 'Blacks switch from one fetish to another at will (*willkürlich*) while other peoples have permanent fetishes' (VPR II 195; LPR II 291). Hegel had only a little earlier suggested that the Chinese were also inconstant in the same way (VPR II 194; LPR II 290), but he believed that he had here found a point of difference that separated the fetishes of Africa proper from the more developed forms of worship found in ancient Egypt. This was important not only because it showed that treatments of Egyptian religion like that of de Brosses were reductive, but also because it performed the important function of establishing a difference between African and European forms of superstition. Bosman had noted the parallel between certain Roman Catholic religious practices and those found among Africans.[63] The Capuchin friar Cavazzi had made the same point, unwittingly, as Hegel observed:

> Cavazzi reports that many negroes were torn to pieces by wild beasts despite the fact that they wore amulets, but that those who had received them from him escaped unharmed.
>
> (VPW 269; LPW 218)[64]

Hegel himself recognized in African sorcery a parallel to European witchcraft (VPW 223; LPW 181). He could afford to do that, even though in general he wanted to show the gulf between Europeans and Africans such that 'we must put aside all our European attitudes' (VPW 218; LPW 177), because he had established the doubly arbitrary character of African religion: arbitrary in its selection of the fetish and arbitrary in its change to some other object. This was in keeping with the standard and long-standing caricature of Africans as 'governed by caprice' (*regitur arbitrio*).[65]

By the time that Hegel's discussion of what passes for African religion is over, the case about Africans lacking a consciousness of objectivity, in the form of consciousness of either nature or God, is complete (VPW 224; LPW 182). As a result, Hegel's discussion of human relations among Africans seems at first sight to be gratuitous. It is true that, within the context of the *Philosophy of Right* with which the *Philosophy of World History* belongs as the Philosophy of Objective Spirit, Hegel would consider that once he had shown that Africans lacked a sense of freedom and had no political institutions, then he would have placed them outside the realm of world history (cf. VPW 216–7; LPW 176).[66] But he went much further than that. He not only insisted that Africans did not respect themselves or others, such that their attitude toward law and ethical life had as its basic determinant complete contempt (*Verachtung*) of death and lack of respect for life (VPW 224 and 227; LPW 182 and 185), he also argued that African society fell outside the opposition between what was just and what was unjust in terms of world history. This is the coda that governs Hegel's discussions of cannibalism as compatible with the African principle of sensuousness and of slavery as something that Africans do not regard as improper (VPW 225; LPW 183). Most readings of Hegel's discussion of Africa have paid little attention to these remarks. I shall offer an interpretation that explains their place in his argument.

Hegel tried to take the emphasis away from the European involvement in selling slaves to America by focusing on slavery as something endemic to African society: 'Since human beings are valued so cheaply, it is easily explained why *slavery* is the basic legal relationship in Africa' (VPW 225; LPW 183). Hegel claimed that 'blacks see nothing wrong with it, and the English, although they have done most to abolish slavery and the slave trade, are treated as enemies by the blacks themselves' (VPW 225; LPW 183). On this point, Hegel does indeed find partial support in both Dalzel and Bowdich. Dalzel included in *The History of Dahomey* a speech made by King Adahoonzou in response to news of a parliamentary inquiry into slavery in which he allegedly made the pro-slavery case, but doubts have been raised about the authenticity of the text.[67] However, Bowdich's report of the desire on the part of the Ashanti to see the English become involved again in the slave trade undoubtedly has some basis in fact.[68] The slave trade had been of such huge proportions that it had transformed social relations in Africa, making its abolition impossible to achieve without disrupting those relations. Nevertheless, this did not mean that Hegel was right when he suggested that slavery was 'the basic legal relation' in Africa (VPW 225; LPW 183).[69] His suggestion that slavery was also the only essential connection that Blacks had with Europeans also suggests, among other things, a total disregard for the kind of treaty that Bowdich had negotiated. However, more important still is a further conclusion that Hegel drew.

Contrasting African slavery with slavery in America, Hegel judged that the condition of slaves in Africa is 'almost worse' than their condition in America:

> For the basic condition of slavery in general is that the human being does not yet have consciousness of his or her freedom and thereby sinks to being a chattel, something worthless.
>
> (VPW 225–6; LPW 183)

Hegel's sources about Africa had given him an exaggerated sense of the readiness with which slaves were executed, but he was not ultimately concerned with the empirical question of whether slaves were treated better in Africa than in the United States. When he moved the discussion of cannibalism to the point where 'the sensuous negro' was allegedly incapable of recognizing that the human flesh he or she was eating was the same as that of his or her own body, Hegel had established the compatibility of cannibalism with the African principle, irrespective of any empirical claims about the occasion or frequency of cannibalism (VPW 225; LPW 183).[70] Now he sought a principle that differentiated African slavery from the European slavery of Africans essentially, thereby saving him from the need to conduct a comparison to determine where slaves were treated worst. He found it again in the figure of the association of the African with arbitrariness.

> In all the African kingdoms known to Europeans, slavery is familiar (heimisch); it dominates there naturally (sie herrscht dort natürlich). But the slave and the master are distinguished arbitrarily.
>
> (VPW 226; LPW 183)

If in Africa the distinction between masters and slaves is arbitrary, that marks it off from the Greek idea of slavery, where slaves are slaves by nature. African slavery is natural, but it works in an arbitrary way. There is an implication that one of the reasons why African slavery is 'almost worse' than slavery by Europeans is that in the former the question of who is master and who is slave is arbitrary. It is determined in contingent fashion by victory in war. By contrast, for the Greeks the slave is a slave by nature, which meant that only certain people could properly be enslaved. Hegel in his *Philosophy of History* presents freedom for some as a stage on the way to freedom for all. On Hegel's analysis, it is only by being enslaved by Europeans that Africans learn this idea of freedom.[71]

This provides the basis for Hegel's fundamental claim:

> The lesson we can draw from this condition of slavery among Blacks, and which is the only interesting aspect for us, is, as we already know in terms of the idea, that the state of nature is itself the state of absolute and thorough (*durchgängig*) injustice.
>
> (VPW 226; LPW 183–4)

Hegel used the phrase 'absolute and thorough injustice' to suggest an injustice beyond the opposition of the just and the unjust. Hegel said of Africa as the state of nature that 'every immediate stage between it and the actuality of the rational state admittedly has moments and aspects of injustice' (VPW 226; LPW 184). However, he made clear that it is only when slavery occurs 'within a state' that it is 'a moment in the progress from pure isolated sensuous existence, a moment of education (*Erziehung*), a way of coming to participate in higher ethical life (*Sittlichkeit*) and the culture (*Bildung*) that goes with it.' African slavery, as Hegel described it, is not only not regarded as unjust within Africa, it is explicitly outside the theodicy that would make sense of it.[72] It is this that makes it a condition of 'absolute and thorough injustice.' Just as Hegel's graphic descriptions of cannibalism have the function of making this idea plausible, so his other remarks on slavery in this context are dedicated to this purpose.

There is a remark that is usually taken as Hegel's response to calls for the total abolition of the Atlantic slave trade.

> Slavery is unjust in and for itself, for the essence of man is freedom; but he must first become mature before he can be free. Thus, it is more fitting and correct that slavery should be eliminated gradually than that it should be done away with all at once.
>
> (VPW 226; LPW 184)

The context, however, seems to suggest that the primary focus of the passage is the enslavement of Africans by Africans. Hegel's point was that the African must pass through the stages of spirit in order to be free. Slavery in the absence of an organized state is outside history.

> But when it occurs within a state, it is itself a stage (*Moment*) in the progress away from purely fragmented sensuous existence, a phase in

man's education (*Erziehung*), and an aspect of the process whereby he gradually attains a higher ethical life (*Sittlichkeit*) and a corresponding degree of culture (*Bildung*).

(VPW 226; LPW 184)

Hegel's argument was that by taking Africans out of Africa as slaves, Europeans had already released them from a barely human existence, even if they were not yet free. Nevertheless, it is clear that Hegel judged slavery to be against reason so that ultimately it could not be tolerated. He spelled this out in his 1824–25 lectures on the *Philosophy of Right*.

> An historically grounded right can be rejected by philosophy as irrational; so, for example, slavery in the Indies is justified historically by the fact that among the Negroes too these slaves were slaves and were faced with an even harsher fate; by the fact that the indigenous population is thereby relieved; by the fact that the Negroes are more capable of work, that the settlers have a property right over them, that the colonies would otherwise have to perish. Despite this justification, reason must maintain that the slavery of the Negroes is a wholly unjust institution, one which contradicts true justice, both human and divine, and which is to be rejected.[73]

Even though Hegel evoked slavery in this context only as an example, there seems little doubt that this was also his considered opinion on the subject. The fact that some of the arguments here identified as merely historical justifications were arguments that Hegel himself employed underlines the care with which one must read Hegel to discover the due weight to be placed on every argument made. But by giving a positive role to the enslavement of Africans by Europeans from the perspective of human development, he gave comfort and resources to those who rejected abolition. It is no wonder that the owners of slaves in the United States saw him as an ally.[74]

The account of Africa in the *Lectures on the Philosophy of World History* also had severe repercussions in another context. These are most clearly apparent when the discussion of Africa is read in the light of the *Philosophy of Right*. The crucial link between the two texts lies in the role played by the notion of the uneducated, uncultured, or uncivilized (*das Ungebildete*). In the *Philosophy of Right*, Hegel identified as uneducated, among others, the poor, Arabs, savages, children, and the mad. If Africans are not specifically mentioned in the *Philosophy of Right*, it is nevertheless clear from other texts that they could have been. In consequence, they would, with the other groups, have found themselves treated by Hegel as legitimate targets of 'pedagogical coercion,' coercion directed by the educated against the uneducated as part of a war on savagery and barbarism (GPR 179; PR 120). Barbarism is a fault to be corrected, if necessary by violent means. Hegel's *Philosophy of History*, read in conjunction with the *Philosophy of Right*, does not simply legitimate this course of action; the texts advocate it as a necessary course of action. Hegel believed generally that so-called 'civilized' peoples could legitimately interfere with those at a lesser stage of development.

> The same determination entitles civilized nations (*Nationen*) to regard and treat as barbarians other nations which are less advanced than they are in the substantial moments of the state (as with pastoralists in relation to hunters, and agriculturists in relation to both of these), in the consciousness that the rights of these other nations are not equal to theirs and that their independence is merely formal.
>
> (GPR 507–8; PR 376)

Extending this to his own day, Hegel proposed colonial expansion as a way of addressing some of the problems of civil society, especially poverty. As Tsenay Serequeberhan recognized, Hegel has no ready answer as to why this does no more than export those problems elsewhere.[75] Hegel was blind to this concern. Hegel himself may not have drawn the consequence explicitly himself, but the conclusion to which his theorizing led was that the colonization of Africa would complete the process of introducing Africans to history, a process that had begun when the first slaves were transported to America. Colonialism was the destiny to which Africa had to submit.[76] Hegel's modification of de Brosses's argument about fetishism had the effect of making Africans the prime candidates for the civilizing mission of colonialism. And the argument about giving Africans a knowledge of freedom by taking them out of Africa as slaves could easily be supplemented by a parallel argument that colonialism would bring the idea of freedom, especially if the comments about climate with which Hegel began could somehow be minimized.

Hegel was clear that in rational states there would be no slaves, but he believed that outside such states slavery was necessary when it was 'a moment in the transition to a higher stage' (VPW 226; LPW 184).[77] Nevertheless, according to Hegel, African slavery fell outside this justification. Africa was not a moment in such a transition until it came into contact with Europe. Until that time it was neither just nor unjust, in the sense of justified or unjustified. Only contact with Europe could redeem it. It was to support that conclusion that

Hegel presented his diatribe against Africans, leading him to distort the travel literature at his disposal.

## III

The aspect of Hegel's discussion of Africa that has received most attention is his claim that Africa is unhistorical. Although it might not seem the most striking charge at first sight, within the context of Hegel's system it can readily be seen to be so, because it serves as the principle of exclusion.[78] 'Africa proper' is introduced before the account of world history gets underway (VPW 237; LPH 136), or at its threshold (VPW 234; LPH 190),[79] in order that it can subsequently be left behind. However, what Hegel meant by the unhistorical has been largely misunderstood in the light of subsequent discussions about the difficulty or impossibility of writing Africa's history except from the standpoint of its contacts with Europe.

When Hegel started to outline the African character in the light of what he had learned from reading Cavazzi, Dalzel, and Bowdich, he observed that it is difficult to grasp because this character is different from 'our' culture (*Bildung*). His conclusion was that the African is incapable of development and culture. The Africans of Hegel's times were, he insisted, the same as they have always been. This was what Hegel meant by saying that Africa is unhistorical. He had already read it in Bowdich, where Sir William Young was quoted in a footnote as saying:

> And here I cannot but remark that those accounts, when compared, shew how little manners and minds improve in Africa, and how long, and how much society has been there at a stand: Jobson saw, in 1620, exactly what Park saw in 1798.[80]

Hegel clearly believed that the comparison of the reports of Cavazzi and Bowdich would lead to the same conclusion: 'Anyone who wishes to study the most terrible manifestations of human nature will find them in Africa. The earliest reports concerning this continent tell us precisely the same, and it has no history in the true sense of the word (*eigentlich keine Geschichte*)' (VPW 234; LPW 190).

Hegel was not unaware that the kind of political history that consists of listing the succession of rulers could be reconstructed for Africa. He had probably read Dalzel's *History of Dahomey* as well as Bowdich's attempt to write an 'imperfect history' of the Ashanti.[81] Nor was the question of whether the

Africans were 'unhistorical' reducible to the question of the extent of their contact with Europeans, as if increased contact might yet bring Africans within the narrative account of history. To be a world historical people is to have a distinct principle and, even though it may occupy several positions, it can only occupy first place once (VPW 187; LPW 152). Du Bois's 'The Conservation of Races' is written somewhat from this perspective.[82]

According to Hegel, Africans do not have a culture of their own; they have character. Furthermore, just as Africa is without history, the African is said to possess a character that cannot change. Hegel called it intractability (*Unbändigkeit*). But the Mohammedans had brought Africans closer to culture (*Bildung*) (VPW 217; LPW 177) and just as Africa can enter into European history, so Africans can take on European culture. In the course of his discussion of Native Americans, Hegel noted that Blacks are 'far more susceptible to European culture (*Kultur*) than the Indians' (VPW 202; LPW 165). Similarly, in his Berlin lectures on the *Philosophy of Spirit*, Hegel explained that

> One cannot deny that Blacks have a capacity for culture (*Fähigkeit zur Bildung*), for not only have they occasionally received Christianity with the greatest thankfulness and spoken movingly of the freedom that they have gained from it after prolonged spiritual servitude, but in Haiti they have even formed a state on Christian principles.[83]

Nevertheless, in the very next sentence Hegel denied that Blacks have 'an inner tendency to culture (*einen inneren Trieb zur Kultur*).' So even when Blacks revolt against slavery, as they did successfully in Haiti, this would seem, in Hegel's view, to be because they have come in contact with European views about freedom.

Hegel also argued that Africans could lose their intractability while still remaining in Africa. Describing the effects of a violent migration to both the east and west coasts, Hegel wrote: 'When their fury has abated, and when they have lived for a time on the slopes or in the coastal region and become pacified, they prove mild and industrious, although they seem completely intractable at the time of their initial onslaught' (VPW 216; LPW 176). This seems to introduce a temporality into Hegel's general perception of the African as characterized by 'good-naturedness (*seelisch Gutmütigkeit*) coupled, however, with completely unfeeling cruelty' (VPW 212; LPW 173).[84] In that case, the tendency of the Africans to combine contrary tendencies, so that they are good-natured (*gutmütig*) but liable to fanaticism, was the symptom of the fact that Africans were already undergoing a transformation (VPW 231; LPW 188).

What we do know of these hordes is the contrast in their behaviour before and after their incursions: during their wars and forays, they behaved with the most unthinking inhumanity and revolting barbarity, yet subsequently, when their rage had died down and peace was restored, they behaved with mildness towards the Europeans when they became acquainted with them.

(VPW 216; LPW 176)

This would mean that Africans were identified with an unthinking inhumanity that only arrival at the coast and, therefore, contact with Europeans could alter. For Hegel, the coast is already in a sense Europe, as, geographically speaking, coastal regions correspond to the principle of Europe (VPW 212; LPW 172). Africa has a very narrow coastal strip (VPW 215; LPW 174), but perhaps the 'terrible hordes' that from time to time descend from the mountains to the coasts are unwittingly already conforming to the march of world history towards Europe (VPW 216; LPW 175–6). Nevertheless, the culture that Africans adopt comes to them from Europe. It is not indigenous. Nor, one remembers, could it be, because of the climate, although one cannot help noticing that Hegel's arguments about the constraints of climate have now at this stage of the discussion indeed been somewhat forgotten.

Whereas North America had long been understood by Europeans, contrary to the facts and with devastating consequences, as a land without inhabitants, Hegel produced the image of Africa as a land without history and without *Bildung*. This description combined with his account in the *Philosophy of Right* of the legitimacy of coercion against the uncivilized provided a potent justification for the exploitation of a continent. I do not know of any evidence that Hegel had a direct impact on the development of colonialism or even that colonialism awaited such a justification, but he certainly contributed to the climate in which there was relatively little scrutiny of the conduct of Europeans in Africa. For Hegel, contact with Europeans could only be to the benefit of Africans, whatever the nature of that contact. This underlies Hegel's defence of slavery, which was not conducted on the basis that Africans were naturally inferior, but on the basis that European slavery would transform African slavery to the advantage of Africans.

Hegel's treatment of Africa and its inhabitants is not without its contradictions, none more damaging than the fact that he announces the African character as 'still unknown to us' (VPW 268; LPW 217) before he proceeds to characterize it. There is no doubt that Hegel, like many of his European contemporaries, was perplexed by Africa.[85] And yet, however confusing Hegel may have found Africa, he approached it across the *Philosophy of Subjective Spirit*, the *Philosophy of Right*, and the *Philosophy of World History* with systematic intent. H. S. Harris, one of the leading Hegel scholars of our time, excused Hegel for not recognizing the structure and cultural traditions of pre-colonial Africa, because they were not the topic of scientific investigation at that time. Harris judged that 'we need not complain at Hegel for interpreting the African evidence that he had in the way that he did – no matter how politically convenient that interpretation may have been for the European imperialism of the century after 1830.'[86] An examination of Hegel's sources shows that they were more accurate than he was and that he cannot be so readily excused for using them as he did. Given the fact, conceded by Harris, that Hegel was writing prior to the main period of European colonization of Africa, this is a serious accusation indeed. It calls for a revision of our assessment of Hegel's philosophy, but, given the undoubted importance of Hegel for subsequent thought, its reverberations go much further. Questions remain about the extent to which contemporary ideas, for example of social development, remain tied to a model that can best be described as colonialist.[87]

# 2

# Of Spirit(s) and Will(s)

*John H. Smith*

What does Derrida say about the will, especially Hegel's will and the last will and testament of German idealism? Why does he have so little to say about the will, this major concept of the Western philosophical tradition and the center of discussions of human freedom, agency, and politics? It is tempting to see the absence of a discussion, even of a deconstruction, of will as an 'avoidance'; but what will interest me here is the trace of (Hegel's) will in some of Derrida's writing and the significant effects that a retracing of that will could have on politics and interpretation.

In 1987, Derrida delivered a long lecture entitled *Of Spirit: Heidegger and the Question*.[1] In exploring the avoidance, and then the return, of *Geist* in Heidegger's writing from 1927 to 1953 (from *Sein und Zeit* to the essay on Trakl in *Unterwegs zur Sprache*), Derrida shows that Heidegger's *Geist* has a number of ghosts. He acknowledges that one of these is the ghost/*Geist* of Hegel and hints that Schelling haunts Heidegger's language as well.[2] But if these two are the ones he thinks of and thereby circumscribes in his deconstruction of Heidegger, what are the unthought ghosts in Derrida's own text?[3] To get at this question, I will switch images: How else, besides as *Geister*, do the dead appear, and in particular, speak to us after death, beyond the grave?[4] The question is legitimate, since death and the voice of the dead from the crypt are central concerns of Derrida in this lecture and in *Glas*.[5] Since we are not speaking here of 'real' ghosts, we must consider the way in which the dead in fact speak up every day, namely in and through their wills, their last wills and testaments, in their 'remains' and legacies that we inherit.[6] Through these associations, I come to consider Hegel's transcendental will to be his ghost in Derrida. Hegel's will lives on in Derrida. I shall resurrect it, or let it speak, less to deconstruct the deconstructor (i.e. less to bust the *Geist*-buster) than to reintroduce a term foreclosed[7] by Derrida. I am interested in using the will as that which can speak to us beyond the grave of idealism to open up a richer dialectic than we find in either a metaphysics of Spirit or its deconstruction.

By 'open up a richer dialectic' I mean a number of things: (1) Derrida's deconstruction of *Geist* unfolds thanks to a series of dualisms (Spirit vs. letter, body animal; purity vs. contamination).[8] The will, however, *is* these opposi- tions. Derrida does not draw out this dialectical status, given his tendency to identify will with Spirit and to limit will to a 'metaphysics of subjectivity.'[9] I hope to show that the concept of the will offers a hermeneutic that accounts for *both* an objective disseminating and a subjective gathering of meaning. (2) Derrida is interested in the 'politics' of Spirit from Hegel to Heidegger,[10] but this question is approached more fruitfully from the perspective of the will, *the* central concept of politics. Three reasons for this are that Hegel's *Philosophy of Right* focuses on the will;[11] that the text referred to only obliquely by Derrida via Heidegger, Schelling's *Philosophical Inquiries into the Nature of Human Freedom* (1809), grounds freedom in a groundless *Wille* as *Ursein*; and that Heidegger's own thoughts 'turn' in the 1930s around the concept of the will and will to power (they perform a *Kehre* from will to Being and, according to Derrida, *Geist*).[12] The will as a concept inextricably linked to ethics and politics in the West, and particularly in post-idealist thought, merits analysis. (3) Where Derrida writes on Hegel (especially in *Glas*), the 'family' is not far behind; but he never deals with the fact that the family, as a moment of communal ethics (*Sittlichkeit*, according to the *Philosophy of Right*), represents a constellation of the *will*, or with the way that this constellation dissolves into 'civil society' by means of a transition through analyses of last wills, inheri- tance, and testaments (§§177 – 81).[13] That is, I show in textual analyses that Derrida's work on Hegel and the family already involves the will. I wish to address and draw out the consequences of this present absence in Derrida. (4) And finally, wherever the individual and the social, the personal and the political intersect – and where do they not, according to both Derrida and Hegel? – the will is not far behind. Indeed, the will, more than most other concepts, allows us to grapple with this nodal point of power and *not* reduce our analysis to subjectivity, spirituality, identity.

Thus, we shall see through and over Derrida's corpus, that the last will of idealism, from Schelling and Hegel, has left a legacy of the will and its repression in Derrida. Not only can the will *not* be avoided, for it will return ghostlike speaking from the dead, but also, I believe, we should attend to its words, which can help us to think *through* otherwise unproductive dualisms (subject/system, individual/state, spirit/body, reason/drive, etc.). By turning to Hegel's will in and after Derrida, we can unearth a concept that can redirect discussions of freedom, agency, and politics.

Before turning to Derrida on Heidegger, Hegel, and Spirit, let us take a brief detour back to Derrida's earliest work on Husserl to see how he narrows and restricts the concept of the will. We see here the way he limits it explicitly, and I shall argue, problematically and needlessly, to a 'metaphysics' of *Geist*. Consider the passage from the chapter 'Meaning as Soliloquy' (*Speech and Phenomenon*) that deals with the creation of (linguistic) 'expressions' (*Ausdrücke*).[14] Derrida follows Husserl's argument closely to show that for Husserl expression involves the conferring of a meaning, constituted ideally, intentionally, and internal to the subject, onto a sign that is capable of externalization. In this way, Derrida sees two strands of thought coming together in Husserl's account of intentional meaning, namely an opposition between Spirit and letter/body on the one hand and a concept of the will on the other. He writes: 'There is no expression without the intention of a subject animating the sign, giving it a *Geistigkeit*.' And further: '. . . expression is always inhabited and animated by a meaning (*bedeuten*), as *wanting* to say' (p. 33). In other words, according to Derrida, for Husserl and the Western philosophical tradition in general, 'willing' is a general case of 'wanting-to-say,' whereby that *vouloir-dire* is understood as the investment of a prior Spirit into an independent sign. Thus, Derrida continues, 'intentionality never simply meant will, [but] it certainly does seem that in the order of expressive experiences. . . . Husserl regards intentional consciousness and voluntary consciousness as synonymous.' This means, for Derrida, that Husserl's 'concept of intentionality remains caught up in the tradition of a voluntaristic metaphysics – that is, perhaps, in metaphysics *as such*' (p. 34f). The will appears to be 'metaphysical as such' because Derrida identifies it with a concept of Spirit that is 'pure' and devoid of the physical. This explains, according to Derrida, why Husserl must distinguish between meaningful expressions (intended, willed, imbued with *Geist*) from involuntary bodily gestures, i.e. 'why everything that escapes the pure spiritual intention, the pure animation by *Geist*, that is, the will, is excluded from meaning (*bedeuten*) and thus from expression' (p. 35). The visible and spatial 'as such' must be excluded, he continues:

insofar as they are not worked over by *Geist*, by the will, by the *Geistigkeit* which, in the word just as in the human body, transforms the *Körper* into *Leib* (into flesh). The opposition between body and soul is not only at the center of this doctrine of signification, it is confirmed by it; and, as has always been at the bottom the case in philosophy, it depends upon an interpretation of language. Visibility and spatiality as such could only destroy the self-presence of will and spiritual animation which opens up discourse. *They are literally the death of that self-presence.*

(p. 35)[15]

My claim is that this is an unfortunate collapse of two traditions. I am by no means claiming that Derrida's deconstruction of Spirit is inappropriate.[16] But the slippage that allows Derrida to speak of Spirit and will as identical 'in philosophy' and 'as such' in fact has excluded the will as a separate category of analysis. What we can learn instead from Hegel (and Schelling and Nietzsche, and indeed from much of Western philosophy) is that the will does not involve the same phantasm of purity as does Spirit. At least there is no conceptual necessity tying will to Spirit, and the most interesting treatments of them keep them essentially separate. The will's reality – its realization in action by means of a representation – is as much of its 'essence' as any abstract, metaphysical subjectivity. Thus, we shall read in Hegel: 'A will which . . . wills only the abstract universal, wills *nothing* and is therefore not a will at all' (§6, Addition). The identity of the subjective and objective, the externalization of the internal, is not *secondary* to the will, and thus contaminating, deadly, but the very core of its nature *as* will. Or, as we shall see in the discussion of 'last wills' at the heart of the *Philosophy of Right*, the opposition is not as Derrida would have it here between life and death, since it is precisely the arbitrarily willed letter of the testament that keeps the will of the deceased alive in familial and non-familial heirs. The last will marks both the finality of a death and the continuation of life for the family and society.[17] Derrida's early association of *Geist*, will, and 'metaphysics as such' therefore has the consequence of allowing the will to persist unexplored and unexplicated throughout his entire work on, and deconstructions of, Spirit.

Let us now smoke out the ghost of Hegel and the traces of the idealist will in *Of Spirit*. It does not take long for Derrida to mention Hegel. In introducing his interest in Heidegger's use and avoidance of the concept *Geist*, Derrida early on relates it to his readings of Hegel: 'This attention paid to *Geist*, which recently gave me my direction in some readings of Hegel [*Glas*], is today called forth by research I have been pursuing for a few years now in a seminar on philosophical nationality and nationalism' (p. 7). The footnote attached to this self-reference stresses *Glas*, which 'treats the word and concept of *Geist* in Hegel as its most explicit theme' (note 1, p. 117). And likewise, a bit further into *Of Spirit*, Hegel occupies the only footnote in Chapter III. In the passage being annotated, Derrida relates the special status that *Geist* has for Heidegger in his *Daseinsanalyse* (namely a question prior to the other sciences of the soul or psyche), to the way Hegel gives philosophy of Spirit priority over both rational psychology and 'pneumatology.'[18] And in the note, Derrida says: 'I must quote this paragraph [§378 from the *Philosophy of Spirit* in the *Encyclopedia*] to anticipate what will be said later about spirit, liberty, and evil for Heidegger' (note 1, p. 118). Thus we see Hegel appearing as 'one of the most obsessing ghosts among the philosophers of this alchemy' (p. 99), an alchemy that includes the following kinds of ingredients: politics, nation, liberty, decisions, families. What is the nature of this *Geist*, so important to Derrida, which can go nowhere without its Hegelian ghost?

I shall approach what I consider the central concern of Derrida's analysis, namely his foreclosure of a dialectical will, by focusing on an oppositional spirit, by considering his strategy. I see it proceeding as follows: Heidegger initially claimed it was important to 'avoid' the term *Geist*, but then it appears (during and after the 1930s) in key places in his texts as that which he wants to keep 'pure.' Derrida's deconstruction would demonstrate the incessant processes of 'contamination,' the breakdown of the dualisms that Heidegger (like Hegel before him?) would establish between Spirit *and* letter-body-animal-matter.[19] Let us consider two passages where Derrida discusses this and its stakes explicitly.

In the first, Derrida is reviewing the threads of his argument and mentions one that relates to his interest in Heidegger's conception of technology. He would see a link between the contamination by technology and that of Spirit:

The concern, then, was to analyze this desire [in Heidegger] for rigorous non-contamination and, from that, perhaps, to envisage the necessity, one could say the fatal necessity of a *contamination* – and the word was important to me – of a contact originally impurifying thought or speech by technology. . . . It is easy to imagine that the consequences of this necessity cannot be limited. Yet *Geist*, as I will try to suggest, also names what Heidegger wants to save from any destitution (*Entmachtung*). It is even perhaps, beyond what must be saved, the very thing that saves (*rettet*). But what saves would not let itself be saved from this contamination.

(p. 10)

This thread of the necessary contamination of that which would be pure explains much of the deconstructive strategy of Derrida's lecture. But the political stakes are higher than one might think. For in dealing with Heidegger's fateful Rectorship Address (1933), Derrida shows the consequences beyond Heidegger of failed attempts like Heidegger's to maintain an impossible opposition between a pure *Geist* and the impure letter or body. The passage is complex and will require a lengthy quote and analysis since it seeks to resist dualisms that might be taken for granted in our politics:

> What is the price of this [Heidegger's] strategy? Why does it fatally turn back against its 'subject' – if one can use this word, as one must, in fact? Because one cannot demarcate oneself from biologism, from naturalism, from racism in its genetic form, one cannot be *opposed* to them except by reinscribing spirit in an oppositional determination, by once again making it a unilaterality of subjectivity, even if in its voluntarist form. The constraint of this program remains very strong, it reigns over the majority of discourses which, today and for a long time to come, state their opposition to racism, to totalitarianism, to nazism, to fascism, etc., and do this in the name of spirit and even of the freedom of (the) spirit, in the name of an axiomatic – for example, that of democracy or 'human rights' – which, directly or not, comes back to this metaphysics of *subjectivity*. All the pitfalls of the strategy of establishing demarcations belong to this program, whatever place one occupies in it. The only choice is the choice between the terrifying contaminations it assigns.

(p. 39f)

A number of things need to be pointed out here if we are to see the aims and limitations of Derrida's reading strategy. First, it is not by chance that the phrase 'freedom of (the) spirit' is glossed with the footnote I cited earlier when referring to Hegel's passage in the *Encyclopedia* on spirit and liberty. Derrida, too, is concerned with formulations of politics and freedom, but he would reject any foundations in a 'free spirit' and hence here clearly strives to place Hegel in the margins, citing him even if as a note.[20] Second, we have here Derrida engaged in a head-spinning deconstruction that, I believe, pulls him into its *mise-en-abîme*. The whole point of this passage seems to be that

Derrida would challenge a 'politics of spirit' that would rest on a 'demarcation' *vis-à-vis* its contaminating other, like naturalism or biologism – even if that politics occurs 'in the name of' causes Derrida would ascribe to, like anti-fascism, anti-racism, etc. But he does so for problematic reasons. He would see such a demarcation as 'fatal', because in so doing the Spirit becomes caught in the 'metaphysics of subjectivity.' But in rejecting such a demarcation, Derrida is in fact following Heidegger in making a literal bogeyman out of subjectivity – he refers to this as 'its bad double, the phantom of subjectivity' (p. 41); and as we know, the logic of such ghosts would always have them return to haunt the exorcist.[21] And third, a different way of seeing the problem I am trying to raise here, the almost offhand comment by Derrida that would see no difference between the 'unilaterality of subjectivity' (i.e. its Cartesian or Kantian self-enclosed 'one-sidedness' opposed to all otherness) and 'its voluntaristic form' is, I believe, itself 'fatally' reductive (and clearly an echo of the logic we saw in the earlier passage on Husserl). Derrida is missing the opportunity here indeed to deconstruct the politics of the isolating/isolated, or purifying/purified spirit and to move on to a politics of the will, according to which the subject precisely 'in its voluntaristic form' transcends subjectivity. My point will be to show that a turn to the will – the ghost in both Derrida and Hegel – would make possible a non-dualistic politics that could avoid the phantasm of pure spirit and the metaphysics of subjectivity, both of which would either 'fatally' exclude or be contaminated by the letter, the body, matter, animality, etc. But to see what could be at stake here in a different reading of the will in Derrida, we should consider briefly Schelling's legacy.

Schelling is another phantom of Derrida's lecture.[22] Schelling's spirit is invoked because Heidegger delivered lectures in 1936 on Schelling's *Philosophical Inquiries into the Nature of Human Freedom* (1809). Given the potential significance of these lectures for an understanding of Heidegger's thought in general, and his politics and discussion of *Geist* in particular, it is remarkable that they receive minimal treatment by Derrida.[23] He points a couple of times to Schelling's concept of the spirit as 'gathering' (*Versammlung*, pp. 77 and 107). And he points out, in a phrase that signals for us a significance belying Derrida's brevity, that 'Schelling leaves traces' in Heidegger's reading (p. 78).[24] These traces are not without their effects. According to Derrida, the appearance throughout Heidegger's work from 1936 to the 1950s of a continuous reference to Schelling is 'both natural and troubling' (p.102). And Derrida explains why:

Because the 'Schellingian' formulas which sustain this interpretation of Trakl seem to belong, following Heidegger's own course, to that metaphysics of evil and the will which at the time he was trying to delimit rather than accept.

Derrida seems to be implying that the presence of Schelling in Heidegger leads to a kind of 'contamination' of the spirit by a metaphysics of evil and the will.[25] But perhaps precisely this place of the will in Heidegger and Derrida would be, *as* the site of contamination, the very site of 'salvation.' Could it not be that Schelling's and Hegel's last will and testament to us would be located here?

Let me briefly indicate what I think we can hear Schelling saying to us of spirit and will. He begins with a long introduction establishing his position dialectically between *Realismus* and *Idealismus*, or between a systematic, apparently 'fatalistic' philosophy (Spinoza's pantheism) and a faith in an arbitrarily independent God. The two positions become linked as body and soul.[26] But it is important to see this not as a mere union of two separate and therefore metaphysical principles. Rather, the very movement of thought and life itself is generated out of the internal contradiction that, and this is crucial, makes up the 'wanting of spirit': 'without the contradiction between necessity and freedom, not only philosophy but every higher *willing/wanting of the spirit* (*Wollen des Geistes*) would die the death appropriate to any field of knowledge that would not engage that contradiction' (German, p. 35; English p. 9, my emphasis). I think it is appropriate to exploit a nuance in English and to understand *Wollen* here as a 'wanting' in the double sense of a lack and driving desire. He tries to explain this contradictory essence, which would make up the 'concept of becoming' (German, p. 53f; English, p. 33f) as follows:

> If we want to bring this being closer to us from a human standpoint, we can say: It is the longing (*Sehnsucht*), which the eternal One feels, to give birth to itself. It is not the One itself, although it is co-eternal with it. To the extent that it wants to give birth to God, that is to the unfathomable (*unergründliche*) unity, it is itself not yet that unity. It is, therefore, as such to be considered a will . . . a will of the understanding, namely its longing and desire; it is thus not a conscious will but an intuitive one, whose intuition is (the) understanding.
>
> (p. 54)

For us, looking at things with our limited, non-dialectical understanding, the world appears or reveals itself to be made up 'entirely of rules, order, form.' And yet, he continues:

the unruly always lies in the base (*im Grunde*), as if it could break out again, and nowhere does it appear that order and form are at the origin (*das Ursprüngliche*) but, rather, that a primal unruliness has been brought to order. In all things, this is the ungraspable basis (*Basis*) of reality, the indivisible remainder (*der nie aufgehende Rest*), that which even with the greatest effort cannot be resolved by the understanding but remains eternally in the base (*im Grunde*).

That is, becoming is possible only because inherent in Being is a will-to-be (or, in Lacanian terms, a 'want-to-be'), a primal non-entity whose 'wanting of itself' as lack and drive is the precondition of both identity and difference.[27] This 'wanting' or willing of Being, which is fundamentally (*im Grunde*) split in itself and hence *grundlos*, *unergründlich*, or *abgründig*, is the conditionless condition of human freedom insofar as it is also split in itself between good and evil.

Thus, through the traces of Schelling in Heidegger and Derrida, we get to something in spirit, its wanting/willing of Being (hence Schelling calls it *Ursein*; German, p. 46; English, p. 24), which I believe is not unlike something Derrida would have us recognize – in his terms, an 'origin-heterogeneous' and the possibility of a different 'testament.' Consider the passage, then, where Derrida indicates the direction of something 'positive' to be gotten out of this reading of Heidegger, i.e. a message beyond the grave, a testament, that 'can still say something to us – at least I imagine it can – about *our* steps.' He refers to it as a 'promise' which

would in truth be of an *other* birth and an *other* essence, *origin-heterogeneous* [*hétérogène à l'origine*] to all the testaments, all the promises, all the events, all the laws and assignments which are our very memory. *Origin-heterogeneous*: this is to be understood at once, all at once in three senses: (1) heterogeneous from the origin, originarily heterogeneous; (2) heterogeneous with respect to what is called the origin, other than the origin and irreducible to it; (3) heterogeneous *and* or *insofar as* at the origin, origin-heterogeneous *because* it is and *although* it is at the origin. '*Because*' and '*although*' *at the same time*, that's the logical form of the tension which makes all this thinking hum. The circle which, via death, decline, the West, returns towards the most originary, that towards which we are called by the *Gespräch* between Heidegger and Trakl, would be quite other than the analogous circles or revolutions that thinking of which we have inherited, from what are called the Testaments up to and including Hegel or Marx, not to mention some other modern thinkers.

What Derrida seems to be saying here is that there is, in spite of all 'metaphysical' attempts at purity, a primal heterogeneity in Heidegger. *That* is what speaks to us beyond the grave and 'seems to designate, beyond a deconstruction, the very resource for any deconstruction and the possibility of any evaluation' (*Of Spirit*, p. 14f).[28] But is it so easy to separate that 'inheritance' from the other last wills and testaments, especially when we see that it is in the discussions of the will (e.g. Schelling) that we see the 'traces' of such an 'originary heterogeneity'? Could we not say, with Derrida, that the 'continuity' between Schelling on the *Wille* as *Ursein* and Derrida on a radical 'origin-heterogeneous' is both 'natural and troubling,' both of these because it implies an inheritance passing from idealism to Derrida that makes him either a part of the idealist family or, at least, a very special friend?

I would claim, then, that Derrida's deconstruction of the Spirit here is interesting not because it so completely breaks with a tradition of testaments but, rather, helps us call forth other 'last wills' that reveal a 'wanting in/of the spirit,' a ghost in *Geist* indeed, a willing and unwilling ghost – *not* reducible to a subjectivity – inhabiting Derrida's deconstruction as well. We can enrich Derrida's position by welcoming this unwanted guest of the will in his house.

So let us turn to that text of Derrida's which 'treats the word and concept of *Geist* in Hegel as its most explicit theme' (*Of Spirit*, note 1, p. 117) and look there for traces of a last will. We are thus led back to *Glas* and 'what, after all, of the remain(s), today, for us, here, now, of a Hegel?' (p. 1). The Hegel column is about the family, Hegel's 'remains,' his legacy after the death(-knell) of idealism and Spirit. Could we not read Hegel then after Derrida to find in the concept of the (last) will, arising out of the remains of *Geist*, a means, also for politics, of dialectically relating the 'metaphysics of subjectivity' and the deconstruction of Spirit?

If the will is remarkably absent from the argument of *Glas*, we need to look for places where this absence is marked and significant. I focus first on a key turn in Derrida's unfolding 'legend' of the family and the Spirit. It occurs when he steps back to consider the structural parallels that make up the passages in Hegel's dialectic from religion to philosophy, from a representational knowledge to Absolute Knowledge, and from the family unit to civil society. Derrida asks:

The most general question would now have the following form: how is the relief [*Aufhebung*] of religion in(to) philosophy produced? How, on the other hand, is the relief of the family structure in(to) the structure of civil (bourgeois) society produced? In other words, how, within *Sittlichkeit* . . . is the passage from the family syllogism to the syllogism of bourgeois society carried out?

(p. 94)

The parallel is crucial for Derrida's entire project in *Glas* because he is, with considerable textual evidence on his side, assuming that Hegel's thought is traversed by this structural parallel between the family and other forms of Spirit. And what Derrida is doing is providing a 'literal' reading of this metaphorical parallel, i.e. seeing what happens to the other passages when we do not merely read past the images of the family in Hegel.

But what I find remarkable about the way Derrida approaches his own question is not that he poses it (it offers him in fact a powerful tool for his reading), but the fact that he does not look precisely to that place in Hegel where the family is 'dissolved' into the more abstract formations of civil society – and eventually, here hinted at already, the State. He does not address the actual transition in Hegel that he inquires after. That place is the section of the *Philosophy of Right* concluding the 'Section 1' of *Sittlichkeit*, i.e. those paragraphs dealing with divorce (*Scheidung*, §176), the 'ethical dissolution of the family' (§177), 'the natural dissolution of the family' (§178), and culminating in the paragraph on 'The Transition of the Family into Civil Society' (§181). These paragraphs will be dealt with in more detail below, but let it suffice here for me to point out that Hegel's central issue of right in this 'disintegration' (§179) of the family into 'self-sufficient and rightful persons' (§180) is none other than last wills and testaments, i.e. the way in which a family (upon the death of its head/patriarch) passes on its property to 'rightful' heirs.

This 'avoidance' on Derrida's part (he instead goes on to raise a quote from a late section of the *Phenomenology of Spirit*, and to deal brilliantly with myriad topics on marriage, sexual difference, religion, etc.) is not just a matter of a philological failure to analyse directly the place where Hegel himself directly works through the transition from family to civil society. (Although the fact that he does not deal with this transition even as he refers to its significance is quite remarkable.) My point is, that in not treating of the 'last wills and testaments' Derrida's entire text on *Geist* is haunted by the ghost of the will in general.[29] After all, how could a book so much about Hegel's 'remain(s),' and death, and families, and 'passing on' after death, and the laws or political economy regulating these, *not* be affected by the absence of a discussion of (Hegel's) will(s)?

Let us consider some of the recurrences of this avoidance. While it is certainly dangerous to speak of the 'architectonics' of a text like *Glas*, there is a kind of 'centrality' to the family and hence to the (absence) of the will that regulates its formation and dissolution.[30] Derrida clearly sees a political point in focusing on the family.[31] As he says, he will be following the 'thread' of the 'law of the family' in the 'major expositions of the *Encyclopedia*' and the *Philosophy of Right* (p. 4). He indicates how the exposition of the family is located within the sections on *Sittlichkeit*, but he never points out that the 'precise point of departure' for the discussion of *Recht* in general is the will.[32] Likewise, he points to the overall architectonics, the movement of the 'great syllogism' from family, to civil or bourgeois society (*bürgerliche Gesellschaft*), and finally to the State, but, as we saw, he does not indicate the transition from the first to the second in the issue of the 'last will' or the testament and inheritance. Note that he does come close to pointing out the location (in Hegel) of discussions concerning inheritance when he comments on a father's supposed highest duties toward his son (p. 13f); but he never points to the key here, last wills and testaments. Needless to say, this issue is in the background (or, as he says, 'to be left to one side, to be held on the margin or a leash'); for he asks (p. 6): 'Is there a place for the bastard in ontotheology or in the Hegelian family?' and this issue is clearly one related to wills and testaments, because the main issue involved in 'bastards' is legal inheritance. Thus, it is legitimate to ask what the place of the will, of last wills, would be, for by Derrida's own 'logic,' by his own focus on the *Philosophy of Right*, politics, and the family and its dissolution, he is as much in the realm of the will as in that of Spirit.

To sight the absent will, we can begin with the end of the section on Sophocles' *Antigone*. Derrida's analysis is contextualized by the overall discussion of the collapse of the family. As we have seen, Derrida begins the discussion with the question of how Hegel could deal with the end of the family and its 'relief' into civil society. And he approaches this question by pursuing marriage and sexual difference. When he turns to the breakup of the family, he brings Antigone onto the stage (p. 145).[33] Derrida concludes this literally central analysis with the following summary:

Thus does the family collapse, cave in, 'engulf itself,' 'gulp itself down.' The family devours itself. But let one not go and see in this, precipitantly,

the end of phallocentrism, of idealism, of metaphysics. The family's destruction constitutes a stage in the advent of *Bürgerlichkeit* (civil and bourgeois society) and universal property, proprietorship. A moment of infinite
reappropriation, the most reassuring metaphysical normality of idealism, of
interiorizing idealization.

(p. 188)[34]

Derrida goes on after two sentences to begin the next part of his argument:
'You have come back, without ever having left it, to the middle of the
*Philosophy of Right.*' In many ways, that is true since Hegel refers to Antigone
(and his own analysis in the *Phenomenology of Spirit*) in §166. But in a crucial way
it is *not* true. For Derrida does *not* take us back to the section of the *Philosophy
of Right* on the 'collapse of the family.' If he had, we would be dealing (as we
shall below) with the issues of the (last) will and the passing on of the family's
'resources' (*Vermögen*). Indeed, the implicit reference to that discussion in the
*Philosophy of Right* is what makes the mention of 'property, proprietorship'
sensible.

I see this unthought moment in Derrida, i.e. the conspicuous absence of the
way Hegel treats testifying beyond the grave, functioning parallel to the way
Derrida says that Hegel does not deal with the voice of the crypt. That is, just
as Derrida says that Hegel does not deal with the power of the dead to live on,
so too does Derrida not deal with the (last) will of the dead. Derrida's point
about Hegel's treatment of Antigone is that Hegel tries to contain and neutralize the voice of the dead. He says:

Crypt – one would have said, of the transcendental or the repressed, of the
unthought or the excluded – that organizes the ground to which it does not
belong.

What speculative dialectics means (to say) [*veut-dire*] is that the crypt can
still be incorporated into the system. The transcendental or the repressed,
the unthought or the excluded must be assimilated by the corpus, interiorized as moments, idealized in the very negativity of their labor. The stop,
the arrest, forms only a stasis in the introjection of the spirit.

(p. 166)

What I see going on here is that Derrida is certainly right regarding the attempt
of the Spirit of speculative dialectics to want to say that the speaking dead, their
will and testament, can be arrested. But I would propose that precisely the
place of this wanting and will(s) within speculative dialectics would be the place

in Spirit that drives it beyond itself. For by staying within the dualisms, triangles, or squares organized oppositionally around Spirit rather than pursuing its 'wanting,' we miss the opportunity to unfold a different kind of politics of the will out of the death of Spirit.

Let us then read the will of Hegel, read what Hegel wants to say about last wills, about the wanting of the spirit, over and after Derrida's corpus. I will move in expanding circles within the *Philosophy of Right* from Hegel's discussion of the dissolution of the family to the opening of the third section on *Sittlichkeit*, and finally to the conceptual frame of the entire work in the Introduction.

Derrida's analysis of issues from the *Philosophy of Right* stops at §175. In his extensive discussion of the family, he deals with Hegel's analyses of marriage, sexuality, the difference between the sexes, and the education of children; and all of these analyses can be found in the *Philosophy of Right*, §§158–75. But there is no actual treatment by Derrida, despite the reference to it, of the transition to civil society that begins with §176. There, as we see in the Addition, Hegel turns to the 'dissolution (*Auflösung*) of the family,' which takes three forms: divorce, the maturing of the children, and the death of the parents. Of these, the last takes up the most space and indeed includes the longest paragraph of this entire section on the family (§180). Why is this so important for Hegel and how could it be for Derrida? We will see that the question of last will introduces a simultaneously legal and uncontrollable element of agency into the formation of regulated society. What I would like to argue is that we have here one of the most tortuous arguments in the *Philosophy of Right* because Hegel is dealing with the 'containment' (in the double sense of the term) of the 'arbitrary' within the 'necessary': precisely at the crucial turn from the family to society he must deal with the paradoxical unavoidability of the arbitrary in order for the dialectics of freedom and the will to proceed. The intractability of the contradictions in the issue of last wills is, I believe, fruitfully paradigmatic.

Let us begin at the end of Hegel's discussion. Consider how Hegel sees the transition from family to civil society *having happened* as a 'natural' and 'calm' process:

> The family disintegrates [*tritt . . . auseinander*], in a natural manner and essentially through the principle of personality, into a *plurality* of families whose relation to one another is in general that of self-sufficient concrete persons and consequently of an external kind. . . . The expansion of the family, as its transition to another principle, is, in [the realm of] existence,

77

either a peaceful expansion whereby it becomes a people or a *nation*, which has a common natural origin, or a coming together of scattered family communities.

(§181, 'Transition from the Family to Civil Society')

In other words, it would seem as if the spirit of *Sittlichkeit* has been marching along towards ever wider social structures in which human freedom will be able to unfold with increasing regularity. And yet, the 'natural' dissolution of the family is anything but resolved and orderly. With the step (*auseinandertreten*) out of one stage into another, enters (*eintreten*) a disruptive moment. As we shall see, its model concerns less a burial as in *Antigone* than willful inheritance as in *King Lear*.

The natural dissolution of the family occurs, according to Hegel, with the death of its (male) head and the need for arranging the inheritance: 'The natural dissolution of the family through the death of the parents, particularly of the husband, results in *inheritance* of the family's resources' (§178). We have here a natural act that opens up a place for the entrance of a radical arbitrariness (he twice refers to an *eintreten*) because while on the one hand the end of a 'natural' family leads to the family's and its members' integration into a larger social order, on the other hand that very integration makes the passing on of the family's resources (*Vermögen*) increasingly arbitrary (unnatural).[35] That is, because a family as an *ethical* (*sittlich*) unit contains, indeed is organized around, its resources, by means of which it hopes to care for and maintain itself (§§170–72), there needs to be some *ethical* (*sittlich*) way of passing these resources on over generations. And yet, what Hegel is dealing with here is precisely the natural dissolution of the family and so an open question about the status of the family's resources is raised ('Where this particular [family] is dissolved – no universal one is present any longer – what's to do with the resources? *wohin mit dem Vermögen?*' [note to §176]). Hence, the question of how to pass on an inheritance becomes a paradigmatic case of the will of *Sittlichkeit*: the greater the ethical content of Spirit, the less nature and hence the greater the arbitrariness. Hegel seems to be arguing then, perhaps even against his own will, that there is no *freier Wille* without *Willkür* (free choice, willfulness, arbitrariness); arbitrariness is necessary to freedom.[36] We see this if we look at the contorted way in which the arbitrary moment is 'contained' in this transition.

At the heart of this transition are the will, last wills, and testaments. As we see in the notes to §178: 'Inheritance. As *transition* of *property* to another individual, [remains] *abstract* — it can only be transferred via wills.' Hegel considers a number of possible ways in which the transition could occur. In the background is the unspoken possibility that the family passes on its resources 'naturally.' But if that is the case, then we never leave the realm of nature and the family. Thus, he must deal with the *fact* of the natural family's dissolution and the need for some other way of regulating inheritance, namely through a 'testament' representing the last will of the deceased. In other words, the very ground of the phenomenon of testaments (passing on a family's resources) is the same as the ground of the transition to civil society, namely the dissolution of the family ('basis of the testament — dissolution — disintegration of the familial bond'; 'Grund des *Testamentes* — Aufgelöstsein — Auseinandersein des Familienbandes'; note to §178). This dispersal of the family (he calls it 'individuating dissemination'; '*verselbständigende Zerstreuung*' in §178) is the ground for both arbitrariness and freedom:

> The disintegration [of the family into the civil society] leaves the arbitrary will [*Willkür*] of the individual free either to expend his entire resources in accordance with his caprices, opinions, and individual ends, or to regard a circle of friends, acquaintances, etc. so to speak as taking the place of a family and to make a pronouncement to that effect in a *testament* [*Testamente*] whereby they become his rightful heirs.
>
> (§179)

Here again we have the imagery of the 'entrance' of a radical arbitrariness into the ethical order precisely as that order is being established. The reason is that once families are dispersed across society, an individual can, through his (rarely her) last will and testament, make a different, non-natural 'family' out of a 'circle of friends.'[37] But this condition of freedom from nature and the beginning of a wider ethical order introduces the potential for its own disruption:

> The formation [*Bildung*] of such a circle as would give the will an ethical justification for disposing of resources in this way — especially in so far as the very act of forming this circle has testamentary implications — involves [*eintreten*] so much contingency, arbitrariness, intent to pursue selfish ends, etc., that the ethical moment is extremely vague; and the recognition that the arbitrary will [*Willkür*] is entitled to make bequests is much more likely to lead to infringements of ethical relations and to base aspirations and equally base attachments, and to provide an opportunity and justification for foolish arbitrariness [*törichter Willkür*] and for the insidious practice of

attaching to so-called benefactions and gifts vain and oppressively vexatious conditions which come into effect after the benefactor's death, in which event his property in any case ceases to be his.

(§179)

Clearly, Hegel would want to see a 'limit' imposed on the degree of arbitrariness that last wills introduce into the development of the ethical will.[38] But these attempts to contain *Willkür* reveal only how it is unavoidably contained.

For example, Roman law would give all power to the father, who can even sell his sons. But this regulation, clear as it may be, is just a heightened form of arbitrariness and thus *unsittlich*.[39] Likewise, other forms of giving priority to certain familial heirs – say to sons over daughters, or to the first-born son – might make possible the continuity of a bloodline, but not the *family*, since, the implication is that some of its members suffer deprivation.[40] Moreover, while the equal parceling out of the resources to each family member would seem to have an ethical priority (§180), this possibility was ruled out precisely by the development of a more ethical society in which families have become dispersed and therefore the individual members are not equally present. And finally, if one wanted to pass on the inheritance on the basis of the ethical principle that is for Hegel behind marriage, namely love, then the door is opened to the arbitrariness of the *individual*, for love is not universalizable.[41]

Thus, we are left at this stage of the Spirit with a double bind, or rather an inextricable knot of many strands. The dissolution of the natural family introduces the possibility of the ethical society. That disseminating dispersal (*Zerstreuung*) makes the *natural* passing on of resources from one generation to the next impossible. Enter arbitrariness with this new-found freedom of choice (*Willkür*). Thus, some order must be found to delimit the extent of arbitrariness. Yet any such regulation is founded on the notion of last wills and testaments, which only increase the amount of arbitrariness and *Unsittlichkeit* (indeed, he refers to the quasi-institutionalization of the unethical, the 'Versittlichung des [Unsittlichen]'; Addition, §180). This is what Hegel refers to as 'the difficult and mistaken element in our inheritance law' ('das Schwierige und Fehlerhafte in unserem Erbrechte') and it reaches deeper than Hegel would, in spirit, admit. For his hope that last wills and testaments would be introduced only in those (limited?) cases where the family is dispersed is undermined precisely by the march of the spirit that is dispersing it. We are in the situation of King Lear, who has no way to pass on his kingdom legitimately.[42] Think of him as a possible implicit referent for the following passage marking the passage to civil society:

> Wills in general have a disagreeable and unpleasant aspect, for in making my will, I identify those for whom I have an affection. But affection is arbitrary [*willkürlich*]; it may be gained in various ways under false pretences or associated with various foolish reasons, and it may lead to a beneficiary being required to submit to the greatest indignities. In England, where all kinds of eccentricity [*Marotten*] are endemic, innumerable foolish notions are associated with wills.
>
> (Addition, §180)

And we can add, not just in England, but in the very essence of the (last) will enabling this transition from family to society, we encounter an intractable contradiction. The (last) will, therefore, *is* this fusion of necessary order and arbitrariness.

My point is not that this is the site of a 'deconstruction.' It would be so only if one expected of wills a kind of 'purity' of spirit, a freedom from contradiction. But, rather, I am arguing that Hegel's analysis of the freedom of will inherent in last wills and testaments, i.e. his sense of the 'absolute ground of inheritance – inheritance [as] unfortunate capital – everything topsy-turvy' ('absoluter Grund der Erbschaft – Erbrecht unglückliches Kapital – Alles durcheinander' [notes on §178]) and the inherent necessity of arbitrariness, points to an insight beyond either the spirit or its deconstruction. Hegel's focus on the will, and here I would recall Schelling, for all its efforts to 'contain' the contradictions, reveals precisely the very nature of the will *as* contradiction, or, to use Derrida's terms, as 'origin-heterogeneous.' At the heart of the ethical/social is a wanting will that *cannot* be contained since it marks the very point of 'transition' or 'going/passing over' (*Übergehen*, *Übergang*) that is the ethical. The story of last wills, therefore, needs to be read for a different kind of Hegelian legacy than his *Geist*, one that he bequeaths to us through his recognition of the necessity and impossibility of thinking through both arbitrariness and order in a 'passing on' from one human agency to another.

If the problem of testaments for Hegel is the fact that they mark the point where legalized control of property meets the arbitrariness of individuality, where the *letzter Wille* could be *willkürlich*, where the 'natural dissolution' of the family in death can lead to its unnatural propagation in strangers (their ownership of the family's property), and thus where the transition of the family into a larger principle (*Volk*, or nation) bequeaths as well a moment of 'something disagreeable [oppositional, contrary, revolting] and unpleasant' (*etwas Widriges und Unangenehmes*) – then the problem of *Sittlichkeit* in general is to deal with these same contradictory determinations inherent in the will at the level of the social in general. These determinations can be formulated as oppositions between the individual and the institutional (general), the subjective and the objective, the instinctual and the rationally known. Let us look to the wider context of this analysis of last wills to see the insistent contradictions at work in the will in general. My goal here is to dislodge the will from its reduction either to a mere 'metaphysics of subjectivity' or to the externally imposed law. I want to argue for a power, indeed a 'truth,' in Hegel's analysis of *Sittlichkeit* and freedom, one that cannot be 'deconstructed' the way that Spirit is, because we refuse to spiritualize the dialectics of will.

As I implied earlier (notes 29 and 30), Derrida himself contextualizes the role of the family in the discussion of 'the general concept *Sittlichkeit* that defines the general field in which something like a family upsurges' (*Glas*, p. 13). But at no point does Derrida refer to the concept of the will. In the notes to the opening paragraph of this third part of the *Philosophy of Right*, however, we find the definition: 'What is *Sittlichkeit*? That my will is posited as adequate to the concept. Its subjectivity is sublated' ('Daß mein Wille als dem Begriff gemäß *gesetzt sei* – seine Subjektivität aufgehoben sei . . .' [notes to §142]). What we need to keep in mind here is that while for Hegel *Sittlichkeit* may be a certain stage of Spirit, namely 'objective spirit,' we nonetheless need to ask what *that* is. The answer is clearly that it is a certain formation of the *will*. And as such it makes more sense, as we shall see, to define it, in keeping with a general logic of the will, in inherently contradictory terms (subjective/objective, individual/general, etc.). That is, to understand *Sittlichkeit* we need to understand the will, for the former is glossed as 'freedom, or the will which has being in and for itself' ('die Freiheit oder der an und für sich seiende Wille' [§145]). The will, therefore, has, in order even to exist *as* will, two moments (its *Ansichsein* and its *Fürsichsein*). The reason they are 'moments' is that they do not have any independent existence; i.e. to the extent that the one appears, the other will also.[43] While the entire first two sections of the *Philosophy of Right* was an unfolding of each moment and the demonstration of their 'flipping' into the other,[44] Hegel summarizes them in a way that reveals the relevance of these discussions of the will for contemporary cultural studies. *Sittlichkeit* (or the *sittliche Substanz*), as the will *an und für sich*, consists, he writes, in both an objective existence over and above the individual and that individual's primal identification with such objectifications. Hegel writes:

In relation to the subject, the ethical substance and its laws and powers are on the one hand an object [*Gegenstand*], inasmuch as *they are*, in the supreme sense of self-sufficiency (*Selbständigkeit*). They are thus an absolute authority and power, infinitely more firmly based than the being of nature. . . .
On the other hand, they are not something *alien* (*Fremdes*) to the subject. On the contrary, the subject bears spiritual witness (*es gibt Zeugnis des Geistes*) to them as to *its own essence*, in which it has its *self-awareness* (*Selbstgefühl*) and lives as in its element which is not distinct from itself — a relationship which is immediate and closer to identity than even [a relationship of] *faith* or *trust*.

(§§146 and 147)[45]

We have here the beginnings of a conception of man and culture that runs through Max Weber to Clifford Geertz, whose famous definition of culture, now a quasi-motto for cultural studies, echoes Hegel on the will of *Sittlichkeit*: 'Believing, with Max Weber, that man is an animal suspended in webs of significance that he himself has spun, I take culture to be those webs. . . .'[46] We are born into a pre-ordered world, structured by wills over which we have no control, if for no other reason than they were always already there. And yet, precisely because this fact of a symbolic order is a condition for my subjectivity, I have a primal relationship, or has Hegel calls it, a 'relationless identity' (*verhältnislose Identität*; §147) to it, which makes my experience of it as subjective as it would seem objective. It is 'subjective' because there is no experience of a world whatsoever that does not consist of the individual's living, with various degrees of reflection, the categories of *sittliche Substanz*.[47]

Hegel seems to me to be formulating something here that as yet has not been approached by a deconstruction, namely a conception of will that accounts for the reality of and the contradictions inherent in our agency and activity. According to Hegel, the will is not to be ultimately equated with a 'metaphysics of subjectivity' (although it must be noted that Hegel *did* have a tendency to use 'will' in the context of radical individualism, false 'moral' autonomy, and romantic irony, etc., both in the *Phenomenology of Spirit* and in the second part of the *Philosophy of Right* on morality).[48] In order for the will to be in accordance with its concept, it must also be engaged with the outside world.[49] The will is also not to be equated with the imposition of law on the subject, even by the subject him- or herself in a Kantian sense, for as a concept it would make no sense to speak about the will in terms of pure determinism.[50] What Hegel is attempting to think together in the concept of the will is the

83

simultaneity in my wanting (also my wanting to say, *vouloir dire*, meaning) of something general *and* the fact that, as a wanting, it is grounded in an irreducible individuality.[51] My wilful engagement in the social is subject to a moment of contingency. That is, we see in the overall analysis of the will of *Sittlichkeit* and of the 'last wills' forming the transition from family to civil society at *Sittlichkeit*'s core how Hegel is maintaining the Schellingian 'contradiction of necessity and freedom,' individuality and system, arbitrariness and law. But for the general discussion of this key conceptualization of a contradiction, we need to go to the beginning.

In the Introduction to the *Philosophy of Right*, 'Concept of the Philosophy of Right, of the Will, of Freedom, and of Right Itself' (§§1–32), the will is defined as the 'more precise location and point of departure' ('nähere Stelle und Ausgangspunkt'; §4) of right (whereas its 'basis [*Boden*] in general is the realm of the spirit [*das Geistige*]'). All of the 'dialectical syllogisms' that proceed from it therefore bear its mark. We could say that to the extent that the *Geist* is related to death ('*Geist* is also consonant with death according to Hegel, spiritual life with natural death'; *Glas*, p. 8), its ground is a cemetery, and the will is the 'exit' (point of departure, *Ausgangspunkt*), the possibility of 'passing on' to a new life without denying the reality of death. But that act of the last will, we saw, is intimately bound up with the arbitrariness of *Willkür*, the freedom of the testament bound up with the undecidability of the choice (e.g. of who is named in my will). So now we must turn to Hegel's general discussions of will, *Willkür*, and freedom. I can give only some indications of the resourcefulness of Hegel's analysis, i.e. what remains for us to think through.

The will is at the heart of his idealism since it is defined as 'die wahrhafte Idee' (§21). But here one must be careful not to identify the will as 'true idea' with metaphysics as some spooky realm of ideas independent of reality. As Hegel explains in the Addition: 'Truth in philosophy means that the concept corresponds to reality.' And while he gives a traditional example of body and soul ('Ein Leib ist z.B. die Realität, die Seele der Begriff'), the reflexivity of their relationship needs to be underscored: 'But soul and body ought to match *one another* (*sollen* sich *angemessen sein*; my emphasis). Neither has any truth independent of the other. Truth means the *Aufhebung* of a contradiction, whereby there is no reason to see in this notion some kind of harmonious or beautiful product, the balancing of opposites. Rather, the point is to insist on the necessity of maintaining the simultaneous tension and exchangeability of these opposites, to resist the 'one-sidedness' that Hegel associates with metaphysics and the understanding.[52]

Let us focus on one of the main points of tension and contradiction, the relationship between inside and outside, nature and reason. The will does not begin as something 'pure' but as 'the *drives, desires, inclinations* (*die* Triebe, Begierden, Neigungen) by which it finds itself naturally determined' (§11). In man, it is not the absence of these natural forces but their indeterminate vicissitudes, their generality, and the fact that they have 'all kinds of objects and can be satisfied in all kinds of ways' ('vielerlei Gegenstände und Weisen der Befriedigung'; §12)[53] that creates the possibility of opening up to a 'real' or 'effective will,' a will that engages both a 'neutral' potentiality and the choice of a particular:

> Inasmuch as the will, in this double indeterminacy, gives itself the form of *individuality* [*Einzelheit*], it is a resolving will (*beschließend*), and only in so far as it makes any resolutions at all is it an actual will (*wirklicher Wille*).
>
> [This is also an act of] 'deciding' [*sich entschließen*], [a phrase] which indicates that the indeterminacy of the will itself, as something neutral yet infinitely fruitful, the original seed of all existence [*Dasein*], contains its determinations and ends within itself, and merely brings them forth from within.
>
> (§12)[54]

This is the will that is confronted with various possibilities but becomes only a *wirklicher Wille* insofar as it actually decides and acts. The will, therefore, is never merely abstract potentiality but unfolds only in a radical particularity that is not subjectivity. It is not as if there is a pure will that then acts, but the will constitutes itself in its actions.[55]

The will contains the contradiction, therefore, that it is *both* the ability to 'stand above' options, an essential undecidability, *and* simultaneously the inability to remain ultimately beyond such concrete choices:

> The finite will, purely with regard to its form, is the self-reflecting *infinite* 'I' which is with itself [*bei sich selbst*]. As such, it *stands above* [*steht über*] its content, i.e. its various drives, and also above the further individual ways in which these are actualized [*Verwirklichung*] and satisfied. At the same time, since it is only formally infinite, it is *tied* [*gebunden*] to this content as to the determinations of its nature and of its external actuality [*Wirklichkeit*]; but since it is indeterminate, it is not restricted to this or that content in particular.
>
> (§14)

The reality of the will, its 'truth,' consists in the simultaneity of its ability to choose out of a state of indeterminacy and the necessity of its making *some* choice. Insofar as I exercise will, I give up any hope for a 'purity' or independence from all real 'content' in the world, although I at the same time embrace my ability to choose among the 'contents.'

This is the contradiction that is *Willkür*. *Willkür* is that aspect of will that contains the opposition between freedom to choose and the dependence on some choice, that is on 'free reflection, which abstracts from everything, and dependence on an inwardly or externally given content and material' ('die freie von allem abstrahierende Reflexion und die Abhängigkeit von dem innerlich oder äußerlich gegebenen Inhalte und Stoffe'; §15). What is its relationship to the will? Consider the earlier discussion of 'last wills.' There, the will was an essential moment in the transition from family to civil society, and precisely in that transition we found the element of arbitrariness, since to write a will means that the 'naturalness' of the family is dissolved. A will (testament) contains the arbitrariness in the double sense: it has it (indeed brings it about) and would control it by its binding force. Here, in the conceptual Introduction to the entire work, *Willkür* is likewise an essential moment of will: 'Since I have the possibility of determining myself in this or that direction – that is, since I am able to choose – I possess an arbitrary will (*Willkür*)' (§15, Addition). But it is not the 'real, effective (*wirklicher*) will,' because it maintains precisely the opposition between inside and outside that the will would disrupt. *Willkür* holds on to its radical undecidability *vis-à-vis* independently existing choices, whereas the will holds on to these *two* as interrelated or 'corresponding.' Thus, to fuse Hegel's and Derrida's terminology, *Willkür* is the contradiction that the 'truth' of will would (always already) deconstruct: 'Instead of being the will in its truth, arbitrariness (*Willkür*) is rather the will as *contradiction* (*der Wille als der Widerspruch*' [§15]; see also the opening of §17: 'Der Widerspruch, welcher die Willkür ist . . .'). The will would not be what it is (would not be real, true, free) if it did not maintain this opposition between arbitrary free choice and the objects of choice *and* overcome this very opposition by recognizing that there is no real, free, effective choice without the objects. Now we can appreciate the intractability of the argument about the arbitrariness of last wills and testaments: both the will in general and a last will and testament in particular include within themselves this opposition and the movement toward recognizing its untenability.[56]

In the most general terms, Hegel plays out this essential dialectic of the will in terms of a movement between subject and object. (Consider the gloss of 'the activity of the will' as 'sublating [*aufzuheben*] the contradiction between subjectivity and objectivity'; §28.) The will might initially be conceived of (by the 'understanding') as a form of 'metaphysical subjectivity,' an inner choice that is secondarily 'externalized.' But this metaphysics cannot be upheld, and certainly should not be identified with a theory of the effective will, because the very movement is propelled by a 'lack' in the subject, a lack precipitated or inscribed always already because of the subject's being as a will 'inmixed' with objectivity.[57] Hegel writes of the purpose motivating will: 'At first, this end is only *subjective* and internal to me, but it should also become *objective* and throw off the deficiency [*Mangel*] of mere subjectivity' (Addition, §8). But he by no means stops with this apparent subjectivity of presence, since he emphasizes that the starting point of the will is a lack (*Mangel*), and the reason for the *Mangel* is that from the start the subjectivity of my purpose was not 'pure,' but already 'beyond itself' in/with the objective.[58] This prevents us from reading the will as a movement from a kind of pure, self-present interiority to an impure, alienated exteriority, 'for to us, freedom and will are the unity of the subjective and the objective' (Addition, §8).

The freedom of the will, or the freedom that Hegel sees as identical with the will, needs to be understood in its contradictoriness. It is certainly not an abstract and negative will/freedom ('freedom from everything'). If that is one's sense of freedom, then Hegel certainly agrees with Nietzsche that there is no such thing as 'free will,' some independent *causa sui*.[59] Rather, it is real and effective only as the will *to* something, whereby that 'something' is never itself objectively binding or radically other than the will but is, in and of itself, self-superseding like the will.[60] Again with Nietzsche, therefore, one could say that the will (to power) can only will (or act upon) other wills. The will's wanting is neither a stable balance of forces nor a unidirectional objectification, but, rather, a radical 'confusibility' of binary poles like subject-object, abstract-concrete, individual-universal, form-content, independent-dependent. Hegel writes:

> In the will . . . [as opposed to in the understanding] such antitheses — which are supposed to be abstract, yet at the same time determinations *of the will* which can be known only *as the concrete* — lead by themselves to their own identity and to a confusion of their meanings [*die Verwechselung ihrer Bedeutungen*], a confusion into which the understanding quite unwittingly [*bewußtlos*] falls.
>
> (§26)

Unique to the will, and inhabiting Spirit and Being, is the effective reality, i.e. the experience and recognition, of a radical heterogeneity. Unlike the Kantian will, whose autonomy is granted on the basis of a pure formalism, Hegel's will is free in embracing a heteronomy.

Thus, the *Philosophy of Right* will unfold not according to the logic of the Spirit but to that of the will. Hegel introduces the Subdivisions of the *Philosophy of Right* (§33) with the statement: 'In accordance with the stages in the development of the Idea of the will which is free in and for itself, the will is . . .' and then goes on to give the different forms that the will can take (abstract, subjective-moral, self-reflexive-communal-*sittlich*). This is not to say that Hegel is not a (indeed, the) 'philosopher of Spirit.' But in a crucial sense he is very much an anti-metaphysical philosopher of will.[61] Consider, for example, the analysis of drives (*Triebe*). He rejects the notion of a 'purification of the drives' (*Reinigung der Triebe*), which would strip them of their nature and arbitrariness; rather he would see them as the 'rational system of the will's determinations' ('vernünftiges System der Willensbestimmung'), which, given what we know about the will, means: the drives are what the will has to work with. We deal with them first according to the principle of 'happiness' (*Glückseligkeit*; §20); but Hegel asks what principle is driving *it*, i.e. what is 'beyond the pleasure principle.' And that is the will that wills itself *as* sensual and rational (not a rational will opposed to drives) (§21). The point is not to see the will as the 'purification' of the drives, or as a subjectivity transcending them, but as that wanting – uniting both lack and desire – around which they are organized for a subject. That is, the will and the drives are structurally co-constitutive. And because of this, the deconstruction of the oppositions around the Spirit leave the will and its very incorporation of these contradictions largely unaffected.

But where does he leave us? What does remain? What are Hegel's remains, what is his legacy for us? I would say there are two major problems for 'us,' 'here,' 'now,' reading Hegel. The one is that the concept of *Aufhebung* has been tainted with the sense of (false) harmony and order. The other is that the details of his analyses are false, anachronistic, absurd, laughable, suspect, etc. Derrida has focused his reading on both of these aspects by disrupting apparent balances and hierarchies and by highlighting the untenable (Hegel on marriage, on the sexes, etc.). While there is clearly nothing wrong with doing this, I think that Derrida's specific focal point in the Spirit has led to an unfortunate moment of exclusion in his own reading. He has deconstructed Spirit as falsely 'pure' by using the 'letters' and 'bodies' against it but does not provide a reading of

Hegel's (last) will. There we see a concept whose truth rests precisely on the simultaneous institution and breakdown of dualisms. By embedding the analysis of 'last wills and testaments' within the analysis of will in general in the *Philosophy of Right*, we see that there is a willful 'origin-heterogeneous' at the heart of it all. My point is therefore *not* to avoid the contradictions in Hegel. On the contrary. They are the most important places. But where Derrida stresses their 'contaminating' consequences for a philosophy of spirit and avoids the dialectics of the will, I would begin there to see how Hegel is initiating a more powerful response to 'metaphysics as such' (a development culminating perhaps in Nietzsche's 'will to power'). Thus, I am by no means calling for a return to a Hegel before Derrida; rather, this reading of Hegel after Derrida, in locating the will as an un-thought in Derrida that is a center of Hegelian thought, returns us to a rethinking of both.

Derrida, therefore, might be right about Spirit. It does generally represent the attempt to delimit and purify radical contradictoriness and the exchange-ability of dualisms. As such, it can be 'deconstructed,' its 'contamination' revealed, its stability destabilized. But are not the more interesting moments, the key ones in Hegel, Schelling, Heidegger, and even Derrida, those where the 'origin-heterogeneous,' that which is being delimited and contained, is shown 'in action'? For example, there where the 'last will and testament' for Hegel is revealed to be the arbitrary ground of the civil society; there where Being is revealed to rest on a *Wille* as groundless *Ursein* in Schelling; there where *Ausgangspunkt* of will leaves the *Boden* of the Spirit; there where the will is not captivated by a 'metaphysics of subjectivity'; there where the will, with full mutuality, implicates the individual and the social; there where *Gelassenheit* for Heidegger entails a simultaneous *Wollen-nicht-Wollen*. I would argue, then, that the concept of the will I have been trying to develop out of Hegel has more to do with the *Wille zur Macht* than, say, with Schopenhauer's metaphysics of the will. We can thus create a different kind of lineage, including Schelling, Hegel, Nietzsche, Heidegger, and Derrida, all of whom see the force of an 'origin-heterogeneous' to an extent in will. The goal of a 'deconstruction' (also this one of Derrida) would be to work out the traces of the will there where these thinkers cover it with, say, Spirit or Being.

To have shown the contradictory moments of the will, i.e. to have shown the 'wanting' of the Spirit, is thus, in one sense, once again to deconstruct the Spirit, because the attempts by speculative dialectic to contain the will, to silence the last will buried in the crypt, to obscure the 'origin-heterogeneous' (wanting) within spirit, have been shown to collapse under the weight of their own willfulness. But in another sense, my reading seeks to reveal Derrida's own deconstruction of Spirit to be 'wanting,' to have excluded the question of the will. Thus, my attempt to resurrect the will is neither a return to Hegel's Spirit nor a destruction of the idealist project. Rather, I hope to have isolated a central moment repressed or unthought or problematically buried in both Hegel and Derrida, a moment that allows us to talk about agency, freedom, politics after the end of any 'metaphysics of the subject' or decline of philosophies of Spirit. What is at stake is not a separating out of 'what is living and what is dead' in Hegel's philosophy, but *after Derrida* to find what speaks to us, *nolens volens*, from beyond the grave of *Geist* and to explore how a legacy of an internally divided individuality can be passed on for us, be we members of Hegel's family or not. And while it is certainly not the case that Derrida's thought and un-thoughts 'give us nothing' (*Of Spirit*, p. 13), the reading of Hegel's will hands down to us more than the deconstruction of the Spirit. As executors of Hegel's testament, we thrive on his death by neither spiritualizing him nor fixating on the deconstructed corpus, but by reading the will literally for what it says to us about the contradictory conditions of freedom.

# 3

# The Surprise of the Event

*Jean-Luc Nancy*

This title ought also to be written or read as 'The Surprise: Of the Event,' for the 'surprise' is not only an attribute, quality, or property of the event, but the event itself, its being or its essence. What eventuates in the event is not only that which happens, but that which surprises – perhaps even that which surprises itself (turning it, in short, away from its own 'happening' [*arrivée*],[1] not allowing itself *to be* event, surprising being in it, not letting it be, unless by surprise).

But let us begin at the beginning. We will find it in that sentence by means of which undoubtedly something began to happen to modern thought, something began to surprise itself in modern thought, something with which we are still not finished:

> Philosophy is not meant to be a narration of happenings but a cognition of what is true in them, and further, on the basis of this cognition, to *comprehend* that which, in the narrative, appears as a mere happening [*événement*].[2]

These lines are taken from 'The Concept in General,' the introductory text of 'The Doctrine of the Concept,' Volume II of Hegel's *Science of Logic*.

This sentence may be read in two ways. According to the first reading – which is the more obvious because it conforms to what passes for a canonical reading of Hegelian thought – this sentence means that philosophy has the task of *comprehending* that of which the event is only the Appearance (*Erscheinung*). More precisely: for philosophy, there is first of all the truth contained in that which happens, and then the comprehension, by the light of that truth, of its very production or of its execution, which appears outwardly, inasmuch as it

91

is not comprehended, as 'mere [*bloss*] event.' Here the eventfulness of the event (the arising, the going-on, the taking place – *das Geschehen*) is only the outer face, obvious and flimsy, of the actual presentation of the true. The advent of the true as real – the content of the concept – eclipses the event – simple narrative representation.

However, this first reading cannot just rest there. Strictly speaking, the *logic of the concept* into which we are entering here should not be a logic of the category or of the idea thought as 'abstract universality' (as in Kant); on the contrary, it should be a logic of the 'identity of concept and thing' (as stated a bit further along in the text (p. 590)). According to this logic, the concept comprehends (seizes, posits, grounds) all the determinateness, all the difference and all the exteriority of real effectivity. And this is why the concept in this sense is the element in which it is revealed (still in the same text, p. 591) that 'the Appearance, far from being incompatible with essentiality, is a manifestation of essence.' The concept, in truth, is the Appearance grasping itself as truth, rather than the opposite of a merely phenomenal appearance.

It is thus not clear – remaining in the straight and narrow of a 'canonical' reading – that the expression 'mere event' may be understood in a unilateral sense, as if predicates determined the essence of the subject: that is, as if the event as such was necessarily and only a 'mere' (inessential) event. On the contrary, a quality proper to the event that is not 'mere' may – and indeed must – subsist. In other words, the *comprehended* event might very well remain the comprehended *event* – and from this several consequences may be drawn.

(It is to be noted that this double constraint about the subject of the event may be found elsewhere in Hegel. That this constraint constitutes a general law for Hegel may be seen, for example, in the introduction to the *Philosophy of History*: 'In the pure light of this divine Idea (which is no mere ideal) the illusion that the world is a mad or foolish event [*Ein verrücktes, törichtes Geschehen*] disappears.' Here too the question of the status of the predicates comes up: are all events mad [*insensé*]? If the world is a sensible [*sensé*] event, is sense independent of its eventfulness?)

It is therefore necessary to undertake a second reading, paying greater attention to the difference articulated in the lines from the *Logic*. This difference is between, on the one hand, knowledge of the truth to be found 'in' the thing (reality, the subject) *that* happens and, on the other hand and 'further' (*ferner*), comprehension of what appears as simple event, that is, not the thing that happens (the content or the non-phenomenal substrate) but *the fact that* it happens: to wit, the eventfulness of its event (or, yet again, its event rather than its advent). Unquestionably, this eventfulness, when comprehended in terms of the truth of the thing, distinguishes itself from the Appearance [*phénomène*], and indeed, opposes itself to it: but it does so only insofar as this eventfulness is the non-phenomenal truth *of the phenomenal itself as such*, that is, as event, as *Geschehen*.

In this sense, the task of philosophy breaks down into:

1 knowing the truth of *that which* took place; and
2 comprehending the taking place as such.

By means of this difference – which is certainly less apparent and in any case analysed less or not at all for its own sake (and which is nonetheless quite distinct ('*ferner*')) – Hegel sets philosophy the task of comprehending, *beyond* the truth, the taking place of the truth: the truth, that is, of the taking place of the truth – or, if you will, beyond the *eventus* of the true, its *evenire*, the truth of the *evenire* such that it cannot be reduced to its *eventus* without failing to be its truth, and consequently, a truth beyond truth itself.

With this difference, with this excess of truth – not the truth about the truth, but the truth of the taking place of the true – Hegel opens modernity. The opening of modernity is nothing other than the opening of thought to the event as such, to the truth of the event *beyond* all advent of sense. In the opening of modernity (or, if one can put it this way, in the closure of metaphysics, which is itself but the event of the opening, the event opening thought to that excess that originarily overflowed it, there is this gesture towards the event *as such*.

In fact, what is at stake is the following: the task of philosophy is not to substitute for the narrative *Geschehen* some substrate or subject that would not happen,[3] but that would simply *be* (which, as *sup-posed*, would always already have been – the 'being-which-it-was,' Aristotle's *to ti èn einai*).[4] Beyond the truth of what happens, and which consequently *is* happening, or which *is* in its happening (which is as much to say *has happened*, and which has always already happened in the happening itself), it is necessary to think *that* it happens – the happening or rather the happen*ing* 'itself' – 'it,' which is not precisely 'the same' as 'that which it was,' since it has not *happened*. One might say: it is necessary to think sameness itself, as being the same as nothing.

This is perhaps how one must think *Geschichte* in Hegel, as being less 'history' as we understand it (and as Hegel himself primarily understands it) than the whole act or being, the entelechy of *Geschehen*. *Geschichte* would then not only or primarily be the productive succession of different states of its subject. More than a development, a process or procession, it would be the happening, the coming – and perhaps even 'happening,' 'coming,' 'taking place,' a verb both unsubstantiated and unsubstantiable. This is why Hegel refuses to identify philosophy with a developmental narration, with its episodic ups and downs. What he rejects thereby is *not* the dimension of the 'happening' as such, for which he would seek to substitute the simple stable identity of being and of having-always-already-been. Upon closer scrutiny, we perceive that he is rather rejecting an understanding of *Geschehen* – the active essence of *Geschichte*, the historiality of history, if you will – as mere episodic events (*blosses Geschehen*). (the pages preceding the quote from which we began may be reread from this perspective.) The event is not an episode; it is, if it must be said that it is – *that there be*[5] – that is, that there be something, something different from the indifference of being and nothingness, if one wishes to put this in the terms of the matrix logic of *becoming*. The event points to what is to be thought at the heart of becoming, as something both more inaccessible and more decisive than the 'passage' (*Übergang*) to which one ordinarily reduces it. As 'passage,' becoming points above all to that into which it passes: the having-become of its result. But for movement to take place, in the steps of the movement [*pas du passer*], there must first be 'agitated instability' (*haltungslose Unruhe*) (*Logic*, I, 1,1,C,2), which has not yet come to pass and which *as such* does not come to pass – but happens.

Hegel thus wants to think – or else at least, Hegel's thought tends towards this thought as if towards its vanishing point – of the essence of *Geschehen* as *Geschehen*. That is, he wants to think of it as the essence of precisely that which shies away from a logic of essence understood as substance, subject, or ground, in favor of a logic of the 'happening' [*arriver*], the whole essence of which lies in the 'agitation,' which consists in not subsisting (*haltungslos*). Moreover, the semantic origins and usage of the word *Geschehen* refer us less to process and what is produced than to the movement and the leap, to precipitation and suddenness. (Incidentally, and in contrast with the French 'événement,' *Geschehen* does not have the sense of 'remarkable event,' for which there are other terms in German, such as the similar *Geschehnis*. The small difference between the two reveals all the more the verbal, active, mobile character of *Geschehen*.)

Certainly, it must be admitted that we thus reach the extreme limit of what it is possible to make Hegel say. What is in question here is neither the commission of interpretive violence against the text, nor dragging Hegel, against his own precepts, out of his time. Rather, what is at stake is simply indicating that it is necessary in any case to make Hegel say this, however surprising such a statement may seem to 'Hegelians' (if they still exist), and indicating that the era proper to Hegel in philosophy, the period of the modern closure/opening, consists itself of this surprise: gnawing anxiety (*Unruhe*) about the event.

To think the event in its eventful essence is to surprise Hegelian thought from within. Hegelian thought closes to this undoubtedly as quickly as it is opens itself to it. Hegel, finally, lets *Geschehen* come and go without getting a grasp on it, yet he states nothing less, as that which is beyond his own discourse, than that it happens upon him and that it is this that must be thought.

One might alternatively say that Hegel grasps the *Geschehen*; he halts it or examines it in its coming and going. He fixes the concept (it is *Geschichte*). But in so doing, he puts in new relief that it is precisely in grasping the *Geschehen* that he will have missed it *as such*. He thereby opens, *nolens volens*, the question of the 'as such' of the *Geschehen*.

The 'as such' of the event would be its *being*. But from this point, it would have to be not the Being of *what* happens – that is, of what is *happening* – nor yet the being *of* the 'that it happens,' but rather the being-happening, or better still, the being-*that*-it-happens. Or again: not the 'there is' [*il y a*], but *that* there is, that *that* without which *there* would be nothing. The difference between 'it is' and 'there is' consists in precisely what the 'there' marks: the proper instance of the taking place of being, without which being would not be. *That* there is equals the being *of* being, or the transitive being of intransitive or substantive being, the event of being that is necessary for being to be, but which is in no way substance, subject, or foundation of being. The event of being,[6] which is not at all like being insofar as it is being 'itself' – it is the same, if you will, as that which it *was not*, or, more exactly, the same as that which it has not been, the same as nothing.

The question of the 'as such' of the event opens something on the order of a negativity of the 'as such.' How does one think 'as such' when the 'as' does not refer back to any 'such'? Thought is caught by surprise in the strong sense of the word; it is caught short of thought. It is not that thought had not spotted its object, but rather that there is no object to spot if the 'event' cannot even be spoken of or aimed at 'as such' – that is to say, in short, if one cannot articulate the 'event' without concealing its eventfulness.

Let us dwell on the nature of this surprise.

There is then something to be thought – the event – the very nature of which – the eventfulness – can only arise [*relever*] from surprise, can only take thought by surprise. What is to be thought is how thought can and should be surprised, and how, perhaps, it is precisely this which makes thought think. Or again, how there would not be any thought without the event of thought.

To think the surprise of the event (which no doubt amounts to thinking the heart or the leap of Hegelian *Geschehen*, the dialectical mainspring at the point of which, before being the resources and motivating force, has to be the trigger or instigation, and hence its negativity *itself*) must be something other than the solicitation of the unthinkable, whatever the style of address. And it must be something other than capturing surprise in order to spurn its surprise by confining it to quarters as a concept. What concerns us here is thus less the concept of surprise, than a surprise in the very concept [*à même le concept*],[7] surprise essential to the concept.

That this be the task of philosophy – and that philosophy be *thought surprised* – is perhaps what must be understood in returning, well before Hegel, to the Platonic and Aristotelian *topos* of 'astonishment.' One harps on this *topos* as if to work oneself up to an original 'wonderment' – simultaneously rapture and avowal of innocence – which would set off the process of its auto-appropriation, that is, of its auto-resorption.

Now, as Aristotle tells us, assuming we have read *Metaphysics* A,2 attentively, 'philosophy' is the science, neither 'practical' nor 'poetic,' that proceeds from astonishment insofar as the latter opens the way to a science that has only itself as an end. Astonishment then does not amount only to a lack of knowledge to be filled or an aporia to be overcome – a characteristic that would not really distinguish one science from others: it amounts instead to a disposition towards *sophia* for itself. Thus, astonishment is properly *philo-sophic*. One can even push this interpretation to say that astonishment is already, by itself, in *sophia's* element, and that, in a symmetrical manner, *sophia* retains in itself the moment of astonishment. (In the same passage, Aristotle states that the *philomuthos*, the lover of myths and their astonishing marvels, is himself also in some ways a *philosophos*.) Retained and not repressed, the moment of astonishment would be that of a surprise kept at the heart of *sophia* and constitutive of it inasmuch as it is its own end. On the one hand, knowledge that is oriented towards nothing else amounts only to its own arising; on the other hand and conversely, this arising in itself is the only real object of knowledge – provided that it is an object. *Sophia* must surprise itself; the surprise must be 'known.'

Thus the surprise of the event would not only be a limit situation for a knowledge of Being; it would also be its essential form and end. From the beginning of philosophy until its end (which re-enacts its beginning all over again), this surprise would constitute the sum of what was at stake – in a literally interminable game.

Still, is it necessary to *remain* precisely in the element of astonishment, that is, in what cannot exactly be an 'element,' but rather an event. How is one to remain in the event? How can one hold oneself in it, if this can be said, without making an 'element' or a 'moment' out of it? Under what conditions can we keep thought in the surprise which thought has the task of thinking?

Let us turn to examine at least some of these conditions, or at least the preliminary conditions.

Let us begin once again, taking as a starting point that 'the surprise of the event' is a tautology. We must begin by articulating the nature of this tautology. The event surprises, or it is not an event. The main thing is to know what a 'surprise' is.

In a birth and in a death – examples that are not examples, that are more than examples, that are the thing itself – there is an event, however anticipated it may have been. One might also formulate this in the following way: what is expected is never the event, but is instead the advent, the result, what happens. At the end of nine months, one expects the birth; but the structural unexpectedness of that expectancy is found in *that* it takes place. Or to be still more precise, the unexpected – and the unexpect*able* – is not 'the fact that' it took place, to the extent that this 'fact' may itself be circumscribed as a sequence in a process and as a given in an experiment. It is not 'the fact that,' but the *that* itself of 'that it happens' or of 'that there is.' Better yet, it is the 'it happens' distinguished from all that comes before it and from all that in which it is co-determined. It is the pure present of 'it happens' – and the surprise has to do with the present as such, with the presence of the present inasmuch as it happens.

That *it happens* is a *quiddity*, but not that of 'what happens,' nor even that of 'that it happens,' nor yet of the succession nor of the simultaneity of that 'that' within all the 'thats.' In order to think something that comes up in a series, it is necessary, says Kant, to conceive of it as a change in the substance (which remains one and identical: *First analogy of experience*), and to link this change to

97

causality (*Second analogy*). 'The concept of change supposes the same subject with two opposing determinations as existent and consequently as permanent.'[8] Outside this concept of change, there is quite simply no concept of a 'something,' for then there would be the 'birth or death of the substance,' which could not take place 'in time,' but rather or exclusively *as time itself*. Thus 'time cannot be perceived in itself.' Pure arising [*survenir*] (*das blosse Entstehen*), otherwise called the *ex nihilo*, or equally, the *in nihilum*, is not anything of which there is a concept, or it is time 'itself,' its paradoxical identity and permanency as 'empty time.'

The event as such: empty time, or presence of the present as negativity, that is, as it happens, and, consequently, as non-present and all this in such a way that it is not even 'not *yet* present' (which would reinscribe the whole thing in a succession of presents already available 'in time'), but, on the contrary, in such a way that nothing precedes or succeeds it: time itself in its arising, as the arising it is.[9]

But empty time, that is, the emptiness of time 'as such,' this emptiness that is not the vacuity inside a form, but the condition of the formation of all forms, this empty time is not a 'thing in itself' out of reach, accessible to an *intuitus originarius*. 'Empty time' – or the articulation *nihil/quid* as non-successive, as arriving [*arriver*] or deriving from something in general – is time itself, insofar as time is not successiveness, but rather that which neither succeeds nor is a permanent substance. One ought to say: permanence without substance, the present without presence, and more than the coming [*la venue*] the coming-*up* [*la* sur-*venue*][10] of the thing itself. Neither time (successive), nor place (distributive), nor thing (being) – but the taking place of something, the event. Thereby we move from a ponderous word to a huge tradition that we will have to problematize later: creation.

Empty time, or negativity as time, the event, itself makes up the 'in itself' of the 'thing in itself': this is no doubt exactly what Kant could not grasp, and what Hegel and all of us who come after him, in the insistent transmission of a thinking of the event, keep aiming at. 'Time' or the 'event' (both terms no doubt still too subjected to a thematics of succession, continuous–discontinuous) perform or *are* the 'site of existence' as such: the *nihil/quid* which could not even be articulated as a 'from *nihil* to *quid*.' The event of Being, not as an accident nor as a predicate, but as the being of being.

Under these conditions, the event is not 'something' beyond the knowable and the expressible, and as such reserved for the beyond-speech, the beyond-knowledge of a mystical negativity. It is not a category, or a meta-category, distinct from being.[11] It is rather being itself [*à même l'être*], the necessary condition for categorizing being: for saying it, for aiming at it, for interpolating it at the level of the surprise of its coming-up [*survenue*].

As such – *als Geschehen, als Entstehen, als Verschwinden*, as taking place, appearing, disappearing – the event is not 'presentable' (in this sense, it exceeds the resources of phenomenology, even though it is the only thing that has ever galvanized the phenomenological theme). But the event is not, for all that, 'unpresentable' as another hidden presence; it is the unpresentable, or rather the unpresentifiable of the present lodged within [*à même*] the present itself. The unpresentifiable of the present, as has been known from Aristotle to our days, passing via Husserl and Heidegger, is its structuring difference. That this structuring difference of the present is not presentable does not mean that it is not thinkable – but it may mean that thought, to think this structuring difference, beyond just seeing and knowing, must surprise itself by/in its 'object.' A becoming-surprise of thought, to put it in a Deleuzian way, must answer to the coming-up of the present (of being).

Following this, there will not be any event 'as such.' For the event *as* event – that is, *quo modo*, in accordance with the mode that is its own (*evenire quo modo evenit*), the event in accordance with the property and the measure of the event itself – is not, to repeat once again, what is produced and what one can show (the spectacular, the born child, the dead man) but it is the event *as* it outcomes [*é-vient*], *as* it happens. One immediately perceives that in such a case, the modal 'as' gets mixed with the temporal 'as' (the 'as' one uses in saying 'as it happened, there was a flash') Here, *quo modo* = *quo tempore*.

The mode of the event – its 'as such and such' – is time itself as the time of the coming-up [*la survenue*]. And the time of the coming-up is 'empty' time. The emptiness of time, or better yet, emptiness *as* time, emptiness *in the mode of* time, will then be 'negativity for itself' (by which Hegel defines time, *Encyclopedia*, §257) – but this negativity understood not, as in Hegel, as 'abstractly related to itself' (which returns us in short to the Kantian 'emptiness'). For in that case, one would still be subject to a model of a succession of presents, separate and linked by this abstract negativity. On the contrary, the relationship of negativity to itself – that is, 'birth and death,' as Hegel says in the same place – must be understood as the non-abstract, which is nevertheless not the result (which is exactly what Hegel lets fall by the wayside, but which he comes close to when he calls time 'existent abstractness'). Coming-up is neither abstraction nor result: negativity 'for itself,' but for itself as a site of Being or of existence.

This positivity of negativity is not its dialectical fecundity: let us say, in order not to reopen the deconstruction site of the dialectic, that it is the exact opposite of such a fecundity and also not, of course, a sterility that would be paired with this fecundity. It is being or being neither engendered nor not-engendered, but come-up [*survenu*], coming-up [*survenant*] or even 'created.'

Negativity, here, does not negate itself, and does not raise [*relève*] itself out of itself. It does something else; its operation or its in-operation is other and obeys another mode. One might say that it extends itself: tension and extension − by which alone something will be able to appear as 'passage' and 'process' − extension neither temporal, nor local, of the taking place as such; spacing by which time arises; tension of nothing that opens time − *Spanne*, as Heidegger says.[12]

Coming-up: nothingness strained to the point of rupture and the bursting-upon of the happening [*au saut de l'arriver*],[13] wherein presence presents itself.

There is rupture and leap: not rupture with the temporal continuum one would have presupposed, but rupture as time itself, that is, rupture as that which admits nothing *pre*supposed and not even, above all, a *pre*supposition, in which time has antecedence over itself. Rupture of nothing, and leap of nothing into nothing: yet again, extension of negativity, or more exactly − since the negative is not something that can be stretched like an elastic − negativity as tension, and tension that is not progressive, but all at once, in one stroke − the tension/extension of being, 'that there is.'

If the event of the 'that there is' has negation 'and not nothing' as a corollary, it is not as its negative − that is, not as another inverse and symmetrical possibility: that there be 'nothing' *in place of* something. For, to be precise, there is no place for the taking place of 'nothing' in the guise of 'something.' 'And not nothing' does not mean that it is not 'nothing' that exists. It means, on the contrary, that nothing exists except 'something' and that 'something' exists without any other *pre*supposed except its very existence, to wit, the extension of 'nothing' as the tension of its coming-present, of its event.

(That in all this the thought of existence is an ordeal of 'nothing,' one may only grant. But the ordeal of nothing is not necessarily or exclusively the anguish of nothingness − which clearly risks carrying with it the projection of this 'nothingness' as the abyssal *pre*(and *post*-)supposed of being. The ordeal of nothing is rather what we are trying to approach: the surprise-thought of the event.)

What then is surprise?

This is exactly what one can no longer ask. The surprise *is* nothing. It is not a newness of being that would surprise in relation to already given Being. Once there is event – whether there be but one, for the totality of Being, or whether there be many, diverse, dispersed, and uncertain (it amounts to the same) – it is the 'already' that leaps out, along with the 'not yet.' Leaps into all the presented and presentable present – and this leap *is* the coming, pres-ence or *prae-ens* itself without the present.

Once 'the child is born,' as Hegel says in the famous passage from the *Phenomenology*, the event is not that it has been born, for that was established in the order of the process and the modification of the substance. The event is rather the interruption of the process, the leap that Hegel represents as the 'qualitative leap' of the 'first breath' (or even, elsewhere, as the 'trembling' that traverses and divides the maternal substance *in utero*). Being born or dying is not 'being' but a 'leap into being,' to speak this time with Heidegger.

Thinking the leap can be done only by a leap of thought – by thought as a leap, as this leap that thought knows and senses itself necessarily to be. But thought knows and senses itself thus *as surprise* (surprise in its knowledge and in its sense, surprise as knowledge and as sense). Surprise is nothing – but the leap right into being [*à même l'être*], this leap wherein event and thought are 'the same.' In its own way, a thought of surprise repeats the Parmenidian sameness of being and thought.

It leaps – what 'it'? nothing, no one: 'it' is only in this leap. That is, it exists – if the ek-sisting of existence is made of the tension and extension between being and being [*étant*], between nothing and something. It leaps into nothing, and thereby it exists. It is this from leaping into nothing. It is itself the articulation of the difference between nothing and something – and this difference is also a *différend (ein Austrag*, dispute, conflict, distribution, sharing, cf. *Nietzsche*, II, p. 167). There is *discord* between being and being [*étant*]: being is in conflict with the present, given, and registered beingness of being [*étant*]; and being [*étant*] is in conflict with being's substantial, founding essentiality. The discord is discord with that which, *in bringing being in accord with being* [*étant*], *would have unleashed ek-sistence.* Thus, discord makes the event: the non-presence of the coming to presence, and its absolute surprise.

But it is not a surprise for a subject. No one is surprised, just as no one leaped. The surprise – the event – does not belong to the order of representation. Surprise is the leap – or the 'it,' the 'some*one*' who comes about in the leap and, indeed, as the leap 'itself' – that surprises itself. It *is* surprised; inasmuch as it is surprised, it is. And, if you will, it is as surprise, surprising itself, that it is caught in the act of being-present. The leap surprises itself precisely inasmuch as it neither represents 'itself' to itself, nor its surprise. It coincides with this surprise; it is only this surprise that is not yet 'its own.'

The tension, the extension of the leap – the spacing of time – the discord of being as its truth: this is the surprise. The *Spanne* surprises, not because it would come to disconcert or to destabilize a subject that was there, but because it *catches hold of* some*one* there *where it is not*, or rather in that the *Spanne* takes it, grasps it, transfixes it, inasmuch *as it is not there*.

And this 'not being there' is exactly the most proper mode of 'being there' once it is a question of 'leaping into being,' or of existing. 'Not being there' is not to be already there, but to be the *there* itself (this is the primary existential condition of *Dasein*). The 'there' is the spacing of tension, of ex-tension. It is space-time – neither space, nor time, nor the coupling of the two, nor a source-point outside of the two, but the originary excision and chiasmus that opens the two to each other.

Surprise is the leap into the space-time of nothing that stems from 'beforehand' or 'elsewhere': it is thus the leap into the space-time *of* space-time 'itself.' It is the taking place of place, of the 'there,' which is not a place 'for' being, but being as place, being-the-there, not present being, but the *present of being as it happens* and which it therefore is not.

The surprise of the event is thus negativity itself – but not negativity as a resource, as an accessible foundation, as nothingness, as an abyss from the depths of which would come the event: for this 'event' would still be a result. Nothing (to retain this harsh word and its caustic effect on all 'abysses' and their depths), nothing that is nothing 'at bottom' and that is only the nothing of a leap into nothing, is the negativity that is not a resource, but the affirmation of ek-sistent tension: its intensity, the intensity or the surprising *tone* of existence.

Under these circumstances, if we need a schematism of surprise – and we do need one, it is what concerns us here – then we must give ourselves the *a priori* conditions for grasping surprise as such, for a surprised grasp of surprise. One might say that this is precisely *the* schematism itself. For if the schematism is the product of a 'pure vision,' anterior to all figure, and if the 'pure vision' is itself the ex-position of time as 'pure affection of oneself' (cf. *Kantbuch*, §§22 and 35), this is because, in the pure affection of oneself, vision sees itself seeing and *thus* sees – nothing(ness). The schematism in general is principally the visibility of nothing as the condition for the possibility of the visibility of something. In all views of something vision sees itself first of all as pure vision, seeing nothing, seeing nothing *there* – and nevertheless already 'vision' [*déjà vu*] and as such ahead, outside itself, nothing of a figure and figure of nothing – this surprising figure without figure traced in one flash by the event of being.

Thus, the schematism – and transcendental imagination in its entirety – would not be at all of the order of 'images' (as we already knew), and not of the order of an archi-image either, any more than of a sublime abyss of dissolving images: more simply, more unimaginably, it would be the *scheme-event*, the flash of the outline strained to nothingness itself and the pure affirmation of existence. Not even, to conclude, 'birth' or 'death,' but only what these excisions carve out: the being of a being [*étant*], its event.

Will it now have to be said that this event is unique – in the manner in which Heidegger speaks of the 'fundamental event in *Dasein*'?[14] Undoubtedly. In a certain way, there is only one event, and there is no 'of the event,' scattered here and there with no connection to essential eventfulness. There is an event, a surprise – and the existent does not pull itself back together, it does not get over it: that is what it is to exist.

But the unicity of the event is not numerical. It does not consist of a single point of origin gathered into itself (for ontology, there is no Big Bang). Because the unicity of the event is or makes a surprise, it is by nature and by structure dispersed in the chance of events, and consequently also in the chance of what is not an event and which hovers discretely in the imperceptible continuum, in the murmur of 'life' for which existence is the exception.

If the event were fundamental and unique in the ordinary – or 'metaphysical' – sense of these words, it would be given, and that gift would also be the originary dissolution of all eventfulness. There would not be any surprise. Because it *is* not *given*, rather it happens; there is surprise, and the aleatory multiplicity of what one might henceforth name the happenings [*arrivées*] (or all 'happen*ings*' ['*arrivers*']) of the unique event. In this sense, there are only events, which means, more precisely, that 'there are' *is* eventful (*Sein, Ereignis*). Which means, further, that events are not just diverse, discrete, and dispersed, but also rare. Or, if you will: the event is simultaneously unique, innumerable, and rare.

The event is never finished happening – and surprising. Thought is never done with surprising itself in watching it arrive, its gaze open onto its own exiguous lucidity. A thought is an event: what thought thinks occurs to it there where it is not. An event is a thought: the tension and leap into the nothing of Being. It is in this sense that 'to be and to think are the same,' and that their sameness takes place according to the cutting ex-tension of ek-sistence.

It is in this sense as well that one may say that the creation of the world is the thought of God. We can think that henceforth if – the unconditioned having ceased to be subject to the condition of the Supreme Being – we can think henceforth that it can be thought without 'God' and without 'creator.' This one may term the exigency of a thinking of the event, such as it comes to us since at least Hegel.

'At least' because it is perhaps necessary to give renewed attention to that which, in Parmenides himself, inscribes ontological truth in the narrative of an event.[15] After all, the poem opens on the present of a fast race – 'the horses that carry me' – of which nothing formally indicates the end. The chariot of the speaker clearly enters into the realm of the goddess, but this realm is presented as the route opened wide by the gaping opening that *Diké* has agreed to open. He does not get out of his chariot, the 'young man,' he who 'knows' and 'sees,' whose route 'crosses all cities.' Without stopping, in passage, he is instructed by the goddess, not about being, but about *it is*. Passing through the gap, he sees that it is there [*qu'il y a*], this is all that happens to him, and nothing else ever happens – once something happens.

But even that must be said and thought – there is only that to be said and to be thought. All sense is there.

What then is sense? That which makes it happen that 'there is.' That which destines or what provokes being to happen. That which passes being by in-coming/going. What is all this? It cannot be represented as an axiom, or as a fact. Let us call it an 'it is necessary' [*il faut*]

Under the title of the last movement of his opus 135, the quartet in F – 'The decision taken with difficulty' – Beethoven noted, as is well known: *Muss es sein? Es muss sein*'[16] (Which may be translated as: 'Must it be? It must be.'). If being simply was, nothing would happen and there would not be thought either. Thus the 'it is necessary' is not the pronouncement of a simple immanent necessity (of a nature or of a destiny). Necessity itself can be only the decided response of thought to the suspense of being wherein it is surprised: *muss es sein?*

Translated by Lynn Festa and Stuart Barnett

# 4

# (The End of Art with the Mask)

*Werner Hamacher*

Irony: this is the end of art. Yet if art is the presentation of the substance of the social world and its deity and, accordingly, if it is the art of political religion, then the end of art — irony — is also the end of substance, the end of political, religious society and its god.

At least Hegel would have it so. In a passage from the *Phenomenology of Mind*, apparently little read and rarely cited in the discussion of the end of art proclaimed by Hegel, he has the 'religion of art' end with comedy and its irony (412/748).[1] This end of art and 'art-religion' is not simply its passing away; it is, rather, foremost the limit immanent to art, its aim, its sense and thus in every sense the determination of art-religion: its requisite, definition and determination. Whatever may figure as artistic presentation of politically organized society is from the very beginning aimed at this end as the goal and thus as the completion of this presentation. Art ends with irony, but in this ending art is also to complete itself and in this way become art for the very first time. It would be neither art nor art-religion — that is, the highest form of the appearance of substance — if art were not, to begin with, already at its end and thus at the point of irony about art-religion, if it were not already the limit of substance and hence the dissolution of its own principle of the production and presentation of something enduring in itself. Any presentation that was not also the presentation of the end, of the furthest limit, of the finitude and fragility of presentation, would be incomplete. Any presentation, as long as it was merely complete, would be incomplete. Therefore, in order to be art, art cannot simply be itself; it must also be the art of the dissolution of art.

The irony of comedy with which Hegel has art end in the *Phenomenology* is therefore not the sheer disappearance of art and of the celebration of man and

105

God it contains. On the contrary, it is only in the dissolution of its objects, representations, contents, and meanings that art becomes – and religion becomes – itself. If for Hegel irony marks the end of art, then it is only in the teleological and perhaps eschatological sense that the truth of art – namely, the truth that it contains no substantial truth – is realized in this irony. Art ends and culminates in irony because irony is art itself; irony is the *self* of art and hence the destruction of its substantial contents and forms. Only a completely desubstantializing art – an ironic art – is with itself and 'at home.' In comedy and its irony about the substantial powers of society, art becomes conscious of itself, thereby becoming self-consciousness itself and proving itself a power absolute even beyond those substances that art itself generates, and that therefore it alone has the freedom to dissolve. At its end, in the irony of comedy, art shows itself as the sole subject of substance in its disappearance, showing itself – but only in the disappearance of its showing – as the phenomenon of dephenomenalization, the aesthetic of the anaesthetic. Comedy, accordingly, is nothing other than the completed subjectivity of society liberating itself from its substance. Comedy is this society itself, disintegrating and still playing with the disintegrating art form 'society.'

Just as Hegel, at the end of the second part of his phenomenology of the religious spirit (after 'natural religion' and at the transition to 'revealed religion'), considers comedy not simply as one literary genre amongst others but the artistic genre *par excellence*, the art of all art and hence the dramatic form of the articulation of absolutized social self-consciousness, so too does he consider irony, the characteristic technique of comedy, not merely a rhetorical figure or one communicative procedure amongst others, but a manner of speaking and acting in which all figures and acts come to their limit – to their end – and hence come to themselves as evacuated substance. To be sure, irony still offers itself as a figure, but it does so as the liminal figure of all figures and only as such, as the figure of figurality itself – that is, as one that is itself, subjectivity without substance, only in separating itself from every figure and every essence. Irony – and here, as everywhere, Hegelian prepositions are to be taken seriously – is the figure *an sich*, *at* its limit, in the proximity to and distance *from* itself. 'What this self-consciousness beholds,' the final sentence of the section 'The spiritual work of art' in the chapter 'Art-Religion' begins, 'is that whatever assumes the form of essentiality as against self-consciousness, is instead dissolved within it – within its thought, its existence and action – and is quite at its mercy. It is the return of everything universal into certainty of self' (412; 748–9). Art – in its extreme, as irony – discharges itself of all the forms of sensate appearance and becomes, in this discharge, the recognition and certainty of itself as something equally without appearance and content.

As odd as the identification of irony and self-certainty may sound, it is not a capricious philosophical gesture but a gesture well-prepared in the general conception of the *Phenomenology* and emphasized in the presentation of art-religious consciousness. Yet it remains odd. This identification states that self-consciousness is essentially comic, that its language is irony and its history a comedy. If Hegel's idea of the end of art is to be understood, then it must be understood in precisely this oddness, that is, precisely as the thought of an estrangement of self-certainty and the wonder at its presentation. For what is consciousness conscious of when it is conscious of *itself*? And how does a consciousness that expresses its self as actual substance speak? What is the language of consciousness and certainty, of self and substance; and how does this language act *on* this substance? What speaks when 'Selbstbewußt*sein*,' self-conscious-*being*, speaks? And does it speak at all as being?

Self-conciousness speaks – thus begins the section 'The spiritual work of art,' which ends with the presentation of comedy – first of all as the language of the assembly of different peoples, or 'national spirits,' and thus as the language of 'universal human nature,' which concentrates itself in a 'common act' and therein 'embraces the whole of nature, as well as the whole moral world' (401/732). 'Thus it is that the separate artistically beautiful national spirits combine to form a Pantheon, the element and habitation of which is Language' (401/731–2). In this phase of its historical constitution, language is the home not of Being, but of the 'universal substances' (401/732). Language is the habitation and temple, the site of the assembly and preservation of the customs and rules of behaviour that have become objectified in divine figures; language is this 'Pantheon' as 'the earliest language, the *Epic* as such' (402/732). For Hegel, social universals come together not in the abstraction of thoughts but as external representations, as deities, heroes, and 'national spirits' in the pantheon of the epic, presumably *The Iliad*. Those 'universal substances' that inhabit the temple of epic language – the social universals of various peoples, on the one hand, and their deities, on the other – do indeed confront each other as discrete powers and individual figures, but in the events narrated in the epic they follow a single principle and are realized in the same acts – and are realized, consequently, at least twice. 'Hence both gods and men have done one and the same thing' (402/734). The language of the epic, therefore, presents itself as essentially overdetermined, and its manner of representation as a duplication and excess. And Hegel leaves no doubt that this excess in the 'first language' – which would necessarily make this language itself into a double and excessive beginning – is already under the principle of the final language of the 'spritual work of art,' the language of comedy. He writes: 'The seriousness with which those divine powers' – that is, those universal powers of moral substance, the gods – 'go to work is a ridiculous excess, since they [i.e., men] are in point of fact the moving force of the individualities engaged in the acts; while the strain and toil of the latter again is an equally useless effort, since the former direct and manage everything. Over-zealous mortal creatures, who are nothing, are at the same time the mighty *self* that brings into subjection the universal beings, offends the gods, and actually procures for them reality and an interest in acting' (402–3/734). Hence the gods of epic art-religion are just as ridiculous as the heroes of the Greek epic and their labor is just as useless, that is, just as supernumerary and superfluous: their seriousness is a 'ridiculous excess.' The language that makes them present is 'in point of fact' a language about a nothingness that it turns into something, a vacuous language and an annihilating power that is the creative power of the *self*. Thus it is in this language that the substantial powers of the moral world, the 'eternal and resplendent individuals' of the Olympian gods, upon entering into conflict with mortals, necessarily lapse into, as Hegel says, a 'comic self-forgetfulness of their eternal nature' (403/735): they act, solely by *acting*, in contradiction to their substantial being; they abandon and forget their immutable constancy and can do nothing other than perform a pantheological comedy in the conflict between their being and their acting. At the same time, all mortal action against them is merely 'a contingent and futile piece of bravado, which dissolves at once, and transforms the pretence of seriousness in the act into a harmless, self-confident play with no result and no issue' (403/735). The language of the epic, the first language of art-religion and the first language of art, is thus the language of a self-démenti in which actual subjects go astray in a futile play 'with no result and no issue,' and in which substance, a superfluous and therefore ridiculous doubling, cannot cease ending up in comic conflicts with itself. Art and art-religion begin in a language that is mere excess, sheer excendence beyond any given statement, a language out of which a self and a substance result whose relation to one another, in turn, cannot be contained in a fixed pair of figures, for this language makes them into 'superfluous' duplicates of one another and 'liquidates' them: self and substance, heroic individuals and moral powers of domestic and communal life are, paradoxically, figures of liquidation. Any self emerging in the 'first language' of art is already in excess and contingent; any substance is already desubstantialized and empty.

In the field of representational language, self-consciousness is possible only in such a way that all positions of the self and consciousness are eliminated in 'comic self-forgetfulness.'

Whereas the 'dispersion of the whole' is completed in the pantheon of epic language and in the 'dissolution of the subject' into 'contingent and inherently external personality' (406/739), the 'higher language, the *tragedy*,' organizes the dispersed moments of the substantial and effective world into two opposing groups: into the agents of dramatic action and, opposed to them, the instances of their unknown substantial laws. These latter are no longer, as was still the case in the epic, the objects or contents of a narration recited diegetically by another voice; rather, they present themselves in 'their own words' (405/737) – present *themselves* by confronting one another in an acting language in which the disparity of their selves is articulated. This second language of art is of necessity dramatic and tragic because in it opens up a difference between the consciousness of subjects and these same subjects as substances incapable of consciousness. This 'higher language,' the first language of social action, is tragic because as action and communication it miscarries, because in it the constitution of self-consicousness trying to give itself the form of acting speech fails. The drama of self-consciousness is executed in speech acts that refer to a power of which this consciousness itself is unaware, negating its knowledge and thus its acts, but in this negation determining them as well. Hegel writes: 'Spirit when *acting*, appears, *qua* consciousness, over against the object on which its activity is directed, and which, in consequence, is determined as the *negative* of the knowing agent. The agent finds himself thereby in the opposition of knowing and not knowing' (406/739). This opposition – between consciousness and that which is unknown to it, and hence also between acting and its aim – now divides consciousness as well as the objects in which it tries to ascertain itself, such that acting consciousness remains hidden to itself in its aims and, consequently, also in its action. Since consciousness does not yet know what it acts towards (and it cannot know this as long as this aim remains to it external and pre-posited), consciousness must, without knowing what it does, go astray in unconscious actions – and thus not in actions but in fatal contingencies – as well as in a deceitful language – and thus in a language that means something other than what it says, a language that perhaps says nothing and that therefore may not be a language at all. The 'higher language' of tragedy is, to be sure, that of an enlightened consciousness, of the conscious investigation of the laws of nature and of the polis; it is the language of the '*Lichtseite*,' the 'aspect of light,' in which the substantial forces of life should be revealed; but it is also the language of concealment, of merely contingent and unconscious actions and of the power 'lurking in the background' of this enlightenment: There is no de-concealment that would not emerge from the concealed and not still be retained in this concealment; there is no revelation and no enlightenment that would not still be caught in the darkness of something closed in upon itself; no action that would not still be hampered by the inaction from which it arises. Phoebus, the sun god, as Hegel remarks, is 'the god of the Oracle, who . . . knows all and reveals all. But the commands of this truth-speaking god, and his proclamations of what *is*, are really deceptive and fallacious. For this knowledge, in its very principle, is immediately non-knowledge, because *consciousness* in acting is inherently this opposition' (406–7/ 740). Consciousness is caught in the opposition between what consciousness unveils in its objects and aims – but also thereby in its own determination – and what must remain hidden to consciousness as long as they remain its mere objects and external determinants. Action, including linguistic action, and any performative speech act must encounter something irreducibly unconscious as long as it, as an act, is directed to an aim external to it: in that aim, acting is external to itself, inaccessible, unperformable. Precisely insofar as acting is intentional, the goal of its intentions and therewith its own determination as acting must evade it, and the intentional consciousness tied to acting must remain in principle limited and incapable of comprehending itself. When this acting is directed towards moral aims and hence towards the confirmation and verification of its own social capacity for truth, when as linguistic acting it can be called *performative* and therefore equally *verformative* (formative of a *verum*), then this acting language has of necessity already inverted itself – with respect to its unfulfilled intention, to its unfulfilled determination and thus its structural disorientation – and become *perverformative*, an unconscious acting toward aims no longer moral, with no determination or capacity for truth and universality. This internal inversion of acting language and of the language of action, of the 'higher language, the tragedy,' in which language falls victim to its intention, breaking intention off, is expressed for Hegel in the ambiguous revelations of the sun god, who 'speaks truthfully' but whose oracle deceives. The *Lethe* in the aletheia of the 'truth-speaking god' renders his statements about what *is* a deceit, and renders consciousness of this being a fundamental being-deceived.

For Hegel, the paradigmatic figure in antiquity of a consciousness that tries to conceive of itself in acting, thereby destroying itself, is Oedipus, and in modern times it is Macbeth: 'He, who had the power to unlock the riddle of the sphinx, and he too who trusted with childlike confidence, are, therefore, both sent to destruction through what the god reveals to them. The priestess, through whose mouth the beautiful god speaks, is in nothing different from the equivocal sisters of fate, who drive their victim to crime by their promises, and who, by the double-tongued, equivocal character of what they gave out as certainty, deceive the man when he relies upon the manifest and obvious meaning of what they say' (407/740). In turning its language, as it must, towards the object from which it receives its determination, consciousness first of all becomes consciousness of *something*; but since it does not penetrate the object and its determination as long as it still confronts the object as a some-thing foreign to it, consciousness must of necessity be the language of deception about the object and itself. Self-consciousness is self-deception as long as it refers, in its speech and in its acts, to rules and laws, knowledge and structures without being able to recognize itself and its own force in their universality. But it *cannot* recognize itself in the orders of universality – the orders of both the physis and the polis – because in its speaking and acting, in its speech-acting, consciousness remains unavoidably singular; and just as unavoidably it refers to a universal, to *its* universality. Torn apart by the conflict between these irreconcilable determinations, it must be pulled into equivocation, must be deceived and duped. An action unaware of itself in all its implications and consequences is as blind as an intuition lacking its concept – and is accordingly not an action but a mis-action, not praxis but parapraxis. A performative act that posits not exclusively itself but always something else as well – reprodu-cing or only transforming something forced upon it by its context – no longer corresponds to the emphatic concept of the act: it is inactive to the extent that it merely submits itself to pre-posited rules, unconscious to the extent that it does not, in an originary positing, produce its own conventions. Hegel has in mind this insoluble remainder of unconsiousness and inaction in the speech act of the dramatic subject when he remarks of the tragic heroes of antiquity and modernity – Oedipus, Macbeth, and Hamlet – that their 'consciousness in acting is inherently' this opposition between knowledge and non-knowledge. This does not mean that consciousness does not conceive this other, the non-knowing and not-acting but, instead, that consciousness does not conceive its inconceivability and accordingly its own disjuncture. It does not mean that the individual speech act misses its aim and leaves its universal rules unfulfilled; rather, this failure to take up explicitly into its act the lapse of its speech rules, and therewith of the act itself, renders the utterances of consciousness a deception of both the universality and the individuality of its speech act and prevents consciousness from coming to itself in this act and becoming transparent to itself in clear, unmitigated self-consciousness. The speech act of the dramatic subject, and accordingly of the subject of art, is always a speech pact with precisely what hollows out and subverts every act, and breaks every pact – an aporetic act of deactivation.

The mis-action of the universal self, of substance, and the deceit of the individual act, of consciousness – that is, the structural selflessness and the corresponding structural unconsciousness of action – are not effects of a private mystification or the limitations of the tragic genre, nor do they arise from an epochal delusion of Greek antiquity or dialectically unenlightened mythical thinking. They are the unavoidable effects of the structure of acting in general, of language and of consciousness. If there is to be any possibility of a self-consciousness that moves beyond its disjuncture and its inherent mis-action, then it could only be a self-consciousness that experiences itself *in* this disjuncture. In the diremption of consciousness into itself and its object, consciousness has 'forgotten' that it determines this object itself and is in turn determined by it. This forgetting, which belongs unsublatably to the structure of consciousness, even if it and its objects and aims are thereby impaired, this oblivion is the truth of consciousness. This is why the tragic conflict between the instances of individuality and universality must also find its result, its truth, in oblivion. 'The truth, however, of the opposing powers of content and consciousness,' Hegel writes, 'is the final result, that both are equally right and, hence, in their opposition (which comes about through action) are equally wrong. The process of action proves their unity in the mutual overthrow of both powers and both self-conscious characters. The reconciliation of the opposition with itself is the *Lethe* of the *nether world* in the form of Death – or the *Lethe* of the *upper world* in the form of absolution. . . . Both are *forgetfulness*, the disappearance of the reality and action of the powers of the substance' (408/743). Hence just as in the first language of art, the epic, consciousness was divided from itself by an excess and had to be dispersed in the 'comic self-forgetfulness' of gods and men, so too is consciousness split in the 'higher language' of tragedy, still haunted by this excess, by this overdetermination and determination over and beyond itself, into two rival powers, which, for their part, are determined by a mutual forgetting and are, therefore, opposed to each other in their injustice, in the untruth about each other and about themselves. The truth (that they are in untruth), the consciousness (that they have no consciousness of one another), is, however, *not* recovered in recollection: there is nothing to remember, for the split between knowing and not knowing, the finitude of consciousness, the forgetting is primary. Truth and consciousness are recovered in the disappearance of both, in oblivion, in the *Lethe*: in death and absolution. Like the language of the epic, the language of acting, the language of the higher art or art-religion, the linguistic drama of the tragedy, is the *aletheic* language of disclosure, unveiling, clarification and light; but – since language is only the process and the movement of this light, disclosure, and revelation, and therefore can never emerge in its entirety from the undisclosed and concealed – it is just as much a *letheic* language, in its structure unsublatably submerged into oblivion; it is, therefore, the language of conscious action only in that it is also the language of fatality and contingency; it is the language of self-consciousness only in that it is, precisely for this reason, also the language of the forgetfulness of self and substance. When Hegel writes: 'The reconciliation of the opposition with itself is the *Lethe*,' it means that both the truth of consciousness and the truth of its substance lie in their oblivion, that self-consciousness, the reconciliation of subject and substance, lies solely in its being forgotten, and that the truth of linguistic action lies only in its 'inactivity' (409/743).[2]

If there is self-consciousness, then it must fall prey to a consciousness of forgetting: the consciousness of deceit in its speech act, the consciousness of a dispersion into the multiplicity of its discrete figures, and the consciousness of its lack of substance. In every one of these phrases, the genitive is to be understood as both subjectivus and objectivus: it is the oblivion that has to be thought of as the distinct, most extreme form of consciousness, the form of its disintegration; and it is consciousness that has to recognize this oblivion as the event of unity with itself and its universal rule, as an imperfection, as a breach of its intentions and evacuation of its substance. It is the dispersion of consciousness in which, however, it also has its only possible reality: as finite and passive consciousness and as consciousness issuing from this passivity. Consciousness for Hegel is consciousness out of the experience of its loss; language is the medium in which the ruin of its capacity for cognition, communication, and action is registered. The structural *Lethe* – oblivion, death, absolution, which in the language of art, the moral world and religion, further still, in every language and every linguistic action – submerges into itself both individual subjects and the social laws that should govern their interaction – has for Hegel above all the consequence that all its substantial figures, all the figures in which subjectivity could present its substance, are lost: this *Lethe*, the extreme and medium of language, 'completes the depopulation of Heaven' (409/743). The deities in which the laws of the natural and social world are

113

manifested show themselves in the tragic process as deceptive representations, as hypostases of structural elements of social action that must fall prey to the *Lethe*. From this, Hegel draws the conclusion: 'The expulsion of such insubstantial ideas, which was demanded by the philosophers of antiquity, thus already has its beginning in tragedy' (409/743). The continuation of tragedy and its language of forgetting and deception is carried out in comedy and its irony; the 'depopulation of Heaven' begun there is completed in ironic language, for here 'actual self-consciousness represents itself as the fate of the gods' (410/745). Like Feuerbach and after him Marx, Hegel here already assumes that the substantiality of the divine is nothing more than the unreal abstraction of the real conditions of existence for social subjects. Divine figures, precisely by virtue of their abstract individuality in which each single trait – love, beauty, artistry, revenge – appears isolated from a complex multiplicity of experiences, are for Hegel nothing more than masks. That these masks can be played with, that these abstractions are manipulatable and detachable from every visage means, however, that the substances represented in them can be consigned to oblivion. The consciousness that plays with these masks is a consciousness that plays with its self as oblivion: aletheia of the *Lethe*, the completed depopulation of Heaven, comedy.

Hence Hegel's characterization of the comic play with substance: 'The actual self has no such abstract moment as its substance and content. The subject, therefore, is raised above such a moment, as it would be above a particular quality, and when clothed with this mask gives utterance to the irony of such a property trying to be something on its own account. The pretentious claims of the universal abstract nature are shown up and discovered in the actual self; it is seen to be caught and held in a concrete reality, and lets the mask drop, just when it wants to be something genuine. The self, appearing here in its significance as something actual, *plays with the mask,* which it once puts on, *in order to be its own person*; but it breaks away from this seeming and pretence just as quickly again, and comes out in its nakedness and commonness, which it shows not to be distinct from the proper self, the actor, nor again from the onlooker' (410/745, my italics).[3] The subject, Hegel writes, the self plays with the mask. The formulation is decisive for the entire theory of comedy, art, and art-religion developed in the *Phenomenology of Mind*. It indicates not only that the real subject, the actor or the social agent, performs his play masked; and it indicates not only that social subjects act as actors who occasionally set aside and then resume their civic *persona* and thus only play with it. 'The self plays with the mask' indicates both at once: that it plays *with* the mask and only *plays*

114

with the mask, that it is essentially a masked subject and nonetheless only plays with its masquerade as though with something inessential and deceptive; it indicates that this self *is* itself a mask or a person, and that it only *plays with* itself, with its self as this mask, with itself as the appearance of abstract substantiality or abstract individuality. That the self plays with the mask thus indicates that it plays with the mask of the self, with the *prosopon* of its being or the *persona* of its universal, political, and religious significance; it indicates that it, the self, plays with itself and plays this self only ever as another. Accordingly, Hegel writes that the spectator of this desubstantializing and desubjectivitizing comedy 'is perfectly at home in what is presented before him and *sees himself playing* in the drama before him' (412/748, my italics). To play oneself, however, means to be distinct from the played self to the point that its play can be seen from without and can at the same time be a 'home' within this seeing, that this 'home' itself can be only played, a non-home, and the play can always be the opening up of another. Not only the actor specially delegated to do so plays himself, not only the member of the demos or participant in the cult, but the self also plays itself in every scene of its realities: the self is the actor and spectator of itself only when, and precisely when, it no longer loses itself in the imaginary substances of the political or natural world. Whereas the hero of tragedy was still said to 'break up into his mask and the actor, into the person of the play and the actual self' (410/745), there is no longer any question of such a disjuncture and hence of '*hypocrisy*' in comedy. Hegel writes: 'The self proper of the actor coincides with the part [that is, with his *persona*, the mask] he impersonates' (412/748) – but this coincidence, as he specifically emphasizes, is not the unconscious unity achieved in cults and mysteries; it is the coincidence of an actor with a role that he knows can be set aside. The role is insubstantial and as such, precisely because it is insubstantial and detachable, the actor always plays *himself* with this role and only ever *plays* himself as another. The play is the alteration of the self and only as such the event in which the self absolutizes itself, in which it detaches itself from its substance and, precisely in its veil, becomes unveiled sheer substance. The play plays out the subjectivity of the subject in its absolute alterity.[4]

The self that plays with the mask is thus not simply this or that subject determined in some way or another; rather, it is a subject only insofar as it treats its This or That and *any* imaginable substantial determination as a mask that it can just as well assume as let drop. It is a subject only insofar as it plays with itself, with itself as a mask, loosens itself from the mask, detaches itself through it, donning and discarding the mask and itself at will; it is a self insofar as the mask dissolves itself for the self and into it. It is the 'actual self' thus only as the analytic force – Hegel writes 'the negative force' (412/748) – which releases the mask from the appearance of its substantiality, thus releasing the mask from the mask and the self from the self. And only as this detachment and release is it what Hegel calls 'this *absolute* power' – that is, the power to detach, dispatch, and absolutize, the power against all external determinations, the free and independent power to determine from case to case and from assumption to assumption, a power, however, for its part, utterly indeterminate, the power of the absolutized, dispatched, detached mask. The play of the self with the mask is the form – yet a form no longer determinable by anything else, not even thoroughly determinable by its 'self,' by its form, and which is thus the *transform* – in which the self plays with itself as though with another, with another as itself, and thus the 'form' of the absolutizing and dispatch of the *persona* of the self. The subject is no longer the agent of this play – it is merely the play's actor – for the position of the agent, absolved, is reduced to a mere element of this play, into which it finds admission only passively. If the subject, because it is *exposed* to this play in every one of its possible determinations, demarcations or maskings *is* only ever *played*, then this play is that event which precedes the egologically determined, self-disposing subject identical with and autonomous over itself and in which this subject can figure only as a subject forever other, forever detachable. The self that has become mask is the site at which the self as subject can first appear – and can take its leave. It is an open site – the mobile vacancy of a subjectivity without substance and thus without a substantial subject.

Hegel's insistence that the self plays with the mask 'in order to be its own person' – that is, in order to be its *persona*, its *prosopon* – and that it sets it aside to emerge again 'from this seeming and pretence . . . to its own nakedness and commonness' (410/745) emphasizes not only the capacity of the subject to realize its being in the mask – the self in the mask *is its* person – but equally emphasizes the complementary capacity to disengage itself from this being of the person: the self is its *prosopon*, but it is this autoprosopon only in that it is both *prosopopoeia* and *prosopolysis*, it can only be *autopoesis* in that it is also *autolysis*. It is the process of the dispatch of the mask (and) from the mask *Self*. Its performation, closely tied to the tragic one, is *imperformation* and, in every sense that can be conferred upon the word, *impersonation* – the embodiment of another in a role, its denunciation as mere role and the detachment from it. The subject, which detaches itself from itself in this information or adformation and *afformation*, and does not stop exercising its 'absolute force' in the démenti

116

of its substantial reality; this subject, 'comic consciousness' (414/752), is not comic incidentally or for contingent reasons. It is comic because it can experience itself only as exceeding its every objectification, even while it recognizes itself in every one of them. Enacting the detachability, fragility, and finitude of its persona, the subject is structurally comic. And only this structurally comic or essentially substanceless subject can be the absolute subject, relating freely to itself as something altogether different. At the end of its passage through the stations of art-religion, self-consciousness would not be comic self-consciousness liberated from its substantiality if it were not from its very beginning, in its very structure, a comedy. Its language can only be an essentially ironic one, rebounding from its statements as from something inessential, merely apparent and only apparently meaningful. It is the language of an *absolution (Freisprechung)* from all linguistic determinations, and as such, it is the absolute language. The art of this language is to give up every art and every art-religion as a mask over which no *subject* has power, because they follow the impulses of an emptied subjectivity alone. The play of this comic language is not a play on the stage, in the state or the world, without first being a play *with* the stage, *with* the state and *with* the world as its masks. The ontology of this free language of self-consciousness: a *prosopontology* and *proso-ponto-theo-logic* in which even the knowledge of the masks 'self,' 'being,' 'god,' and 'reason' is a mark in a play not graspable or regulatable by any other, more potent knowledge.

In becoming comedy, self-consciousness shows itself as 'absolute essence.' To know itself does not mean to muster itself as representational content, but to recognize the substantial figures in which consciousness has externalized itself as unavoidable forms and yet artificial and therefore detachable forms. Knowing itself in this way, the subject becomes in comedy – and only in comedy – power over substance. Hegel calls this movement, ambiguously, 'Leichtsinn,' frivolity or light-hearted folly, and writes: 'The proposition, which gives this frivolity expression, runs thus: *The self is absolute essence.* The essence which was substance, and in which the self was the accidental element, has dropped to the level of a predicate' (412–13/750).[5] The *Leichtsinn* of the proposition is that essence, substance – and concomitantly precisely the sense the proposition contains – has become something light, a frivolity, and even a vacuity. But this *Leichtsinn* of the 'absolute essence' redefines in turn the subject of the proposition, the self, declaring it a 'frivolous' self in which its sense and its essence evaporate. Nor does Hegel hesitate to claim that in this self-consciousness, 'against which nothing appears in the form of objective essence,' spirit 'has lost its consciousness' (413/750). As in the comedy of self-consciousness, in the comedy that self-consciousness *is*, consciousness is lost – retained only as forgotten or vacant, as substance emerging only as a 'nothing' or as a powerless 'accidental element.' The language of tragedy, the language of oblivion, of *Lethe* and deceit, is heightened and intensified in the language of comedy. Comedy is comedy only when it performs the comedy of tragedy. At the same time, the comedy of absolute self-consciousness continues to play the epic by staging once again its 'ridiculous excess' (402–3/734) and the 'comic self-forgetfulness' of its gods (403/735). Yet forgetting, deceit, and excess appear in comedy no longer as a fate to which the agents of the action are helplessly subjected but as the ostentatious fiction of a spectacle in which the actors are only masks, the actions only citations from the props of the history of myths and the theatre, and sense only simulation. Comedy still plays with forgetting, deceit, and excess. It plays with the epic and tragedy, with art and its religion, it plays with the entire history of art-religion as the self plays with the mask. But comedy can play like this only because the structure of self-consciousness is none other than the *Leichtsinn* in which all that has sedimented as the substance of the subject is cast off, liquidated as something superfluous, denounced as deceit, and pleasurably surrendered to oblivion. The play of self-consciousness is lethal for both consciousness and the substantial self. What survives and enjoys itself is solely the play as the infinitely open form, the opening form in which a self and its consciousness can first appear and disappear.

Not only art but the whole of 'formally embodied essence' falls prey to the comic play of absolute subjectivity. And nothing is excluded from this 'formally embodied essence' [*gestalteten Wesenheiten*]: neither nature, nor political communal existence, nor the rational thinking articulated in philosophy. What connection this comic play has with the autonomy of nature – Hegel calls this nature's 'independent substantiality' [*Selbstwesenheit*] – is already evident in the use of natural materials as ornament, abode and sustenance: 'in the mystery of the bread and wine' celebrated in the cults of Bacchus and Ceres, as Hegel writes, self-consciousness makes natural materials 'its very own . . . together with the significance of the inner essence, and in comedy it is conscious of the irony lurking in this meaning' (410/746) – of the irony, that is, that every natural figure which appears autonomous can be made to serve the purposes of self-consciousness and that its mystery can be betrayed to knowledge. If the irony of the natural shape lies in its dissolution into the purposes of self-consciousness and in the loss of itself as figure, then the irony of communal existence, of the polis, lies in the contrast between its claims to universality and the particular interests it falls victim to — Hegel calls this contrast again 'ridiculous' and sees in the comedy of democratic politics 'the entire emancipation of the ends and aims of the mere individual from the universal order and the scorn the mere individual shows for such order' (411/747). Thus once again, as immanent contrast, irony shatters the figure — in this case, that of the demos organized in the polis — and liberates its elements, political individuals: they become actors in a political comedy who self-consciously use the masks of the abstract legal person for their own ends. More distinctly than the corrosion of art-products and the transformations of nature, the dissolution of politics reveals what Hegel calls irony, scorn, ridiculousness, and comedy to be an asymmetrical phenomenon: abstract universality, essence, or substance falls victim to its elements. Irony is the process of the disintegration of natural and political totalities; comedy is the spectacle of the inconsistency of substance and substantial subject. This is true *a fortiori* of the universals of rational thinking. After the gods have been stripped of their anthropomorphic appearance in comedy and philosophy, 'they are left, as regards their *natural* aspect, with merely the nakedness of their immediate existence; they are [as in Aristophanes' *Nephelai*] clouds, a passing vapour;' but, 'having passed in accordance with their essential character, as determined by *thought*, into the *simple* thoughts of the *Beautiful* and the *Good*, these latter submit to being filled with every kind of content' (411/747). The highest ideas, successors to the divine substantial universals, pure thoughts in which consciousness is to find its last hold, are necessarily empty precisely because of their universality, and can be invested only with contingent particular interests. 'The pure thoughts of the Beautiful and the Good,' Hegel writes of the highest Platonic Ideas, 'thus display a comic spectacle — through their being set free from the opinion [. . .] they have become empty, and, on that very account, the game of the private opinion and caprice of any chance individuality' (411/747–8). The pure *eidos*, the *idea*, does indeed offer an ironic spectacle and object of comic speculation, for the universal envisioned with it, the ground and background of every particular design, must represent itself as exactly what it should not be: a contingency and play of individual designs. The performance of the comedy in the Platonic domain of Ideas presents the powerlessness of 'self-conscious pure knowledge' (411/746) to think a 'formally embodied essence' (410/746) that would not be ruined by this very thought.

That the figure, and indeed any one, including the figure 'thought'; the support, including the support that consciousness could offer, dissolves itself, and the ideas turn into 'clouds, a passing vapour' just like the gods; that this analytic anamorphosis and anasemiosis liquidates nature, political society and philosophy, all artistic figures and religious ties into a torrent of contingent and unsupported details; that the only remaining relation is to the dissolution of all relations – this is what Hegel calls comedy, irony, the play with the mask, the end of art. The comedy of nature and art, of politics and philosophy, no longer offers substantial figures but, rather, presents the desubstantialization and defiguration of everything that could be its object. Art – and even the art of politics and philosophy – which had begun as a pantheon is, at the end, its cenotaph.

The end of art in comedy is not merely the end of a figure of consciousness, but the end of consciousness as figure. Like Athenian democracy, like the Platonic theory of Ideas and like art in its irreligious conclusion, the self-consciousness articulating itself in them also has the structure of comedy. It relates to itself as something detached, put aside, and hence treats itself as its end: its *Lethe*, oblivion, and death. Just as art at its end – and it is only therefore *end* – forgets itself, consciousness forgets itself in self-consciousness. 'Here, then, the Fate, formerly without consciousness,' Hegel writes, 'consisting in the empty rest and forgetfulness, and separated from self-consciousness, is united with self-consciousness' (411–12/748). The lack of consciousness, the 'forgetfulness' and the 'empty rest,' is united with self-consciousness. That is, the destitution of self-consciousness is constitutive for consciousness insofar as it is consciousness of its productions, and accordingly, of itself as something departed, dead, and forgotten. It is *self*-consciousness only as the self of an impotent and deadened consciousness. When the self plays with the mask, it plays with its own death, with a death mask. Hegel writes: 'The *individual self* is the negative force through which and in which the gods, as also their moments (nature as existent fact and the thoughts of their determinate characters), pass away and disappear. At the same time, the individual self is not the mere vacuity of disappearance, but preserves itself in this very nothingness, holds to itself and is the sole and only reality' (412/748). When the self preserves itself in this nothingness as the ruined gods and the corroded thoughts of substance, when it preserves itself as its own disappearance, then it 'holds to itself' only by 'holding to' its death, and 'holds to' its death only by being death's force, 'the negative force,' itself. The self is its own *Lethe*. It is autolytically constituted. Self-consciousness is essentially the experience of the finitude of self and consciousness only by being *its* death, its *own* death, its reality, its *own* reality. Likewise art in its lethal conclusion: in its disappearance art ex-poses itself as *its* end, its *own* end, and 'preserves' itself and can only 'preserve' itself because it takes hold of itself as disappearance. Just as 'the life of the mind is not one that shuns death, and keeps clear of desertification [*Verwüstung*]; it endures death and in death preserves its being' (29/93), so too does art first fully become art when it endures its end and preserves itself in this devastation or desertification. Art 'preserves' itself, as Hegel writes in the *Phenomenology*, in comedy. Comedy is its devastation. Only because art at its end, in comedy, is no longer anything but the exhibition of the finitude of art — and indeed of its *own* finitude — can it be called complete. Hegel writes: 'The religion of art is fulfilled and consummated in it [the individual self in its disappearance in comedy], and has completely turned into itself' (412/748). And in the same sense in the *Vorlesungen über die Ästhetik*, which in many ways follows a strategy different from the *Phenomenology*, he writes: 'Yet at this peak [of art], comedy leads at the same time to the dissolution of art altogether.'[6] And he continues: 'But if comedy presents this unity [of idea and appearance] only in its self-destruction,' the presence of the absolute 'asserts itself only in a negative form, that everything which does not correspond to it is sublated and only subjectivity as such shows itself at the same time self-confident and self-assured in this dissolution.'[7] Only subjectivity as such, we are to understand, is 'at the same time' dissolved and assured of itself, assured thus only by virtue of its dissolution and assured only because subjectivity can still conceive of its dissolution as its *own* work — a subjectivity beyond every individual subject and even beyond subjectivity *itself* — and yet a subjectivity that, in this beyond, can still play with its destruction, can play with it as its *own* destruction. The death of art in comedy is thus *assured* death, its *own*, and comedy is accordingly the art that realizes itself in the devastation of art: an art beyond individual arts and beyond art altogether, an art that still plays with its death mask, but only with its *own*. Therefore Hegel can regard death as an event without terror, without the pain of devastation, but instead, remarkably — because for the first and last time, for the only time — as happiness. At its end — and only therefore can it be called completion — art savors its death as its self-appropriation and is happy. It savors — that is: experiences as real and present — the death of the final god of representation, the death of art itself.

Hegel speaks of the 'perfectly happy, the comic consciousness' into which 'all divine reality goes back' (414/752) and writes: 'What this self-consciousness beholds, is that whatever assumes the form of essentiality as against self-consciousness, is instead dissolved within it — within its thought, its existence and action — and is quite at its mercy. It is the return of everything universal into certainty of self, a certainty which, in consequence, is this complete loss of fear of everything strange and alien, and complete loss of substantial reality on the part of what is alien and external. Such certainty is a state of spiritual well-being and of self-abandonment thereto, on the part of consciousness, in a way that, outside this kind of comedy, is not to be found anywhere' (412/748–9). And once again in the *Vorlesungen über die Ästhetik* he writes about Aristophanes: 'Without having read him, one can scarcely know how damned well-off [*sauwohl*] a person can be.'[8] In the same sense he says of modern comedy that it restores 'what Aristotle achieved to perfection in the field of the Ancients,' that its 'keynote' is 'cheerfulness, assured exuberance,' 'inherently and fundamentally blissful foolishness.'[9] But in these and similar passages, particularly in the talk of the 'bliss and ease of subjectivity'[10] has not Hegel forgotten that self-consciousness – that is, precisely this subjectivity – has become one with its emptiness and 'forgetfulness' and hence with its death? Has he not forgotten that the self in comedy has 'lost its aspect of consciousness' (413/750) and therefore that its experience is not merely an experience of the lack of substance, but is itself without substance and consciousness? If these questions are answerable with the suggestion that the foolishness, the 'inherently and fundamentally blissful foolishness' is precisely nothing other than the necessary movement in which consciousness disengages from its hold to a self, giving itself over to its lack of substance – then has Hegel, frivolously, not taken seriously his own formulation of the devastation in which the self 'preserves' itself, forgetting that 'desertification' which it does not 'keep clear' of but instead suffers on itself? It is clear that for Hegel the happiness of the 'perfectly happy, the comic consciousness' (414/752), touches this suffering and thus the seriousness and the pain of the negative. But precisely because the labor of sense in comedy touches on the play of *Leichtsinn* and the dialectic of comedy, the former can, frivolously enough, be forgotten in the latter. At this tangential point, the point between an art that is no longer art and a philosophy that has not yet become substantial, the two are barely distinguishable. But if pain is to be forgotten in happiness, as Hegel will apparently have it, then it is also in order to include this happiness of foolishness in an enclave and keep it pure, to localize it historically and geographically, staving off contamination with anything else and enclosing within limits whatever in this happiness might become dangerous to the seriousness and labor of philosophical sense – and whatever in this meaning, in turn, could be harmed by foolishness. Hegel ascribes to comic consciousness a 'spiritual well-being and self-abandonment . . . that outside this kind of comedy is not to be found anywhere' (412/749). This claim of exclusivity keeps apart from comedy both the pain and the horror

122

over the annihilation of the 'formally embodied essence.' The enjoyment of disappearance and the pleasure in the death of all gods is warded off and reserved for Attic comedy, kept from infecting other genres, other epochs, like the era of Christianity for example, or speculative philosophy. The thesis of the end of art in comedy – however radically it may present art as the agent of political and religious, philosophical, and aesthetic disintegration, and even of the disintegration of self-consciousness – this thesis also entails putting an end to the ending of art and limiting the radicality of the experience of finitude and happiness disclosed in it. For end is here conceptualized as a completion and closure in which a praxis or an epoch of consciousness realizes its determination, force, and concept: itself. End for Hegel is a conceptualized end and, accordingly, the privileged mode of self-possession and self-appropriation. If comedy and its irony of the substantial powers puts an end to art, does it play only in the service of dialectical labor? Does its self-loss stand in the service of self-appropriation? Is comedy then exclusively the moment of a dialectic that, for its part, is no longer comic and no longer vulnerable to any comedy?

The protective limit around the happiness of comedy is as porous as the defensive limit against its analytic threat. Where irony turns up among Hegel's contemporaries, in particular among the misleadingly named Romantics, to compete with speculative dialectic, Hegel finds himself obliged to distinguish irony as the formal speech of vanity from true comedy.[11] His most aggressive attacks are directed, as is well known, against Friedrich Schlegel, whom he charges with the vain hubris of the formal, empty I and whose presumptive theory of 'absolute self-complacency' he scolds as a 'lonely mass of itself.'[12] But in 1794, in Schlegel's *Vom ästhetischen Werte der griechischen Komödie*, Hegel might already have read about the 'political intermezzo, the parabasis' – the exemplary case of a demystifying play with the mask: 'The greatest agility of life must have an effect, must destroy; if it finds nothing beyond itself, it turns back to a beloved object, to itself, its own work; it then injures to stimulate, without destroying.'[13] And in 1800, Schlegel's *Über die Unverständlichkeit* claims that 'Socratic irony' was 'the freest license, for through it one is moved beyond oneself; and yet the most lawful license, for it is absolutely necessary'(Ath II 243).[14] Both texts celebrate not self-complacency but register – in one case historically, in the other structurally – a movement beyond the self executed in the ironic interruption of role-playing.[15] What Hegel fears in Schlegel is presumably not so much the hypertrophy of subjectivity but the transport of the analytic force of irony and of the comic into fields that lie beyond the historical and structural limits established by Hegel. What he distorts and attacks as 'self-complacency' in Schlegel's texts was a theory of enjoyment that he wanted to reserve for the Attic comedy in his *own* presentation, which he accordingly wanted to reserve for *himself*. What Hegel may have found unbearable in Schlegel was not only the sustained mobility of the negative force of the dialectic as infinite paradox and 'permanent parabasis' instead of their being bound in the unity of subject and substance, but also that *his* end, his *own* end, the end *itself* was thereby contested. However, the end, death, was only as one's *own* end, only as a death *conceptualized* by the self as a force – and, in fact, the force of substantialization – while, as the death of *another* or as an inconceivably *other* death, it could attest only to the impotence of the concept, always receding, defiguring, distant from the subject and alien to substance. What repelled Hegel in Schlegel was in the end perhaps the onomastic double, the echo of his name, the 'ridiculous excess' of a meaningless sign that with involuntary irony draws attention to the fact that the limits of person, work or concept are contingent and mobile like masks.

The end of art in 'comic consciousness' shares this mobility of the mask. And this end is mobile above all *as* this mask. If the *prosopon*, the *persona*, was for tragic consciousness the abstract individuality of substance in which the actual self had to deceive itself and find itself forgotten; if this same *persona* was for comic consciousness only the externalized substance of itself, with which it could play as though with the deceit and the forgetting of consciousness – this same *persona*, the mask, migrates into the Roman 'condition of right or law' and 'its *Leichtsinn* clarifies and rarifies it till it becomes a "person" and attains the abstract universality of right' (413/751). The *Leichtsinn* of the structurally comic consciousness was the proposition that 'the self is absolute essence' (412), and it is this dispatch of the self from every substantial fulfillment through the 'national spirits,' through laws, conventions or the contents of faith that dilute the subject, reduced to its most abstract form, into a 'spiritless,' 'disembodied' 'individual person' – to a legal person as the absolute mask that no longer conceals anything and is worn by no one but 'fate.' The proposition of *leichtsinnigen*, comic consciousness that marks the end of art – that the self is absolute essence – is now given greater precision in the proposition: 'The self as such, the abstract person, is absolute essence' (413/751). This proposition, in one or another of its variations, as the proposition of the comic *persona* and as the proposition of the abstract legal person, has the same content: that the self – whether as *persona* or person – is without content, empty and unreal. It states the mask character of both comic and legal consciousness. Having triumphed over substance, the self retains the mask as a trophy – the armature of past, emptied, and vacuous essence and the insignia of the continuing sovereignty of the self. But with its triumph over substance, the self has won a Pyrrhic victory, for it has defeated only its *own* substance – and wears from this the *persona* as a mark and mask of its *own* emptiness. The abstract legal person is the mask with which no particular individual plays any longer. But it plays on by 'itself.' In becoming a formal person, the comic *persona* has, frivolously and dialectically unburdened, exceeded the end of art, has exceeded the end of art *as* this end which it is, and now roams as a mobile vacancy 'spiritlessly' in the new, the Roman epoch of the spirit. With this, the mask, the play-form of comic consciousness, the end of art, under a barely noticeable changed name, under the 'mask' of another name for the mask, no longer as 'person' (410; 412/746; 748) but as 'person'(413/750), has become the determining instance of the epoch of formal legal consciousness. With this, the detached form of the detachment from itself, the end of art has abstracted itself and made itself autonomous, has traversed itself, the limit, and exceeded its determination. The end – the mask – in a way other than itself and as an other than its self, migrates. The concept 'person' has become a limit to the concept, a conceptual mask that tears itself away from its term, doubles, evacuates and with its indetermination contaminates and con-terminates the further history of conceptual knowledge and action.

Even in the last passage of the chapter on art-religion, the ambiguity of the mask – as both persona and person, marking both the emptiness of substance and subject – is given an ambiguous formulation: the self 'preserves itself in this very nothingness' (412/748). This means, in its context, that the comic subject and therefore the subject *par excellence* continues to preserve itself as consciousness *in the face of* the nothingness of the substantial figures of its art. And it also means that this subject preserves itself *in* this nothingness and thus only as vacuous, selfless, and consciousless, as a mask. Both of these meanings, which still play off one another in the chapter on art-religion and characterize 'comic consciousness' only in their doubling – this double meaning of the *persona* is now, in the prelude to revealed religion, separated into its two tendencies. 'Comic consciousness' is now called the 'complete externalization of substance,' but also the preservation of knowledge of itself as an empty self—and thus requires the radicalizing complement in another consciousness that has lost not only substance but also the knowledge of this loss and thus the knowledge of itself. Hegel calls this knowledge, by now completely voided, knowledge without knowledge, the 'unhappy consciousness,' the 'counterpart and complement' of 'comic consciousness' (414/752). 'Comic consciousness'

125

is thus first complete when it also embraces 'unhappy' consciousness; it is the ultra-comic consciousness of the fact that even its knowledge of the loss of its substantiality is lost. It is, as Hegel writes, 'just this loss become conscious of itself, and is the surrender and relinquishment [*Entäußerung*] of its knowledge about itself.' And again: 'In the condition of right or law, then, the moral world has vanished, and its type of religion has passed away in the mood of Comedy. The "unhappy consciousness" is just the knowledge of this *entire* loss. It has lost both the worth and dignity it attached to its immediate personality [as a legal person] as well as that attaching to its personality when reflected in the medium of *thought*' (414). And once again: 'It is consciousness of the loss of all *essence* in *this certainty* of itself, and of the loss even of this knowledge of certainty of self – the loss of substance as well as of self; it is the bitter pain which finds expression in the hard words, *God is dead*' (414/752–3). Comic consciousness knows itself as the loss of its substance; unhappy consciousness still knows itself as the loss of this knowledge and this subject: no longer simply as the death of the gods but of the one God – the knowing subject – in its person. If ironic consciousness could still be expressed in the *leichtsinnigen* proposition of the *docta ignorantia*: 'I know that I know nothing,' then the lament of utterly unhappy consciousness in its *indocta ignorantia* must run: 'I do not know whether anything can be known at all, and thus also do not know whether it is I who knows nothing and does not know that I know nothing.' With the evacuation of both knowledge and the self from self-consciousness, however, comedy and its irony, radicalized by its 'counterpart and complement,' has extended even beyond the end of art, into the abstract legal person and its 'pure thoughts.' Thought, too, is a *persona*, a mask, a dead god – and the escalating comedy of spirit must set aside this mask as well and devastate this thought.

If knowledge can be a mask, it can no longer be known what is mask and what is not mask. The extreme of irony is the devastation or desertification of even the consciousness that it is consciousness of something without substance: it must thrust this consciousness, lethally, into oblivion. The extreme of the play with the mask is the devastation of the mask – not an unmasking, which would reveal behind it the reality of the subject or the thing itself, or the truth of consciousness – but the exposure of the sheer mask without the suggestion that something other than it exists, that this mask might still be recognized, known or thought as such. It is the devastation of every conceivable limit and foremost of the limit apparently reached with the end of art, the devastation of the end that comedy is supposed to mark, the devastation of the end of art.

'The statues set up are now corpses in stone whence the animating soul has flown, while the hymns of praise are words from which all belief has gone. The tables of the gods are bereft of spiritual food and drink, and from his games and festivals does not return to man the joyful sense of his unity with the divine Being. The works of the muse lack the force of the spirit which derived certainty and assurance of itself just from the crushing [*Zermalmung*] of the gods and men' (414/753). This characterizes the end not only of art, but the end of the end of art, of comedy: from the play that pursues the 'crushing of the gods and men,' consciousness no longer returns to itself and no self-assurance issues from it. The subjectivity that savored the devastation of substances finds its own consciousness devastated – and does not find itself again. The circle of self-reflection is broken and falls apart into the disparate fragments of a world equally void of consciousness and objects. But if art is supposed to reach its completion and truth, the stance of absolute subjectivity, in comedy, and if this art, outré, evacuates even subjectivity in the abstract legal person and its absolute scepticism, then art is the devastation of art and its truth: subjectivity; then it is the play with the mask that devastates this play, the end that devastates the end. Then comedy is, in its extreme, the death of god – the death, namely, of that assurance which could still conceive of the 'crushing of the gods and men' and by virtue of this concept could survive.

There is thus no end of art, of comedy, of devastation, of atheology. And there is, from the very beginning, nothing other than the end of art, comedy, desertification. The end of art thus does not cease, *malgré soi* and anachronistically, to end. It is a *suspended* end, an endless end, one that can be neither known nor thought; an *a priori* masked end, an end of art within – and without – parentheses. This (end) can no longer simply be the object of a theory, of a conceptualizing intuition, certainly not of a theory of the aesthetic or even of an aesthetic theory, for after its 'crushing' there remains of art only dust – Hegel speaks dryly of 'specks of dust' (415/754) – not the appearance of essence, no 'formally embodied essence' still sensately stimulating. From its theory, neither assurance nor knowledge nor belief is to be expected. The (end) is, if it is an end, an outré comedy of the end, an ultra-comic end, a 'ridiculous excess' of ending and a 'comic self-forgetfulness' that art and its end still plays out against itself, against the very idea of an end. It has ceased to be a known, regulated, *proper* end and the end *itself*.[16]

What remains at the end of art, art-religion, its gods, and its God is a desert. And in this desert (the end of art) – the most extreme and unregulatable of ironies – is born, not *after* the end of art but *out of* it, the (as Hegel

127

would have it) last religion, 'revealed religion.' 'The self is absolute essence' is the *leichtsinnige* proposition of comic consciousness. That of legal consciousness is more precise: 'The abstract person is absolute essence.' Now this abstract person, the removed mask into which the subject has gathered itself together, is utterly empty, a mere schema without the force to grasp the complexities of any content, and without the stability that could protect the subject against the attacks of sceptical doubt as to whether it is stabile and enduring at all. The pure form of abstract consciousness can do nothing but cast away the self in which this form could find sustenance and present itself as the death mask of the dead god of art-religion. This god, the last and paradigmatic spectator of comedy, who 'is perfectly at home in what is represented before him, and sees himself playing in the drama before him' (412/748) of necessity died at the loss of his consciousness, which was relinquished to the mask-self of comedy. Knowledge exists henceforth only as an 'externalization of the knowledge of itself,' as knowing without knowing and thus merely as its form without content and object. But if self-consciousness is vacant, then the content, without its sustaining form, must for its part be an unsustained tumult of formless elements, conflicting interests, conceptless disparate individuals. Hegel calls them 'the desertifying wildness [*verwüstende Wildheit*] of content with its constituent elements set free and departed' of that abstract legal person (415/755). This content, now unsustained, is a desert of every immediate, material this, non-objective matter, material as the sheer dispersion of unschematized elements. The god deceased in the vacant mask, on the one hand, and the desert, on the other – these are the two extremes of the ultra-comic self-consciousness whose structure is articulated in the proposition that the person is absolute essence. Yet, how ever far apart they lie, mask and desert are joined by a copula and generate – that is: a dead, purely formal and therefore contourless consciousness and an amorphous, devastated subject – generate together, 'each becoming the other,' the mask becoming desert and the desert becoming mask, 'actual self-consciousness,' the incarnate God, Christ. Christ is the offspring of desert and mask, he himself being both of them. 'It can be said,' Hegel writes of this self-consciousness, 'if we wish to use the terms drawn from the process of natural generation – that it has a *real* mother but an *ansich*-existing father' (416/756). The father, this is why he is called '*ansich*,' is dead, a death mask; and the reality of the mother lies in the 'desertifying wilderness' of all the isolated elements of the material world. Precisely for this reason, however, their sexual-logical copula, which produces the figure of the Christian son of God, is none other than the elementary unity of being and thinking, of self and consciousess, and thus of subject-mask and subject-desert, in self-consciousness: the unity of a self, unsustained and unstabile in its sheer material being-there, and a consciousness that has forgotten everything and even itself (419/761). It is this unity of the extremes of sheer being and thinking, extremes that have become absolute and absolved even of themselves, which the *Phenomenology of Mind*, even in the chapter on art-religion, envisions throughout as speculative *onto-logic*. As such, that is, as the *thinking* of *being*, this onto-logic legitimizes itself only when, in the sequence of the figures it thinks, it can point to at least one in which thinking is 'immediately existence' (419/761). And this single figure, for Hegel, is Christ, his ontology is the Christian ontology of a self-conscious This, a christology of spiritual singularity. This is how Hegel, as must be understood from his officious proclamations, understood himself. But even if his christology is hardly compatible with any 'orthodoxy,' he would presumably have thought it blasphemy to admit the comic into his christo-ontology. He was candid enough, courageous and – ironically – systematic enough, however, to leave in the text of his *Phenomenology* no doubt that only the comic suspension of substance in its union with the unhappy devastation of the subject could produce the one personal God, the God *in persona,* and therewith first produce the actual concept of subject and substance at all. That the Christian system of self-conscious singularity proceeds out of the coincidence of mask and desert and 'itself' can be nothing other than this contingent union of extreme and excessive experiences, which at least deranges every system, if it does not render it impossible.[17]

Hegel does not state it, but his text clearly propounds that the conjunction of desert and mask – a desert that can be nothing other than a mask, a mask that can be nothing but a desert, both of which, accordingly, can simply be only other than *themselves* and other than *being* – that this absolute coincidence of the absoluta in Christ and his onto-logic, and therefore the speculative ontology *in its totality* is the continuation of this 'ontology' of the mask, an outré *prosop-ontology* and comic. The personal god, the actual concept, and in its wake even absolute spirit, remains as a mask – and not as the mask *itself*, but its devastation, which can no longer be grasped in the concepts of self, being, or concept, and thus not in the ruling concepts of Hegelian doctrine, namely, substance, subject and their unity.

Hegel thought of the end of art – comedy, irony – only as its completion, as its historical regionalization and domestication, as its self-appropriation and self-possession. The point, however, is to think of this end not as completion – that is, to think of art as finite and as incompletion, as mobile, porous and *released* from itself and even from the substantiality of the subjectivity of its ending. The point is to think of both art and its end as a detaching of the mask, as a release of matter without contour and of a thinking without schema, as a dispatch in which *with* art something other *than* art, something other *as* art, is promised and exposed.

Translated by Kelly Barry

# 5

# Eating My God

*Stuart Barnett*

Ingredients:  'The Spirit of Christianity' (finely chopped)[1]
1 column *Glas*, sliced
1 sign of divinity
1 loaf of bread
1 jug of wine

garnish with *pleroma* à la Hamacher
(feeds twelve)

A piece of Hegel remains. Perhaps several pieces. Of that early essay 'The Spirit of Christianity and Its Fate' we know that many pieces are lost, for ever. The whole – which we know to be the truth – will never be known to us. Yet much remains. Much more, moreover, remains untouched by us. Was this intentional? Are we glutted on Hegel and thus find it an easy matter to leave pieces of this feast to propitiate the gods? Or do they remain indigestible? Do they remind us that we are having some difficulty digesting what we have taken in?

Written in Frankfurt between 1798 and 1800, this text belongs to the early writings of Hegel, writings that seem to beg discussion of whether they announce crudely the coming system or reveal a repressed alternative to that very system. First published by Nohl in 1907, this early essay was part of the material that allowed the twentieth century to reassess Hegel. From Dilthey and Lukács on to the present day, it has been clear that this text – among other writings from this period – is not simply a mere instance of juvenilia. Indeed, it seems that to discuss these texts is to put the very concept 'Hegel' at stake. Derrida comments that for this reason these texts have been subject to the logic of biological development. Their difference from the mature system accordingly becomes the incipient, adolescent form of that very system. These texts, then, will always have been a part of Hegel; but they are – in a crucial sense – not yet Hegel.[2]

Setting aside the issue of the genetic development of Hegel's work, it is not clear whether one can employ a biological, organicist logic even within a single text from this period – especially such a text as 'The Spirit of Christianity.' As Gisela Schuler reminds us, we should wonder whether 'these manuscripts can at all be characterized as a completed whole, as Nohl offers it to us.'[3] And as H. S. Harris points out:

> The long essay published by Nohl as 'The Spirit of Christianity and Its Fate' is really a series of essays with absolutely no determinate sequence. The essays themselves were put together by Hegel during 1799, or even perhaps early in 1800, by cutting up, revising, and making lengthy additions to, a set of meditations written in the last few months of 1798 and the first months of 1799. . . . In any case the sequence of the manuscript in its original form cannot now be restored; all we can say with certainty is that the ordering of topics and arguments was in places very different from that of the second draft.[4]

In short, 'The Spirit of Christianity' is a collection of fragments whose order and structure is impossible to determine. It is an essay that exists perhaps in a form closer to *Glas* than many would care to admit. Indeed, it is not an essay in any conventional sense.[5] A dilemma then lies at the heart of these text(s) – can one render an interpretation, a reading, that is not a violation of what is interpreted and read? Is reading necessarily the forging of a unity that does not exist?[6] Ironically, in order to consider these questions in their turn it will be necessary – in order to bring forth the radical implications for reading itself – to read, to undertake the very same violation that this essay, by its very status, renders embarrassingly thematic. Thus here too this essay will be treated as both completed and as a piece of a larger whole. The saving grace in this procedure is that the violence of reading is exposed rather than rendered transparent.

This essay forces upon us what at first seems a trivial philological issue and yet which quickly becomes a problem that lies at the very heart of Hegelian philosophy. Can one read this act of rememberment that is actually a forgetting contained within the act of reading? Can one disrupt this relation, which genetically links passage, part, and text, to work, genre, and discourse? Disruption as such is no doubt impossible. For every reader is necessarily a

Hegelian – just as all reading is always already Hegelian. Yet in Hegel we can trace the stakes involved in such reading. Let us accept, then, Hegel's invitation to the last supper of reading, the final course of which is philosophy. Yet we should be aware: to consume only a fragment is to enter into communion with Hegel.[7] Take this, he seems to say. Take this piece of writing, and read from it. For it is of my corpus.

This text(s), then, divides its considerations between the spirit of Judaism and the spirit of Christianity. It must be made clear at the outset, however, that theological issues are, despite their apparent prominence, not the main issue that Hegel seeks to address. Again, it is easy to be led astray by the manner in which this and other essays have been presented to us. It might perhaps be best not to think of this, as Nohl would have us, as a theological text. Indeed, as has been suggested, these early essays might be better thought of as anti-theological texts.[8] Hegel was seeking in these essays to address an ethical dilemma, a dilemma that both philosophy and religion had failed to surmount. This was due to Kant's having introduced – by means of the categorical imperative – an intractable disunity into ethics, indeed, into humanity itself. For the categorical imperative operated on the premise that it was necessary to enforce the rule of reason upon quite irrational instincts. Reason therefore was in a state of permanent war with what humanity was understood to be. Kantian ethics, in turn, was little more than an uneasy peace treaty in an ongoing war within the individual subject. The self-enforcement of the categorical imperative might allow individuals to coexist as atoms in a society. Yet it would never allow them to live together as a community. This wounding blow to community – which defines modernity henceforth as the search for a community lost or imagined – is intolerable to Hegel.

Hegel begins to define the terms of this dilemma in his delineation of Judaism. As appallingly anti-Semitic as his reflections are, it must be made clear that for Hegel the relations between Judaism and Christianity were, for the most part, a malleable vocabulary within which to consider the implications of Kantianism. In this text the Jews are a figuration of Kant. The earlier history of Judaism thus serves to present the story of the Kantian society. Hegel focuses therefore on the irrevocable separation of the Jews from the divine. Just as Kant renders God a regulative idea that is necessary but unknowable, so do the Jews sunder humanity from God. Not only did the Jewish God not manifest himself, but man was not to broach any form of mediation with the divine. Thus images and words that would purport to 'represent' the divine were not permissible: 'The infinite subject had to be invisible, since everything visible is something restricted' (K191/N250). This separation has decisive consequences for the Jewish community. This Hegel sees inscribed in the very origins of Judaism, in the actions of Abraham:

> The first act which made Abraham the progenitor of a nation is a disseverance which snaps the bonds of communal life and love. The entirety of the relationships in which he had hitherto lived with men and nature, these beautiful relationships of his youth (Joshua xxiv, 2), he spurned.[9]

Thus, not only is the Jewish community separated from God and nature, but it is also divided against itself. It is a fragmented society. What holds this society together are commandments from God. This does not entail the manifestation of God or the establishment of an enduring relation with God. Rather, the Jews are left to apply these laws to themselves. The very existence of the laws underscores their separation from God.[10] The commandments, moreover, are not merely a prefiguration of the categorical imperative. They stand for determinative judgment, the application of concepts to particular instances. Thus in addition to the categorical imperative, Hegel also challenged the more fundamental principles of rationalism itself.

Hegel's ambition is to find an alternative to this projection of a Kantian society. Christianity accordingly provides him with the vocabulary with which to articulate a critique of Kantian ethics. Before this critique can be explored, however, it must be made clear that Hegel's final verdict is that Christianity ultimately fails to provide such an alternative. For Christianity finds its very origins in a gesture of separation similar to that of Judaism. Jesus, for instance, isolates himself not only from Jewish society, but also from all familial and sexual relations:

> Therefore Jesus isolated himself from his mother, his brothers, and his kinsfolk. He might love no wife, beget no children; he might not become either a father of a family or a fellow-citizen to enjoy a common life with his fellows. The fate of Jesus was that he had to suffer from the fate of his nation.
>
> (K285/N328, translation slightly modified)

Jesus must separate himself from the society of separation. In doing so, however, he only sustains that very same separation. This is the first indication of the 'fate' awaiting Christianity. Hegel also points out that Christianity will be ineffective in transforming the society of separation and disunity:

Jesus did not fight merely against one part of the Jewish fate; to have done so would have implied that he was himself in the toils of another part, and he was not; he set himself against the whole. Thus he was himself raised above it and tried to raise his people above it too. But enmities like those he sought to transcend can be overcome only by valor; they cannot be reconciled by love.

(K205/N261)

The love of Jesus will be overwhelmed – by Christianity. Christianity, for its part, will endure as the institutionalization of the separation from society. Thus the fate of Christianity is to fail as community. Despite this failure awaiting Christianity, Hegel argues that there is much in the New Testament which one might yet use to search for an alternative to the Kantian society.

The prime focus for Hegel in this search is the notion of love. For the spirit of Christianity is drawn together in love. Love defines the distinction between Jesus and the law of the Old Testament, the law of Kant. Love does not command or punish. It does not seek to bind concept to particular instance. Indeed, love is the very limit of conceptual thought. For not only can love not be commanded, but it hardly allows itself to be spoken of:

It is a sort of dishonor to love when it is commanded, i.e., when love, something living, a spirit, is called by name. To name it is to reflect on it, and its name or the utterance of its name is not spirit, not its essence, but something opposed to that. Only in name or as word, can it be commanded; it is only possible to say: Thou shalt love. Love itself pronounces no imperative [Sollen]. It is no universal opposed to a particular, no unity of the concept, but a unity of spirit, divinity. To love God is to feel one's self in the 'all' of life, with no restrictions, in the infinite.

(K247/N296)

Language is necessarily the medium of reflection, division, and disunity. Love, accordingly, is neither a command nor a concept. It does not partake of the law. Indeed, it *is* not. Love precedes conceptuality and relationality. It is the quasi-transcendental that marks the possibility of a relation. To think love is to think relation before any institution of relation.

What love brings to light is that the problem of the command lies at the heart of language. For language is not only the medium of the command; it is also the originary command as such. Language is predicated upon judgment, upon the determinative application of concepts. Language commands the thing as well as being to be equivalent to, to submit to, the concept. Hegel provides an example of this power of language:

> It is still more alien to love to call the other a fool, for this annuls not only all relation with the speaker but also all equality, all community of essence. The man called a fool is represented as completely subjugated and is designated a nonentity.
>
> (K216/N269)

The particular being in this instance is subjugated by the judgment to the concept. This is not merely the case with this example, but with every instance of judgment. For what does not obey the law of concept is either banished or repressed. The law of the concept – as well as the concept of the law – functions by means of excision and exclusion. As a result, this violence of language annuls community.

Therefore it is not that a particular command of the Jews is unjust. Rather, it is language itself that works to undo community. For concepts are in a state of war with being. Indeed, being cannot be in this siege. Philosophy, moral philosophy, is the purest expression of this war:

> The description of a thing [Sache] is always a represented thing; if he [the speculative moralist] compares this representation, the concept, to what is living [Lebendiges], he says that this is how that which lives should be – there should be no contradiction between the concept and the modification of what is living other than that this is something thought and that this is something living . . . but his thing [Sache] is actually to conduct war against the living, to polemicize against it, or to calculate only with lifeless concepts.[11]
>
> (N276)

The exercise of judgment, the application of the law of the concept, seeks to end contradiction – which always originates in being. As Hegel notes: 'So long as laws are supreme, so long as there is no escape from them, so long must the individual be sacrificed to the universal, i.e. be put to death' (K226/N278). And where being cannot be, beings-in-common cannot come to be. Hence community – being-in-common – is not possible in such a regime. The only community here is the community of the concept. And in this community being is always on the way to the gulag.

Paradoxically, then, love would seem to gesture towards community at the same time that it resists communication. The problem for Hegel becomes how

– if love resists language itself – does one (im)part love?[12] Can love, for its part, be commanded? Can one say: thou shalt love? Hegel seeks to explore how Jesus addresses this paradox. For it would seem self-defeating to make love a commandment. To do so would be to submit it to the language of the law, to the reign of concepts. And yet one must (im)part the message of love. If not command, one must 'teach' love. Thus Hegel turns to consider how Jesus teaches love. Jesus does not teach love of himself, or love of God. Rather, Jesus teaches love of the other:

> In this feeling of harmony there is no universality, since in harmony the particular is not in discord but in concord, or otherwise there would be no harmony. 'Love thy neighbor as thyself' does not mean to love him as much as yourself, for self-love is a word without meaning. It means 'love him as who you is' [*liebe ihn als* [*einen,*] *der du ist*].
>
> (K247/N296)[13]

The difficulty with teaching love is that for love to enter language is for it to be deformed. The process of its deformation, however, deforms language in turn. This results in statements that seem to defy logic and grammar. The command of love is not to love one's neighbor as one would oneself. This, for Hegel, is senseless. The command of love is: love him as who you is. He (is/are) you. The temporality of reading itself is suspended – much as being is suspended here – so that one can read this sentence both ways, backwards and forwards, until the verb – the impossible conjugation of being – becomes distorted beyond sense. Here Hegel turns the violence normally directed against being against concepts, against language itself. For language is the being of concepts. Yet, in order for love to happen, language must be violated. It is in the cracks, the interstices of language, that difference, the other, is glimpsed. One only confronts the other by means of a disruption of language and conceptuality. Yet contained within Hegel's reflection is another message, a warning perhaps for the love of Hegel. To equate oneself with the other, to elide the difference of the other (you is he) is to violate being itself.

Love thus disarticulates the command. It is still not clear, however, how love can (im)part itself. In search of a solution, Hegel turns to the Last Supper. For the Last Supper is a communal celebration of love that confronts the problem of its own (im)parting. However, Hegel must also confront here the problem of religion. For it is in the Last Supper that Christianity finds the inspiration for its own institution. The Last Supper provides Christianity with the ritual and signs

137

of religion. Despite these traits, Hegel argues that the Last Supper is always not yet religion:

> Love is less than religion, and this meal, too, therefore is not strictly a religious action, for only a unification in love, made objective by imagination, can be the object of religious veneration. In a love-feast, however, love itself lives and is expressed, and every action in connection with it is simply an expression of love. Love is present only as an emotion, not as an image also.
>
> (K248/N297)

Love is only present as a feeling; it should not be an image or sign. Yet there is an objective form of love at the last supper – the bread and wine. It is this that makes this meal hover [*schweben*] between a meal among friends and a religious act.

The fact that love becomes objective in the Last Supper – that is, assumes the structure of a language of sorts – becomes then a problem for Hegel. Strictly defined, according to Hegel, love is a feeling, spirit, that inhabits the lovers. To assume material form would be to confine, to restrict – to determine – love into a lifeless objective form. Thus love should not submit to the finitude of mediation. Hegel must accordingly address the status of the bread and wine, which clearly function as material signs of the love of Jesus – indeed, of Jesus:

> The common eating and drinking here is not what is called a sign. The connection between sign [*Zeichen*] and referent [*Bezeichnetem*] is not itself spiritual, life, it is an objective connection; the sign and referent are strangers to one another, and their connection lies outside them in a third thing; their connection is only a connection in thought. To eat and drink with someone is an act of union and is itself a felt union, not a conventional sign.
>
> (K248/N297, translation slightly modified)

The bread and wine are not signs that have a natural, ostensive function. There is no real connection between the sign and the referent. Hegel thus defines the sign in a very modern way. It is defined as the relation between a signifier and a signified. Community, in turn, is defined as the establishment of this relation, as the harnessing of the potentially arbitrary nature of the sign.[14] In as much as a sign cannot by definition be private, the sign comprises the space of community.

Hegel, however, must further qualify the sign in relation to community. Thus, according to Hegel, divine love, the love of Jesus, should not enter the realm of the signifier. Ideally, it would exist, much as Schelling's Absolute, in a point of absolute in-difference with the objective. Yet, as the Last Supper demonstrates, the signified — in this instance, God — must become flesh, must enter into the material world of the signifier. What the Last Supper seems to force upon Hegel is that it is only by means of this finite realm of the signifier that community can be founded. The problem that Hegel must address is the difficulty of founding community by means of finitude and yet maintaining the purity of love. The possibility of resolution is offered by the very nature of the signifiers in the Last Supper.

As stated, Hegel argues that, properly speaking, the bread of the Last Supper is not a sign. Its referent, after all, is God. Yet it is and is not a sign. This allows the Last Supper to achieve the minimal condition of a religious event while at the same time renouncing it in order to remain an act of love:

> Jesus is in them all, and his essence, as love, has divinely permeated them. Hence the bread and the wine are not just an object, something for the intellect. The action of eating and drinking is not just a self-unification brought about through the destruction of food and drink, nor is it just the sensation of merely tasting food and drink. The spirit of Jesus, in which his disciples are one, has become a present object, a reality, for external feeling. Yet the love made objective, this subjective element become a thing, reverts once more to its nature, becomes subjective again in the eating.
>
> (K250–1/N299)

Love, like God, must (im)part itself; it must assume material form in order for finite beings to take part in it. Only in this way can love become communal. Yet the sign of love can exist only as part of its disappearance.[15] This is why bread is for Hegel the consummate sign. It is consumed and destroyed in the very act of signification. The gestures of understanding, comprehending, and destroying are one. The signifier is ingested and all that remains is the subjective feeling, the signified. Love thereby partakes of finitude only in the most minimal and fleeting manner — just enough to establish itself as communal love.

With this fine distinction, Hegel seeks to avoid the problem of reflection, for 'every reflection annuls love, restores objectivity again, and with objectivity we are once more in the territory of restrictions' (K253/N370). Yet how can this transcendence into a disembodied signified, into the love of Jesus, be achieved at the same time that finitude is maintained? This is the question that plagues Hegel's thought and which the notion of spirit will seek to resolve.[16] What we see Hegel beginning to articulate here is the passage of the Absolute through the finite. Just as God must appear as Jesus, so must the love of Jesus appear as the bread and wine of the Last Supper. With just as much necessity, however, these manifestations must disappear. They must produce the effect of their appearing (the signified), disappear, and leave no trace (erasure of the signifier). The shared bread of the Last Supper – precisely because it is communally consumed – becomes then the perfect medium of love. It offers a model of finitization that nonetheless resolves itself in communal transcendence. It is, in short, the minimal structure of the *Aufhebung*.

The aim of the Last Supper therefore is to prepare for the destruction of the material form of the sign of God. This takes the form of eating what is in essence the flesh of Jesus. Yet what does it mean to meditate thus the gesture of eating one's God? It can only mean to think the death of God – to think of participating in the death of God. More precisely, it entails thinking of participating in the death of *one's own God*. For Jesus is – for every Christian – always *my* God. Yet for *my* God to become *our* father the community of worshippers must eat their God. This is necessitated according to Hegel because no trace of God should exist as a remainder that could be wrongly worshipped. This would constitute a religion, a veneration of lifeless objects that supposedly exist as signs of an absent God.

What the bread of the Last Supper underscores is that Jesus 'is' only love. As a man, he is always already undergoing his own death. This is what his disciples do not grasp. For them, Jesus is uniquely and solely the divine. For Hegel, this indicates that the lesson of the Last Supper did not take hold among the disciples. Indeed, when the necessary and inevitable death of Jesus takes place, his disciples cannot accept it. As Hegel notes: 'After Jesus died, his disciples were like sheep without a shepherd' (K291/N333). Yet, as he explains, not only is Jesus's death necessary, it is also necessary that this death be accepted by his followers:

> So long as he lived among them, they remained believers only, for they were not self-dependent. Jesus was their teacher and master, an individual center on which they depended. They had not yet attained an independent life of their own. The spirit of Jesus ruled them, but after his removal even this objectivity, this partition between them and God, fell away, and the spirit of God could then animate their whole being.
>
> (K268/N314)

The sign of God must undergo a dematerialization so that a community might be made possible. For Hegel, Christianity must be defined by the realization that Jesus is only a signifier whose unfortunate necessity must be dispensed with. This is what the death of Jesus was meant to teach his followers. For love cannot reside in any finite form.

Once the signifier of God is destroyed, only a subjective unity – which, in fact, constitutes community – exists. God would then truly 'be with' the disciples. It is the departure of Jesus as the material sign that permits a true bond to be established:

> Only after the departure of Jesus' individual self could their dependence on
> him cease; only then could a spirit of their own or the divine spirit subsist
> in them.
>
> (K272/N317)

It is within this 'or' that the future of Hegelian philosophy lies. With the death of Jesus, then, love is no longer the love of Jesus. Henceforth it is love as spirit that will be at work. Once the material bond has been erased, the disciples can be one with the divine. They join, as worshippers, the community of love that is itself an expression of the divine. Community becomes communion with the divine.

This problematic helps to explain Hegel's fascination with Mary Magdalene, that 'famous beautiful sinner.' Derrida has rightfully drawn our attention to this odd moment in this essay. Following the logic of his argument, Mary Magdalene is the one true disciple of Jesus. At first glance, Mary Magdalene would seem to be an unacceptable figure from the point of view of both Jewish law and Christian ethics. She has transgressed Jewish law. She has also transgressed Christian ethics – as understood by the disciples – in that she has used money that might go to the poor to anoint the feet of Jesus. Yet Jesus claims that this woman full of love has performed a beautiful work:

> Not only did they fail to grasp the beautiful situation but they even did
> injury to the holy outpouring of a loving heart. 'Why do you trouble her,'
> says Jesus, 'she has wrought a beautiful work upon me,' and this is the only
> thing in the whole story of Jesus which goes by the name of 'beautiful.'
>
> (K243/N293)

The act is not a religious act; it is an aesthetic act. It reads Jesus not as a god, but as sign. What truly sets Mary Magdalene apart from the disciples of Jesus is that she understands already the death of Jesus. As Jesus comments, she is preparing him ahead of time for his burial. While seemingly disreputable if not

141

'sacrilegious, Mary Magdalene nonetheless presents a more profound understanding of Christian love than any of the disciples. For love to be truly divine
love – and not religious – Jesus can exist only as his own impending death. The
material sign of love – which Jesus 'is' – must be readied for death and decay.

To end our investigation here, however, would leave a false impression of
Hegel's ultimate assessment of Christianity. For, as already suggested, Christianity, as a new way of thinking and being, must fail according to Hegel
because it has already – through the example of Jesus – sundered itself from the
community as a whole. It seeks not integration, but autonomy. It also must fail
because it cannot help but become a religion. This desire continues after the
Resurrection in the search for relics and miracles – material signs of the divine.
It it this desire that leads to the establishment of Christianity as a religion, as an
institution, as a community within a community.

As Hegel describes it, Christianity begins to meet its fate immediately after
the death of Jesus. This is because 'his spirit had not remained behind in them'
(K291/333). The living presence of Jesus was absolutely necessary for the
disciples as a bond to the divine. He was – and was their link to – God. As
Hegel notes: 'He was their living bond; in him the divine had taken shape and
been revealed' (K291/N334). Love as spirit, then, must fail. For ultimately it
was the love of Jesus – as a finite being – and not love as such that bound
together the believers into a community. The disciples require a finite, material
sign of divinity. Finite beings require finite signs. They require, moreover, that
true mark of finitude, the signifier. Hegel can only accept the notion of the
finitization of God if it follows the model of the Last Supper. Hegel, moreover,
will adopt the gesture and structure of the Last Supper's understanding of this
necessity as the founding insight into his mature system. Spirit will become the
relentless transcendence of the finite signs of the absolute.

Hegel's ultimate criticism of Christianity is that it fails to become one with
the society within which it is embedded.[17] It is necessary, however, to inquire
into the nature of this community that Hegel holds up – with some minor
reservations – as a model. The community Hegel considers here is one in which
community is achieved through the sublation of finitude itself. Love is the
principal means of this sublation. Love is thereby no longer the encounter
between finite beings. While supposedly resisting reflection, it nonetheless
begins to serve a decidedly speculative end. Thus love should function to
permit the experience of the self by means of the other: 'In love man has
found himself again in another' (K394/N322). This is not love as recognition of
the other, but as appropriation of the other. This finds its culmination in the

transcendence of finite beings into the love of Jesus, where they are one. The reduction of love to the movement of self-recognition is implicitly extended to the self-recognition of God via the worship of finite beings. It is a community therefore that has achieved immanence. It is not a community of finite beings-in-common but a community that has discovered its essence exterior to itself and has accordingly understood itself as the emanation of that essence. This, it must be remembered, is the ambition of the Hegelian community.

Thus while it seems that Hegel would prefer to avoid the uneasy compromises of the Last Supper, it nonetheless provides him with the means of thinking the contours of the community he seeks to make possible. Indeed, the fate of speculative thought itself depends on the reading of the Last Supper – or, more simply, on reading itself. Thus Hegel draws the analogy between the Last Supper and the act of reading:

> This return may perhaps in this respect be compared with the thought which in the written word becomes a thing and which recaptures its subjectivity out of an object, out of something lifeless, when we read. The simile would be more striking if the written word were read away [*aufgelesen*], if by being understood it vanished as a thing, just as in the enjoyment of bread and wine not only is a feeling, for these mystical objects aroused, not only is the spirit made alive, but the objects vanish as objects.
>
> (K250/N299)

The act of reading is this celebration of communion. For just like the bread, the sign as signifier – that lifeless, material object – becomes a thought, a signified, becomes subjectivity. Both reading and community are constituted by the passage from the signifier to the signified, the process of the constitution of the sign. Yet reading fails ultimately to be a feast of love; it must remain in part a religious act. For the signifier remains after the consumption of the sign. It remains, precisely, as object. The signifier haunts the signified. For this reason, Hegel argues that the analogy between the Last Supper and the act of reading would be more appropriate if the written word, the signifier, would disappear in the very act of reading.[18]

What is remarkable about this account of Christianity is the way in which it both does and does not fit into the later mature system. As Hegel will later develop it, Christianity does indeed fail because it is a primitive attempt, on the level of pictorial thinking, to understand the Absolute. Nonetheless, Christianity, as the absolute religion, provides the text for philosophy to read. The truth of religion awaits the intervention of philosophy in order to be disclosed. Yet the failure of Christianity in this early essay seems to be final and not open to the *Aufhebung.*

What Hegel will not be able to admit is the extent to which this essay reveals that speculative idealism is predicated upon the impossibility of its own founding premise. Speculative idealism will pursue this impossible dream of reading. It will be unable to articulate itself without the empty, spent signs of the Absolute. Its very task will be to read the history of the Absolute on the basis of these signs of its disappearance. It will seek and assemble signs – relics equivalent to pieces of the true cross. From these signs that should not 'be there,' speculative idealism will craft a philosophy that will be a theory of reading. This manner of reading will always be, once again, a last supper of spirit. Speculative idealism thereby becomes a permanent Last Supper. In this Last Supper signs are eaten, disgorged, and then readied to be eaten again.

Hegel's philosophy, then, is the menu for this last but endless supper. Moreover, every act of reading draws one to the table of this supper. For reading itself seems bound up with the desire for communion, for the incorporation and destruction of the signifier. Yet, as the reading of Hegel demonstrates, there is always a remainder, a material residue. It is this remainder that sticks in the throat and that marks every piece as finite.[19] To bring an end to this supper, it is necessary to savor, to dwell upon, these remainders. To undertake such a relentlessly finite reading – which must necessarily resist communion – will be to prepare for a finite community, one that will not seek its own transcendence in the realm of the signified, but which will be constituted by the experience of its own limit.

# Part II

# AFTER HEGEL
# AFTER DERRIDA

# 6

# The Remnants of Philosophy: Psychoanalysis after *Glas*

*Suzanne Gearhart*

## I. Hegel and the Critique of Phallocentrism

Despite its highly critical relation to Hegel, Jacques Derrida's *Glas* is as much a reflection on the future of Hegelian philosophy as on its past, on its survival as on its death. I say 'as much' because, as most readers of Derrida would doubtless agree, we must weigh both aspects of Derrida's interpretation of Hegel carefully if we are not to distort it. Derrida's title suggests that philosophy, at least in its Hegelian form, is indeed dead, or at any rate, that its death knell has been sounding for quite some time. But taken as a whole, *Glas* also clearly indicates that 'something of Hegelian philosophy' (*de la philosophie hégélienne*), if not Hegelian philosophy itself, lives on in many different forms. One of the most significant of these, in the terms of *Glas* itself, is a certain form of psychoanalysis.

It would be imprecise to say that the relationship between psychoanalysis and philosophy is the central element of *Glas* – or even of the portion of *Glas* devoted to Hegel. The important place that linguistic, poetic, political, ethical, and strictly philosophical concerns also hold in this multi-semantic work argues against assigning a pre-eminent status to any one of them. Moreover, the organization of *Glas* – that is, both its typography (the two or perhaps one should say multiple columns of print, for example) and its fragmented nature (the fact that many sections and *Glas* as a whole begin and end in mid-argument and even in mid-sentence) – is also calculated to undercut the emergence of any center of a thematic or formal nature. It may be true that Derrida's interpretation of Hegel has heretofore elicited few responses or readings and that this alone is sufficient to justify focusing, at least for the moment, on the question of Hegel's place and importance in *Glas*. But it is also true that in concentrating on the relationship between Hegelian philosophy and psycho-analysis, or even on Hegelian philosophy alone, one runs the risk of reading *Glas* in a reductive manner.

Despite the complexity of the form and argument of *Glas*, however, few would deny that a discussion of its importance and significance would be incomplete without a consideration of the manner in which it presents the relation between Hegelian philosophy and Freudian psychoanalysis. As Sarah Kofman has argued, it would certainly be an overstatement to call the relation-ship between psychoanalysis and philosophy the 'transcendental key' to the text of *Glas*.[1] But it is also the case that much of its interest and force stem from the manner in which Derrida exploits the contrast between them to provide a critical perspective on both Hegel and Freud or, alternatively, to draw from each or both the terms of a critique of radical forms of philosophy and psychoanalysis as well as the most traditional forms.[2]

Derrida's interpretation of the figure of the Greek tragic heroine Antigone marks an important moment in *Glas*, because, as I shall argue, it serves as a point of convergence for several of the major themes of Derrida's exploration of the relationship between philosophy and psychoanalysis and his readings of Hegel and Freud. Derrida's analysis of Antigone suggests that, just as Hegelian philosophy lays the ground for and even makes necessary a theory of the unconscious, so psychoanalysis lays the ground for and makes necessary a critique of phallocentrism – that is, of the manner in which philosophy and more generally theory have repeatedly and consistently exploited the difference between the sexes for their own theoretical purposes by interpreting it from within a system of values and concepts that subordinate the feminine to the masculine. In Derrida's interpretation, the figure of Antigone comes to stand for this critique of phallocentrism, not as something originating in or necessi-tated by political or ethical considerations that are extraneous to philosophy (or psychoanalysis), but rather as something intrinsic to its (their) development, as an unavoidable consequence of its (their) own inner logic. This critique of phallocentrism constitutes what I would call an important 'remnant' of philo-sophy and psychoanalysis, because it testifies both to their destruction and to their continuing existence and relevance.

The place of psychoanalysis in *Glas* has, of course, already been treated extensively by Sarah Kofman in 'Ça cloche,' in which she argues that a concept of 'generalized fetishism' is central to Derrida's interpretation of Hegel and Freud.[3] Kofman's analysis contains much that is valuable and, I would even say, beyond dispute. But it leaves aside two issues that seem to me to be crucial in coming to terms with the significance of the place Hegel occupies in *Glas* and hence, in more general terms, with *Glas* itself, insofar as many of its broader arguments are tied to its interpretation of Hegel. In doing so, it also neglects a crucial feature of Derrida's critique of phallocentrism, one that distinguishes it from both Lacanian psychoanalytic theory and even from the position Kofman takes in her essay on *Glas*, indebted though she unquestionably is to Derrida.

The first issue is obvious, but crucial nonetheless: why, in Kofman's terms, does Hegel have any place at all in *Glas*? Her answer is that Derrida wants to 'show that Hegel [before the fact] proposes . . . a powerful systematic articulation' of Freud's concepts of castration and fetishism and his complementary theory of femininity – in short of his phallocentrism. As a result, according to Kofman, Derrida is able to 'graft Freud's text onto that of metaphysics' (p. 100), of which Kofman, like others, argues that Hegelian philosophy is the summation.

There is much in *Glas* that confirms the accuracy of this assessment. It echoes what Derrida himself writes, for example when he asserts that the Hegelian *Aufhebung* 'articulates the most traditional phallocentrism with Hegelian onto-theo-teleology.'[4] As we shall see, in his analysis of the Hegelian *Sittlichkeit* in particular, Derrida repeatedly emphasizes that Hegel's description of family life, of the relations between family and state, and of the relations between the sexes are all structured by what he calls the 'dissymmetry' between Hegel's concepts of the masculine and the feminine – that is, by the manner in which Hegel arbitrarily privileges the masculine. At the same time, after reading 'Ça cloche,' one is left wondering why Derrida chose to give Hegel such a preponderant role in his analysis if it was only to serve as an example of a traditional phallocentrism, which the work of any number of other philosophers could presumably have exemplified with equal force. Even in Kofman's own terms, one wonders what is 'powerful' about Hegel's systematic articulation of the traditional concepts of phallocentrism.

A second issue is Kofman's decision to focus on the theme of 'fetishism,' or 'generalized fetishism.' Here again, she is certainly justified in arguing that 'lots of things become clearer' when one rereads *Glas* from the standpoint of Derrida's reinterpretation of this Freudian concept (p. 113). But in focusing on it, Kofman comes to neglect what I would argue is the complementary and equally important theme of repression. This is a potentially serious omission, because if Hegelian philosophy has a critical role to play in *Glas*, particularly in relation to Freudian psychoanalysis, I would argue that in Derrida's terms at least, it assumes that role because it lays the ground for a radical theory of repression that goes beyond one in which repression is understood primarily in 'empirical terms,' that is, in terms of the specific contents that are the object of repression.

Kofman's relative lack of interest in the question of Hegel's particular role in *Glas* and in the problem of repression is in my view related to her interpretation of fetishism. Despite her critical self-awareness, her understanding of fetishism ultimately grounds it in a reality or a truth that would lie beyond repression and be its object – or its subject. In this respect, it is not just the critical role played by Hegel in *Glas* that is neglected by Kofman, but also a crucial feature of Derrida's critique of phallocentrism.

The problem with Kofman's position is evident in the manner in which she assimilates Freud's (Derrida's) notion of fetishism to Derrida's notions of supplementarity and undecidability. For Kofman, the critical insight implicit in Freud's notion of fetishism (which according to Kofman becomes explicit only in Derrida's interpretation of it) is that fetishism 'breaks with the idea of the penis as 'thing itself,' since the penis for which the fetish is the substitute is a fantasmatic penis, since it has never been perceived as such, and since the penis of the mother, 'the thing itself,' is always-already a fetish fabricated by the child' (p. 102). But Kofman also quickly converts the absence of origin implied by the notion of generalized fetishism into an original absence – and into a corresponding affective state that, despite her critique of the concept of origin, does indeed function in her reading as the origin of the supplementary fictions with which the child/fetishist attempts to mask it: 'There never was any "thing itself," but only the *Ersatz*, the postiche, the prosthesis, an original supplementarity in the form of the panicked reaction of infantile narcissism' (p. 102). The fear or panic that Kofman here imputes to the child is the origin of fetishism as she understands it. Rather than ask if fear is indeed the basis of the fetish, or even, if it is, what could have produced such a fear, she posits it as the spontaneous and natural outcome of the child's perception of 'the sex of the woman' (p. 98).[5] And thus for her the deconstruction of fetishism is implicitly tantamount to an unveiling or laying bare of the underlying 'realities' it masks – the panicked reaction of the (male?) child and 'the sex of the woman.' Kofman's argument 'assimilates . . . the fetishistic compromise . . . to undecidability' (p. 103) in such a manner as to make the woman if not the privileged agent then at any rate the privileged locus of deconstruction. In doing so, she implicitly privileges fetishism as the dominant form or model of undecidability.

Despite the critical nature of her intentions with regard to Freud in 'Ça cloche,' Kofman's view that the fetish should be understood as a denial of the

150

reality of the female sex recalls particularly the three essays on female sexuality that Freud wrote late in his career: 'Some Psychological Consequences of the Anatomical Difference Between the Sexes,' 'Female Sexuality,' and the portion of the *New Introductory Lectures* entitled 'Femininity.' The complementary concepts of castration and penis envy, which Freud develops in these essays, are based on what he similarly holds to be a fundamental, underlying reality in terms of which the psychic life of girls/women can be analysed. The fact that Kofman evaluates that reality 'positively,' whereas for Freud it has a neutral or even, some might argue, a negative value, is in certain respects less important than the similarities in the manner in which that reality is conceived by both. In each case, what is in question can be termed a reality, because it is grasped in a similarly immediate perception (which for Freud, as for Kofman, is typically followed by denial). In Freud's case, the reality is the 'castration' of the girl ('a castration that has been carried out' rather than one that has been merely threatened)[6], which the little girl comprehends 'in a flash' when she sees 'the penis of a brother or playmate, strikingly visible and of larger proportion' ('Some Psychological Consequences,' p. 252). For Freud, penis envy is the spontaneous and immediate consequence of the perception of this reality.

Virtually from the day that it was first presented to the public, Freud's concept of penis envy has been criticized on the grounds that it reflects a masculine bias. But I would argue that some of the most powerful objections that can be made against Freud's concept of penis envy and the terms in which he propounds it are to be found in Freud himself – and, according to the logic of *Glas*, in Hegel. The problem with the concept of penis envy is not only that it violates 'our' sense of justice, or that it conflicts with other theories of the psyche that may (but also may not) be better theoretically or practically grounded than Freud's, or that it neglects the role of social factors in determining the value (or lack of it) attached to the masculine or the feminine – assuming for the moment that it does indeed do one or more of these things. It is that Freud's concept of penis envy and the terms in which he elaborates it are inconsistent with the ultimate implications of the concept of repression – that is, I would say, with the implications of both Freud's own concept of repression and also the one Derrida argues is being suggested by Hegelian philosophy.

The conflict between Freud's approach to the problem of repression in his three late essays on female sexuality and his approach to it in the founding work of his psychoanalytic theory, *The Interpretation of Dreams*, is evident when one considers a crucial footnote to the *Interpretation* in which he clarifies the relationship between the dream-thoughts, the dream content, and the dream-work. In summing up the argument of the *Interpretation* as a whole, this footnote clearly indicates that repression is fundamental to the psychic processes as they are revealed in the dream, so much so that it cannot be derived from any more fundamental process, object, or cause:

> I used at one time to find it extraordinarily difficult to accustom readers to the distinction between the manifest content of dreams and the latent dream-thoughts. Again and again arguments and objections would be brought up based upon some uninterpreted dream in the form in which it had been retained in the memory, and the need to interpret it would be ignored. But now that analysts at least have become reconciled to replacing the manifest dream by the meaning revealed by its interpretation, many of them have become guilty of falling into another confusion which they cling to with equal obstinacy. They seek to find the essence of dreams in their latent content and in so doing they overlook the distinction between the latent dream-thoughts and the dream-work. At bottom, dreams are nothing other than a particular *form* of thinking, made possible by the conditions of the state of sleep. It is the *dream-work* which creates that form, and it alone is the essence of dreaming – the explanation of its peculiar nature.
>
> (v. V, note, pp. 506–7)

Though the term 'repression' does not appear explicitly in this passage, in effect it criticizes those who do not acknowledge the distinction between the dream-content and the latent dream-thoughts for their failure to understand the role played by repression in the creation of the dream. They have not grasped that the dream-content is not simply 'there,' but that it has been produced by a process of repression and must be analysed accordingly.

But those who understand the dream in terms of the latent dream-thoughts commit an equally serious error: they appear to accept the existence of repression, but in fact they too fail to take account of it. That is, they fail to understand that the 'essence of dreaming' cannot be separated from the process of repression. Although Freud insists elsewhere in the *Interpretation* that dreams take the form they do because of the exigencies of a censoring agency, what he reveals in this passage is that the process of censorship or repression cannot be understood in terms of what is repressed, that is, the latent content, but only in terms of repression itself. This means that repression must be conceived of first and foremost as an ongoing process that has always-already begun rather than simply as a punctual activity occasioned by specific events.

If one compares Freud's three essays on female sexuality with this note from the *Interpretation* and to the *Interpretation* as a whole, it is difficult not to conclude that they constitute a repudiation of his earlier conception of repression. In the most succinct terms, the closely related ideas of penis envy and castration elaborated in those essays imply that repression can indeed be understood above all in terms of what is repressed – in terms of the unpleasant fact of castration, which the process of repression in both the girl and the boy is designed to resist or deny.[7] And these essays also convey that the theoretical task of psychoanalysis is or should be understood in terms very similar to those in which Kofman 'deconstructs' fetishism. In each case, the aim would be to lift the veil of repression in order to reveal the reality underlying it, whether that reality is conceived of as the penis of the boy, the castration of the girl, or the sex of the woman.

If one analyses what Freud says about the notion of castration in his article on fetishism and what Hegel writes in connection with the wanderings of Abraham and the rite of circumcision, the suggestion of *Glas* appears to be that what Freud and Hegel are conveying is profoundly similar – as Kofman argues. It is true, Derrida pauses to note, that 'Hegel puts forward neither the concept nor the word "castration"' (pp. 52, 42e). But this fact, Derrida goes on to argue, does not necessarily mean that the two discourses – the Hegelian and the psychoanalytic – cannot be assimilated in terms of a common concept of castration, despite the absence of the term in Hegel's text. The differences between Hegelian philosophy and psychoanalysis with respect to 'this symbolic castration across which Hegelian discourse slides [or upon which it slips]' (pp. 51, 41e) could be 'secondary, exterior, non-conceptual' (pp. 52, 43e).

If one looks at the relationship between Freud and Hegel in terms of the problem of repression, however, it becomes possible to defend Hegel's 'theory of repression' against the Freud who writes the three late essays on female sexuality referred to above. Or perhaps it would be more accurate to say that Derrida's reading of Hegel suggests the possibility of a Hegelian (Derridean?) psychoanalysis that would be potentially more rigorous than was Freud himself in working through the implications of his insights concerning repression and in particular in elaborating their consequences in relation to the problem of 'the feminine' (and 'the masculine').[8] Once repression is seen as an ongoing process, then models of experience such as those proposed by Freud to describe the nature of the sexes can be understood more critically, because they appear not so much as the reflection of stable structures, attitudes, and identities, but rather as something more closely resembling dream-images, whose meaning is never fully transparent in either their manifest or latent content. In a similar manner, fetishism no longer appears as the model instance of repression, but instead as one instance of a process whose other forms are equally significant or exemplary.

It should be noted that Derrida has explicitly argued that 'logocentric repression is not comprehensible on the basis of the Freudian concept of repression.'[9] And in view of the limitations Freud places on the concept of repression in his three essays on female sexuality and in other texts as well, it is not difficult to understand why for Derrida 'the deconstruction of logocentrism' cannot be conceived of as 'a psychoanalysis of philosophy' (p. 196). But in *Glas,* Derrida suggests that psychoanalysis does have a critical role to play in the process of deconstruction, as, for example, in his lengthy discussion of the contrast between Kantian philosophy and Hegelian philosophy, a contrast that he draws in large part on the basis of the relationship of each to psychoanalysis. Derrida summarizes that contrast when he writes that, unlike Hegel, 'Kant tries to exempt [before the fact] his discourse from the authority of psychoanalysis' (pp. 241, 215e). In making such an assertion, Derrida indicates not only what is for him the greater critical value of the philosophy of Hegel in relation to Kant but also the critical value of psychoanalysis itself in relation to the philosophical tradition.

## II. Repression and the *Aufhebung*

We have seen that, according to Kofman, Derrida's reading of Freud and Hegel shows how the work of the former is 'grafted' onto the philosophy of the latter and through it, onto metaphysics as a whole. The notion of grafting, which Kofman borrows from Derrida, is equally useful for understanding the manner in which Derrida's interpretation of Hegel and Freud creates the possibility of relating Freud's concept of repression to Hegelian philosophy, and in particular to his concept of the *Aufhebung*. Derrida does more than show that Hegel's concept of the *Aufhebung* and the closely related concept of the transcendental prefigure the Freudian concepts of repression and the unconscious. When the Hegelian concept of *Aufhebung* is contrasted with the concept of repression as it is presented in many of Freud's texts, particularly the three essays on female sexuality, one can see that in important respects it is Hegel, rather than Freud, who treats repression as an ongoing process, and that, in this sense, the Hegelian *Aufhebung* is a post-Freudian concept.

Just as in his 'Introduction' to the French translation of Husserl's 'The Origin of Geometry' Derrida highlighted what was particular about Husserl's concept of the transcendental by contrasting it with that of Kant,[10] so in *Glas* he contrasts Hegel and Kant in a similar spirit:

> It is not possible to describe a phenomenology of the Spirit, that is, according to the subtitle, an 'experience of consciousness,' without recognizing in it the onto-economic work of the family. . . . Here we have the principle of a critique of transcendental consciousness [conceived of] as a formal *I think* (it is always a member of a family who thinks) but also of a concrete transcendental consciousness [conceived of] in the manner of Husserlian phenomenology. . . . It is impossible to 'reduce' [in the manner of a phenomenological reduction] the family structure on the grounds that it is a vulgar, empirical-anthropological annex of transcendental intersubjectivity.
>
> (pp. 154, 135e)[11]

In Derrida's terms, the contrast between Hegel and Kant is not one between a purely rational philosophy on the one hand and a predominantly historical or historicist philosophy on the other. In fact, Hegel's break with Kant would not be so decisive or radical in Derrida's terms had he simply turned his back on the purely rational or transcendental and made the concrete, historical existence of human beings the object of his thought.

This point is repeatedly confirmed in Derrida's early work when he writes of the complicity or solidarity between such apparently antithetical tendencies as empiricism and idealism or historicism and transcendentalism.[12] Rather than dogmatically denying the validity of Kant's concept of the rational subject, Hegelian philosophy situates that subject in terms of a process that produces it. In the passage quoted above, as in much of *Glas*, Derrida portrays Hegelian philosophy as analysing the production of rational consciousness through his description and interpretation of the family and the effects of its 'onto-economic work' in its constitutive relation to rational subjectivity.

The Hegelian family – both the family as an element of the Greek *Sittlichkeit* and the Holy Family – thus plays a central role in Derrida's reading, because it is through the dialectical philosopher's interpretation of the family that he goes beyond the imperatives of transcendental philosophy, even as (or perhaps one should say because) he at the same time respects them. The life of the family serves Derrida as a model of what Hegelian philosophy describes as an ongoing process through which rationality is produced – the process of the dialectic itself, or, in other words, the *Aufhebung*.

When considered in terms of its exemplification in family life, the *Aufhebung*

155

can be seen as having a dual status. It is in a sense eminently rational, insofar as its end or purpose is the production of the rational or the 'conscious' subject, who leaves the family and 'goes out into the "bourgeoisie" [*Bürgerlichkeit*], into civil society' (pp. 185, 164e). In doing so, the subject attains rationality, because he enters into what Hegel calls 'the ethical life that is conscious of itself and actual,' that is, the life of the citizen.[13] But the process of the *Aufhebung* also escapes reason or lies beyond it, in the sense that the reason that it constitutes cannot be there from the beginning to control that process. If it were there from the beginning, then the process would have no necessity or determining function. This is why Hegel describes the law of the family, which the subject leaves behind in order to become a self-conscious citizen, as 'an ever-lasting law, and no man knows at what time it was first put forth.'[14] The law of the family is not one that the rational subject creates freely for itself, but rather one whose origins are obscure or even unfathomable to human reason.

Insofar as the *Aufhebung* is both constitutive of rational (self-)consciousness and also pre-rational, operating in a sphere beyond the control of reason and therefore even beyond its theoretical grasp, it can be considered equivalent to (a form of) what Freud would later call 'repression.' This is what Derrida indicates in a particularly dense passage in which he discusses the close connection between these two concepts. In the passage in question, Derrida begins by asking 'can repression be thought according to the dialectic?' (pp. 214, 191e). He continues by noting the multiple terms in Hegel's philosophy that relate to a common notion, which he translates as 're-striction' and which he suggests should perhaps be seen as 'forms of *Aufhebung*.' (This list includes *Hemmung*, *Unterdrückung*, *Zwingen*, *Bezwingung*, *Zurückdrängen*, and *Zurücksetzung*.) He indicates that the number and relative heterogeneity of these terms is one of the things that makes it less than self-evident that the dialectic and repression can be thought in relation to each other. Furthermore, he argues that, even were one to subsume these multiple forms of 'restriction' under the concept of *Aufhebung*, it would still be unclear what exact position the Hegelian concept of *Aufhebung* would hold in relation to repression, or at least 'what is imagined today, still very confusedly, in connection with this word' (pp. 214, 191e).[15] Derrida asks if the concept of *Aufhebung* or the concept of repression should be seen as the broader or more inclusive concept.

In spite of the difficulties involved, difficulties that he himself has emphasized, Derrida concludes by answering his initial question in the affirmative: 'If one asks '*what is* repression?' '*what is* the re-stricture of repression?' in other words, 'how can it be *thought*? ['comment la *penser*'],' the answer is The

Dialectic' (pp. 214, 191e). That is, the answer to Derrida's initial question is affirmative not only inasmuch as the dialectic can give us the means to think repression but, even more, because repression, the 're-stricture' of repression, can be thought of as the dialectic.[16]

The basis for this affirmative answer, however, becomes fully apparent only with the addition of the qualification that follows it. Derrida goes on to indicate that the conclusion that the *Aufhebung* and repression are two names for a single process should not be taken to imply that the process of repression is a conscious or self-conscious process ultimately comprehended by reason alone. On the contrary:

> To say that re-stricture – under the name of repression – remains today a confused notion [*une imagination confuse*] is perhaps only to designate what, in the eyes of philosophy, does not let itself be *thought* or even inspected through a [*arraisonner d'une*] question. The question is already stricturing.
>
> (pp. 215, 191e)

The dialectic, then, must be thought of as repression, because it escapes reason even though it is already at work in the process of questioning in which reason begins to emerge ('the question is already stricturing'). Or in other words, the dialectic must be thought of as repression because it roots reason not in consciousness but in 'what . . . does not permit itself to be *thought*,' that is, I would say, in an unconscious. In this sense, repression – and the dialectic – cannot be 'thought' at all.

The consequences of this point in relation to Hegelian philosophy as a whole are crucial from Derrida's perspective. If the dialectic is not exclusively or even essentially rational or conscious, then the end of the dialectical process, which lies in the realization or concretization of the ideal, can be thought of not just as the attainment of Absolute Reason, but equally well or perhaps even better as the fulfillment of what is unconscious or repressed. In a comment on the final paragraphs of Hegel's *Philosophy of Nature* that illuminates this point, Derrida argues:

> What is in question here is the full realization of the teleology inaugurated by Aristotle and revived by Kant, the concept of internal finality having almost been lost in the interval between them, in modern times. This internal finality is not conscious, as the position of an external aim would be. It is of the order of 'instinct' [*Instinkt*] and remains 'unconscious.'
>
> (pp. 125, 109e)

The Absolute Consciousness that serves as the telos of nature should be conceived of as 'unconscious.' The paradox that Derrida elaborates here in commenting on the ambiguity of the telos of Hegel's philosophy of nature is of course equally evident in the manner in which he designates Absolute Knowledge throughout *Glas* – as *SA*, that is both '*Savoir Absolu*' and, in spoken French, the 'ça,' or id.

The complex and at the same time critical relationship that Derrida establishes in *Glas* between Hegelian philosophy and psychoanalysis is to a significant extent a result of the manner in which he focuses on the link between Hegel's concept of *Aufhebung* and Freud's concept of repression. By keeping open the question of whether or not the dialectic can be thought of as repression, Derrida is able to distinguish, at least to a certain point, between the side of Hegel's argument that closes off any possible inquiry into the questions of the unconscious and sexuality, and which is thus idealist in the most traditional and narrow sense, and another side that implies the necessity for psychoanalysis. Equally importantly, by continually questioning Freud's concept of repression in terms of Hegel's concept of *Aufhebung* and *vice versa*, he is able to keep before the reader the complexity of the (Hegel's? Freud's? Derrida's?) concept of repression in general and, more specifically, the undecidability of its effects and processes in relation to language, concepts, and experience.

To be sure, in Derrida's terms all discourse is characterized by undecidability, insofar as the simple addition or subtraction of quotation marks can radically change the sense of any given utterance: 'By simply playing with quotations marks [*un simple jeu de guillemets*] one can change a prescriptive utterance into a descriptive utterance; and the simple textuality of an utterance makes possible such a putting in quotation marks' (pp. 222, 198e). But in Hegel's case this most general form of textual undecidability is complemented by what I would call a conceptual undecidability that relates to the substance of his philosophy. Undecidability is a quality intrinsic to a reason that defines itself through an ongoing process of 're-striction' or repression, inasmuch as such a reason represents the fulfillment as much of instinct as of its own more properly rational ends.

In their *Vocabulary of Psychoanalysis*, Jean Laplanche and J.-B. Pontalis argue that Freud's concept of sublimation represents one of the 'lacunas' of his theory (p. 467). In terms of Derrida's logic in *Glas*, however, it seems possible to argue that the sketchiness of Freud's discussion of this term is less of a limitation than they seem to suggest. For what is perhaps most valuable in the concept of sublimation is the manner in which it permits the exploration of the undecidability of the process of repression/*Aufhebung*. Like the dream-work as described in the previously quoted footnote from Freud's *Interpretation of Dreams*, repression does not *simply* restrict, devalorize, ignore, delete, or suppress. It also creates significance and value. The *Aufhebung* is not just the negation of reality; it is also the production of the ideal (and of that authentic reality Hegel calls 'the concrete'). Thus, in terms of the concept of repression that is suggested by *Glas*, sublimation is not at all distinct from repression but is rather an integral component of its complex, contradictory functioning.

The idea that sublimation and repression are two facets — and not particularly distinct ones — of a single process is closely connected to a point that is underscored more than once in Derrida's reading of Hegel: the 'fulfillment of a wish' to borrow from Freud (or 'desire,' to speak in more Lacanian terms), is inseparable from repression. Insofar as family life and family relationships can be considered the agents and milieu of repression/*Aufhebung*, they thus share its contradictory nature. Family relationships are both repressive in the narrow, negative sense, and also pre-eminently fulfilling. The narrowly repressive dimension of the family is emphasized in the following passage, in which the connection between repression and the process of idealization or the *Aufhebung* is also highlighted:

> Man does not go from feeling [being] to conceiving [being] except by repressing drives [*la poussée*], something that the animal, according to Hegel, does not know how to do. Ideality, understood as the thought of the universal, is born and then bears the mark of a repression of drives. . . . The family is prefigured [*s'annonce*].
>
> (pp. 33, 25e)

In Derrida's terms, the process of idealization can and should be understood as a process 'born of' and 'bearing the mark' of repression, and the ideal — or at any rate 'ideality' — should be understood as the repressed. By asserting that the family 's'annonce' in this process of repression, Derrida suggests that the family and repression are inseparable and even indistinguishable: the family is always-already there in the form of repression.

In the passage quoted above, Derrida stresses the 'negative' aspect of repression, its suppression of the drives and of what Hegel regards as those aspects of the human being that he shares with the animal. But Derrida shows Hegel presenting the repressive work of the family in a somewhat different light when, for example, he stresses that repression, or in this case inhibition, is 'internal and essential' to human desire: 'Human desire is work. In itself. This

159

is because inhibition in general structures it in the most internal and essential fashion' (pp. 139, 122e). Thus, according to a logic that is fundamental to the Hegelian dialectic, the form of desire or love that is the basis of marriage is exemplary in that it restricts itself to one partner without at the same time experiencing this restriction as a restriction. In the case of (the Hegelian concept of) marriage, restriction (or repression) 'is part of the spontaneity of love, . . . is taken on freely by desire' (pp. 43, 35e). In this passage we see with particular clarity the relation between repression and desire. They are, quite simply, inseparable, part of one and the same process.

The critical value of this 'Hegelian' concept of repression can perhaps be better delineated by considering Freud's *Civilization and its Discontents*, where Freud himself takes up the question of repression in his discussion of the development of the super-ego. Freud's reflections on repression in this essay grow out of a dilemma posed by what he calls a 'peculiarity' of conscience or the sense of guilt. It is that 'the more virtuous a man is, the more severe and distrustful is its [the super-ego's] behavior, so that ultimately it is precisely those people who have carried saintliness furthest who reproach themselves with the worst sinfulness' (v. XXI, p. 126). 'Virtue,' or what Freud also calls the 'renunciation of instinct,' does not have the effect one would expect of it – a lessening of the sense of guilt. Instead, it has the opposite effect – it only increases the severity of the super-ego. The question is, why?

Freud's answer in *Civilization and its Discontents* is that the super-ego represents the internalization of parental authority and that, once this internalization of authority occurs, nothing can be hidden from the super-ego. Henceforth it will punish the ego for the crimes – the unconscious, imaginary crimes – of the id. But it could be argued that the process of the internalization of authority, which gives repression its distinctive, unconscious quality, is one that *Civilization and its Discontents* never successfully accounts for. How is it that what is (unconsciously) pleasurable comes to be (unconsciously) renounced? The fear of the loss of love adduced by Freud is clearly a powerful motive for the renunciation of certain activities, but not for renunciation of the psychic aims that correspond to those activities.

In the terms that Freud adopts in *Civilization and its Discontents*, there is no real answer to the question of how it is that desire is repressed. But it could be argued that in Derrida's reading of Hegel there is an answer of sorts, or at least a reformulation of the question. In Hegel's/Derrida's terms the problem of the renunciation of pleasure or desire would not exist in the terms it does for Freud, because there would be no renunciation of desire inasmuch as repression itself is an inseparable component of desire, in other words because for Hegel repression cannot be understood in terms of a 'before' or 'after,' an 'origin' or 'end,' but rather only as an ongoing process that coincides with desire itself.

## III. Repression and/as the Feminine

The various aspects of Derrida's analysis of the relation between speculative philosophy and psychoanalysis come together in his reading of Hegel's interpretation of *Antigone*. But this section of *Glas* does not merely confirm arguments that run throughout the text. It is also the part of Derrida's analysis of Hegel where the Hegelian text is seen not only to anticipate Freud but also to be most clearly at odds with the perspective on repression elaborated in Freud's three late essays on female sexuality and his complementary perspective on femininity.

A significant part of Derrida's analysis of Hegel's *Antigone* does nonetheless confirm the picture of a phallocentric Hegel who in his interpretation of the Greek tragic masterpiece continues to express the most traditional views concerning both the family and the woman. For example, Derrida argues that for Hegel the *Sittlichkeit* is based on the exclusion of the woman from the city and her relegation to the home, an exclusion that is treated as 'natural' due to the woman's purportedly greater proximity to the immediate (pp. 185, 164e). This exclusion, moreover, is not compensated for by a comparable limitation in the sphere of activity – and also a corresponding limitation in the nature – of the man. By being excluded from the city, Derrida writes, the woman is deprived of 'the right to desire as well as of her freedom in relation to desire' (pp. 185, 164e). The man, on the other hand, 'who leaves the home and goes out into the "bourgeoisie" [*Bürgerlichkeit*], into civil society, has the right to desire but also the freedom to overcome this desire' (pp. 185, 164e). And when Antigone disappears, having been entombed by order of Creon, and 'taking with her her womanly [or wifely] desire' (pp. 169, 150e), Derrida writes sarcastically that 'Hegel thinks this is very good, very consoling' (pp. 169, 150e). In making this comment, he emphasizes the manner in which Hegel arbitrarily precludes any possible discussion of feminine desire, and in doing so arbitrarily subordinates the feminine to the masculine.

Equally important and particularly telling from a Freudian perspective, Hegel's interpretation of Antigone privileges the one family relation he considers to be 'without sexual desire' over all other relations and thereby expresses a refusal to enter into a discussion of a form of sexuality that would be an essential dimension of the life of the family: 'Three relationships thus are held to be original and irreducible. They are organized according to a hierarchy with three pegs. Apparently one raises oneself up by appeasing or even by strictly annulling sexual desire' (pp. 167, 147e). The suppression of the question of feminine desire and specifically of the desire of the sister thus goes hand in hand with a more general suppression of the question of sexual desire in the context of family life as a whole. Derrida responds to Hegel's assertion that the sister/brother relationship is 'without sexual desire' with the question, 'Is it possible? Is it in contradiction with the whole system?' (pp. 169, 149e). While here, as elsewhere, more than one reading of Derrida's statement seems possible, one clearly legitimate interpretation is that the question Derrida asks is purely rhetorical. At least from a perspective that treats sexuality as unconscious, such an asexual relation is *not* possible.

It would seem then that nowhere is Hegel farther from Freud – and from Derrida – than in his interpretation of *Antigone*. And yet, according to the logic of the dialectic – or perhaps one could call it the logic of undecidability – the point where two (or three) thinkers appear to be farthest apart is always potentially the point where they are in fact closest together. This seems to be the case here. From Derrida's perspective, what eludes Hegel's conceptual and speculative grasp – but is implicit nonetheless in his analysis of *Antigone* – is highly significant, as Derrida suggests when he writes of Hegel's 'fascination with a figure that is inadmissible to the system' (pp. 171, 151e). That figure is Antigone, who, Derrida argues, is being referred to by Hegel's text even when she is not explicitly named – a situation that testifies all the more clearly to her power (pp. 169, 150e).

To begin with, the critical power of the figure of Antigone derives in part from her association with the family. Although, as we have seen, in certain respects her relegation to the family is interpreted as negative by Derrida, ironically it also has a potentially positive significance. Unlike those who have argued that issues relating to women cannot be explored in terms of the life of the family without prejudicing the outcome, Derrida argues explicitly that the family provides a frame for the discussion of such issues that may not be better but that is no worse than any other. There is no guarantee, according to Derrida, that the 'dissolution of the family,' either in practical or theoretical terms, would mean the end of 'phallocentrism, of idealism, of metaphysics' (pp. 211, 188e). Moreover, when one considers the interpretation that Derrida gives to Hegel's concept of the family, the relative advantage of using a description of family life such as Hegel's as a starting point for a critique of phallocentrism becomes clear: as we have seen, in Derrida's reading, the family is the agent and milieu of repression. Thus, by considering the issue of femininity in the context of the family, Derrida is able to explore it without divorcing it conceptually from the process of repression.

But while Derrida argues that one cannot escape from phallocentrism by dissolving the family, he also indicates that neither does one escape from it by remaining wholly within the family, particularly if it means basing one's critique of phallocentrism on the value of love as the family's binding force. In this sense, Hegel's decision to focus on the sister, who is neither wife nor mother nor daughter, and who is therefore more peripheral to the family in terms of its erotic and conservative interests, is not entirely negative. The same can be said of his insistence on defining the role of the sister in terms of her relationship to death and in particular to her *dead* brother rather than to desire or love. It has a critical value in highlighting another force or other forces in the family and those dimensions of the feminine that are not purely libidinal in nature. These other forces risk being obscured or even repressed in any family portrait that depicts the family as bound together by love and the woman as the primary agent of Eros.

But what exactly are the other, non-erotic forces in the family? In *Beyond the Pleasure Principle*, Freud identifies the aggressive instincts or the death drive as counter-forces to Eros, and in *Civilization and its Discontents*, he goes on to argue that the family and civilization itself are both essentially agents of the latter in its struggle against the former. Like *Civilization and its Discontents*, Hegel's interpretation of the *Sittlichkeit* also gives an important place to death. Unlike Freud, however, Hegel does not depict the family as bound together by the force of love and struggling against death, but rather as itself an agent of death, at least in its human form. This point is underscored by Derrida when he writes that according to Hegel's view of the *Sittlichkeit*: 'One belongs to a family only by busying oneself about the dead person. . . . The family does not yet know the productive work of universality in the city, but only the work of mourning' (pp. 162, 143e). As a result, the woman (particularly the sister), because she is especially charged with the duty of carrying out funeral rites for her dead brother, becomes the representative as much of death as of Eros, and the household economy becomes an economy of the dead [*économie du mort*] as much as of the living (pp. 162, 143e).

A question thus naturally arises as to the connection between the depiction of the family as the agent and milieu of repression, on the one hand, and its depiction as an entity organized by an 'economy of the dead,' on the other.

What exactly is the relation between repression and the death drive as they are represented in this portrait of the family? In a slightly different connection, Jacques Lacan has argued that the death drive and repression have an especially intimate relation: 'When speaking of repression, Freud asks himself where the ego obtains the energy it puts at the service of the 'reality principle.' The answer to this question, Lacan goes on to assert, was not difficult for Freud to find. He needed to 'look no further' than to what Lacan in the same passage calls the "negative' libido' or death drive.[17] In this passage, Lacan describes the connection between repression and the death drive by identifying the latter as the source from which repression draws its energy.

The picture of the relationship of repression and the death drive is somewhat different in *Glas*, because the (positive) libido itself is just as intimately involved in the process of repression as the death drive, as we have seen Derrida indicate at more than one point in his discussion of the family, as well as in the following, dense passage, whose meaning is dramatically complicated by punning and double entendres:

> The end of pleasure [*la jouissance*] is the end of pleasure: period. The snag [*l'os* – also, the bone] of pleasure, its possibility and its loss, lies in the fact that it must sacrifice itself to be there, to give itself its *there*, in order to approach [*toucher à* – also, to touch or to play with] its *Da-sein*. [The] *Telos* [*tel os* – such a bone] of pleasure equals death.
>
> (pp. 289, 260e)

In terms of the logic of this passage, it is impossible to distinguish any longer between, on the one hand, the pleasure principle and, on the other hand, a death drive that now appears not as the external but rather as the *internal* limitation or inhibition of the pleasure principle – that is, as the telos of pleasure. Pleasure is not simply 'there,' because it is finally (and therefore originally) compromised by the death drive, which structures it from within. It would thus not be completely accurate to say that for Derrida the death drive is the source of repression, as is the case for Lacan. Instead, in Derrida's terms it would be more accurate to say that repression is already implicit in the duality of the drives, a duality that can bring them into conflict even though it does not prevent them from reinforcing each other.

If the theme of death has an important role in Derrida's interpretation of the family, then, it is not because he seeks to establish that aggression and the death drive are more central to the family than love. He highlights the theme of death to the extent he does in order rather to stress the undecidable nature of family affect and of affect in general. In her role as the principal representative of the family in its conflict with the state, the sister, Antigone, becomes the representative of the undecidable character of its affect as well.

From all this it is apparent that there is an ultimate irony or paradox in Hegel's interpretation of the figure of Antigone as it relates to psychoanalysis. Hegel appears to diverge most radically from Freud when he describes Antigone's relation to her brother as being 'pure and without desire.' But it is precisely because of the emphasis he places on the overcoming of desire in his analysis of the brother/sister relation in *Antigone* that Hegel can also be said to be Freudian and even to point beyond Freud, to diverge from Freud without simply reverting to a pre-Freudian position. This is because we can now see the overcoming of desire as intimately related to desire. Derrida's question about the absence of desire in the brother/sister relation – 'Is it possible? Is it in contradiction with the whole system?' – turns out to have another sense, which is anything but rhetorical. It is not in contradiction with the whole system, provided we see that system as one open to two very different interpretations that are necessitated by the undecidable nature of its telos, understood as 'the end of pleasure.' This is what Derrida indicates when he writes of Antigone and of the brother/sister relation and refers to the latter as 'this powerful liaison without desire, this immense impossible desire that could not live' (pp. 187, 166e).

Inasmuch as Antigone, the woman-as-sister, symbolizes the deeply ambiguous nature of desire or pleasure, she can also be seen as a figure of the process of repression/idealization itself. That she is such a figure is evident in the terms in which Derrida links her to Hegel's concept of the transcendental. He argues that Antigone does not capture Hegel's attention because she embodies a radical alterity totally removed from the speculative system. Instead, she compels interest as a figure who exemplifies or who even *is* the 'transcendental' itself. But because of the manner in which Antigone is ultimately suppressed by her entombment and the sense of consolation Hegel holds it affords, Derrida asks if she cannot be seen simultaneously as 'what cannot be received, formed, terminated in any of the categories internal to the system. The vomit of the system. And what if the sister, the brother/sister relation here represented the positing, the ex-positing, of the *transcendental*?' (pp. 183, 162e). The image Derrida uses in this passage recalls his argument concerning the manner in which the dialectic, understood as a process of repression, both constitutes reason and at the same time eludes its grasp. When he writes that Antigone represents the transcendental itself as the 'vomit' of the transcendental system, he is suggesting that she represents what is internal and essential to the transcendental system as being simultaneously alien to it.[18] In this sense, she is a figure for the process of repression/*Aufhebung* that makes the entire transcendental system undecidable, the fulfilment as much of desire as repression, the expression as much of instinct as reason.

As we have seen, Derrida focuses on the figure of Antigone in a manner that continually underscores the central nature of the question of femininity not only to the philosophy of Hegel but also to the position he himself elaborates in his reading of the Hegelian text. That this feminine figure plays a central role for Derrida himself is indicated when he explicitly identifies with Hegel and his 'fascination' with the figure of Antigone: 'Like Hegel, I have been fascinated by Antigone' (pp. 187, 166e). But the term 'fascination,' while it testifies to the importance that Derrida attaches to Antigone, also seems to suggest that there is a potential danger of attaching too much importance to her. It is apparently in this spirit that Derrida asks: 'Will it be said that Hegel transformed an empirical situation described in a particular text taken from the history of the tragic genre into a structural and paradigmatic legal form? And did so in order to serve an obscure cause . . . or an obscure sister?' (pp. 186, 165e).

This passage applies explicitly to Hegel, but its interest derives from the fact that it could just as well be applied, with minor modifications, to Freud and even to Derrida himself. Freud, like Hegel, was to transform 'an empirical situation' into a 'structural and paradigmatic legal form' by invoking the authority of another Greek tragedy, *Oedipus Rex*. Freud's 'Oedipocentric' theory – to borrow a term Derrida uses in 'To Speculate – on 'Freud" (p. 361) – is thus prefigured by and is not essentially different from Hegel's speculative system, insofar as it too testifies to a fascination with the protagonist of a Greek tragedy. One could go on and say the same thing with respect to the values or themes expressed in the figure of Oedipus and the figure of Antigone. Like life, Eros, and masculinity, the themes of death, desire, femininity, and repression exemplified by Hegel's (or Derrida's?) Antigone can also become – or already are – conservative values, which may be enlisted in the service of traditional phallocentrism. We have seen Derrida remind his reader that one does not necessarily escape from phallocentrism by leaving the family behind. By the same token, Derrida's remarks on the privilege Hegel attaches to Antigone indicate that neither does one escape from it when one discards the hero of *Oedipus Rex* for another tragic persona, even a feminine one such as Antigone.

There is thus a general danger involved in privileging the figure of Antigone, the danger that theory inevitably faces when it has recourse to literary (or empirical) examples, perhaps especially when it privileges a particular literary text over all others. But in Derrida's terms there is a more specific danger associated with privileging Antigone as a woman. The danger in question is that of identifying undecidability with the woman and thereby determining that fetishism, the form of repression that defines itself specifically in relation to the woman, is not simply one instance of repression among many but *the* instance of repression, the model of all repression. Because if fetishism is the model form of repression, then that can only mean we have accepted castration as the founding reality of psychic experience. Once we have done this, it makes little difference if we affirm castration or attempt to refute it. Either way we are caught in the logic of fetishism itself, as Derrida suggests when he asks at one point: 'As much as one criticizes fetishism . . . will one [thereby] have touched [questioned, tampered with] the economy of metaphysics?' ('Tant qu'on critiquera le fétichisme . . . aura-t-on touché à l'économie de la métaphysique?') (pp. 232, 206–207e).

The limitation inherent in any critique of fetishism or castration is further brought out in a passage from the Genet column discussing castration, fetishism, and sexual difference, where Derrida writes:

> 'This does not mean that there is no castration but that this *there is* has no place [or does not take place]. 'There is' that one can no more sever [*trancher*, which also means 'decide' between] the two contrary, acknowledged functions of the fetish than the thing in itself and its supplement. Or the sexes.'

(pp. 256, 229e)

The problem with the idea of castration is not that it is false. The problem is the 'givenness' (the 'there-is-ness') of castration or of the difference between the sexes that is assumed whether castration is affirmed or denied. It is this 'givenness' that 'n'a pas lieu,' that does not take place or that has no place. Castration, like 'the masculine' and 'the feminine,' is never unambiguously 'given,' even in terms of the supposedly naive perspective of the child, that is, even in order to be negated or transcended.

The reference in the passage quoted above to a Lacanian interpretation of sexual difference is unmistakable. As Derrida had previously argued in 'Le facteur de la vérité,' although Lacan constantly insists on the distinction between the phallus, on the one hand, and both the penis and the clitoris, on the other, at the same time in Lacan's terms the phallus 'mostly and primarily symbolizes the penis.'[19] By the same token, the (symbolic) castration in question in Lacanian theory is a localized one that does indeed *have a place* or *take place* — 'on the immense body of the woman, between the "legs" (*jambages*) of the fireplace' (p. 440) — the place designated metaphorically by the mantle of the fireplace in Poe's 'The Purloined Letter.' In this Lacanian model, neither sex is seen as possessing the phallus, but castration is nonetheless more closely linked to the woman, and in this sense, Lacanian psychoanalysis defines and defends the reality of castration through a negation of it.[20]

In Derrida's terms, then, there is no possibility of ever staging a 'primal scene,' whether of an historical, cultural, or symbolic nature, that would account for — or give a place to — castration. There is no immediate ('at once') recognition of the reality of castration (Freud); no symbolic experience of 'the lack,' whether one is speaking of a lack implied by castration or by the purportedly arbitrary nature of language (Lacan); nor even an experience that takes the form of the child's 'panicked reaction when confronted with the sex of the woman' (Kofman). It is not the content of any of these scenes that is most problematic. It is the 'given-ness' each presupposes, whether that given-ness is understood as natural, cultural, or symbolic. In each case, what is in question is not 'a real event but an economic simulacrum' (pp. 52, 43e). In other words, in each case, the process of repression/idealization has always-already begun. Repression is thus not inaugurated by fetishism but rather presupposed by it. That is why 'you cannot even understand what you mean by castration if you do not take on all of the idealism of the speculative dialectic' (pp. 52, 43e).[21]

But if there is a danger in giving a central place to Antigone as a woman, there is an equally great danger involved in ignoring or suppressing her femininity. Derrida indicates as much in a passage already quoted above when he writes that one cannot 'trancher . . . entre les sexes,' which means both 'sever the sexes [from one another]' and 'decide between them.' If we cannot 'decide' between the sexes, this implies that, like reason and instinct or Eros and death, masculinity and femininity are not just external and hence opposable to one another, but that each structures the other 'in the most internal and essential manner.' If there is thus no pure femininity or pure masculinity, it is nonetheless important to respect the relative specificity of femininity (and masculinity) precisely in order to avoid reducing one to the other and in the process reducing the complex nature of each 'in itself.'

In the end, then, the contrast between Freud's chosen text and Hegel's is what gives Hegel's figure of Antigone the particular critical power it possesses in *Glas*, perhaps precisely because the manner in which it sustains the speculative system compares with the manner in which the figure of Oedipus sustains psychoanalysis. That is to say, it is the mere possibility of this comparison that reveals the arbitrary nature of Freud's choice. By referring so extensively in *Glas* to the figure of Antigone, Derrida exploits the critical potential of the implied contrast between *Antigone* and *Oedipus Rex*, a potential that lies in the equally legitimate but nonetheless in many ways diametrically opposed claim of each of these tragic dramas to be considered what Hegel would have called 'the most perfect work' of all, or what, in the logic of Derrida's argument, might be termed the text that best sustains the system of practices, values, beliefs, and concepts that has been called 'metaphysics.' Indeed, one of the most important effects of *Glas*, I would argue, is to have heightened significantly our sense of the constitutive role played by tragedy in (psychoanalytic) theory and the manner in which Freud's and Hegel's choices of their literary examples or models do not simply reflect but also to an important extent shape their theoretical perspectives.[22]

In the wake of *Glas*, Freud's essays on female sexuality appear as an attempt not only to deal with but also to limit the impact of the question of the feminine on the theoretical edifice he had elaborated. But in terms of the logic of *Glas*, it appears that any such attempt is bound to fail. Because of the manner in which the concepts of repression and femininity are linked, it is clear that the issue of the feminine is not just a specific one that can be treated separately from the whole of psychoanalytic theory. Rather it is a much broader question that implies a rereading of Freud's entire corpus and a reinterpretation of masculinity as much as of femininity. But I say 'rereading' rather than 'rejection,' because it remains true that we are as much if not more indebted to Freud for what could be called an enlarged or primary concept of repression than to anyone else. And any attempt to address the question of sexuality or gender from a perspective that ignores the fundamental nature of repression risks being caught in the logic of fetishism, that is, in a logic that is Freudian or even pre-Freudian rather than post-Freudian.

It is probably inevitable that various forms of 'theory' attempt to grasp the objective nature of sexuality and gender by means of models that purportedly depict their essence or deep structure. But a Freudian/Hegelian sense of the process of repression, while it would not lead us to discard all models, can help us see them in more critical terms, to appreciate their ambiguous significance, to see them as the expression of what are in each case potentially ambivalent feelings.

In a similar spirit, the difficult nature of the question of the development of the child can also be seen, because any 'telos' that one might posit for that development would have to be critically considered in its contradictory ambiguity. In this connection, the idea that one cannot 'sever the link between . . . the sexes' (Genet column, pp. 256, 229e) implies that a masculine (or is it 'feminine'?) telos is always intimately linked to a feminine (or is it masculine?) telos, and thus it is never clear where the 'destiny' of the individual lies. Like the dream-work, the process of development is an open-ended, ongoing one whose structure and essence are to be found in no single, unequivocal origin, end, or model.

As we have seen, the aspects of Derrida's reading of Hegel that I have argued suggest the necessity of rethinking the problem of the feminine in terms of the concept of repression contain many indications as to the theoretical implications of such a project. But the formal and thematic fragmentation of *Glas* also points beyond *Glas* itself and indicates the necessity of having recourse to other texts, other readings, and even other forms of experience in order to continue the work that is begun in *Glas*. The fragmentation of *Glas* testifies to the idea that the *glas* for both speculative philosophy and psychoanalysis has already sounded, because they no longer − if they ever did − have the power to close off the systems they generated, to think those ideas they nonetheless make necessary, or even to supply by themselves the basis of a commentary or interpretation that could fill in their gaps. But of course this fragmentation also serves to underscore the point that the work of philosophy and psychoanalysis − that is, the work of philosophy in psychoanalysis and of psychoanalysis in philosophy − is ongoing and that in a sense it has just begun.

# 7

# Hegel/Marx: Consciousness and Life

*Andrzej Warminski*

*For the philosophers' relationship = idea*. They only know the relation of 'Man' to himself and hence for them, all real relations become ideas.

*Verhältnis für die Philosophen = Idee*. Sie kennen bloß das Verhältnis 'des Menschen' zu sich selbst, und darum werden alle wirklichen Verhältnisse ihnen zu Ideen.[1]

To begin reading the Hegel/Marx relationship, we may as well start with their differing versions of the relation between consciousness and life: 'It's not consciousness that determines life,' writes Marx in a well-known sentence of *The German Ideology*, 'but rather life determines consciousness (*Nicht das Bewußtsein bestimmt das Leben, sondern das Leben bestimmt das Bewußtsein*).'[2] If the sentence is well-known, it is no doubt because both in its content and in its form it expresses what we all know about Marx's relation to Hegel and Hegelian philosophy: that is, an apparently straightforward substitution of 'life,' 'real life,' for 'consciousness,' for the primacy of consciousness in the understanding of the human being, by means of an apparently equally straightforward (chiasmic) inversion or reversal of the terms 'life' and 'consciousness' in a hierarchical opposition or relation. Of course, in context the immediate targets of this operation are the *Young* Hegelians, but it is clear enough that they can *be* its targets because, despite their claims and pretensions, they do *not* challenge the primacy of consciousness (over life) and hence do *not* differ from the Old Hegelians (or, presumably, the Old Hegel). For despite their attempt to *criticize* everything – in particular the concepts of idealist philosophy – by taking it as the product of man's self-alienation in religious or theological projections, the Young Hegelians nevertheless agree with the Old Hegelians in

171

their belief in the rule of religion, of concepts, of the universal in the existent world. In other words, because all they do is to substitute one consciousness for another – for instance, a human, man-centered consciousness for a religious, God-centered consciousness – the Young Hegelians never challenge the primacy of consciousness itself. Rather than changing the world, they manage only to interpret it differently, that is, only to *know* it by means of another interpretation.

All this is indeed very well-known. If I rehearse it here one more time, it is only in order to remind us that from the outset of *The German Ideology*, the main thrust of Marx's critique is directed against those who would *criticize* Hegel or Hegelian philosophy by performing a species of inversion, of mere overturning, of setting the Hegelian philosophy back on its feet by substituting a purported materialism for a purported idealism. As *The German Ideology* never tires of telling us, a mere inversion does nothing to change either the terms inverted or the relation between them. A self-proclaimed 'materialism' that defines itself as the symmetrical inversion and negation of idealism winds up being defined and determined by that idealism as its own determinate negation. This is pithily illustrated by Feuerbach's predicament: in short, because his stress on human sensuous existence, his conceiving man as an 'object of the senses,' is an abstraction from human 'sensuous activity' in given social relations, Feuerbach winds up with an abstract materialism that cannot account for *men* as products of a history of production and hence cannot provide a 'criticism of the present conditions of life.' Whereas as soon as he does try to account for the historical conditions, Feuerbach has to have recourse to idealist conceptions:

> [Feuerbach] gives no criticism of the present conditions of life. Thus he never manages to conceive the sensuous world as the total living sensuous *activity* of the individuals composing it; therefore when, for example, he sees instead of healthy men a crowd of scrofulous, overworked and consumptive starvelings, he is compelled to take refuge in the "higher perception" and in the ideal "compensation of the species" ("*ideelen Ausgleichung in der Gattung*"), and thus to relapse into idealism at the very point where the communist materialist sees the necessity, and at the same time the condition, of a transformation both of industry and of the social structure. As far as Feuerbach is a materialist he does not deal with history, and as far as he considers history he is not a materialist.[3]

The dialectical edge of Marx's critique could not be clearer: an abstract 'materialism' – the ahistorical reification of 'man' and his sensuous existence

– all too easily turns over into an equally abstract idealism. Rather than being a critique of Hegelian absolute idealism, such a materialism only comes up with a more naive, because undialectical, pre-critical idealism.

The upshot would be that whatever Marx may mean by all the formulations that suggest a reversal or an inversion of the terms of a hierarchical opposition – like 'consciousness' and 'life,' for instance – the one thing he *cannot* mean is a *mere* inversion, a mere reversal, for that is precisely the (non-)critique of Hegel performed by the German Ideologists, who thereby fall back into a *pre*-Hegelian position. And, indeed, in the case of the life/consciousness relation, it is easy enough to see that for a dialectical thought it makes no difference which determines which as long as their relation remains one of determination. For Hegel – as for Spinoza – *omnis determinatio est negatio*, and therefore it does not matter whether consciousness is said to determine (*bestimmen*) life or life consciousness – as long as one determines the other, it is mediatable with it thanks to the work of the determinate negative. For life to determine consciousness means for it still to be the negation *of* consciousness, consciousness's *own negation*, which needs to be negated in turn so that consciousness can verify and become itself, consciousness (and so that life can be relegated to an essential, necessary moment [of truth, of verification] of consciousness: consciousness = life sublated, *das aufgehobene Leben*, one could say). So if Marx's statement that life determines consciousness (rather than *vice versa*) is going to make a difference, is going to mean anything different from the eminently sublatable differences of determinate negation, then both the nature of the terms 'life' and 'consciousness' and the nature of the relation (of 'determination' [*bestimmen*]) between them before and after the inversion need to be rewritten, reinscribed: or, schematically put, Marx's operation cannot be one of mere inversion, mere overturning – that is what the Young Hegelians do and he criticizes them for it – but rather has to be an operation of inversion and reinscription – in short, a full-scale 'deconstruction' of both consciousness *and* life and the 'relation' between them. In other words, however symmetrical the chiasmic reversal may seem – and however parallel the determining (*bestimmen*) before the inversion and after the inversion – what Marx is actually saying (and *has* to be saying if he is to be Marx and not just another Young Hegelian or German Ideologist) is that life, real life, determines consciousness in a way that consciousness cannot master, cannot come up against as a merely determinately negative object *of* consciousness, of itself *as* consciousness. In short, life *over*-determines consciousness – it is made up of contradictions and a negativity, call it, that cannot be reduced to (i.e. mediated,

173

sublated, into) one, simple, determined negation.[4] And we do not have to look far in *The German Ideology* to begin to determine what the nature of this over-determination is. Life, the real life of human beings, is not biological, appetitive existence but rather the product of a history of production: men distinguish themselves from animals not by consciousness, not by knowing, but by producing their means of subsistence. In other words, life is not a given, positive fact but rather produced by the labor of human beings, who constitute themselves *as* human in this history of material production. Whereas consciousness is the (historical, material) *relation* of these human beings first to nature and then to other human beings – a relation that is historical and material because it is not one 'mediated' by knowing (and all the determinations that come with it: subject and object, truth and certainty, in itself and for itself, etc.) but by the historical materiality of relations of production (and *its* determinations, like the division of labor, class divisions, etc.). It is no surprise, then, that according to *The German Ideology*, consciousness and its products, when they come into existence, do so as the 'conscious expression' (*der bewußte Ausdruck*) or the 'direct efflux' (*der direkte Ausfluß*) *of* these relations of production, what the text calls 'the language of real life' (*die Sprache des wirklichen Lebens*).[5] Indeed, consciousness, when it comes on the scene, appears not as pure consciousness or as 'pure spirit' but rather as 'burdened' with matter 'which here steps on the scene in the form of moving layers of air, sounds, in short, language.'[6] Only if this language of real life is alienated from itself – only if in addition to the spirit (*Geist*) of real, material individuals a spirit apart (*einen aparten Geist*) is invented, only if a consciousness other than the consciousness of existent praxis is imagined – can consciousness free itself from the world and go over (*überzugehen*) by means of a species of metaphorical transport to the formation (*Bildung*) of 'pure theory,' theology, philosophy, morality – i.e. ideologies.[7] Much is implied about language – about the language of a material spirit or a material consciousness as distinguished from the language of a ghostly redoubled *Geist* or consciousness apart, the language of ideology – and not least of all a certain hint as to *why* a mere demystification of an ideological formation by an inversion or overturning always remains insufficient: that is, if the language of ideology is the projected figure for a second, spectral *Geist* or consciousness apart, then an interpretation *of* those figures that confines itself to unmasking them *as* figures, *as* projections, will only manage to uncover and return to the literality of the *Geist* or consciousness apart – a still abstract, reified consciousness like the sensuous consciousness of Feuerbach. (To demystify the religious realm in the clouds as an alienated projection, a figure, of the secular, earthly realm below – or to show that the Holy Family is an alienated projection of the earthly family – is still not to be able to explain *why* the earthly secular basis needed to divide itself from itself in this way and to project a heavenly realm in the clouds as its own symmetrical, determinate negation – as though it *were* one, unified, homogeneous and not a 'secular basis' riven by over-determined contradictions like those of class divisions which need to be covered by being ideologized into determined contradictions like that between human and divine, earthly and religious, sensuous and spiritual, etc.)[8] This amounts to saying, in other words, that the language of ideology is what one could call an 'allegorical' language: one that represents, figures, one thing but actually *means*, signifies, points to, refers to, something else. Hence it can never be enough to unmask or demystify its phenomenal appearance, its figural, representational function – this would be to fall into the trap that ideologies set for critics – rather its allegorical, pointing, referential (carrying back) function also needs to be *read* in its over-determined historical materiality.[9]

But that is easily said. That is, it may be easy enough to wield terms like 'over-determination' or 'over-determined contradiction' and to insist that what is necessary for Marx to become Marx is not only an inversion but also a 'reinscription' of the life/consciousness relation; more difficult is to take the full measure of what lurks behind these more or less convenient ciphers or place-holders – ciphers or place-holders for what actually *happens*, what is historical and material in the reading (or the writing) of a text. In the case of the text Hegel/Marx, to say that what Marx performs is a 'deconstruction' of the relation of consciousness and life in Hegel does not mean that there is a 'deconstructible' Hegelian relation there 'before' the operation (of inversion and reinscription) and a 'deconstructed' Marxian relation there 'after' the operation (of inversion and reinscription). In fact, to think this about Hegel/Marx (or, for that matter, about deconstruction) is precisely German Ideology – the operation that 'critiques' not Hegel but a caricature of Hegel, not Hegel as the text that *happens* (historically, materially) but Hegel as a cliché of intellectual history. For indeed if 'Hegel' were just some kind of subjective idealist who reduces 'life' to 'consciousness' – all sensuous otherness to sublatable moments in the progress of self-consciousness to absolute knowing, to an utterly transparent self-consciousness of self-consciousness – then it would be hard to understand not only how such a Hegel could be Hegel (rather than, say, a relatively simple-minded Fichte) but also how Marx could ever have become Marx by critiquing (however 'deconstructively') such a Hegel: that is, how Marx could have ever found the resources he needed in

175

Hegel to become Marx, i.e., to *happen* (historically, materially) *as* Marx and not as a Young Hegelian.[10] (As is already legible in the critique of Hegel in the *Economic and Philosophical Manuscripts of 1844*, even the pre-'epistemological break,' apparently Feuerbachian Marx knew better, read Hegel better, than that.) In short, I am asking about that which would be the historical, the material, in, *of*, 'Hegel,' of Hegel's text – whatever it is that made it happen. Or, in other words, what is it that could be said to be *alive*, living, in Hegel's text? Whatever it is, this 'life' of Hegel's text – if it is understood in a Marxian (historical, material) sense – would be a life that exceeds consciousness by *over*determining it and hence a life that threatens to interrupt irrevocably the entire project of a 'science of the experience of consciousness' or a *Phenomenology of Spirit*.[11] So how should we read the life of Hegel's text, a life that would also be the death of the *Phenomenology of Spirit*?

The moment of what Hegel calls 'life' in the *Phenomenology of Spirit* is very precisely determined, and, as it turns out, even thinking its *determinately* negative relation to consciousness is no simple matter. That is, 'life' appears in one of the most difficult passages in the entire *Phenomenology*: i.e., the short introductory section to the chapter on 'self-consciousness' entitled 'The Truth of Self-certainty.' This eight-page passage is *so* difficult, in· fact, that many otherwise diligent commentators simply give up on it – sometimes very explicitly – and prefer immediately to go over to the master/slave dialectic that is its result.[12] Those who do not just skip it and do manage to say something about it nevertheless do not really read it and instead content themselves with telling what *should* happen, what *must* happen, what *must have* happened, in order for us to understand why and how it is that we are reading about a fight for recognition between self-consciousness and self-consciousness that issues in one's becoming master and the other slave. But even a perfunctory account of what should happen or should have happened in the dialectics of life and desire cannot occult the fact of this section's absolutely crucial importance for the project of the *Phenomenology of Spirit*. The passage is crucial most obviously because it marks a moment of transition between the end of the section on 'consciousness' and the beginning of the section on 'Self-consciousness.' Marking this transition has particular importance because its burden amounts to being able to explain why and how self-consciousness *as* self-consciousness is possible. And explaining how and why self-consciousness is possible is absolutely necessary because it turned out that consciousness in order to be what it is – i.e. knowing as knowing something – has to be, has to have *already* been, in truth, in essence, *self*-consciousness, i.e. self-knowing. In other words, consciousness can be what it is only because it is essentially self-consciousness – self-consciousness in its truth – and hence self-consciousness is the new object of knowing that comes on the scene, appears, in this presentation of apparent knowing – the new object (which, clearly, is also a *subject*) of knowing whose claim to truth has to be examined and verified in turn. In short, self-consciousness *is*, what would it have to be in order to *be* (in truth, in essence, in itself, *an sich*) self-consciousness? Formally speaking, the answer is very easy: to go on the model of the dialectical movement of consciousness, if the truth of consciousness is *self*-consciousness, the truth of knowing *self*-knowing, then the truth of *self*-consciousness, of *self*-knowing, would have to be self-consciousness *of* self-consciousness, self-knowing *of* self-knowing – in other words, a redoubling of self-consciousness would be the necessary and the only *sufficient* condition of the existence of self-consciousness *as* self-consciousness. We all know this – this is indeed what has to happen in order to issue in the dialectic of master and slave – but, of course, what *we* know is in fact only the formal side, the formal aspect, of the arising of the new figure (*Gestalt*) and the new object of apparent knowing (as the 'Introduction' to the *Phenomenology* had put it).[13] The *content* of this new figure of apparent knowing has to be gone through, and this can only be done by the consciousness going through the experience of *knowing*, of thinking that first *this* and then *that* is the true object of a certain knowing – the experience of itself, consciousness, on the way to absolute consciousness, absolute knowing. We cannot *tell* it what it has to be in order to be what it is but rather can only observe how on its own it comes to know what it is in and for itself. How does it?

It does it by becoming desire (*Begierde*). That is, when self-consciousness arises as the new object, the new truth, the new in-itself, of consciousness, it appears as *desire*: self-consciousness is first of all desire. Why so? To paraphrase the second paragraph of 'The Truth of Self-certainty' (§167 in Miller's numbering): when the truth of consciousness turns out to be self-consciousness, knowing as the knowing of an other (*Wissen von einem Andern*) turns out to be knowing of itself (*Wissen von sich selbst*). In this dialectical movement of the experience of consciousness, the *other* that consciousness claimed to know in truth would seem to have disappeared – knowing of an other has become knowing of itself. But the moments of this other (of knowing) have at the same time been preserved, they are in fact present as they are in themselves, in their essence – which essence consists of their being essentially (in truth, in themselves) disappearing essences (*verschwindende Wesen*), essences whose essence is to disappear, or, better, to *be* disappearing. As such, these essences are preserved as *moments* of self-consciousness – a self-consciousness that (as the result of the dialectic of consciousness) has turned out to be a reflection out of the being of the sensuous and perceived world and essentially a return out of other-being (*Aber in der Tat ist das Selbstbewußtsein die Reflexion aus dem Sein der sinnlichen und wahrgenommenen Welt und wesentlich Rückkehr aus dem Anderssein*). 'It [self-consciousness] is as self-consciousness movement (*Es ist als Selbstbewußtsein Bewegung*).' But – and this 'but' articulates the negative moment in the dialectic of what will shortly be given the name 'desire' – since these essences of other-being are essentially disappearing essences, the movement of self-consciousness out of the sensuous and perceived world and of return out of other-being remains a tautologous movement in which it goes out from and comes back to only itself because it differentiates *only* itself *as* itself *from* itself. The differentiation between itself and its other-being *is* not, has no being, and hence it falls back into the movement-less tautology of the 'I am I.' And *as* bereft of *movement*, it *is* not self-consciousness, since *as* self-consciousness it is movement.

This dialectic is in fact already the dialectic of self-consciousness as desire. That is, self-consciousness is here desire because it appears under the sign of a double lack, a negativity proper to itself as desire. In brief: because self-consciousness at this (preliminary) stage has only itself, the unity of the tautologous 'I am I,' as its truth, it does not have an other-being that, simply put, is *other* enough for it to be able to verify itself (the unity of the 'I am I') in it, to make itself *true* in an essence (an in-itself, a truth) that would have enough *being*, enough existence, to verify self-consciousness, that is, an essence whose own being, truth, in-itself, essence, did *not* consist in being a disappearing essence. Hence it is desire: desire first of all for self-verification in an other that would be other enough as its own other – the other *of* itself (i.e. the unity of the 'I am I'), of self-consciousness. The other-being of the other of itself, self-consciousness, as desire always turns out to be not *other enough*: it is in fact all too easily annihilated, sublated, like the object of an appetitive desire for nourishment. Take the potato. The two moments of self-consciousness as desire can be demonstrated on it – before and after eating. First, there is the moment of other-being (*Anderssein*). I recognize myself in the otherness of the potato: this is my potato in which I can recognize myself, verify myself, it is my other, etc. In this case – before eating – I depend on an other external to me, to the 'I,' for my identity, my being, and therefore I cannot recognize myself in it *as* a self, *as* an 'I.' I can recognize myself in it only *as* a potato. The 'I' becomes a potato – i.e. *not* a self-consciousness. Then, there is the second moment: the unity of self-consciousness with itself, the 'I am I.' That is, I eat the potato, thereby annihilating its otherness, negating the negativity of its other-being; but, in doing so, I also negate that in which I recognized myself, the other on which I depended to verify myself (albeit as a potato), and hence I am thrown back on my sheer self, the empty, movement-less tautology of the 'I am I.' In short, I negate myself not *as* a self but as a potato – i.e. *not* a self-consciousness. In the first moment – before eating – the other-being of the other is *too* essential, that is, it negates me too immediately to be, to allow me to be, the negation *of* self-consciousness. In the second moment – after eating – the other-being of the other is not essential enough, and my negation of its otherness is too immediate. So in the first case, the potato negates self-consciousness too immediately; in the second case, I negate the potato (*my* negation) too immediately. In the first case, I revert to the position of mere *consciousness* – i.e. that for which the truth of knowing is the otherness of the sensory outside – in the second case, I remain a merely one-sided, abstract, tauto-logous *self-consciousness*. What is the point? The point is that the potato is not yet essential enough for self-consciousness. That is, it is essential enough for self-consciousness *as desire*, but not for self-consciousness *as self-consciousness*. And the point becomes clearer perhaps once we recall that the objects of desire, of self-consciousness as desire, are *living*, are *life*. The potato I desire to eat is the object of self-consciousness as living and desiring – in fact, as desiring to live – and not of self-consciousness as self-consciousness, as self-knowing. This means that in the potato, for example, life is not yet essential enough for self-consciousness. And this sentence has to be read in two registers, as it were, according to two emphases, two stresses: either on the word 'self-conscious-ness' or on the word 'life.' On the one hand, we need to emphasize the word 'self-consciousness' – life is not yet essential enough for *self-consciousness* – that is, life may be essential enough for self-consciousness as living and desiring, but since the essence (truth, *an sich*) of self-consciousness is not the otherness of life but rather the unity of itself with itself (the 'I am I'), life *cannot* be essential enough for *self-consciousness*. But, on the other hand, we need just as much to emphasize the word '*life*' – life is not yet essential enough for self-consciousness – that is, until self-consciousness can make life essential for itself *as* self-consciousness, it cannot become truly self-consciousness but rather remains at the stage of the tautologous 'I am I,' the merely immediate unity of itself with itself. Now the first hand – the stress on the word 'self-consciousness' (life is not yet essential enough for *self-consciousness*) – would certainly be obvious enough in the case of an idealism that would want to dissolve all non-conscious otherness, all merely living existence, into knowing, consciousness, mind, spirit, etc. It is no wonder that life would not be essential enough for *self-consciousness*! But the second, other hand – the stress on the word 'life' (*life* is not yet essential enough for self-consciousness) – should make us pause to elaborate its considerable implications: namely, first of all, the inescapable fact that whatever is going on here in the dialectics of desire and life is not your average, clichéd received idea of idealism. The burden of the passage is not at all a matter of self-consciousness's attempt to rid itself of any otherness that it cannot reduce to itself, but rather, if anything, precisely the opposite. That is, self-consciousness does indeed have to rid itself of all *merely immediate* otherness (because such other-being does not have enough existence, enough essence – it is a merely apparent, i.e. merely *disappearing*, essence) but in order that it may make otherness essential for itself. In short, it is not trying to annihilate, negate, the potato – that it can do easily enough, immediately enough, by eating it – but rather to make the potato essential, other enough, for self-consciousness. Life itself has to become (essential for, the essential other of) self-consciousness.

Another, more general, way to put this is to say that Hegel here does not take the 'easy' idealist way out. He does not begin with some kind of absolutely self-positing 'I' that can then take all 'non-I' as its own negation, but rather arrives at idealism's formula 'I am I' as the result of a dialectical movement of the experience of consciousness. And, to boot, *this* self-consciousness, whose truth (essence) is the unity of the 'I am I,' is not one that can be satisfied by, or verified in, an immediate negation of its other-being. No, it has to make its other-being – the object of self-consciousness as desire that is life – essential for itself, it has to show how it is that self-consciousness can emerge out of life itself, how self-consciousness *as* self-consciousness can emerge out of self-consciousness as desire (whose object is life). This is indeed quite a task that the *Phenomenology* has imposed on itself (by a dialectical necessity) at this point, and the size of the stakes has not gone unnoticed in the commentaries, especially in the 'anthropologizing' or 'existentialist' interpretations of readers like Kojève and Hyppolite, who see the *enjeu* as the question of how man, the human being (who they identify [too quickly] with self-consciousness), can emerge out of merely biological, appetitive, desiring, animal being.[14] How indeed? How will 'life' itself become the essential other of self-consciousness – again, the essential other of self-consciousness as self-consciousness and *not* of self-consciousness as desire? How can life by itself produce, as it were, its other *as* self-consciousness? And lest we think that the answer is easy – as 'easy' as the answer to the question of how self-consciousness is possible – and answer that the only way self-consciousness can emerge out of life *as* self-consciousness and not as desire is precisely by a negation of itself *as* desire, i.e. by means of a 'desire of desire,' let me say straight away that this is *not* what happens in Hegel. It may indeed be what *should* happen, what *must* happen, what *must have happened*, in order for us to arrive by the end of 'The Truth of Self-certainty' at the stage of a self-consciousness for a self-consciousness, but it is not what happens in Hegel's text. What in fact happens is weirder, odder, more *over*determined, hence something that produces a 'Hegel' other than the successfully Hegelian Hegel of Kojève and Hyppolite. Let me begin to spell it out.

What happens is this: in order to demonstrate how it is that life – the object of self-consciousness as desire – can become an other essential enough for self-consciousness to emerge *as* self-consciousness out of it, Hegel's argument goes over to one side of the dialectic of desire – namely, its object, life – and presents its dialectic. The burden on this presentation is clear: it has to be able to show that life itself, the object of self-consciousness as desire, undergoes the same movement, the same process of reflection into itself, as consciousness did in becoming self-conscious by a reflection out of the sensuous and perceived world and a return from other-being. In other words, self-consciousness is going to have to make the experience of the independence of its object – life – and learn that life is in fact independent enough – other enough, say – as independent as self-consciousness at this stage. And for it to be independent enough for self-consciousness, life is going to have to be shown to be self-negating enough for self-consciousness: it will have to negate itself just as self-consciousness does at the stage of desire. This is indeed what takes place, and it is certainly no surprise that it does so, for it is based on the most important element in Hegel's phenomenological presentation of apparent knowing: namely, the fact that for this presentation, knowing is always essentially knowing of something, of an object and a truth that are always determinately *the* object and *the* truth of that particular form of knowing. In short, when the knowing changes, so does the object known, for a new object (of knowing) arises along with a new subject of knowing.[15] So here if consciousness undergoes a movement of reflection into itself – i.e. it becomes self-consciousness as desire – so does its object – the apparently disappearing essences of the figures of consciousness – undergo a dialectical movement of reflection into itself. And *how* it does so is for us of less interest here – in part because the dialectic of life amounts to something of a mirror repetition of what took place on the side of the dialectic of desire – than its result. For short-hand purposes,

181

suffice it to say that in the end the determinations of life – like the subsistence and finitude of the individual and fluidity and infinity of the genus – wind up going through a dialectic of self and other at least like that of self-consciousness as desire: a self-constitution and a self-annihilation of life like that of the desiring self-consciousness and its potato. And whereas eating was an apt analogy for this process in the one case, so procreation is an appropriate analogy in the other: that is, in procreating, the individual living being annihilates itself as individual by rejoining the infinite fluidity of the genus (*Gattung*) *and*, at the same time, also reproduces itself *as* individual living being in the progeny that is the result of this procreative act.

> Thus the simple substance of Life is the splitting-up of itself into shapes and at the same time the dissolution of these existent differences; and the dissolution of the splitting-up is just as much a splitting-up and a forming of members.

> [*Die einfache Substanz des Lebens also ist die Entzweiung ihrer selbst in Gestalten und zugleich die Auflösung dieser bestehenden Unterschiede; und die Auflösung der Entzweiung ist ebensosehr Entzweien oder ein Gliedern*].[16]

This is all well and good for the task that the dialectic of life needs to accomplish. That is, it does indeed succeed in showing that life, in the result of its dialectic – i.e. genus (*Gattung*), the universal reflected (and hence no longer immediate) unity of itself with itself – seems to be independent enough for self-consciousness insofar as it seems to be self-negating enough for self-consciousness.

But sooner or later one has also to ask: is it knowing, conscious – self-knowing and self-conscious – enough for self-consciousness? Or, to put it another way, does life when it negates itself *know* that it negates itself in such a way (i.e. determinately) that its other will have to be knowing, consciousness, self-consciousness? Or, again, is there a necessity in life's self-negation (i.e. death) that necessarily results in the production of knowing, consciousness, self-consciousness? Perhaps the awkwardness of the question can be lessened if we put it in the somewhat jocular terms of the analogy of procreation. In short, does the cat, for example, when it desires to eat and procreate know that what it desires is (essentially, actually) to dissolve itself into the genus (the cat-*Gattung*?) and yet dialectically be reborn as individual? I do not know about you – or the cat – but I prefer to leave the question open. And, as it turns out, so does Hegel – or, at least the 'Hegel' that is the writing of the text. For, in fact, when the dialectic of life is finished up (in *Gattung*), when the argument is ready to take us back to the *other* side of the relation, namely back to self-consciousness, the text does not make the transition by means of a determinate negation that could mediate life and self-consciousness. Instead, what the text actually says is that life – in the result of its dialectic, i.e. genus (*Gattung*) – points to or indicates or beckons towards an other than it (life) is, namely consciousness, for which it (life) can be as this unity, or the genus (*in diesem Resultate verweist das Leben auf ein Anderes, als es ist, nämlich auf das Bewußtsein, für welches es als diese Einheit, oder als Gattung ist*).[17] The implications of this pointing of life towards, at, an other than itself are far-reaching, and I can only begin to outline them here. First of all, it means that whatever happens at this moment of transition, of return, from life back to consciousness and self-consciousness, the transition itself does not take place, is *not* said to take place, by means of a determinate negation. Consciousness here is not the *other* of life as its determinate negation but rather an other pointed to, indicated, beckoned to, referred to, by life. The argument that would demonstrate the possibility of the existence of self-consciousness (*as* self-consciousness) certainly *needs* this pointing operation to be that of a determined negation – and it needs to have this other of life be life's own other – but the text just as surely does not work this way, does not perform *this* operation. Rather what the text does is to introduce something of a 'linguistic moment' into the relation of life and consciousness and, in doing so, threatens to render impossible not only the emergence of self-consciousness (*as* self-consciousness) out of life but also the project of the *Phenomenology of Spirit* as such. Life's pointing introduces this threat because it opens the possibility of an unmediatable break or gap between life and consciousness: that is, if the 'relation' between life and consciousness is 'mediated' not by a determinate negation but rather by an act of pointing that can, perhaps, point to many living things (just as it can point to their 'other,' many dead things) but that can, by itself, never make the other of life – consciousness as consciousness, knowing as knowing – *appear*, then this 'relation' would in fact be a disjunction, the falling apart of life and consciousness. (Another way to put it: life may indeed point, may indeed 'speak,' but that this pointing or speaking 'linguistic' function will make anything appear is doubtful – least of all that it can make the other of life itself – i.e. *death* itself – appear. Again, life can make living things appear and it can make dead things appear, but death itself? No.) And when life and consciousness are unmediated or 'de-mediated' in this way, then the possibility of spirits appearing – the possibility of a phenomeno-logic of spirits appearing in the phenomena of its own self-negations – would also be very much in question. It is in question because a linguistic act or function of pointing or reference cannot make anything *appear* unless it is itself phenomenalized, only if it is given a figure, a face, as it were, only if the *logos*, speech, is made to, *said* to, appear – only if speaking is said to appear, only if the speaking (*logos*) of the apparent (*phenomena*) is said to be the appearance of speaking.

But if the speaking of the apparent can turn into the appearance of speaking only thanks to the figural, rhetorical, function or dimension of language, then the authority for this tropological substitution or transfer – this trope or figure – is most unreliable. It is unreliable because the only authoritative ground for this figure – a figure that would turn life (in its result, *Gattung*) into a determinate figure for consciousness – would be the system of consciousness itself, i.e. the system of (apparent) knowing, here taken as a *closed* tropological system (i.e. a system of substitutions and exchanges based on a *knowledge* of entities and their exchangeable properties). In other words, the only way to stabilize the figure that would turn life's pointing, referential function into a phenomenal appearance (and hence into an object that would be the determinate negation *of* consciousness) would be to ground it in the 'proper sense' of consciousness itself: in short, to know 'language' here, the 'linguisticality' of life's pointing, on the model of consciousness ('proper') and its determinations. The trouble is, however, that the integrity and self-identity of the system of consciousness as a closed tropological system cannot be taken for granted here, for it is precisely the linguistic function of pointing or reference that is said to make *consciousness* possible and not *vice versa*. That is, according to the text, it is only by virtue of life's pointing that anything like 'consciousness proper' – i.e. a system of consciousness that would include life *within itself* (as its own determinately negative other) and thereby constitute itself as a *closed* tropological system – can come into existence in the first place. In other words, consciousness is the only thing that could authorize the trope that turns life into a reliable phenomenal figure for consciousness, but consciousness can emerge, be itself, i.e. *become* itself (self-consciousness), *appear*, only thanks to this trope. Since it is the very burden of this passage to demonstrate how consciousness, and thereby *self*-consciousness (i.e. consciousness in its truth), is possible in the first place as a system of knowing that emerges, as it were, out of life itself and thereby includes life within itself as its own other, consciousness cannot be called upon to validate and verify (as in 'make true') this demonstration as though it were already existent in its truth, as though we already *knew* what consciousness was in its truth – *as though we had already verified it as self-*

*consciousness!*[18] In other words, how understand, how know, 'language' on the basis of the model of consciousness, when 'language' is that which is supposed to make consciousness possible in the first place? And if 'language' turns out to be a disjunction between reference (life's pointing) and phenomenalism (the appearance of consciousness as the determinately negative other of life) mediatable only by a trope that is necessarily aberrant because it is not grounded in any proper sense (but rather is an arbitrary imposition of sense), then 'language' is here also that which makes consciousness *im*possible.[19] That the very 'linguisticality' of this 'linguistic moment' would prohibit the emergence of consciousness as the determinate negation of life is finally not all that surprising, for what Hegel's claim amounts to here is that the limit of life (i.e. in its result, *Gattung*), namely death, is the determinate negation of life and therefore can become the object of consciousness: death is, death becomes, consciousness, insofar as it is the limit of life that pushes consciousness beyond its own immediate existence to its (self-)mediated essence, self-consciousness. But, as Bataille and others well knew, death can become (self-)consciousness — that is, can *appear* as the limit (and therefore the determinate negation) of life rather than *occur* as the random violence of sheer exteriority — only thanks to a subterfuge, a spectacle, a comedy of sacrifice that will allow me both to die and, at the same time, to watch myself die.[20] The subterfuge or comedy of sacrifice here consists in Hegel's wanting to turn an act of sheer linguistic imposition — indeed, the giving of a name (to death!): 'in its result, at its limit, life points to an other than it is, call it consciousness' — into an apparent, knowable, reliable, phenomenal figure of consciousness. To put it as bluntly as possible: at the moment that Hegel's text says that life (in this result: *Gattung*) points to an other than it is, consciousness, 'Hegel,' or at least the Hegel who would want this to be a self-determination and self-negation of life — *this Hegel* hallucinates, he is seeing things, instead of death or the dead he sees ghosts (*Geister*). This Hegel is a *Geisterseher*, and the *Phänomenologie des Geistes* would be the confessions of a seer of ghosts, the speaking of the appearances of ghosts.

The idealizing nature of Hegel's impossible trope is nicely legible here in the word *verweisen*, to point. Even though Hegel presumably would never be caught trying 'to grow grapes by the luminosity of the word "day"'[21] — although let us not be so sure — we can read him here, at least *this* Hegel, trying to make consciousness appear by the light of the verb *verweisen*, which, conveniently enough, comes from the same roots as *wissen*, to know, and hence as *Bewußtsein*, and which ultimately comes from the same root (*weid*) as Greek *eidos* — 'visible appearance,' say — and *idea* — visible appearance *as* visible, visibility as such. The proto-idealist operation is clear: the *Idea*, the spiritually (and truly) existent, is constituted (linguistically) by a (pseudo-)metaphorical transport from that which is visible for the sensuous eye of the body to that which is *in*visible, non-visible, except for the non-sensuous eye of the soul – call it *Idea*. (One could ask, only half-jokingly, why not something like 'Smell-aia,' say, or 'Audea,' etc.? And Heidegger might answer: 'For very good reasons embedded in the destiny [*Geschick*] of Western metaphysics as the history of the forgetting of Being.')[22] Like all such idealizing operations, this is an arbitrary act of linguistic imposition of meaning. And as an imposition, it works not by the determinate negation of the sensuous and physical but rather by a blind marking, naming, which is then taken as the mark or the name of the blindness, of the blindness as a negation of seeing and visibility, etc. In short, it is a catachrestic act, not a substantial metaphor at all but a 'blind metonymy,' as Paul de Man would put it,[23] a mutilated and mutilating metaphor that brings monsters into the world, precisely the monsters necessarily created by the language that does nothing so much as to figure our own self-mutilation by figures, our own self-blinding as we go about our business giving legs, arms, feet, faces, mouths, and eyes to things that are legless, armless, footless, faceless, mouthless, and eyeless.[24] But the catachrestic nature of the aberrant trope that would 'mediate' reference (as a function *of* language) and phenomenalism (reference taken not as a function of language but as an intuition) in this idealizing operation is not the point here. The point is rather that this idealizing operation – the phenomenalization of a linguistic function – would be quite clearly an ideological operation, and *ideo-logical* in the most basic sense: making speech appear, and appear as an *ideal* entity, which is ideological through and through (the representation of an imaginary relation to the real conditions of existence, to coin a phrase) because speaking, if and when it appears, does not 'appear' as ghost or *Geist* but, say, as moving layers of air (in Marx's phrase) or as inscribed letters – that is, as historically, materially over-determined, i.e. made up of contradictions that will not be returned to a master negation, a master dialectic, *dia-logos*, of determinate negation. In other words, although 'Hegel' here might indeed want to be the German super-ideologist who would transform life into consciousness, the text does not, cannot, make the mediation by self-negation of life and consciousness – of self-consciousness as desire and self-consciousness as self-consciousness. Instead, the text writes a 'properly' linguistic moment into the workings of the dialectic of desire – 'linguistic' because it amounts to the introduction of a moment of reference that can be phenomenalized, that can *appear*, only thanks to an aberrant trope (i.e., catachresis) – and thereby threatens not only to make the emergence of self-consciousness (*as* self-consciousness and *not* as desire) impossible but also to turn Hegel's history of the experience of consciousness into an allegory of the mutual interference and inevitable ideologization of linguistic functions.

But in *not* making the mediation, in being unable to make the transition between life and (self-)consciousness – except by way of a 'linguistic moment' – the text introduces what could be called a 'material moment' into 'itself,' indeed, the moment of text *as* text. 'Material' – because it is a moment when 'Hegel,' the text, is simply too much of a materialist, too intent upon having (self-)consciousness emerge *out of* life, from *within* life, to 'fake' the transition here (by saying something like: life determines or negates itself here in such a way that consciousness itself, the other or negation of life itself, appears). Instead, the moment is 'material' because what 'appears' is neither 'life' nor 'consciousness' nor the mediation by negation of the two but rather, what? The text appears, or, more precisely, text *happens* here as a linguistic artifact, a bit of material produced by the workings neither of life and appetitive desire nor of consciousness and its negations but rather the *work* (in a fully Marxian sense) of language in its materiality – i.e. the irreducible referential function, its over-determined potential for meaning, and its inevitable phenomenalization and ideologization in an aberrant trope. And *as* material, this moment is also truly 'historical', in the sense that it is what *happens* – and it happens precisely because it will not allow itself to be inscribed *as* a moment into Hegel's history of the experience of consciousness, of the presentation of apparent knowing. (If it did allow it, it would by definition be a non-happening, a non-event, something whose role is to be *only* a moment in a process whose meaning is the (self-) negation of *all* moments *as* moments – i.e. whose meaning is the phenomeno-logic of the process itself.) If we are right about this historical/material moment – better, event, happening – of the *Phenomenology* – that is, if reading has indeed taken place – then *this* Hegel, the text, would be a Hegel much closer to Marx than most Marxists, and especially closer to Marx than those Marxists who go one better than Hegel, out-Hegel Hegel as it were, and do in fact accomplish the mediation of life and consciousness, of self-consciousness as desire and self-consciousness as self-consciousness.[25]

But lest this 'other Hegel' – a 'Hegel' closer to Marx than to Hegel – get lost in my claims about 'language,' let me recapitulate why and how life's pointing makes such a difference – for Hegel, for Marx, and for us. Going back to the crucial sentence may be the most economical way to do this: 'In this result [namely, the *genus*, the simple *genus*] life points to an other than it is, namely toward consciousness, for which it [life] is as this unity, or as genus (*in diesem Resultate verweist das Leben auf ein Anderes, als es ist, nämlich auf das Bewußtsein, für welches es als diese Einheit, oder als Gattung ist*).' If we bracket the phrase 'life points to an other than it is, namely' for a moment, the essential appropriateness and adequation to one another of life as *Gattung* and consciousness is clear: this result can be only *for* consciousness because it is indeed only consciousness that can have this result – i.e. life as genus, as *Gattung* – for it, for an object that is consciousness's own object. It is only *for consciousness* that life can *be* the 'unity' (*Einheit*) that is genus (*Gattung*). This is certainly clear and understandable enough: life, that which is living, can be the identity of identity and difference that is genus only for a consciousness that *knows* this, that *knows life as* genus. But how ever clear this relation of genus and consciousness may be, it is equally clear that the being of life for consciousness (i.e. genus) is not life's own for itself, it is not something that life can ever have as its own object, that could ever be a unity *for* life. No matter how much life may negate itself and no matter how much consciousness may want to recognize itself in this self-negation of life (as its own, consciousness's, negation), nevertheless the fact remains that life *cannot* have itself as the unity that is genus for an object. In short, life cannot have itself as an object of consciousness, because, quite simply, life is *not* (yet) consciousness, and it is precisely the burden of this passage to demonstrate how it is that it (life) *can be* consciousness. Again, this result, the unity that is genus, can be only for consciousness. This is why life *points* and can *only* point to consciousness. That is, life can be only a sign for consciousness – it can only signify it, refer to it – because by itself it will never be able to go beyond the limits of its immediate existence, as Hegel had put it in paragraph §8 (§80 in Miller's numbering) of the 'Introduction' to the *Phenomenology*, except when it is forced to do so by an other: death.[26] And even though consciousness may be able to make this other – death – its own other, a negation in which consciousness can recognize itself, *for life* this death remains always other, a sheer exteriority in which life will never be able to recognize itself. Again, this is why life *points* and has to point to an *other* than it is. And that this other will be, will *have* to be, consciousness – that which can have life as genus, and therefore death, for an object, for its own object, a negativity proper to it, consciousness – is most uncertain once we take the full measure of this pointing into account. Life may indeed point to an other than it is, but this other will necessarily be consciousness – the determinate negation of life – only for life in its result, the unity that is genus, that is, only for a life, the life, that consciousness can make its own object, only the life that can be (only) *for* consciousness. In other words, the last thing that Hegel's argument wants life to do is to point at an other than it is, for such a pointed-at other need not be a consciousness that would be the result of life's own self-negation (the essential, true, determinately negative other *of* life) but rather could be 'simply' (that is, *over*-determinately) other – an other other, as it were, that could as well be called 'consciousness' but that would not be a consciousness mediatable with life (as its determinate negation, as its essential other). *This* consciousness would indeed be a ghost, and all the more ghostly because *when* it appears, it can appear not in symbolic incarnations or phenomenal figures for the spiritual but rather can only signify itself, point to itself, by a sheer act of signification when it converts sensory appearances into signs, allegorical signs, for itself.

If one could pinpoint this moment of arbitrary allegorical signification in the text's sentence – the moment when spirit, rather than appearing in phenomenal form, signifies itself in an allegorical sign – it would have to be when 'an other' (*ein Anderes*) that life is said to point to gets identified, determined, as the other that is and has to be consciousness: 'life points to an other than it is, namely to consciousness (*verweist das Leben auf ein Anderes als es ist, nämlich auf das Bewußtsein*).' It is perhaps in this 'namely' (*nämlich*) that the mediation of life and consciousness is most legible as *not* a mediation by determinate (self-) negation at all but as a disarticulation of life and consciousness in the act of an arbitrary imposition of a name: life points to an other than it is – writes the text (and in doing so *over*-determines this other as the (historical material) *product* of 'the language of real life') – 'namely consciousness' – says the dialectic of self-consciousness (and in doing so wants to determine this other as the determined other of a life that can be only *for* consciousness). So instead of being able to mediate life and consciousness (and thereby bring us back to self-consciousness) by demonstrating how it is that life could not be life except *as* consciousness, the text converts life into an allegorical sign for consciousness, which points to an other than it is, call it consciousness. In doing so, it brings into 'existence' a ghostly consciousness or *Geist* apart, as Marx might (did) put it (the Marx that, in a sense, read this passage in Hegel very well), *not* consciousness as the product of the historical materiality of the *work* of Hegel's text, but the shadow consciousness that would phenomenalize itself and appear *as* the essential (determinately negative) other of life, life's own negation, death itself. This ideological consciousness – or, better, consciousness as ideology[27] – nevertheless always bears the marks of its material production, and these marks, like life's allegorical pointing, can always be read in turn on the body

189

of the language of ideology, *not* in what that language represents but in what it points to, signifies, refers to – an allegory that has itself to be read allegorically in turn. This is especially the case here in the *Phenomenology of Spirit* at the moment when life catches up with consciousness, as it were, and demands that the arbitrary decision between man as a living creature (the object of anthropology) and man as knowing, as consciousness (the object of phenomenology) – a decision that one might as well locate in the very first sentence of the Introduction to the *Phenomenology* (*Es ist eine natürliche Vorstellung, daß* . . . or, to paraphrase loosely: 'There is knowing, consciousness, what does it have to be to be what it is, for it *is?*')[28] – that this decision (or cutting or *Unterscheidung*) be accounted for. The account offered by the text is to be read allegorically, for it is itself an account of allegory – the allegory of allegory, one could say – the story of how consciousness at the stage of self-consciousness as desire needs to verify itself (as itself) in the disappearing essences that are the (sublated) objects of consciousness and how its attempt to do so fails and has to fail. It fails because the attempt to verify self-consciousness in disappear*ing* essences can only make self-consciousness itself disappear, or, better, itself *be* disappearing. In fact, it would not be going too far to say that this constant, persistent, disappear*ing* is the very 'truth' – the very *allegorical* truth – of self-consciousness. Its disappearing essence is the truth of this infinitely (or rather [irreducibly] finitely) unhappy self-consciousness[29] because the only way it *has* to appear, to verify itself as itself in an other that appears, is to mark, signify, point to, itself by converting this phenomenal other into an allegorical sign for itself. But as an always disappear*ing* essence, this sign can ultimately be the sign only for self-consciousness's own disappearing essence, its constant wearing away and wearing down, the ceaseless erosion of material history.

Although the essay could end here (without ending), it may be helpful to append a version of some remarks that were written for a conference on 'The Future of Deconstruction: Reading Marx's *German Ideology*' held at the University of California, Santa Barbara, in February 1992. Although these remarks may run the risk of self-ideologization – as is inevitable whenever one would spell out the 'theoretical implications' of a reading – they are most appropriate for a volume entitled *Hegel After Derrida*.

Let me end by simply asserting what I think are the implications of this reading – for Hegel, for Marx, for us, and for the future of deconstruction. What this means for Hegel should be clear: namely, that once read, *consciousness* in Hegel is the 'same thing' as *life* in Marx insofar as it is produced, the product of a history of material labour, the *work* of the text. But if consciousness is just as much a product of a history of material production as life is – if, historically, materially speaking, there is no difference between life and consciousness – then Hegel is no longer who we thought he was, or at least no longer *just* who we thought he was: i.e. the absolute idealist master of ideology incarnate, the German super-ideologist. Instead, 'Hegel' would be divided against himself, as it were, his text would be heterogeneous to itself, fissured, cracked, different from itself in ways that no work of determinate negation can simply patch up, put together, or heal. In fact, Hegel would be heterogeneous to himself in a way that we could call, we *do* call, Hegel/ Marx. This other Hegel – the Hegel whose signature is legible in the marks and traces of the text's remaindering (my translation of Derrida's *restance*) – is the Hegel that Marx elaborates, works through, reinscribes – in a reinscription that allows him, Marx, to become Marx or, better, that produces Marx as Marx (and not as a mere inverter of Hegel or a German ideologist). (In other words, what the reading says is: Hegel, the text, points to an other than he is, call him Marx. In saying this, the reading is a repetition – with a difference, or better, with a remainder – of Hegel, the text, its reproduction as it were.) But to say that Marx is in a sense the reinscription of the remainder or remaindering of Hegel's text is not to say that Marx – whoever that would be – is the *truth* of Hegel, the essence of Hegel, etc. It does not even mean to say that what Marx does is to think the 'unthought' of Hegel. No, what Marx does is to *read* Hegel, to read Hegel's text in its difference from itself. That is what makes him Marx and not a Young Hegelian – his countersigning of Hegel's text, as it were, is what allows him to sign *Marx*. But to *sign* 'Marx' is different from *being* Marx – some sort of monolithic, homogeneous document whose own single, simple, liberating 'truth' could be discovered by a hermeneutic activity of unpacking and unveiling – for Marx's own signature needs itself to be read in turn, meaning that his text is also heterogeneous, is also riven by over-determined contradictions that will forever prohibit any easy totalization of 'Marx' into *only* Marx, *just* Marx, into Marx and nothing else. Marx's text, like Hegel's, is also living on in a species of afterlife,[30] it too is still to come in the future, from the future. That is what makes it Marx. And it is also what makes deconstruction – or, better, deconstruction*s* – something yet to come in and from the future. Its – their – future is also coming, on the way, yet to come, any day now – for instance, in the reserve or remainder of texts that *as* texts will have always already *been* the future of deconstruction(s), like Derrida's *Positions,* which twenty years ago (in answer to questions about Derrida's 'relation' to and silence about Marx) says not only that 'the "lacunae" [. . .] are explicitly calculated to mark the sites of a theoretical elaboration which remains, for me at least, *still to come*' but also that: 'when I say "*still to come*," I am still, and above all, thinking of the relationship of Marx to Hegel [. . .] Despite the immense work which already has been done in this domain, a decisive elaboration has not yet been accomplished, and for historical reasons which can by analysed, precisely, only during the elaboration of this work. [. . .] Now, we cannot consider Marx's, Engels's, or Lenin's texts as completely finished elaborations that are simply to be "applied" to the current situation. In saying this, I am not advocating anything contrary to "Marxism," I am convinced of it. These texts are not to be read according to a hermeneutical or exegetical method which would seek out a finished signified beneath a textual surface. Reading is transformational. I believe that this would be confirmed by certain of Althusser's propositions. But this transformation cannot be executed however one wishes. It requires protocols of reading. Why not say it bluntly: I have not yet found any that satisfy me. [. . .] I do not find the texts of Marx, Engels, or Lenin homogeneous critiques. In their relationship to Hegel, for example. And the manner in which they themselves reflected and formulated the differentiated contradictory structure of their relationship to Hegel has not seemed to me, correctly or incorrectly, sufficient. Thus I will have to analyse what I consider a heterogeneity, conceptualizing both its necessity and the rules for deciphering it; and do so by taking into account the decisive progress simultaneously accomplished by Althusser and those following him. [. . .] We will never be finished with the reading or rereading of Hegel, and, in a certain way, I do nothing other than attempt to explain myself on this point. In effect I believe that Hegel's text is necessarily fissured; that it is something more and other than the circular closure of its representation. It is not reduced to a content of philosophemes, it also necessarily produces a powerful writing operation, a remainder of writing, whose strange relationship to the philosophical content of Hegel's text must be reexamined, that is, the movement by means of which his text exceeds its meaning, permits itself to be turned away from, to return to, and to repeat itself outside its self-identity.'[31]

So, despite all our misgivings, the title of the conference – 'The *Future* of Deconstruction: *Reading* Marx's *German Ideology*' – seems to me correct enough, as long as we remember to emphasize the word 'reading' as well as the word 'future.' Like Hegel, like Marx, indeed like 'Hegel/Marx,' the only future 'deconstruction' can have is the future *produced* by a reading that is transformational, i.e. that happens, and *as* something that happens is history – and *as* history has, is, will have been, a future. As anything else – as an institutional fashion, trend, movement, or method, or, for that matter, as a new 'philosophy' (of the 'limit' or whatever) – 'deconstruction' is already over (because it did not happen) and may as well have no future.[32]

# Part III

# READING *GLAS*

# 8

# A Commentary Upon Derrida's Reading of Hegel in *Glas*[1]

*Simon Critchley*

Qu'est-ce qui cloche dans le système, qu'est-ce qui boite? La question est aussitôt boiteuse et ne fait pas question. Ce qui déborde le système, c'est l'impossibilité de son échec, comme l'impossibilité de la réussite: finalement on n'en peut rien dire, et il y a une manière de se taire (le silence lacunaire de l'écriture) qui arrête le système, le laissant désœuvré, livré au sérieux de l'ironie.[2]

## Introduction

*Glas* is a *tour de force* of Hegelian scholarship.[3] Although primarily concerned with the *Philosophy of Right* and the *Phenomenology of Spirit*, Derrida also offers detailed discussions of *The Spirit of Christianity and its Fate*, the *First Philosophy of Spirit* of 1803–4, the 1803 essay *Scientific Ways of Treating Natural Law*, the *Lectures on Aesthetics* and the introduction to the *Lectures on the Philosophy of World History*. In addition – and this list is not exhaustive – there are discussions of and references to the *Logic*, the *Encyclopaedia*, the *Lectures on the Philosophy of Religion*, the *Differenzschrift, Faith and Knowledge* and abundant quotations from Hegel's correspondence.

It must be stressed at the outset that the Hegel column is for the most part a straightforward and closely argued commentary on Hegel, interrupted by a series of excurses on Marx, Feuerbach, Kant, and Freud, and a number of significant allusions to Heidegger. Derrida's persistent mode of demonstration is through quotation rather than reconstruction or exposition. He quotes, often at extraordinary length, rarely making a claim that cannot be textually verified with reference to Hegel's works. When Derrida is read with the care with which he reads Hegel, his reading practice appears largely irrefutable, employing an implicit conception of truth as *adaequatio* between text and commentary. When he wishes to offer a parenthetical remark or a quotation from a different source, he uses the formal device of the judas, a marginal window in the main text, which acts as a commentary upon his commentary and should not be judged to be of subordinate importance to the main text. It should be noted, however, that there are many fewer judases in the Hegel column than in the Genet column.

However, the apparent linearity of the Hegel commentary is disrupted as soon as one glances to the right (reading the Hegel column on the left-hand page), or to both left and right (reading the Hegel column on the right-hand page). These planned or aleatory intertextual effects, in the judases and opposing columns, and the oscillating movement between text and intertext, between commentary and what exceeds it, describe the very rhythm of the deconstructive reading. But however true that may be, I shall try to fix an unblinking, Cyclopean eye on the Hegel column in order to ascertain whether one can begin to formulate an *Einführung* (an introduction) that will lead the reader to an understanding of the reading of Hegel being attempted in *Glas*.

## Method: systematic reading and the family

The only recent secondary text on Hegel that Derrida refers to at any length is Bernard Bourgeois's *Hegel à Francfort: Judaïsme-Christianisme-Hegelianisme* (Gtr83–4a).[4] According to Derrida, Bourgeois reads the Hegelian system as if it were a book of life, where one would speak of an 'adolescent' Hegelianism, an 'early' Hegelianism, an 'incipient,' 'mature,' 'later,' and 'accomplished' Hegelianism, with the truth of Hegel only being actualized at the end of a development. For Derrida, such an approach to Hegel represents 'the logical reading' (Gtr84a) against which he opposes his own, refusing to distinguish the young from the old and objecting that the logical approach overlooks 'the systematic chains' (Gtr84a) at work in the first texts. This passing remark is helpful, for it helps the reader to understand that Derrida gives very much a *systematic* reading of Hegel, a reading that is always focused on the concept of system and that treats individual texts, from whatever period, as morsels or constituent articulations of the greater system. To approach *Glas* as a systematic reading of Hegel illuminates a number of features of Derrida's commentary: first, it explains the privilege that Derrida gives to texts from the Frankfurt and

Jena periods, like *The Spirit of Christianity* and *The First Philosophy of Spirit*. Second, and to choose an example, it explains why, when Derrida wants to give an account of *Sittlichkeit*, he begins with the *Differenzschrift, Faith and Knowledge* and the essay on *Natural Law*, in which Derrida claims to find 'the essential traits of *Sittlichkeit*' (Gtr97a/G137a). These traits are early traces of the 'great syllogism' (Gtr98a/G137a) of *Sittlichkeit* contained in the *Philosophy of Right*. Third, it explains Derrida's choice of the 'thread' ('fil,' Gtr4a/G5a) with which he draws out his reading: the concept of the family. But, one is entitled to ask, why the family?

The opening of the Hegel column is graphically complex and alludes to themes that become clearer as the reading develops. After a brief discussion of two seemingly peripheral passages from Hegel – the paragraph that mentions 'flower religion' (*Blumenreligion*) from the *Phenomenology* (PStr420/PS372) and the short discussion of the phallic columns of India from the *Aesthetics* (A641), which function as *leitmotifs* for both columns and are more fully discussed in the closing sections of *Glas* – Derrida raises the methodological problem of how one is introduced (*eingeführt*) or led into Hegel. Derrida remarks: 'The problem of the introduction to Hegel's philosophy is *all* of Hegel's philosophy (c'est *toute* la philosophie de Hegel)' (Gtr4a/G5a). This familiar issue implies that whatever point one chooses to enter the circle of speculative dialectics will presuppose all the other points on the circumference and thus the entirety of the Hegelian system. The point where *Glas* introduces itself into the system is with the theme of the family. Derrida's central text is the *Philosophy of Right*, where the family is the first moment in the syllogism of *Sittlichkeit*, the other two being Civil Society and the State. The family occurs therefore immediately after the transition from *Moralität* to *Sittlichkeit* (an important transition in *Glas*), that is to say, from the abstract diremption of the Good and subjectivity to their unification in the Concept. As well as being the first moment in the syllogism of *Sittlichkeit* and the beginning of the third moment in the syllogism of Abstract Right, *Moralität* and *Sittlichkeit*, the family also has its own syllogistic structure: marriage, family property, and capital, and the education of children and the dissolution of the family (PRtr111/PR152). Thus, the immediate unification of the family in monogamous marriage and the family's external embodiment in capital are *aufgehoben* in the education of the children, which brings the latter to 'freedom of personality' and 'holding free property' (PRtr118/PR163–4) and leads to the family's dissolution. The truth of the family is its dissolution and transition to Civil Society, 'the stage of difference' (PRtr122/PR168).

Derrida draws on the thread of the family for a number of reasons: first, he admits that this choice, which is far from innocent, is made because 'the concept family very rigorously inscribes itself in the system' (Gtr5a); and again, 'the whole system repeats itself in the family' (Gtr20a). The concept of the family, and this is true of every moment of the dialectic, exemplifies the system of which it is a part. Second, the family is a crucial transitional hinge in the *Philosophy of Right* and the system as a whole:

Its interpretation directly engages the whole Hegelian determination of right on one side, of politics on the other. Its place in the system's structure and development, in the encyclopaedia, the logic, and the Hegelian on-totheology, is such that the displacements or the desimplifications of which it will be the object would not know how to have a simply local character.

(Gtr4–5a)

The transition from *Moralität* to *Sittlichkeit*, from abstract freedom to the actuality of freedom, from Kant to Hegel, hinges upon the passage through the family. However, this is no safe passage in the sense that Derrida's commentary upon the family would leave it and the system intact. Rather, Derrida analyses the family 'in order to make a problematic within the whole field appear in the family' (Gtr16a). Thus, the Derridian claim is that there is something in the concept of the family that both repeats the system and renders its entire field problematic. If Derrida can be said to read Hegel systematically, then this is not done in order to maintain the system, but rather to find a moment of 'rupture' (G5a – a key word in *Glas*) within the system's development. As Derrida writes later in the Hegel column: 'Development then, and rupture: response to the question of method' (Gtr97a). His method of reading Hegel has a rhythm of development and rupture, of 'fits and starts, jolts, little successive jerks' (Gtr5a/G7a), that follows the course of the family and the speculative dialectic 'like a machine (*un appareil*) in the course of a difficult maneuvre' (Gtr5a/G7a). In the closing pages of *Glas*, Derrida describes the dialectic as 'the three-stroke engine (*le moteur à trois temps*)' (Gtr252a/G350a), which seeks to run smoothly through the repeated triadic pattern of in-itself, for-itself and in-and-for-itself. The mechanism of reading in *Glas* attempts to throw a spanner in the works of this engine, transforming Hegel's text into a cumbersome and ineffective machine lumbering slowly across difficult terrain.

It is, then, a deconstructive reading, which rigorously and minutely follows or 'will have to feign to follow' (Gtr6a) the family circle of the dialectic whilst continually disrupting its circumference. In an allusion to Genet, Derrida calls his method of reading, 'a bastard course (*démarche bâtarde*)' (Gtr6a/G8a), a reading of the family in terms of that which exceeds and resists it.

## Christian lore and Hegel's Judaism

Derrida begins with the concept of love, which specifically characterizes the family for Hegel (PRtr110/PR151). After a brief exposition of the transition from *Moralität* to *Sittlichkeit* in the *Philosophy of Right*, Derrida comments on Hegel's introductory discussion of *Sittlichkeit* (PRtr105–10/PR144–51), out of which the concept of the family emerges. The family is defined as the immediate substantiality of Spirit, or, more precisely, 'ethical Spirit' (*'sittliche Geist'*; PRtr110/PR151). The unity of *Geist* in the family, that which unifies the three moments of its syllogism, is love. In a *Zusatz*, Hegel defines love as 'the consciousness of my unity with another' (PRtr261/PR152), a unity where I win my self-consciousness only through the renunciation of my independence or 'selfish isolation' (ibid.). Love has two moments for Hegel: (1) where I do not wish to be an independent person and where I experience my autarky as a lack or defect; (2) where I attain my independence and 'find myself in another person' (ibid.), the beloved. Hegel, and Derrida is following him to the letter here, identifies 'the most tremendous contradiction' (*'der ungeheuerste Widerspruch'* – ibid.) within the concept of love. In a characteristic move, Derrida simply pauses with this contradiction, a contradiction found within Hegel's text and not imposed upon it. He is not interested in turning such a contradiction into a vicious circle, but rather, alluding to Heidegger's *Was heisst Denken?*, Derrida wishes to follow the hermeneutic circle that is the product of an apparent contradiction and which cannot be avoided in thinking (GRtr20). Suspending his commentary on the family in *The Philosophy of Right* at this contradictory moment, Derrida moves on to a further account of the family given in 'a very late text' (Gtr21a), the Introduction to the *Lectures on the Philosophy of World History*.

In the latter, Spirit is defined as the inseparability within self-consciousness of self-knowledge and objective knowledge (Gtr21a). Derrida discusses the relation of Spirit to freedom (Gtr22a), activity (Gtr24a) and the notion of the *bei sich* (Gtr22a), rendered by Derrida as '*être auprès de soi*' (G30a). He shows how the Hegelian concept of Spirit is dependent upon a number of exclusions: first, the exclusion of matter, defined as exteriority, as that which is not *bei sich*.[5] Second, the constitution of humanity is dependent upon the exclusion of animality, the natural, and of everything that Hegel designates with the word

*Trieb*. However, although humanity is spiritual and is constituted upon the exclusion of the natural, the material and the animal – 'a powerful and ample chain from Aristotle, at least, to our day, it binds ontotheological metaphysics to humanism' (Gtr27a) – the human is only an example of *finite* Spirit. As the example of *infinite* Spirit, Hegel names God. However, the infinite is not without relation to the finite, for what distinguishes the Christian religion for Hegel – which raises it above its antecedent, Judaism – is that infinite Spirit can become finite in the person of Christ. In the incarnation, God becomes an object for himself, he knows and recognizes himself in his son. The relation that binds the father to the son, the infinite to the finite, is the Holy Spirit, the third person of the Trinity. Spirit, then, is filiation, a familial relation between father and son.

Derrida then asks: 'What is the function of this Christian model?' (Gtr33a). This brings the reader to the next major transition in Derrida's reading, where, 'within the system' and its 'very precise homology' (Gtr33a), he steps back to Hegel's 1799 Frankfurt text, *The Spirit of Christianity and its Fate*. Note once again that the same systematic reading is at work: 'one enters the analysis of Christianity and of the Christian family elaborated by the young Hegel as the conceptual matrix (*la matrice conceptuelle* – the conceptual womb) of the whole systematic scene to come' (Gtr55a/G78a). Derrida's reading of this text extends for some sixty pages of the translation (Gtr33a-93a) and is one of the most thorough sections of *Glas* and essential reading for anyone researching into Hegel's concept of Christianity and in particular his attitude to Judaism.[6] Derrida's general point here is that the transition from *Moralität* to *Sittlichkeit* described in the *Philosophy of Right*, whose first moment is the family unified by love, is replicated and reinforced in the transition from Judaism to Christianity. That is to say, there is no love before Christianity (Gtr34a). It is the person of Christ who relieves (*relever* is Derrida's French translation of *aufheben*, somewhat inadequately rendered by Leavey as 'to relieve') the abstract rights of Judaism into ethical love. There is no true family before Christianity, for the concept of the family is only unified by love and therefore the Judaic family – Derrida discusses the example of Noah (Gtr38–9a) – is based upon 'dutiful fidelity' (Gtr34a). Thus, the advent of *Sittlichkeit* and the family is synonymous with the *Aufhebung* from a religion based upon duty and commandment to a religion based on love and freedom. To this extent, Derrida parenthetically and provocatively remarks: 'Kantianism is, in this respect, structurally a Judaism' (Gtr34a).

For Hegel, the essence of the family is filiation; it is bound by the thread that binds the father to the son and where the mother is but 'a short detour'

(Gtr36a) into materiality and the daughter does not even figure. The essence of Christianity consists in the filiation of God the Father and God the Son through the material medium of the Virgin birth. The revelation of Christ consists in the loving recognition of his divine incarnation and the realization that human beings are the children of God (Gtr78a). The incarnate human family is an echo of divine filiation.

It is precisely the doctrine of incarnation that Judaism (and Kantianism) cannot understand and that indeed surpasses the formal abstraction of the understanding. With his tongue lodged firmly in his cheek, Derrida asks: 'What do the Jews make of Hegel?' (Gtr84a). He responds: 'They cry out scandal. How can Jesus identify himself with God, regard himself equal to God, and believe that possible by naming God his father?' (Gtr84a). The Jew, then, is 'enclosed in this double, non-dialectical one-sidedness, he accedes neither to the divine nor to the spiritual sense of filiation. For the spirit has not yet spoken in him. He has not yet become an adult in himself' (Gtr85a). Within the system, the Jew understands neither Christianity nor Hegelianism; he is a child who, moreover, does not even understand his childishness (Gtr85a). The Jew does not love, he cannot love, he is the circumcised and dutiful subject of a 'dieu transcendant, jaloux, exclusif, avare, sans présent' (Gtr44a/G62a). The Jew attains neither self-presence nor presence to God, he or she is not *bei sich*, but is rather condemned to wander homelessly and nomadically like Abraham in the desert (Gtr41a). The Jew is a materialist whose circumcision is based upon a materialistic misunderstanding (Gtr44a), and who, like the Gorgon's head, turns everything to stone, petrifying and materializing Spirit (Gtr45a).

Worst of all, the Jews 'have no sense of freedom' (Gtr48a) and cannot become citizens of a *polis*. For Hegel, citizenship in the Greek sense is conditional upon the holding of property rights, where freedom is synonymous with the ownership of private property. On Hegel's reading, in virtue of the fact that Jews hold their possessions on loan and not as private property, they are denied both full citizenship and freedom (Gtr53a). Consequently, a Jewish state could not possess political freedom and would inevitably be governed by violence (Gtr52a). Derrida cites the following chilling passage from *The Spirit of Christianity*,

All the subsequent circumstances of the Jewish people up to the mean, abject, wretched circumstances in which they still are today, have all of them been simply consequences and developments of their primordial destiny. By this destiny – an infinite power which they have set over against themselves and could never conquer – they have been maltreated and will be continually maltreated until they reconcile it by the spirit of beauty and so relieve [*aufheben*] it by reconciliation.

(Gtr55a, SC199–200)

History has given such statements a dangerous irony. In order to indicate some paths of investigation that cannot be followed here, I would suggest that Hegel's attitude to Judaism is not simply or empirically anti-Semitic; after all it could be argued, for reasons to be shown below, that Hegelianism is equally anti-Christian. Rather, Hegel's attitude is perhaps *philosophically* anti-Semitic, that is to say, the conceptual matrix of family, love, community, and property has no place for the Jew, if the latter is defined as the other to Greco-Christian philosophical conceptuality. Can philosophical dialectics approach the otherness of the other, that is to say, can it entertain an alterity that cannot be comprehended or reduced to an object of cognition or recognition? Does the maintenance of the other within the horizon of cognition, self-recognition and the Concept, and the privilege of love over duty, reduce the alterity that ensures respect for the other person? Is the very desire for love, family, community, and cognition predicated upon a reduction of the other's otherness, hence upon a violence to the other person? And if this is the case, then might not anti-Semitism be defined as a failure to respect the otherness of the other?

Opening these questions onto both columns of *Glas*, Sartre remarks in *Saint Genet* that 'Genet is anti-Semitic. Or rather he plays at being so' (SGtr203/ SG192). What is one to make of the arguably pro-Nazi eroticism of Genet's third novel, *Funeral Rites*, or, more recently, the anti-Zionism of his posthumously published *Prisoner of Love*? Is this a philosophical anti-Semitism or a prejudice of a rather more empirical kind? And what of Derrida's relation to this complex anti-Semitism working in both columns of *Glas*? How would it relate to the poignant, seemingly autobiographical remarks on the double-columned *Torah* held aloft by colonists in an Algerian synagogue during Derrida's childhood (Gtr240bi)? Is *Glas* a kind of *anti-Torah*, a memory or 'dream' of the sacred text that would 'organize all the pieces and scenes . . .' (ibid.) of *Glas* whilst continually bringing the authority of the sacred text into question?

## The *Aufhebung* of the family and sexuality

For Hegel, Christianity is the absolute religion, which has the Absolute for its content. As such, Christianity is the *Aufhebung* of Judaism. However, although

Christianity possesses the Absolute as content, it represents this content only in the form of *Vorstellung*, or picture-thinking. Therefore, Christianity must itself be *aufgehoben* in order for Absolute Knowledge to be achieved: religion is superseded by philosophy. As Derrida remarks, Hegel's reading of Christianity is double (Gtr92a), or, more precisely, Christianity possesses this duplicity within itself, where it is both the truth of religion and that which only attains its truth in philosophy. Now, it is precisely this *Aufhebung* of religion by philosophy, the passage to Absolute Knowledge, that is Derrida's most general concern in *Glas* and that ultimately guides the subsequent transitions of his reading. He writes: 'The most general question would now have the following form: how is the relief of religion into philosophy produced?' (Gtr93a). However, Derrida then immediately adds the following question: 'How, on the other hand, is the relief of the family structure into civil (bourgeois) society produced?' (Gtr93a). How are these two questions analogous? Derrida's hint is that the family will have a determining function in the passage to Absolute Knowledge and will somehow disrupt that passage. Alluding to the closing paragraph of the 'Religion' chapter in the *Phenomenology*, Derrida notes how, in the transition from Absolute Religion to Absolute Knowledge, the *Aufhebung* of the form of Christianity, the family reappears in the guise of the Holy Family,

> Just as the *individual* divine Man has a father *in principle* and only an *actual* mother, so too the *universal* divine Man, the community, has for its father its own doing and knowing, but for its mother, eternal love which it only feels, but does not behold in its consciousness as an actual immediate *object*. Its reconciliation, therefore, is in its heart, but its consciousness is still divided against itself and its actual world is still disrupted.
>
> (PStr478/PS421, Gtr94)

The Holy Family thus represents a moment of 'dehiscence' (Gtr221a) or divorce between the 'father *in principle*' (God) and 'an actual (*wirkliche*) mother' (Mary) that produces 'the *individual* divine Man' (Christ) who does not fully reconcile Absolute Spirit and self-consciousness, and because of whom the 'actual world is still disrupted.' On the very threshold of Absolute Knowledge, both the Holy Family and the universal family of the community are dirempt and divorced and thus have to be *aufgehoben*. Thus, by choosing the guiding thread of the family, Derrida foregrounds a concept that is crucial to the passage to Absolute Knowledge or philosophy and with which the latter might be deconstructed.

Looking quickly ahead, Derrida's claim will be that 'the *Aufhebung*, the economic law of the absolute reappropriation of absolute loss, is a family concept' (Gtr133a), and furthermore, that philosophy itself 'is properly familial' (Gtr134a). By this, Derrida appears to be claiming that the movement of speculative dialectics always results in reappropriation, ' . . . the guarding of the proper [*la garde du propre*]' (Gtr134a), bringing back all phenomena within the circle of the proper, of property, of propriety, of one's own – love, home, family, community, cognition. It is precisely the circumference of this circle that Derrida seeks to deconstruct.

After a brief discussion of 'The Need for Philosophy' from the *Differenzschrift* (D10–14), Derrida returns to the concept of *Sittlichkeit*, the context for the family, and traces its emergence in the 1803 essay on Natural Law, the *Philosophy of Nature* and the *First Philosophy of Spirit*. The place of the family in the *First Philosophy of Spirit* is the 'Third Level' of the 'Formal Concept of Consciousness' (FPS231–5). The family forms part of a theory of consciousness, where it is characterized by love, marriage, and procreation and is *aufgehoben* in the transition to 'The People,' or absolute *Sittlichkeit* (FPS242). Derrida's claim here is that, despite some modifications, the treatment of the family in the *First Philosophy of Spirit* essentially predicts the fuller treatment given fifteen years later in the *Philosophy of Right*.

Consciousness, for Hegel, is the *Aufhebung* of nature by Spirit, and this prompts Derrida to make an excursus into the *Philosophy of Nature*, in order to give an account of the natural sex differences that are superseded by the spiritual sexual desire that founds the family (FPS231). Derrida focuses on the short section of *Philosophy of Nature* that treats 'The Sex-Relationship' (PN Vol. III, pp. 172–5). Beneath the apparently anatomical description of Hegel's text, Derrida detects the most traditional, Aristotelian interpretation of sexual difference, which repeats the hierarchical oppositions of male to female, form to matter, and activity to passivity, that characterize classical phallocentrism,

> The clitoris moreover is inactive feeling in general; in the male on the other hand, it has its counterpart in active sensibility, the swelling vital, the effusion of blood into the *corpora cavernosa* and the meshes of the spongy tissue of the urethra.
>
> (PN Vol. III, p. 175)

Derrida shows the wider complicity between phallocentrism and philosophy with a discussion of Kant's *Anthropology from a Pragmatic Point of View*. Kant's account of sex differences is even more repugnant than Hegel's. One reads,

Whenever the refinement of luxury has reached a high point, the woman shows herself well-behaved (*sittsam*) only by compulsion, and makes no secret in wishing that she might rather be a man, so that she could give larger and freer playing room to her inclinations; no man, however, would want to be a woman.

(ANT221,Gtr221a)

However, as well as being sexist and anti-feminist, classical phallocentrism is also *heterosexist*. A possible reading of Hegel that cannot be fully explored here would have to show how homosexuality is excluded from *Sittlichkeit*, where spiritualized sexual desire is at once familial, monogamous and heterosexual. With reference to Jean Genet, it should be asked whether speculative dialectics has a place for the homosexual other than in prison?

## Antigone – the quasi-transcendental

Such themes of sexual difference are taken up and focused in the next major transition in *Glas*. After a discussion of the 'struggle for recognition' in the *First Philosophy of Spirit* (FPS235–42), Derrida moves on to a detailed and fascinating discussion of Hegel's interpretation of *Antigone* in the *Phenomenology of Spirit*. Note that one is once again within the context of *Sittlichkeit*, the first moment of its syllogism, which itself forms the first moment of the great syllogism of *Geist* in the *Phenomenology*. Derrida chooses two 'foci' (Gtr142a) upon which to concentrate his reading: the sepulchre (*sépulture*) and the liaison between brother and sister (*ibid.*). He begins by reiterating the cluster of oppositions that govern Hegel's reading: Antigone/Creon, divine law/human law, family/state, woman/man, law of singularity (*Gesetz der Einzelheit*)/ law of universality (*Gesetz der Allgemeinheit*). With respect to the first focus, it is the function of the family, defined as the space of woman, the singular, the divine, to deal with the burial of the dead. The feminine work of mourning is rigorously distinguished from the masculine labour of the *polis*. Although, within this schema, the sepulchre is the proper or property (*le propre* – Gtr144a) of man, it is the wife or the daughter who is entrusted with the funeral rites (*pompes funèbres*, Gtr143a – which is also the title of Genet's third novel, an extended work of mourning for his dead lover, Jean Décarnin – J. D. – an intertextual allusion that is far from incidental in this context). The building of the sepulchre is woman's work, as is the embalming, shrouding, and interring of the corpse and the preparation and erection of the slab or stele. When the corpse is placed in the sepulchre, its singularity and materiality decompose, allowing it to ascend into the universality of Spirit.

Enter Antigone: for it is she who demands a sepulchre for her brother Polynices in the name of the divine law. This introduces the second focus of Derrida's reading, where he draws on two related phenomena: first, Antigone's declaration:

> I could have had another husband
> And by him other sons, if one were lost;
> But, father and mother lost, where would I get another brother.
>
> (AN lines 906–10)

And second, Hegel's reading of this passage and his consequent privileging of the brother/sister relation over those of husband and wife or parents and children (PStr273–5/PS246–8). The relation of sister to brother is an 'unmixed' ('*unvermischte*' – PStr274/PS247) recognition of spiritual and ethical essence where the two parties neither desire one another ('*Sie begehren daher einander nicht*' – ibid.), nor do they enter into a 'life and death struggle' or a 'struggle for recognition.' Although Antigone is 'never a bride, never a mother' (AN line 911), Hegel recognizes that 'the feminine, in the form of the sister, has the highest *presentiment* of ethical essence (*Das Weibliche hat daher als Schwester die höchste* Ahndung *des sittlichen Wesens*)'[7] (PStr274/PS247). Derrida's argument here is that Antigone and Polynices are

> The two sole consciousnesses that, in the Hegelian universe, relate to each other without entering into war. Given the generality of the struggle for recognition in the relationship between consciousnesses, one would be tempted to conclude from this that at bottom *there is no* brother/sister bond, there is no brother or sister. If such a relation is unique and reaches a kind of repose (*Ruhe*) and equilibrium (*Gleichgewicht*) that are refused to all others, that is because the brother and the sister do not receive their forself from the other and nevertheless constitute themselves as 'free individualities.' – The for-selves (*les pour-soi*) recognize, without depending on, each other; they no more desire one another than tear each other to pieces (*ne se désirent pas plus qu'ils ne se déchirent*).
>
> (Gtr149a/G208a)

Thus far, Derrida has been pushing very hard at these paragraphs of the *Phenomenology*, but following them to the letter. However, he now raises a question with regard to this brother/sister relation: 'Is it impossible [the translation has 'possible' here]? Is it in contradiction with the whole system?' (Gtr149a/G208a). Following Hegel's remark that the relation between the sister and the brother represents the limit at which the life of the family breaks up and goes beyond itself (PStr275/PS248), Derrida suggests that the sister's presentiment of the essence of *Sittlichkeit* cannot be contained within the limits of the system. In virtue of the fact that Antigone and Polynices constitute themselves as free individualities that have not 'given to, or received from one another this independent being-for-self (*Fürsichseyn*)' (PStr274/PS247), and because they do not engage in a 'struggle for recognition,' their relation somehow exceeds the system of which it is a part. The figure of Antigone gazing with impassive rage at the unburied body of her brother cannot be dialectically appropriated and stands outside any attempt at assimilation. She exemplifies the femininity of the ethical relation with the other that is not based upon dialectical structures of recognition, reconciliation, and reciprocity.

The effect of focusing on this 'impossible place' (Gtr151a) within Hegel's reading of Antigone, and *a fortiori* within the family, within *Sittlichkeit* and within the system, is to propose a second question that will radicalize this impossibility:

> What if the inassimilable, the absolutely indigestible, played a fundamental rôle within the system, abyssal rather, the abyss playing . . . [and here there is an interruption of eleven pages, where Derrida cites lengthy passages from Hegel's correspondence with his lover/friend Nanette Endel, his fiancée/wife Marie von Tucker and his friend Friedrich Niethammer, which offer insights into Hegel's opinions on love, friendship, marriage, and teaching] a quasi transcendental rôle and letting be formed above it, like a sort of effluvium, a dream of appeasement? Is there not always an element excluded from the system which assures the space of the system's possibility? . . . And what if the sister, the brother/sister relation here represented the transcendental position or ex-position?
>
> (Gtr151–62a/G211–27a)

These questions, and note that they are still only questions, deconstructively turn the reading and suggest that what cannot be assimilated within the Hegelian system, the abyss, functions as a quasi-transcendental condition of possibility for the system. The peculiar character of Derrida's transcendental claim is that it not only establishes the condition for the possibility of the system, it also indicates the condition for the system's *impossibility*. The figure of Antigone is the quasi-transcendental condition for the possibility and impossibility of the Hegelian system, its *Grund* and *Abgrund*.

The above argumentation very much typifies Derrida's reading practice in *Glas* and elsewhere: he focuses on a seemingly minor point in a text, a point that one might easily overlook in a casual reading, and then shows how this point is the text's blind spot from which its entire conceptual edifice can be deconstructed. He summarizes his reading in the following way,

> Like Hegel, we have been fascinated by Antigone, by this unbelievable relation, this powerful liaison without desire, this immense impossible desire that could not live, capable only of reversing, paralysing or exceeding a system and a history, of interrupting the life of the Concept, of taking its breath away (*de lui couper le souffle*) or, indeed, which comes back to the same thing (*ce qui revient au même*), of supporting it from the outside or the beneath of a crypt.
>
> Crypt – one would have said, of the transcendental or of the repressed, of the unthought or the excluded – that organizes the ground to which it does not belong.

(Gtr166a/G232a)

The twin foci of sepulchre and sister finally combine in the figure of the crypt, where Antigone is imprisoned and hangs herself. Ultimately, for Derrida, it is Antigone's death that sounds the knell or *glas* of the system and announces the end of history: 'Nothing should (*devrait*) be able to survive Antigone's death. Nothing more should follow, go out of her, after her. The announcement of her death should sound the absolute end of history (*la fin absolue de l'histoire*)' (ibid.). Antigone's death *should* bring the system, history, and the movement of cognition to a halt, and yet speculative dialectics incorporates this crypt within itself, making of Antigone a moment to be *aufgehoben*. For Derrida, Antigone's death *should* exceed the Hegelian system and make Spirit stumble on its path to Absolute Knowledge, and yet Spirit barely loses its footing for an instant and relentlessly continues its ascent.

Once again, it should be noted how the choice of the family as the example of the system is crucial here, because Antigone *exemplifies* the family, following its duties to the letter and showing the point at which the family, *Sittlichkeit*, and the system exceed the intentions of Hegel's text and deconstruct themselves. Starting from Derrida's reading, I would want to argue that by exemplifying the essence of ethical life, of *Sittlichkeit*, Antigone marks a place ('an impossible place') within the Hegelian system where an ethics is glimpsed that is irreducible to dialectics and cognition, what I would call an ethics of the singular. Such an ethics would not be based upon the recognition of the other, which is always self-recognition, but would rather begin with the expropriation of the self in the face of the other's approach. Ethics would begin with the recognition that the other is not an object of cognition or comprehension, but precisely that which exceeds my grasp and powers. The formal structure of such an ethics of the singular might well be analogous to that of mourning: Antigone's mourning for Polynices, Haemon's mourning for Antigone, Genet's mourning for Jean Décarnin. In mourning, the self is consumed by the pain of the other's death and is possessed by the alterity of that which it cannot possess: the absence of the beloved.[8] Might not the death of the beloved, of love itself, and the work of mourning be the basis for a non-Christian and non-philosophical ethicality and friendship? Although such remarks give only hints and guesses, my claim is that an ethics of the singular is the perpetual horizon of Derrida's deconstructive reading of Hegel.

Derrida closes his reading of Hegel on *Antigone* by focusing on the final paragraphs of 'Ethical Action. Human and Divine Knowledge. Guilt and Destiny' (PStr287-9), where the combat of Eteocles and Polynices provides the backdrop for the conflict between the spirit of community and the rebellious principle of singularity, of the family (PStr286/PS257). In refusing to administer the proper funeral rites to Polynices, the community represses the singular; but in so doing, the community dishonours and destroys the family pieties that underpin it. The community is avenged, and Antigone revenged, by destructive war with other cities, which results in the ruin of *Sittlichkeit* (PStr289/PS260). In Hegel's much-cited words, womankind, the feminine, the singular, is the community's 'internal enemy (*innern Feind*)' and 'everlasting irony (*ewige Ironie*)' (PStr288/PS259).

At this point, one might attempt a *rapprochement* between Antigone and Genet. Both are criminals, both are imprisoned or entombed, both are orphans (Gtr165-6a), and, more importantly, both are excluded by and reject the human law, what Hegel calls 'the manhood (*die Männlichkeit*) of the commu*nity' (PStr287/PS258). Whatever the community might do to repress the singular, there always remains the everlasting possibility of irony. Irony is the genre of ethical* discourse. Imprisoned at Fresnes, Genet, the effeminate, the homosexual, the masturbator, the thief, silently ironizes the customs and legislature of the community in his writing. In *Funeral Rites*, his irony of the *Libération* in France in 1944, he works over his mourning for Jean Décarnin. Like Antigone gazing at the corpse of Polynices, Genet contemplates Décarnin's face in his coffin, writing of the 'funereal flavor' that 'has often filled my mouth *after love*' (my italics – FR25–7). As Cocteau has remarked, Genet will one day have to be recognized as a moralist (SGtr558/SG513). Sartre extends this insight, arguing that although Genet's works 'are criminal assaults upon his readers, they are, at the same time, presented as systematically conducted ethical experiments' (SGtr559/SG514). However, rather then seeing the ethical content of Genet's work in terms of Sartre's totalizing narrative of liberation, the ethical status of a text like *Funeral Rites*, as well as Derrida's methodology of reading in *Glas*, lies precisely in its resistance to totalization, its everlasting ironization of totality.

## Kant's Judaism, Derrida's post-Hegelian Kantianism

At this point in Derrida's reading, he interrupts his discussion of the *Phenomenology* in order to return to the *Philosophy of Right*, precisely at the point in the discussion of marriage when Hegel mentions *Antigone* and refers the reader back to the *Phenomenology* (PRtr114–5/PR158, Gtr188–9). For Hegel, marriage is in essence monogamy and is characterized as 'ethico-legal love (*rechtlich sittliche Liebe*)' (PRtr262/PR153). It is our 'ethical duty' (PRtr111/PR153) to enter marriage, and therefore, as Derrida remarks, 'the ethical and the political are reached only on condition of being married' (Gtr192) – which, of course, excludes both Antigone and Genet from Hegelian *Sittlichkeit*.

Derrida interests himself in two presuppositions of marriage: inhibition or repression (*Hemmung* – which Knox translates as 'restraint' PRtr114), and the incest prohibition. First, the ethical aspect of love consists in 'the higher inhibition and depreciation of purely natural pressure [*die höhere Hemmung und Zurücksetzung des bloßen Naturtriebs*]' (PRtr114/PR156). Thus, the entrance into marriage, the family and *Sittlichkeit* is founded upon what Derrida calls repression (*refoulement;* Gtr197/G275a) of the natural drive. Second, marriage is founded upon the incest prohibition, where the ethical transaction of marriage is denied to blood relatives like Antigone and Polynices (PRtr115/PR159).

This discussion occasions an excursus into the 'children' of Hegel's philosophy: Feuerbach, Marx, and, very briefly, Kierkegaard (Gtr200ai – see also Gtr232ai-33ai). Derrida focuses on Feuerbach's *Principles of the Philosophy of the Future* and *The Essence of Christianity*, and on Marx's critique of Feuerbach in the 1844 *Economic and Philosophical Manuscripts* and the *Theses* of 1845. The purpose of this rare excursus into Marx in Derrida's work would appear to demonstrate simply that Marx's and Feuerbach's critique of Hegel is largely a critique of religion. For Feuerbach, 'speculative philosophy is the *true, consistent, rational* theology' (Gtr201a).

The mention of religion slowly turns Derrida's reading back, somewhat circuitously, to the problem of the transition from Absolute Religion to Absolute Knowledge and to the guiding question: 'How is the relief of religion into philosophy produced?' After a discussion of fetishism in Hegel's account of African religion in the *Lectures on the Philosophy of World History* (Gtr207–11a), Derrida once again takes up Hegel's critique of Kant's conception of religion. In the Introduction to the *Lectures on the Philosophy of Religion*, Hegel criticizes the Kantian claim according to which 'we can know nothing of God' (LPR36–7, Gtr211a). For Hegel, Christianity is the revealed religion, indeed it is the *only* revealed religion, and the essence of the revealed, *das Offenbare*, is that the content of religion, Absolute Spirit, is revealed to self-consciousness as an object of knowledge in the form of *Vorstellung*. The Hegelian conception of revealed religion is speculatively expressed in the closing pages of the *Encyclopaedia*: 'God is God only in so far as he knows himself: his self-knowledge is, further, a self-consciousness in man and man's knowledge *of* God, which proceeds to man's self-knowledge *in* God' (PM298).

The Kantian claim that God is not an object of cognition fails to comprehend both the nature of revelation and the relation between the human and the divine. In these respects, Derrida claims, Kantianism is Judaic:

> To claim to found Christianity on reason and nonetheless to make non-manifestation, the being-hidden of God, the principle of this religion is (Kant) to understand nothing about revelation. Kant is Jewish (*est juif*): he believes in a jealous, envious God.
>
> (Gtr213a/G297a)

In the *Encyclopaedia* (PM298), Hegel repeats the exclusion of jealousy as a predicate of the divine that was established in Plato's *Phaedrus* and Aristotle's *Metaphysics*.[9] The enigmatic guardedness of jealousy is opposed to the phenomenal revelation of Spirit (PM298), and the former can have no place in either Absolute Religion or Absolute Knowledge,

> In *Sa* (i.e. *Savoir Absolu*), jealousy no longer has a place. Jealousy always comes from the night of the unconscious, the unknown, the other. Pure sight relieves all jealousy. Not seeing what one sees, seeing what one cannot see and who cannot present himself, such is the jealous operation. It always

has to do with the trace, never with perception. Seen from *Sa*, the thought of the trace would thus be a jealous thought.

(Gtr215)

The structural analogies between Kantianism, Judaism, jealousy, and the thought of the trace (i.e. the thought of that which will never have been revealed or incarnated and which exceeds the order of phenomenality and presence) are highly suggestive, recalling the above discussions and provoking others that cannot be followed in this context. If Hegelianism is, as Derrida claims, a philosophy of presence, where philosophy is the truth of religion and where self-consciousness is presented with the Absolute as an object of cognition, then, one might ask, does Kantianism bear a more complex relation to the philosophy of presence? Might not the deconstruction of *Sittlichkeit* and the hypothesis of the ethics of the singular signal a return to a form of *Moralität*? Is *Glas* implicitly postulating a post-Hegelian Kantianism?

Such questions would, at the very least, have to pass through Hegel's critique of Kant in the *Phenomenology* and the *Philosophy of Right* and focus in particular on the status of the Postulates of Pure Practical Reason. It would be necessary to ask whether the postulation of an 'infinite progress' towards the complete fitness of the will to the Moral Law (immortality) and of morality to happiness (God), can be contained within the horizon of presence.[10] Might not the infinite deferral of the presentation of the postulates to self-consciousness open out onto the thought of *différance*, where God and immortality would be present only as traces of that which will never have been present? In this regard, it is worth noting that when Derrida locates the thought of *différance* in Husserl's use of the 'Idea in the *Kantian* sense,' he adds, 'La critique de Kant par Hegel vaudrait sans doute aussi contre Husserl.'[11] My claim is that this remark, read against the grain and in the knowledge of *Glas*, is a good deal more Kantian or Husserlian than might at first appear.

## Luminous essence – the non-metaphysical gift of holocaust

Derrida continues with the extraordinary *mise en scène* of a fictive dialogue between Kant and Hegel (Gtr216–8a), with parenthetical remarks by Freud (Gtr217ai), before summarizing the relation between religion and philosophy with Hegel's remark: 'Thus religion and philosophy come to be one . . . . Philosophy is only explicating *itself* when it explicates religion, and when it explicates itself it is explicating religion' (LPR20, Gtr218a). Indeed, it is the precise and paradoxical nature of the limit that divides and unites religion and philosophy at the end of the *Encyclopaedia* and the *Phenomenology* that fascinates Derrida here. The paradox is that Absolute or Revealed Religion is not yet Absolute Knowing and yet it is already Absolute Knowing. Derrida expresses this structure more elegantly and untranslatably as 'l'absolu du déjà-là du pas-encore ou de l'encore du déjà plus' (Gtr219a/G306a). Although a digression would be necessary here upon the function of the 'we' and the concept of *Erinnerung* in the *Phenomenology*, as well as upon the circle metaphors that recur in Hegel's text (cf. PStr488/PS429, PRtr225/PR17, A24–5), it can justifiably be claimed that Absolute Religion is only the *Vorstellung* of the unification between self-consciousness and Absolute Spirit, a unification only 'in principle (*an sich*)' (PS425/PStr483) and therefore neither actual nor fully present.

> The reconciliation has produced itself and yet it has *not* yet taken place, it is *not present*, only represented or present as remaining before, ahead of, to come, present as not-yet-there and not as presence of the present. But as this reconciliation of Being (*l'être*) and the same (*même*) (reconciliation itself – *même*) is absolute presence, absolute parousia, we must say that in religion, in absolute revelation, presence is present as representation.
>
> (Gtr220a/G308a)

*Parousia*, as the presence to self-consciousness of the consciousness of the Absolute and the completion of Spirit's circular phenomenology, is minimally but decisively deferred in Absolute Religion. Absolute Knowledge is the unification of the content of religion, substance or being-in-itself (PStr478/PS421), with the form of Spirit (PStr409/PS362), subject or being-for-self, in the thinking of the Concept, what Hegel calls 'comprehensive knowing (*begreifendes Wissen*)' or *Science* (PStr485–6/PS427–8). It is only with Absolute Knowledge that the Concept attains its passage into consciousness and where the latter experiences the certainty of immediacy, thereby returning to the beginning of its phenomenological path in sense-certainty (PStr491/PS432). Thus begins the labour of recollection.

Derrida ascends with Hegel to the peak of Absolute Knowledge, but instead of remaining at the summit, he descends a little into the 'Religion' chapter of the *Phenomenology*. As I will show, such a move is neither contingent nor a product of vertigo. Derrida schematizes the three moments of religion: natural, aesthetic, and revealed (Gtr236a). The immediacy of natural religion (light, plants and animals, and the artificer) is superseded by the religion of art (the abstract, living and spiritual works of art), and these two forms are unified in revealed religion, which is the true shape (*'wahren* **Gestalt***'* PStr416/PS368) of Spirit. Now, although Christianity is the true shape of Spirit, this shape will itself have to be overcome in order to pass over into Absolute Knowledge. Derrida infers from this that 'le *Sa* n'a pas de figure' (Gtr237a/G330a), and that it is precisely shapeliness or figuration that must be superseded in Absolute Knowledge. From this inference, Derrida draws a circle around the syllogism of religion in order to link up the immediacy of natural religion with that of Absolute Knowledge (Gtr237a). This would appear to be justified insofar as the first moment of natural religion, *Das Lichtwesen* (translated by Miller as 'God as Light', PStr418; and by Hyppolite as '*L'essence lumineuse*', PE Vol. II, p. 214 – Derrida follows the latter translation), shares the the same shape, or rather 'shape of shapelessness (*Gestalt der Gestaltlosigkeit*)' (PStr419/PS371; cf. LPR Vol. II, p. 78) as sense-certainty. Crudely stated, the *Phenomenology* contains two movements, that from subject to substance in Chapters I to VI ('Sense-Certainty' to 'Spirit'), and that from substance to subject described in Chapter VII ('Religion'). All that remains in Chapter VIII ('Absolute Knowing') is for these two moments to be unified into the comprehensive thinking of the Concept.[12] Thus, the return to sense-certainty that occurs at the end of the *Phenomenology*, as well as being a return to the beginning of Chapter I, is also a return to the beginning of Chapter VII; although, of course, religion presupposes that the moments of consciousness, self-consciousness, Reason and Spirit 'have run their full course' (PStr413/PS365). Thus, for Derrida, the discussion of natural religion is an oblique way of analysing the claim to Absolute Knowledge and of answering the question that appears as the subtitle to the French paperback edition of *Glas*: 'Que reste-t-il du savoir absolu?'

I would argue that the pages of *Glas* that deal with natural religion (especially Gtr236a-45a), together with the discussion of *Antigone*, constitute the core of Derrida's reading and the clearest deployment of its thesis. Perhaps the enduring importance of these pages for Derrida can be judged by the fact that he quotes from them at great length in a 1987 publication, *Feu la cendre* (FC26–32). What specifically interests Derrida here is the page and a half of '*Das Lichtwesen*' and the precise nature of the transition to 'Plant and Animal.' The 'shapeless shape' of the first moment of natural religion ' . . . is the pure, all-embracing and all-pervading *essential light* of sunrise, which preserves itself in its formless substantiality (*das reine, alles enthaltende und erfüllende Lichtwesen des Aufgangs, das sich in seiner formlosen Substantialität erhält*)' (PStr419/PS371). As Derrida points out, this conception of religion, that of ancient Parsis or Persia, corresponds to the Zoroastrian cult of light discussed by Hegel in the

*Lectures on the Philosophy of Religion* (LPR77). In Zoroastrian religion, light is worshipped not as a symbol or sign of the Good, but as the Good itself, its pure manifestation (LPR76 & 78).[13]

Essential light is, Derrida writes, 'pure and without shape (*figure*), this light burns all (*brûle tout*). It burns itself in the all-burning (*brûle-tout*) that it is, leaves of itself, of itself or anything, no trace, no mark, no sign of passage' (Gtr238a/G332a). The 'torrents of light' or 'streams of fire' emanating from *das Lichtwesen* are 'destructive of all structured form' (PStr419/PS371). Hegel concludes that the content of essential light is 'pure *Being*' (*das reine Seyn*), 'an essenceless by-play (*ein wesenloses Beyherspielen*) in this substance which merely ascends, without descending into the depths to become a subject (*Subject zu werden*)' (ibid.). Essenceless substance without subject, 'the many-named one' that 'lacks a self' (*ibid.*), is the thought that interests Derrida here. To express this differently, to think essenceless substance without subject is akin to thinking Being (*das Sein*) prior to its determination with regard to particular beings (*das Seiende*). Derrida asks: 'How can the self and the for-itself (*pour-soi*) appear?' (Gtr239a/G334a). That is to say, how can the transition from the in-itself to the for-itself that opens dialectics and history begin? How is the transition from this oriental sunrise to occidental sunset to be accomplished?

As always, it is a question of a transition from immediacy to mediation, or being-in-itself to being-for-self. Derrida, citing and retranslating what is perhaps the most important passage from Hegel for his reading, writes:

> But this reeling (tottering, tumultuous, *taumelnde*) life must (*muß*; why must it?) [*pourquoi doit-elle?*] determine itself as being for self and give its evanescent figures a stable subsistence. . . . Pure light disseminates (*wirft . . . auseinander*) [Miller has 'disperses' and Hyppolite '*éparpille*'] its simplicity as an infinity of separated forms and gives itself as a holocaust to the for-itself [*se donne en holocauste au pour-soi*] (*gibt sich dem Fürsichseyn zum Opfer*) [Miller has 'sacrifice' for *Opfer*, Hyppolite also has '*holocauste*'], so that the singular [*das Einzelne*] may take its subsistence from its substance.
> (PStr420/PS371–2/PE Vol. II, p. 216, Gtr241/G336)

Thus, the total burning and consummation of essential light gives itself to being-for-self as a holocaust, that is, as a whole (*holos*) that is burnt (*caustos*). With the advent of this gift, the fire of light goes out and the sun begins to set; the dialectical, phenomenological, and historical movement of occidentalization that will result in Absolute Knowledge has begun. Within the syllogism of natural religion, there occurs a transition from the religion of light to the pantheism of the religion of flowers, a move that mirrors the transition from sense-certainty to perception (PStr420/PS372) and that lets Derrida complete a circle that refers the reader back to the beginning of the Hegel column and the prefatory discussion of flower religion (Gtr2a). Yet, one might ask, why is all this important? As Derrida writes: 'What is at stake in this column?' (Gtr241a/G337a) He responds:

> This perhaps: the gift, the sacrifice, the putting in play or to fire of all, the holocaust, are in the power of ontology (*en puissance d'ontologie*). They bear and overflow it but cannot give birth to it. Without the holocaust the dialectical movement and the history of Being could not open themselves, engage themselves in the annulus of their anniversary, could not annul themselves in producing the solar course from the Orient to the Occident.
>
> (Gtr242a/G337)

*En puissance d'ontologie*: ontology would here seem to be understood simply as discourse (*logos*) about beings (*onta*). As discourse about beings, ontology always thinks that which is – Being – with respect to its determination through beings. Heidegger defines metaphysics as onto-theo-logy, that is to say, the Aristotelian investigation of *to on on*, Being *qua* Being, which asks after the totality of beings with respect to their most universal traits (ontology), but also with respect to the highest and therefore divine being (theology). Metaphysics or, more properly, first philosophy, conceives of beings in terms of a unifying *ousia* and ultimately a divine *ousia*.[14] Heidegger therefore describes metaphysics as discourse that states what beings are as beings ('*Die Metaphysik sagt, was das Seiende als das Seiende ist*' p. 19, tr. p. 275). However, in its discourse upon beings (*das Seiende*), what does not get asked about is Being itself (*Sein*) prior to its determination in terms of beings. Heidegger writes: 'Metaphysics, insofar as it always represents only beings as beings (*das Seiende als das Seiende vorstellt*), does not recall Being itself (*das Sein selbst*)'(p. 8, tr. p. 266).

Returning to Derrida, his claim would appear to be that although the gift of the holocaust is in the power of ontology *qua* metaphysics, it simultaneously bears and overflows ontology and the dialectical or metaphysical determination of Being in terms of the subject, or being-for-self. Derrida is here attempting the thought of a sacrificial giving, which is a moment within the Hegelian text which that text cannot master and which engages and exceeds ontology, dialectics, and metaphysics. Recalling the above discussion of *Antigone*, the gift of holocaust is perhaps the condition for the possibility and impossibility of the Hegelian system. Derrida continues:

Before everything, before every determinable being (*étant*), there is (*il y a*), there was (*il y avait*), there will have been (*il y aura eu*) the irruptive event of the gift (*don*). An event which no longer has any relation with what one currently designates under this word. One can no longer think the giving (*la donation*) starting from Being (*être*). . . . In *Zeit und Sein*, the gift of the *es gibt* gives itself to be thought before the *Sein* in the *es gibt Sein* and displaces all that is determined under the name of *Ereignis*, a word often translated by event (*événement*).

(Gtr242a/G337a)

With this allusion to Heidegger's 1962 lecture *Zeit und Sein,* the ultimate orientation of Derrida's reading of Hegel becomes apparent. There are scattered references to Heidegger in *Glas*, but the above allusion is the most important.[15] Derrida appears to be understanding Hegel in terms of the ontological difference between *Sein* (*être*) and *Seiende* (*étant*) and focuses in particular upon the thought of the gift contained in the phrase *es gibt Sein* ('it gives Being' or 'there "is" Being'; in French, *il y a être*), which returns the thinking of Being to that of a primordial giving.

In *Zeit und Sein*, his continuation and radicalization of the thinking begun in *Sein und Zeit*, Heidegger's seeks to raise the question of Being and time anew as a matter for thinking. To think Being in terms of beings, where the former is the ontological ground for the latter, is to think metaphysically (SD4/TB4). Heidegger replaces the customary expressions, namely that 'Being is' or 'time is' ('*Sein ist, Zeit ist*' SD5/TB5) with the formulations '*es gibt Sein*' and '*es gibt Zeit*' (ibid.). Thus, Heidegger displaces the problem of Being and time onto the horizon of an 'it' that 'gives' or provides the primordial donation of Being. This giving is ultimately thought as the appropriating event (*das Ereignis*, SD20/BT19; in French *l'événement*), or, more precisely, as the appropriating of appropriation ('*das Ereignis ereignet*' SD25/BT24), which permits a thinking of the conjunction of Being and time without regard for beings, that is, without regard for metaphysics ('*Sein ohne das Seiende denken, heißt: Sein ohne Rücksicht auf die Metaphysik denken*' SD25/BT24).

What fascinates Derrida in the formulation *es gibt Sein* is the way in which Being is divorced from the language of metaphysics and shown to belong to a prior giving, the giving of an 'It' ('*Sein gehört als die Gabe dieses Es gibt in das Geben*' SD6/BT6). The gift of an 'It,' in Derrida's text *Ça*, and the homophone for *Sa, Savoir Absolu*, exceeds the metaphysical determination of Being. For

Heidegger, Being *is* not ('*Sein ist Nicht*') but rather gives 'It' as the unconcealing of presence ('*Sein gibt es als das Entbergen von Anwesen*' SD6/BT6).

To think Being without beings, the essenceless, burning by-play of light, is to think without metaphysics. The aim of Derrida's deconstructive reading of Hegel is the location of a non-metaphysical moment within dialectical metaphysics. Yet this non-metaphysical moment of *das Lichtwesen* completely burns itself, becoming a holocaust that is then given to being-for-self, *das Seiende*, and from which the metaphysical movement of the dialectic begins. Hegelian dialectic thinks the meaning of Being with regard to beings, as self-conscious subjectivity. Yet Derrida's claim appears to be that, in its destination, as Absolute Knowledge, and in its beginning, as sense-certainty and *das Lichtwesen*, Hegelian dialectic contains that which it cannot contain: the primordial and non-metaphysical donation of the gift. To formulate this more radically, one might say that Absolute Knowledge (*Sa*) transforms itself into an It (*Ça*) that gives.

Derrida continues:

> The process of the gift (before exchange), process which is not a process but a holocaust, a holocaust of the holocaust, *engages* the history of Being but does not belong to it. The gift is *not*, the holocaust *is not*, if at least there is some (*il y en a*). But as soon as it burns (the blaze is not a being) [*un étant*] it must [*il doit*], burning itself, burn its operation of burning and begin to be.
>
> (Gtr242a/G338a)

The blaze of fire is not a being, yet in its burning it *must* (and the ethical modality of this *doit* and its corresponding duty or *devoir* is of interest here) become a being, begin to be and set the history of Being – understood as Being's oblivion in the history of metaphysics – in motion. Derrida generalizes his claim, writing:

> The dialectic of religion, the history of philosophy (etc.), produces itself as the reflection-effect [*l'effet-reflet*] of a *coup de don* [a gift's blow] in holocaust. But if the blazing is not yet philosophy (and the remains) [*le reste*], it cannot not nevertheless give rise [*donner lieu*] to philosophy, to dialectical speculation.
>
> (Ibid.)

Philosophy, understood historically and dialectically as metaphysics, is the effect of a *coup de don*, a primordial giving that is otherwise than philosophy.

Philosophy begins with a non-philosophical event that it cannot both contain and not give rise to philosophy. This claim has the status of a *necessity* in *Glas*:

> There is there [*il y a là*] a *fatum* of the gift, and this *necessity* [my italics] was said in the 'must' (*muß*) we indicated above: the *Taumeln*, the vertigo, the delirium *must* determine itself as for-itself and take on subsistency.
>
> (Gtr242–3a/G338a)

It is necessary for the gift to be given, for the non-philosophical event that gives rise to philosophy to be received as philosophy's beginning. At this point in the text, inexplicably, Derrida slips into the language of personal pronouns: 'I give you [*je te donne*] – a pure gift, without exchange, without return – but whether I want this or not, the gift guards itself and from then on you must, you owe [*tu dois*]' (Gtr243a/G338a). The necessity of giving the gift without receiving anything in return also implies the necessity of receiving the gift. I am bound to give you the gift, and from that moment you are duty-bound in a responsible relation where you must respond, where you owe (*dois*) the gift to me. The discourse of philosophy has as its unthought horizon an event of holocaust, of primordial giving that informs and exceeds it: 'The gift [*don*], the giving of the gift [*la donation du don*], the pure cadeau does not let itself be thought by the dialectics to which it, however, gives rise [*donne lieu*]' (Gtr243a/G339a).

Yet, once again it is necessary to ask, what is at stake in this column? Derrida's tireless labour of reading results in the location of the thought of the gift and the holocaust, notions that deny dialectical or even philosophical comprehension. Such a gift *must* (*doit*), however, give rise to philosophy. It is the nature and fatality of this *must* and its association with a notion of ethical duty (*devoir*) that is of interest here. Connecting this discussion with the reading of *Antigone* and the hypothesis of an ethics of the singular and of mourning, might one not ask whether *Glas* is also delineating an ethics of holocaust, of a primordial gift or sacrifice that is the unthought limit of philosophical conceptuality? Can philosophy think holocaust, its ashes, its remains? Can ontology, even fundamental ontology or the question of the truth of Being, responsibly break its silence on the holocaust? What is at stake here?[16]

This perhaps: the gift or holocaust that I must give to the other and that the other owes to me is to regard the other as he or she for whom I would sacrifice myself. Prior to my concern with myself, with my death and with all that is proper to me, arises the primacy of the other's death over my own and the consequent possibility of regarding myself as a sacrifice or holocaust for the other. An ethics of holocaust would describe a radical expropriation, a movement of charity, where I give to the other without hope of remuneration and yet, from that moment, you are obliged.[17]

## At the origin of literature

However, *Glas* does not end with the discussion of the gift. Indeed, the text does not have an end, in the sense of an organized *telos*, like Absolute Knowledge, towards which the reading tends. The final pages (Gtr245a-62a) continue the reading of Hegel, working through the remaining sections of 'Natural Religion' and discussing the first two moments of 'Religion in the Form of Art' (PStr424–39/PS376–88). Derrida begins by examining flower religion and digresses onto Hegel's remarks on plants from the *Philosophy of Nature* (PN67-91). Bringing together themes from both the Genet column and the discussion of *Antigone*, Derrida writes: 'The plant is a sort of sister' (Gtr245a), that is, it is innocent, without desire, its subjectivity is 'not yet for-itself' (Gtr245a). The plant or flower, Antigone or Genet, becomes a figure for the singular entity that receives the gift of the light, the life-giving sustenance of the sun, and in so doing, recognizes its debt, its *devoir*. From the innocence of the flower religion and 'the guilt of *animal* religions' (PStr420/PS372), Derrida passes onto the third moment of 'Natural Religion,' 'The Artificer' (*'Der Werkmeister'*). By focusing on the way in which the artificer employs 'plant life' as 'mere ornament' (PStr422/PS374), he joins a further textual circle and returns to the passage from the *Aesthetics* that was the second of the figures with which he began his commentary. The phallic stone columns of India themselves derive from plant forms (A657–8) and become objects of religious adoration.

The final pages of the Hegel column discuss the moments of abstract and living works of art, analysing the notions of hymn, oracle, and cult (PStr427–35/PS378–85), before returning once again to what was called above the *Taumel*, the scene of 'Bacchic enthusiasm' (PStr439/PS388, Gtr261a). Derrida follows Hegel's discussion of Dionysian religion, where, 'the mystery of bread and wine is not yet the mystery of flesh and blood' (PStr438/PS387), and where Dionysus must pass over into the figure who represents revealed religion, the person of Christ. This explains the closing lines of *Glas*, where Derrida writes of 'a time to perfect the resemblance between Dionysus and Christ. Between the two (already) is elaborated in sum the origin of literature' (Gtr262a). In Dionysian enthusiasm, the self is in rapture and 'beside itself (*ausser sich*)' (PStr439/PS388), it has become a god. Yet, Hegel argues, the self in rapture is unbalanced and the only element in which a balance between the self and the Absolute, or the interior and the exterior, can be achieved is through language (*die Sprache* – ibid.). However, language here understood is no longer that of the hymn, oracle or Dionysian 'stammer' (*ibid.*), but rather *literature*: epic (Homer), tragedy (Sophocles and Aeschylus), and comedy (Aristophanes). *Glas* ends at the origin of literature and the overcoming of Dionyisian religion in a development that recalls the analyses of Nietzsche's *The Birth of Tragedy*.

The Hegel column finishes with the following incomplete sentence, 'But it runs to its ruin [*elle court à sa perte* – it is heading for disaster], for having counted without [*sans*]' (Gtr262a/G365a). The pronoun 'elle' seems to refer back to 'littérature' in the previous sentence, and indeed Hegel's analysis of literature ends with the dissolution of both divine transcendence and, significantly, Greek *Sittlichkeit*, in the irony and mockery of Aristophanean comedy. But what does literature count without? Does it count without Genet, the thief who single-handedly destroys and reinvents literature (SGtr439/SG407)? Is the reader encouraged to progress from the reading of Hegel to the beginning of the Genet column? Perhaps. Although joining the two columns together in this manner risks missing the graphic complexity of *Glas*. For this is a book that seeks to escape linearity and circularity, the metaphorics of speculative dialectics. By concluding without climax or apocalypse – without even a full stop – *Glas* nevertheless makes its point. During his discussion of Genet, Derrida notes that 'the object of the present work, and its style too, is the morsel [*morceau*]' (Gtr118b/G166b). By repeating the Hegelian system, largely in the manner of a commentary, and by letting Hegel speak for – and against – himself, the system somehow begins to decompose, morsels fall off and remain outside the grasp of the dialectic. The rhythm of reading Hegel with Derrida is not governed by the smooth three-stroke engine of the dialectic, but rather by a jerking rhythm of interruption and recommencement – the music of Genet's masturbation – a vast and inefficent reading machine slowly lumbering across the terrain of the text.

## Ascesis and the experience of language

Although I have given a broadly sympathetic reading of *Glas*, this is not to say that I think the text is without shortcomings. In this context, I shall list two criticisms that are relevant to the reading of Hegel:

1 The almost complete absence of footnotes and references in *Glas* obliges the

English-speaking reader to rely upon the accompanying *Glassary* in order to locate the specific texts and passages that Derrida deals with. Derrida's scholarly practice leaves him open to the charge of obfuscation and mystification. In the preface written for the English translation, Derrida notes that *Glassary* 'has restored the references I thought I had to omit' (GL19). My question is: why did Derrida feel he had to omit them?

2 Who is Derrida addressing in *Glas*? What is the audience for this deconstructive reading? *Glas* could not be described as an introductory reading of Hegel (although, as was noted, the problem of *Einführung* is thematized by Derrida), in the sense that the text is difficult to follow for readers with little knowledge of Hegel's work, and in particular of the *Phenomenology*. But if *Glas* is more accessible to advanced readers of Hegel, then the problem of audience remains unclear because much of Derrida's commentary, for example Hegel's critique of Kant, the passage from Judaism to Christianity or the transition from revealed religion to Absolute Knowledge, will be familiar to anyone who has begun to grapple with Hegel.

So why does Derrida proceed in this way in *Glas*? Perhaps it is the very status of commentary and its repetition of the main text that is at stake here. *Glas* is precisely a repetition of Hegel, a devotional labor of reading, translating and writing, what Jean Hyppolite called, with reference to his translation of the *Phenomenology*, his '*travail de Bénédictin*' (GSxxvi). In contradistinction to certain platitudinous *idées fixes* with regard to Derrida and deconstruction, I would suggest that *Glas* is a profoundly *ascetic* text, rigorous in its exegesis and austere in its denial of any fixed interpretative key, grid, or schema. It is an arduous writing that resists the temptation of critique and obeys no other law than to carry on with the labor of reading and writing and keep open a space where thinking can take place.

By way of conclusion, is *Glas* a plausible reading of Hegel? Is it even correct? The plausibility of Derrida's reading consists, I would suggest, in its demonstrability. Derrida traces, with austere rigor and ascetic patience, the circumference of the circle whose totality comprises Absolute Knowledge. He works within – rather than with – the text that is being read, producing a commentary that does not seek to impose an interpretative meta-language upon the text but which rather, to use Heidegger's formulation, undergoes an experience with language itself.[18] Within and through this commentary, this experience of language, Derrida leads the reader to focus upon certain privileged moments in Hegel's text that cannot be fully mastered by the dialectical method and that perhaps constitute the unthought towards which Hegel's thought tends. To be persuaded by Derrida's reading would entail first checking his commentary against Hegel's text and seeing whether the selection of those moments which are said to exceed the system can, in fact, be justified, i.e. assessing the necessity of Derrida's reading. I have attempted, in the guise of a commentary, to show the plausibility of Derrida's reading of Hegel in *Glas*. However, the essential work of demonstration remains to be done by more expert readers of Hegel. *Glas* is not so much an introduction as an invitation to Hegel, both to his texts and to his readers.

## Abbreviations

A — *Aesthetics: Lectures on Fine Art*. Translated by T. M. Knox. 2 vols. Oxford: Clarendon, 1975.

AN — *Antigone* (in *The Theban Plays*). Translated by E. F. Watling. Harmondsworth: Penguin Books, 1947.

ANT — *Anthropology from a Pragmatic Point of View*. Immanuel Kant. Translated by Victor Lyle Dowdell. Revised and edited by Hans H. Rudnick. Carbondale: Southern Illinois University Press, 1978.

D — *The Difference Between the Fichtean and Schellingian Systems of Philosophy*. Translated by Jere Paul Surber. Atascadero: Ridgeview Publishing Co., 1978.

FC — *Feu la cendre*. Paris: Editions des femmes, 1987.

FPS — *System of Ethical Life and First Philosophy of Spirit*. Edited and translated by H. S. Harris and T. M. Knox. Albany: State University of New York Press, 1979.

FR — *Funeral Rites*. Jean Genet. Translated by Bernard Frechtman. London: Anthony Blond, 1969.

G — *Glas*. 2 vols. Paris: Denoël/Gonthier, 1981.

GL — *Glassary*. John P. Leavey Jr, Lincoln and London: Nebraska University Press, 1986.

GS — *Genesis and Structure of Hegel's Phenomenology of Spirit*. Jean Hyppolite. Translated by Samuel Cherniak and John Heckman. Evanston: Northwestern University Press, 1974.

Gtr — *Glas*. Translated by John P. Leavey and Richard Rand. Lincoln and London: Nebraska University Press, 1986.

LPR — *Lectures on the Philosophy of Religion*. Translated by Rev E. B. Speirs and J. Burdon Sanderson. 3 vols. London: R.K.P., 1895.

PE — *Phénoménologie de l'Ésprit*. Translated by Jean Hyppolite. 2 vols. Paris: Montaigne, 1941.

PM — *Hegel's Philosophy of Mind: Part Three of the 'Encyclopaedia of the Philosophical Sciences.'* Translated by A. V. Miller. Oxford: Clarendon Press, 1971.

PN — *Hegel's Philosophy of Nature*. Edited and translated by M. J. Petry. 3 vols. London: George Allen & Unwin Ltd, 1970.

PR — *Grundlinien der Philosophie des Rechts*. Edited by Helmut Reichelt. Frankfurt: Ullstein, 1972.

PRtr — *Philosophy of Right*. Translated by T. M. Knox. Oxford: Oxford University Press, 1952.

PS — *Phänomenologie des Geistes*. Gesammelte Werke Band 9. Edited by Wolfgang Bonsiepen and Reinhard Heede. Hamburg: Felix Meiner, 1980.

PStr — *Phenomenology of Spirit*. Translated by A. V. Miller. Oxford: Oxford University Press, 1977.

SC — *The Spirit of Christianity and its Fate*. Translated by T. M. Knox. pp. 182–301 of *Early Theological Writings*. Philadelphia: Pennsylvania, 1948.

SD — *Zur Sache des Denkens*. Martin Heidegger. Tübingen: Max Niemeyer, 1969.

SG — *Saint Genet: comédien et martyr*. Jean-Paul Sartre. Paris: Gallimard, 1952.

SGtr — *Saint Genet: Actor and Martyr*. Translated by Bernard Frechtman. London: Heinemann, 1988 (1963).

TB — *On Time and Being*. Martin Heidegger. Translated by Joan Stambaugh. New York: Harper & Row, 1972.

# 9

# On Derrida's Hegel Interpretation[1]

*Heinz Kimmerle*

Of all the deconstructions Derrida has carried out — be they of Husserl or Levinas, Nietzsche or Freud, De Saussure, Lévi-Strauss or Rousseau, Plato or Hegel — it is Hegel who seems to have necessitated the greatest engagement. Indeed, the new praxis of writing that is bound up with this activity has taken shape in the clearest and most insistent manner in the reading and deconstruction of Hegelian texts. Hence *Glas* assumes a unique position among the works of Derrida. The particular characteristics of this book — which might be better characterized as an anti-book — have often been described. The unity of the book is broken up in that a plurality of texts are assembled, all of which are without beginning and end. The unity of the book is at the same time doubled. There are two books in one here — one column on and by Hegel and another on and by Genet. According to Derrida, if one can read a book within a book in this manner 'the abyss, . . . the bottomlessness of infinite redoubling,' opens up. 'The other is in the same.'[2] Yet this eccentric position is also a transition. It functions as a transition in that realm of transitions that Heidegger, together with Nietzsche, terms 'nihilism.'

In the limited confines of this essay, a thorough treatment of *Glas* is not possible. In this text there are a vast array of different dimensions, positions, allusions, and critical access points. In *The Post Card* there are numerous references to *Glas*, in particular to its psychoanalytic dimensions.[3] A thorough treatment would necessitate an investigation of Derrida's earlier readings of Hegel. For the openness and incompleteness of *Glas* refer explicitly to these texts. As representative of the earlier and later interpretation of Hegel I will discuss the brief article on Bataille, 'A Hegelianism Without Reserve,' from *Writing and Difference*. The question to be asked here is: is Bataille laughing at

227

Hegel or at death? For the discussion of *Glas* the following question is central: what remain(s) perish in the holocaust of absolute knowledge?[4]

Before these questions can be worked through, it must be emphasized that in his recent books Derrida no longer operates in a deconstructive manner. His object is no longer comprised of texts from the European philosophical tradition or the history of metaphysics. He has turned to art. This has already begun in *The Truth in Painting* (1978); and it progresses from this and acquires a new dimension in the explication of the poetic works of Blanchot and Celan. The attempt to approximate these works also means having to renounce the attempt to transcend them.[5] They are what they say: a shibboleth.[6] This remain(s) to be thought. Finally, Derrida comments on the poetic and painting/sketch work of Antonin Artaud and their interrelation in his 'pictograms' by pondering one word − 'subjectile' − a word that Artaud uses three times in his work. This word, which means essentially the backdrop of a painting or sketch, does not exist in the German language. He ponders not to understand its meaning, but to undo its meaning. I will not address this turn in Derrida's texts.

## Is Bataille laughing at Hegel or at death?

Derrida characterizes Bataille's interpretation of Hegel as a 'Hegelianism without reserve.'[7] Derrida wants to suggest with this notion that Hegel himself has certain reservations; he does not follow through to the final consequences of his thought. According to Bataille, Hegel's thought is a thinking of death. For every movement of the *Aufhebung* entails the destruction of a specific content. The elements of the content thus destroyed become moments of the higher unity that follows thereupon. The *Phenomenology of Spirit* is concerned with the forms of knowledge. In its totality it is the elaboration of all forms of knowledge in 'its absolute disunity.' The form of knowledge that discerns this pervasive negativity of all its forms is 'absolute knowledge.'[8]

Hegel's reserve, characterized by Bataille as his 'failure,' is founded on the assumption that the thought of pervasive negativity is everything. Thought in all its guises, i.e. reason, is all encompassing. According to Bataille, however, there is a phenomenon in Hegel that is not taken up in this totality of the negative. In the 'Preface' to the *Phenomenology of Spirit* one finds the following sentence: 'Impotent beauty hates the understanding.' For beauty is not capable of giving itself substantiality, of tolerating death and the negative and of maintaining itself in this. If one could dispel the fear of the 'beautiful soul' that it would lose its purity if it acted and mediated itself with the real world, a form of action would arise that would not be subject to the totality of reason.[9] According to Bataille, this action is carried out in 'naïve behavior,' that is, as 'sacrifice' – not as thought, but, rather, as a 'ritual of death.'[10]

In his 1955 article on Hegel, Bataille explains that Hegel, in his concept of the *Aufhebung*, thought out in complete clarity what occurs in this naive or unreflective conduct. There is, according to his understanding, only *one* difference. For Hegel, death can only be a 'holy terror.' He could see only the sorrow and disunity. In the sacrificial rituals, however, death is also desire. Bataille speaks of 'joyous anguish' and 'anguished joy.'[11] Because he knows death, and orients his life towards it, man distinguishes himself from animals. This is the basis for fear and terror, but also for joy and desire. Hegel overlooked this doubleness in that he declared thought and reason (in their negativity) to be all-encompassing. Thus real sacrifice and the thought of death stand opposed to each other as negativity. And he asks himself which is indeed more naive; in which does a less one-sided absolutization take place.[12]

Thus Bataille laughs neither at Hegel nor at death. But he wants to save the laughter at death that finds expression in sacrifice from Hegel's one-sided interpretation of death. This interpretation of Hegel arose on the basis of the commentary of Alexandre Kojève on the section on the master and the slave in the *Phenomenology*. Bataille, however, makes Hegel more one-sided than, in fact, he is. For Hegel fully acknowledges a moment of desire and pleasure in the movement of negativity. Destruction is always at the same time a preserving, a resurrection always follows death. Hegel acknowledges not only the 'speculative Good Friday,' but also a speculative Easter. At the end of the *Encyclopedia* he says that in the movement of the *Aufhebung* 'the eternal in-itself and for-itself existing idea acts, creates, and enjoys itself as absolute spirit' and 'that cognition takes part in this.'[13]

More frequent than Bataille's misunderstanding – and the critique of Hegel that is founded upon it – is the opposite argument: reconciliation is ultimately stronger in Hegel's system. Thus negativity is not taken seriously enough. Adorno addressed this issue with the greatest clarity. According to Adorno, dialectics is determined – as Bataille presupposes – purely negatively in Hegel. Hence, the reconciling synthesis is absent in Adorno; it cannot be justified in the face of reality. Nonetheless, for Adorno this means that negative dialectics is not everything; it does not encompass the whole and makes no claims about the totality.[14] In this regard he is closer to Bataille and Derrida than Hegel.

Derrida errs in his supposition that Bataille laughs at Hegel. The 'cunning of life, that is, reason' – the fact that death does indeed occur, but that 'life' remains – is, according to Bataille, not laughable, but, rather, the precise philosophical representation of the experience of death, as it finds expression in the sacrifice ritual.[15] For in the sacrificial ritual the participants experience the death of the other (for example, of a sacrificial animal) as their own death; and they survive by means of this experience. Through this experience their lives are human. By knowing death, they distinguish themselves from animal life.

Derrida, on the other hand, proceeds with a more precise understanding of Hegel. He understands that for Hegel death is always followed by a resurrection. It is this interpretation of death that, according to Derrida, prompts the laughter of Bataille. In all actuality, it is not that Hegel takes death too seriously; rather, he does not take it seriously enough. Therefore Derrida also wants to correct Bataille's interpretation of the *Aufhebung*. In this matter he agrees with Bataille as well as Adorno. The preservative moment of the *Aufhebung* in Hegel is too strong, too self-evident, too certain of itself. Thus it must be said: there is too much joy in the 'joyful fear' and the 'fearful joy.' As a consequence, Derrida wants to replace the notion of the *Aufhebung*, as he understands it, with another one. One cannot adequately describe with the concept *Aufhebung* what Bataille, in fact, does with Hegel. For then it would remain within the discursive, the all-encompassing system of reason, the circulation of meanings, which ultimately are not sacrificed, but rather remain in effect. Instead of *Aufhebung*, the concept of displacement would be more appropriate in order to indicate the transition that Bataille acts out: the transition from the thought of death to real sacrifice.

If we adopt this interpretation of Hegel, which is more in accord with the texts, then the result is that the laughter at death that arises in real sacrifice turns out to be a joyfulness of an entirely different sort from the moment of pleasure in the *Aufhebung*. This laughter is a much more anguished expression of fear than the knowledge of the resurrection from the dead. Thus the joyfulness that emerges out of this is much more joyful and liberating than that in the transition to a greater form of knowledge or spirit. Only in this way, according to Bataille, is human existence at all possible. Bataille, Derrida, and Adorno can agree therefore that beauty is not 'powerless', because it is not taken up in the series of dialectical mediations in Hegel; rather, it opens up the system of reason to experiences that exceed its parameters. Indeed, Bataille would claim, beauty transcends the mediation between subject and object and moves in the direction of a language of the sacred, of poetic language. Therein lies its specific power, by means of which it partakes of 'sovereignty.'

According to Bataille, 'sovereignty' is not attained in the sacrificial ritual as such. This is just as true both for the conceptual articulation of the sacrifice in Hegel (that is to say, of its negative aspect) and for an understanding that Bataille assumes is Hegel's. 'Sovereignty' is attainable, if, first of all, thought and reason are understood as subordinate to life – for they belong to the order of labor. Second, the beauty of the sacrificial ritual must be accorded a power that it in itself does not have.[16] To an astonishing extent this perspective is similar to the understanding of the late Adorno. According to this perspective, nothing else remains for us in the contemporary global situation – existing as we do 'after Auschwitz' and without a prospect for a positive form of truth – but to allow negative dialectics and the aesthetic dimension to persist as two separate realms and to experience them as such.

Derrida's praxis of writing is a means of moving forward in the context of this situation. What Bataille in another context said about the libidinal economy, Derrida employs in order to elucidate the 'displacement' in the semantic field of the spiritual process that Hegel characterized as *Aufhebung*. He rightly connects the economy of lack and the totality of the operations to overcome it with Hegel's dialectics of *Aufhebung*. Bataille contrasts a 'general economy,' which assumes that life in its vital functions always produces an excess, to this 'restricted economy.' This excess leads in general to a build-up of energies that can only be resolved through an explosive discharge. Thus Bataille proposes an economy of expenditure, which should help to avoid such build-ups and their explosive discharges. He finds an example of such an economy in anthropologist Marcel Mauss's descriptions of North and Middle-American Indian cultures. The exchange of gifts, in which the givers try to outdo each other in the giving-away of their own wealth, is termed in these cultures the potlatch.[17]

Derrida takes up this example in connection with the question of *Aufhebung* or displacement. What he wants to achieve is a displacement of meanings. The discursive texts of the philosophical tradition are read in such a manner that their words become ambiguous, they make diverse interpretations possible and therein unfold a play of differences. What thus arises is a 'potlatch of signs.' Fixed meanings are sacrificed; and sense is dissolved and diverted into the no longer meaningful. As a result, an aesthetic order comes into play. For the tragedy of this sacrifice is at the same time a comedy, an expression of joy that proceeds out of its literary genre. In the place of the 'we' of the *Phenomenology of Spirit*, which consciously takes part in the transition to the new forms of knowledge as transformations of sense, a 'we' is posited that joins the world of sense to the world of non-sense. This 'we' sees the 'un-ground of play' as the background before which the history of sense with its *Aufhebungen* and its negativities plays out.

## What remain(s) are annihilated in the holocaust of absolute knowledge?

The movement of the *Aufhebung* in its complete form or the mediation through the concept is, for Hegel, intimately bound up with the essence of labor. Marx clearly saw this and even expressly formulated it in relation to the *Phenomenology of Spirit*. By tracing the history of the genesis of the *Phenomenology* in the sketches of the Jena system, we can now see that he was, in fact, accurate. Labor plays a far greater role there than in the later system of philosophy. Marx did not know of this text, because it had not yet been published from the manuscripts of Hegel. He derived his thesis through a precise and thorough reading of the *Phenomenology* itself. Derrida is quite familiar with the texts of Hegel from the Jena period, yet he has not precisely grasped the meaning attributed in these texts to labor – when what is at stake is the constitution of the I, that is, consciousness or the self – in addition to language.

The labor that plays such an important role in the *Phenomenology* is, however (other than the chapter on the master and the slave), the labor of spirit. Marx formulated this clearly as well. The labor of spirit is more accurately described as the completion of nature inasmuch as this forms the constitutive element of knowledge.[18] Absolute knowledge is the self-cognition of knowledge. This means that even the other of knowledge is not nature, externality, objectivity; it is, rather, itself knowledge. At both ends of this relation there is knowledge on the side of the subjective (or knowledge) as well as on the side of the objective (or the known). The structure of absolute self-relation is attained; the return of knowledge out of the other of itself back to itself is completed. What has to be completed through the spirit seriatim, of which finally only remain(s) are left, is thus the independent object, the non-internalized externality – in a word: nature. What do the remain(s) of nature consist of? How can these remain(s) also be disposed of? Which holocaust is it, in which, according to Derrida, these remain(s) perish?

*Glas* begins with the question: 'What remain(s) today, for us, here, now, of a Hegel?' This question is immediately developed on the first page into the other question: what remain(s) for us to think after absolute knowledge? Thought since then is the thought of these remain(s). Derrida wants to articulate this thought by telling a legend, the legend of Hegel's family.

On the first page of *Glas* there is – as there is on all the following pages – a second column, which should wrap around the first column by and about Hegel like an envelope or enclose it like a sheath. Through this the first column is reversed, repeated, replaced, marked, and circumcised in an incalculable manner. In the second column we also read that at issue is the collapse in *one* movement of a monument and the erection of a tombstone. Through the tones of the death knell (*glas*) something else is at the same time rung in for Hegel. The movement of deconstruction, as it should be carried out in relation to Hegel, is thereby more closely circumscribed – without this word being used. In fact, this movement is every time also another movement, so that in the long run it is not appropriate to stick to this word.

Derrida allows the legend of Hegel's family – and that means the family in Hegel, in his thought, and in his life – to begin at the chronological beginning, which is intentionally also understood teleologically. This beginning is love. In the fully elaborated system of Hegel only *one* side of love is spoken of. As affection, love precedes marriage. Inasmuch as it grounds marriage as an ethical reality, love is immediately 'transformed into a *spiritual*, into a self-conscious love.'[19] This thought, according to Derrida, is already present in rudimentary form in Hegel's early writings, especially in the fragments 'The Spirit of Christianity and Its Fate.' The community of love between Jesus and his disciples attains its completion by means of being spiritual in the purest sense. The physical aspect of love must, inasmuch as it is possible, be overcome. Eating and drinking at the Last Supper become symbolic actions, even if the physical acts of chewing, swallowing, etc. cannot be dispensed with entirely. Shame is grounded ultimately in the fact that love cannot be completely spiritualized. In this course of thought begins the process that utterly determines the *Phenomenology of Spirit* and thereby the attainment of the standpoint of the speculative system: the completion of nature.

In connection with the story of Mary Magdalene, the 'beautiful and famous sinner,' Derrida investigates the women in Hegel's life. He indicates that Hegel's mother, his wife, and his daughter who died shortly after birth all bore the name Maria and that Hegel associated the name primarily with 'the pure virgin.'[20] The model for women is beyond sexual activity and expresses thereby their inner overcoming of the natural. The *immaculata conceptio* (IC) and absolute knowledge (*Savoir absolu* – Sa) belong inextricably together for Derrida. Here is to be found the point of access for a psychoanalytic reading within the context of deconstruction. Hegel attempts to repress the sexual in relation to woman. It is, in any case, questionable whether Derrida thereby represents carefully the views of Hegel in the early writings. Obviously Julia as well as Mary plays an important role at this time. Erotic elements can be discerned in the flow of language itself, as in the phrase the 'unity in otherness.'[21]

In the column by and on Genet next to the Hegel column Derrida discusses Genet's as well as his own obsession with this name. He cites from *Our Lady of the Flowers* and *Miracle of the Rose* passages on the genitalia of flowers that are turned entirely outward, and whose form and shape are described in detail. In these texts an 'anagrammatization' of the name Genet is carried out such that the flower is thereby described, symbolized, presented, and made into a rhetorical figure. This 'twofold anatomy lesson in the margins, and in the margin of the margins,' [55] exceeds my interpretive capabilities.[22] It forms the other to Hegel's family in such a paradoxical manner that the relation appears in principle to transcend intellectual comprehension.

I would like briefly to address the discussion of love, marriage, and family in Hegel's Jena writings and Derrida's relation to them. It seems noteworthy to me that Derrida demonstrates that all detailed discussion of the distinction between the sexes and the physical aspect of sexual life are relegated by Hegel to the philosophy of nature. This supports the notion of repression. Yet Derrida does not acknowledge and thus cannot demonstrate that Hegel in the first years of his Jena period acknowledged a 'natural *Sittlichkeit*.' Hegel's great interest in the philosophy of nature arises doubtless on the basis of the collaboration with Schelling and the contact with Goethe. Yet he worked through more thoroughly – and for his own motives – what the naturalness of man expresses. Labor, as material labor, is made here a point of departure for practical philosophy. Through the use of the tool man breaks off his living relation to living nature and places a relation oriented to his goals in its place.[23] This leads to man's effort to separate his own sphere of consciousness from natural contexts. The negative effects of this effort are readily apparent to Hegel. With the improvement of tools and the invention of machines, human work becomes itself more and more machine-like, dulled, and spirit-less.

Unlike in the *Philosophy of Right*, what happens in the family belongs to the labor process. On the one hand, Hegel accords an equal place to the productive labor that is carried on in the family. He does not just dismiss the family into the realm of mere reproduction. On the other hand, he considers the raising and educating of children as well as the administration of the family property as labor. The relations between man and wife are not affected by this: 'Here the living should not be determined through cultivation.' Children are not produced. But in the children and through the children the social totality reproduces itself. In this way this totality becomes an infinite relation.[24]

An important step in the deconstruction of the Hegelian system could have consisted in demonstrating how labor, in the development of this system during the Jena period, is gradually and increasingly understood as the labor of consciousness and spirit. Material labor, which is directed towards objects of nature, acquires a limited, increasingly subordinate position. But this interpretation of the developmental history of Hegelian thought between the early writings and the *Phenomenology of Spirit* of 1807, which is not to be found in Derrida, could not have explained why Hegel in the *Phenomenology* suddenly accorded the role of the sister such a central position in the treatment of familial relations. Or why she is employed to present the tragic prehistory of the state of law and the organization of the state. This does not seem to be derivable from the developmental history of Hegel's thought.

Hegel had indeed already discussed earlier the tragic determination of bourgeois society and hence of the state in connection with Aeschylus. I am thinking of the famous passage in the *Natural Law* essay on the 'tragedy in the *Sittlichen*.' That this is bound to the role of the sister, as it appears in Sophocles' *Antigone*, is, however, entirely unexpected and points to the unconscious dimensions of Hegel's discourse. This cannot be expressed better than in Derrida's succinct formulation: 'Enter(s) on the scene Antigone.'[25] The unconscious dimensions that Derrida exposes in this passage address the relation of Hegel to his sister Christiane.

The entire correspondence between the siblings until the tragic end of Christiane is documented in *Glas*. The relation to Nanette, who grew up in the house of Hegel's parents, also plays a certain role in this context. She was much like a sister and yet she aroused the first sexual feelings in Hegel.

The tragic situation of Antigone is well-known. She stands for the bygone order of the 'old gods' that watch over and protect the law of the family. This law, however, has not entirely disappeared. The goddesses of revenge still have a place in the subterranean realm of the temple. Hence the new order of the polis rests upon that which it excludes. 'The visible spirit has the roots of its power in the underworld.' What is excluded is the family, in which the woman played a decisive role. Femininity is, for the new community, that which 'it represses and yet that which is at the same time essential to it.'[26] For this reason, femininity is its inner enemy. And nowhere is it clearer that the state depends on the family being ruled by the man and by the woman being kept in her place than in the tragic role of the sister. She exists on the border of reason just as it reigns over the state, because her relations to the others, even the male members of the family, cannot be disrupted by sexual desires. For otherwise there would follow the penalty of death. According to Derrida, therefore, the grave of Antigone lies at the beginning of the organization of the state. In this grave the unification with the beloved takes place; at the same time it functions as the subterranean refuge of the excluded.[27]

The completion of nature demonstrates itself, in a decisive sense, in the exclusion of the feminine. The essential relation in the family is now the father son relation. The meaning of this act for the family is summed up in the grooming of the son to assume the role of a father. At issue here, in principle, is the relation of the father to himself. The upbringing of the son comprises the other, out of which the father returns to himself. The relations in the earthly family comprise, according to Derrida, not *one* of many mediations in the system of philosophy. This mediation is central and expresses the structure of the *Aufhebung*/mediation in nuce. This is evident in the fact that precisely these same relations return at the pinnacle of the system, where the form of mediation with the most highly determined content – in the doctrine of the holy Trinity – finds expression. The earthly family is the model of the holy family – based on how the family is thought out in the internal relations of the Trinity.

The role of the mother in the Trinity is still present in the *Phenomenology*. Yet she is reduced to bearing and raising the son. Jesus, the son of God, had a 'father existing *in himself*' (ansich*seiende Vater*) and, moreover, '*a real mother*.'[28] The latter seems unavoidable because spirit, which is in and of itself the unity of substantiality and subjectivity, has left the form of substantiality in the earthly son. His actuality is bound up with his naturalness. Therefore he was born and raised by a human mother. This constellation occurs also in the religious community, in which the holy spirit has its earthly existence. It is still a community of love, founded on an earthly feeling, and not yet the definitive form of spirit in which subjectivity itself has its substantiality. For comparison, Derrida could have here referred to texts from the early Jena period in which the mother of Jesus assumes a much more important role in the Trinity. Without her and her love, which lives on in the religious community, there can be no reconciliation in which God is reconciled to himself.[29] On the other hand, the position of the *Phenomenology* could have been clarified by reference to the *Encyclopedia*. In the outline of the system of the *Encyclopedia*, the first edition of which appeared ten years after the *Phenomenology*, the mother of Jesus is no longer present in the relations of the Trinity. Out of three conclusions the

Trinity forms one conclusion, in which the structure of the *Aufhebung/* mediation finds expression without disturbing difficulties.[30]

The exclusion of the mother – and thus of woman and the feminine from the holy family – does not yet, however, comprise the destruction of the remain(s) of nature in the transition to absolute knowledge. The self-relation of the father to himself through the son still contains something natural that must perish in order to make the self-cognition of knowledge possible in its pure conceptual form. Derrida shows that this last transition no longer has the structure of the *Aufhebung*. The relation between the 'already' (*déjà*) and the 'not yet' (*pas encore*) of the preceding transitions is no longer the same here.[31] From the point of view of the content, the structure of the mediation in the revealed religion of Christianity, especially in the understanding of the Trinity, is 'already' completely attained. There is nothing else that would not be 'not yet' worked out and developed. Simply with regard to form, a final transition must take place. The form of representation, which in the religious understanding is still present, must be transposed in the form of the concept, into which the same structure finds expression, without reference to actual existing represented relations. At the juncture of this final transition is the grave of Jesus, out of which he arises. This representation of the reconciliation must still be sacrificed so that its pure conceptual structure can come to light.

The decisive step of this last transition consists in the 'annulment' of time.[32] This expression demonstrates that the usual form of the *Aufhebung* is no longer applicable here. More force is necessary than with the usual *Aufhebung*, which always destroys and preserves at the same time. The 'annulment' of time is the destruction of the remain(s) of nature. The structure of self-cognition of knowledge lies outside of time. It is absolute presence that was always already what it is, in which nothing is 'not yet' realized and which is therefore not transitory. It forms the eternal, infinite precondition of all finite mediation. This act of the 'annulment' of the remain(s) brings Derrida to the thought of the holocaust. He makes clear that the increased force that is necessary here was already secretly at work in the preceding *Aufhebungen*. What happens to the remain(s) is only the final consequence of the entire process of the completion of nature. How is this holocaust related to that other holocaust, which Adorno summed up in the word 'Auschwitz'? Here the ultimate catastrophe of a thought that has a long prehistory is revealed. If this thought does not change, it can make catastrophes possible of which 'Auschwitz' was only a prelude.

If we consider the course of Hegel's thought we see that the 'annulment' of time is not successful. The system of philosophy that is to be derived from the self-cognition of knowledge does not allow itself to be brought coherently to conclusion. This reveals itself in the fact that up until his death Hegel attempted to reach this goal in always new and different ways. This attempt makes clear that the conclusion was not successful. The timeless truth of pure thought that Hegel presupposes and sets forth (by means of a disclosure that, of course, does not take place in time) in his *Science of Logic* is not to be applied to the real relations in nature and the human world without remain(s). The most important result of Hegel is finally the 'authentic movement of failure' that Bataille established and that Derrida cited. Only under this precondition is a 'Hegelianism without reserve' appropriate. The opposite, the *contre-épreuve*, is the beginning of another thought, a thought in which the most important point of orientation is formed — emerging from the grave of Jesus — by the merging of Dionysus and Christ.

'But it [ça] does nothing but begin, the labor, here, from now on. As soon as it [ça] begins to write. It [Ça] hardly begins. No more than one piece is missing.'[33]

Translated by Stuart Barnett

# 10

# Hegelian Dialectic and the
# Quasi-Transcendental in *Glas*

*Kevin Thompson*

Two basic enigmas may be said to organize all of Derrida's work: one, an enigma of affinity, the other, of simultaneity.[1] Derrida himself has constantly reminded us of the first: the continuum of constitutive syntheses that his writings have attempted to expose (supplementarity, writing, iterability, and *différance*, to cite only those most well-known) maintain a 'profound affinity' (M/15/14) with that very discourse that '*summed up* the entire philosophy of the *logos*' (DG/39/24), the Hegelian dialectic. Through the speculative posit-ing and interiorizing of negativity, the very movement of *Aufhebung*, this summation brings to its circular limit, to its closure (*clôture*),[2] the history of metaphysics as the comprehension of exteriority within the absolute self-identity of *Geist*. Similarly, the quasi-transcendental infrastructures, as differ-entiating relations, may be said to make possible, to inscribe, this speculative *parousia* through their simultaneous movement of spacing and temporization. Hence, a deep affinity becomes manifest between the concept of *Aufhebung* – the 'speculative concept par excellence' as Derrida recalls (ED/377/257) – and *différance*, to invoke the most immediately relevant infrastructure within this context, that is itself, as Derrida has noted in a now infamous formulation: 'Neither a word nor a concept' (M/7/7). Given its 'almost absolute proximity' (P/60/44) to that most speculative of concepts and the entire onto-theological system it sanctions,[3] the chain of infrastructural relations would seem to emerge – 'unable to break with that [Hegelian] discourse' (M/15/14) – as a simple repetition of the fundamental gesture of philosophy itself: the conceiving and positing of limitation in order to master and transcend it.[4] In this sense and to this extent, Derrida's thought remains faithful to the very intention embedded within the philosophical tradition itself and, more specifically, to the Hegelian system of speculative science as this tradition's culmination. However, this simple repetition and affinity remain enigmatic in that it is precisely the Hegelian constriction of negativity, as a moment appropriated within a teleological economy of absolute presence, that Derrida's work has most forcefully sought to call into question, i.e. to solicit. How then is this proximity to be understood?[5] With this question we pass to the second and most obscure enigma within Derrida's thought, the 'very enigma of *différance*' (M/20/19) itself.

Derrida claims that, within the affinity of onto-theology and deconstruction, 'a kind of infinitesimal and radical displacement' (M/15/14) of Hegelian speculation is carried out. Uncovering this displacement necessitates demonstrating that *différance* not only makes possible the identity of speculative knowledge but also that it, simultaneously (*à la fois, du-même-coup*) and necessarily, fissures this ultimate identity by inscribing it within a non-totalizable and interminable negativity, within what Derrida calls the remains (*reste*),[6] which in turn can be neither elevated nor interiorized. The synthetic movement of *différance* is thereby conceived as the simultaneity of the speculative economy of absolute presence and the general economy of absolute alterity; it is an originary contamination of pure identity and pure difference. This perhaps unthinkable enigma of simultaneity, what Derrida elsewhere calls a 'non-Hegelian identity' (D/285/253),[7] is the moment within Derrida's thought where the very movement of *Aufhebung*, and thus the speculative project of philosophy itself, is displaced and refigured within an originary contamination of interiority and exteriority. It is only through this function of displacement, Derrida maintains, that the very specificity of the infrastructural syntheses is established in relation to the appropriative movement of *Aufhebung*. Moreover, it is only then that it becomes possible to isolate the precise 'point of rupture with the system of *Aufhebung* and with speculative dialectics' (P/60/44) that Derrida's work carries out.

Derrida claims that in order to undertake such a displacement as this the concept of *Aufhebung* itself had to be designated as the 'decisive target' (D/280n45/248n53) of a fundamental critique in which the Hegelian 'constriction (*rétrécissement*)' (M/81/71)[8] of negativity would be submitted to a rigorous examination. This task and its inherent reinscription of the concept of *Aufhebung* is what fundamentally takes place in the left-hand column of Derrida's 1974 work, *Glas*.[9] Yet, so as properly to prepare a reading of one crucial moment within that text's intricate interrogation of Hegel's speculative logic, we must uncover the formal elements of this critique as it organizes the enigmas we have sought to elucidate. We will do so by drawing upon an operation constant throughout Derrida's work from 1967 to 1972; i.e. from the year in which Derrida's proposal for a thesis on Hegel's semiology was submitted[10] to the first announcement of the project that ultimately became *Glas*, the period of Derrida's most intense and sustained engagement with Hegel's work.[11]

## Negativity, Articulation, and Simulacrum: The Law of the Family

For Hegel, the movement of *Aufhebung* ceaselessly demonstrates that negativity is intrinsically necessary for the constitution of truth, meaning, and ideality. Most importantly, it is through this movement that *Geist* may be said to produce itself as a kind of pure repetition such that any moment, any entry point, within its development is always already grasped as the result (*das Resultat*) of the preceding moment. The function of negation arises in this movement in two distinct forms. There is an immediate relation to alterity, 'abstract negation,' through which any immanence or immediacy is brought into distinction and formal differentiation. However, at each transition in the progression of the dialectic, the abstract negation of the previous moment of immediacy reveals the essentiality of that movement that maintains and repeats itself in and through this destructive power. In a second speculative form of negation, the immediacy of the previous moment is transcended through the appropriative movement of *Aufhebung* that interiorizes abstract negativity. This movement thus negates, as its proper contradiction, the initial wholly abstract negativity and, in and through this now 'determinate negation,' the production of *Geist* as pure repetition is made possible. By conceiving abstract differentiation in terms of the interiorizing movement of *Aufhebung*, Hegel interprets negativity, i.e. difference, as a moment within the constitution of a specific *telos*, a specific determination of being: the pure and infinitely free repetition of *Geist* as being-with-itself (*das Beisichselbstsein*), *parousia*. Thus, in the passage from abstract to determinate negation, which is a passage from merely external difference to speculative contradiction,[12] lies a specific determination of the purpose of negativity – a constriction of difference – within a teleological progression towards speculative self-relation. As Hegel says – in a phrase to which Derrida has repeatedly drawn our attention and that bears the entire weight of the problematic at issue here: 'Difference in general is already contradiction in itself (*Der Unterschied überhaupt ist schon der Widerspruch in sich*)' (WL/279/431).[13]

Derrida's thought has attempted to meditate precisely upon nothing other than this binding passage as the fundamental logic of *Aufhebung* and it is this teleological determination of negation that forms the guiding problematic of *Glas* itself. Derrida has maintained that the Hegelian critique of pure difference, abstract negativity – as it is articulated in the *Science of Logic*[14] – serves, within his own work, as 'the most uncircumventable theme' (ED/227n/320n).[15] Indeed, as he has shown in essays on Levinas, Artaud, and Bataille, conceiving negativity as a pure and unmediated relation to alterity reduces difference to non-difference, to an immediate identity, and thereby to an uncritical and merely external presence.[16] *Différance* is thus not abstract negation, purely external differentiation. Yet neither is it determinate negation, difference understood as speculative contradiction. Interpreting any constitutive differential relation as a mutually determining contradiction, according to Derrida, restricts the movement of negation and makes possible its interiorization, through *Aufhebung*, within the absolute Idea.[17] In fact, Derrida has specifically claimed that he has:

> attempted to distinguish *différance* . . . from Hegelian difference . . . at the point at which Hegel, in the greater *Logic* determines difference as contradiction only in order to resolve it, to interiorize it, to lift it up (according to the syllogistic process of speculative dialectics) into the self-presence of an onto-theological or onto-teleological synthesis.
>
> (P/59–60/44)

Though *différance* cannot be equated with the moments of either abstract or determinate negation, it is nevertheless marked within the determining movement articulated by these moments as that juncture wherein the continuity of the chain of speculative logic is 'necessarily fissured' (P/103/77), displaced and disjointed. Yet, if *différance* is neither a mere uncritical exteriority nor a determinate moment taken up within the life of *Geist*, how are we to understand its unique and irreducible negativity such as it is thought within the Hegelian determination of difference? Would this not ultimately require thinking difference beyond the Hegelian model of negation itself? Is such a conception as this even possible? It is this basic problematic, as the formal law permeating all of Derrida's both explicit and oblique readings of Hegelian speculation, that structures the left-hand column of *Glas*. To determine the precise moment within the structural logic of the Hegelian system, somehow 'between' abstract and determinate negation, wherein the contaminating negativity of *différance* is marked, is to ascertain the quasi-transcendental structure of the remains (*reste*) at the limit of the history of metaphysics. It is ultimately to the disclosure of the infinitesimal non-coincidence of deconstruction and dialectics that serves to give rise to the very enigmas within Derrida's work with which our examination began.

Yet if, as Hegel claims, the categorial relations he exhaustively interrogates in the *Logic* are already 'displayed and stored in human *language* (*Sprache*)' (WL/20/31)[18] such that discourse itself is structured by the teleological determination of negation, then how would one be able to present a quasi-transcendentality that exceeds the determinations of speculative logic? How could such an irresolvable relation, the very displacement of *Aufhebung*, be articulated within a discourse always already given over to the onto-theology one is attempting to call into question?

Throughout his work on Hegelian speculation, Derrida has recognized this intertwining of the problem of negation and the question of language that uniquely presents itself in the closure wrought by the Hegelian summation of the history of metaphysics. Whether through the Bataillean figures of 'laughter,' 'sacrifice,' and 'heliotrope,' the 'hymen,' 'fan,' and 'mime' of Mallarmé, or even a 'machine' defined solely in terms of the purity of its functioning, Derrida has constantly insisted upon engaging the discourse of Hegelian onto-theology, which is to say the discourse of metaphysics itself, through recourse to simulacra.[19] The necessity of such engagement arises from the recognition that the Hegelian system presents itself as an hermetic totality that has, in and through its summation of the history of metaphysics, taken into account any and every rejection as well as affirmation of its absolute self-relation.[20] Derrida thus claims that, given this infinite closure, one can articulate a non-totalizable structure of negativity only through a 'simulated repetition' (ED/382/260) of Hegelian discourse and system, through a repetition by means of which the stricture of negation is displaced and functionally inscribed within its own non-ontological 'space of possibility' (G/226a/162a), what Derrida ultimately calls the 'irresoluble, impracticable, nonnormal' (G/7a/5a), the remains.

The problems of negation and articulation are thus bound together within the Hegelian system and it is finally in the left-hand column of *Glas* that Derrida submits this interwoven problematic to its most thorough and decisive examination. He engages in a simulated repetition, a 'critical displacement' (G/6a/5a), of Hegelian onto-theological discourse and system by drawing upon one structure, 'one thread (*fil*),' within Hegel's thought: the 'law of the family' (G/5a/4a). According to Derrida, the family is a 'party to (*partie prenante*) the system of the spirit' (G/27a/20a)[21] in that it is both a part and the whole of the system. As with every moment within Hegel's thought, 'the family is marked twice' (G/28a/21a). On the one hand, it is a finite and particular moment passed through but once in the history of the formation (*Bildung*) of *Geist*. As such, it has a determinate place within the system. On the other hand, the movement of *Aufhebung*, the pure and constitutive repetition of *Geist*, takes place within the structures of the family moment. Derrida is thus able to claim that 'this finiteness *figures* . . . the system's totality' (G/29a/21a), which is to say that the family, as a specific moment within the movement of *Geist*'s pure repetition, is able to simulate the general structure whereby *Geist* comes to repeat itself infinitely; in other words, the passage from abstract to determinate negation. The law of the family thus imitates or figures the general system of the teleological repetition of *Geist*, i.e. the system of *Aufhebung*. In this sense, focusing upon the law of the family and tracing the genesis of this concept throughout Hegel's texts draws the problems of negation and articulation together around the question of being. For, as Derrida notes with regard to the Hegelian system and its *telos*, '*Aufhebung* is being, not as a determinate state or the determinable totality of beings, but as the 'active,' productive essence of being' (G/47a/34a). Hence, in taking up the law of the family as a simulacrum for the free self-production of *Geist*, Derrida seeks to understand the way in which this 'familial schema' (G/29a/21a), at the point at which the self-relation of *Geist* may be said to 'detach itself within the family hearth' (G/30a/22a), inscribes the Hegelian determination of being within a non-totalizable and non-ontological alterity. As such, the attempt to articulate a negativity that is neither abstract nor determinate, yet still marked within the movement of *Aufhebung*, becomes focused here around the relations that constitute the familial moment. Due to its figurative function then, uncovering an irresoluble and non-totalizable negativity at the limit of the familial structure will serve to call into question not only this particular moment within the formation of *Geist* but the entire onto-theological system as well. As Derrida notes: 'The displacements or the disimplications of which it [the family] will be the object would not know how to have a simply local character' (G/6a/5a).

Having ascertained the formal elements of Derrida's engagement with Hegelian discourse and system, we can now take up, by way of an exegesis of some crucial passages in the *Phenomenology of Spirit*, one moment of *Glas'* reading of the Hegelian family. Focusing directly upon Hegel's text, we will be able to understand the perplexing questions that Derrida's reading proposes, questions that serve to disclose the quasi-transcendental structure of the remains within which the Hegelian dialectic is displaced and inscribed. Yet, so as to elucidate the radicality of these questions as well as the negativity they attempt to expose, we must also take up a 'hinge of the greater Logic' (G/234a/168a), as Derrida says, that provides the categorial structure for the constitution of the familial moment: a hinge that, though operative throughout Derrida's work on Hegel, has never been the subject of his direct textual scrutiny. Having grasped through this analysis the specificity of quasi-transcendental negativity, we can then circle back to the initial enigmas with which our inquiry began.

### The Ethical World, Equilibrium, and Sexual Difference: The Bond between Brother and Sister

As with any discussion focused upon a particular moment within the 'history of the *Bildung* of consciousness' (PhG/56/50), extracting Hegel's account of the family from the speculative unfolding that truth is not only substance but subject as well runs the risk of stilling the very movement of immanent necessity whose 'formal aspect' (PhG/61/56), Hegel says, raises this seemingly arbitrary succession into a 'scientific progression' (PhG/61/55).[22] So as to mitigate against this necessary interpretive violence and, more importantly, to disclose properly the underlying movement from abstract to determinate negation that structures Hegel's account, one must attend to the context and developments within which these analyses are carried out. Derrida, recognizing this dilemma, prepares his own reading of the *Phenomenology* through an extended discussion of the interrelated development of the concepts of *Geist* and family as presented in various texts from Hegel's early Jena period. For us, it will suffice to indicate the general problematics and developments of the *Phenomenology* within which Hegel's analysis of the familial moment takes place.

Hegel's discussion of the family is situated within perhaps the most important chapter of the *Phenomenology*, namely chapter six, which is entitled simply *Geist*. Hegel defines the fundamental issue of this chapter as the 'self-supporting, absolute, real essence' (PhG/239/264) that, when it is aware of itself as actually existing, comes into its truth as the 'ethical life of a people (*eines Volks*)' (PhG/240/265).

This 'living ethical world' (PhG/240/265), however, itself undergoes a constitutive movement in which its immediate substantiality perishes with the advent of the formal universality of right (*Recht*) and is ultimately taken back into the essentiality of subjectivity in the shape of conscience (*Gewissen*); an unfolding of *Sittlichkeit* into *Moralität*. It is within the immediacy of ethical life, i.e. within *Sittlichkeit*, that the family first becomes manifest as a shape of *Geist*.

Hegel's concern in the *Phenomenology* with *Sittlichkeit* is focused upon the way in which the concept of action (*Handlung*) enables right (*Recht*) to attain formal universality in the shape of legal status such that the living immediacy of the pure will and the ethical substance, the *Volk*, perishes.[23] Yet, Hegel tells us, just as any object of perception shows itself as a unified thing with various properties, so 'a given action is an actuality with many ethical relations' (PhG/241/267). This plurality of relations forms a structured totality, a world, within which activity is carried out. As such, these structural relations function as the enabling condition or horizon for ethical action. As manifestations of ethical substantiality, again paralleling the structural moments of perception, these relations already bear within themselves the distinction, the implicit contradiction, that is ultimately only posited and overcome in action itself: the split between the 'law of individuality' and the 'law of universality' (PhG/241/267).

The embodiment of the 'law of universality,' in terms of ethical substance, is found in the codification of the prevailing customs of the ethical community and, as a moment of consciousness, in the legitimate authority of the government. Together these moments constitute what Hegel calls *Geist* as 'human law' (PhG/242/268). The realization of the 'law of individuality' is to be found, on the side of consciousness, in a 'natural ethical community' (PhG/243/268), the family, that has its immediate existence not in a posited legal code but in the unwritten and eternal laws of the 'subterranean realm' (PhG/246/273) that underlies the manifest public sphere. Together these moments constitute what Hegel calls *Geist* in the form of 'divine law' (PhG/242/268).

The relation between human and divine law sets forth the constitutive tension of the ethical world.[24] Yet, despite their intrinsic contradiction, this horizon forms, Hegel maintains, an 'immaculate world, a world unsullied by any internal dissension' (PhG/250/278). Its intrinsic movement is merely a 'stable becoming' (PhG/250/278) of human and divine law into one another such that an 'equilibrium (*Gleichgewicht*) of all the parts' (PhG/249/277) — which Hegel here identitifies with 'justice (*Gerechtigkeit*)' (PhG/249/277) — is established within this ethical whole. This living equilibrium and stability is the maintenance of *Geist*'s self-relation, its being-with-itself (*das Beisichselßstsein*).

The ethical significance of both the universal community, the government, and the individual community, the family, must, for Hegel, be understood in relation to this *telos*. Therefore Hegel claims that the work of *Aufhebung* is achieved within this sphere through the unique ethical task carried out by each. Specifically, the ethical community has an intrinsic tendency to articulate itself according to the needs of particular groups and associations rather than in accord with the good of the people as a whole. By forcing its members, in a kind of 'downward movement' (PhG/250/278), into the task of warfare and thus submitting them to their proper 'lord' (PhG/246/273), death,[25] the government is able to reassert the universality of the whole and its common interests over the particularity of specific needs. While in a kind of 'upward movement' (PhG/250/278), the family, due to its immediate and natural bond, is able to interrupt the movement of death's abstract negativity by entombing their deceased loved ones, thereby reaffirming their blood-relation such that the deceased is returned to the ethical community. These tasks together overcome the already implicit conflict between human and divine law and in so doing reveal this tension to be nothing other than both the 'authentication and suspension (*Bewährung*) of one [law] through the other' (PhG/250/278).[26] But how precisely is the underlying movement from abstract to determinate negation, the logic of *Aufhebung*, manifested in this suspension? As we shall see, it is at the limit of the family structure that the stable passage (*Übergang*) between these laws is accomplished. It is this limit – and specifically its differential structure – upon which Derrida's text focuses. It is this that constitutes the point of detachment and return through which *Geist* circles back upon itself.

Having established that the ethical realm is constituted as a sphere at peace with itself, as a just, coherent, and enclosed world, Hegel reveals the centrality of the family structure for the genesis of this circular enclosure and, in so doing, sets forth the question of difference, sexual difference, as this sphere's decisive issue. Due to the intrinsic unity of ethical substance and ethical consciousness, Hegel tells us, the downward movement of human law is accomplished through man, while the upward movement of divine law takes place through woman. The passage from one power to the other is thus made possible for Hegel by an 'active middle,' the 'union (*Vereinigung*) of man and woman' (PhG/250/278). This bond is the living element that enables the downward and upward movements of the ethical sphere to be properly under-stood as a unitary becoming, as a generative movement that forms the ethical world into a completed totality. It therefore becomes clear that it is through this relation that *Geist* may be said to accomplish its circular self-relation, its *Beisichselßstsein*. The *Aufhebung* of the implicit conflict between the laws of universality and individuality is accomplished in and through a familial union of sexual difference. What is accomplished, however, is not the simply abstract, external, and indeterminate difference of man and woman, but a more specific and unique sexual difference. *Aufhebung* here, as always, is a matter of abstract difference becoming determinate, becoming here a speculative sexual contradiction. The question concerning the genesis of the ethical world thus becomes transformed into a question concerned with ascertaining the precise structure and nature of this union such that it permits a passage between this world's powers. Above all, it becomes evident that this passage is organized around the issue of difference and negativity, around a relation of determinate sexual difference.

It is therefore in terms of this unique bond that Hegel takes up an analysis of the essential structural relations of the family.[27] At issue here is the concept of recognition (*Anerkennung*) whose exploration had only begun with chapter four's setting forth of its structural moments.[28] Ethical duty, as a universal and necessary prescription, is only possible given the presence of genuine freedom. Such freedom, Hegel holds, arises only where there is a relation of mutual and uncoerced recognition that is not given over to the contingency of nature, the merely consumptive immediacy of desire (*Begierde*). Thus, if woman is to carry out the task of entombment and if man is to be subject to the law of conscription, then each must recognize the other and themselves in each other as free and independent individuals; each must be a being-for-self (*Fürsichsein*). A confluence between the levels of desire and recognition would reduce the universal ethical character of the tasks to the level of mere particularity, transitoriness, and chance. The being-for-self of both man and woman must therefore arise from a truly reciprocal relation rather than simply out of a natural immediacy. It is based upon these considerations that Hegel makes his most puzzling yet central claim: the bond of reciprocal recognition that accomplishes the enclosure of the ethical world is the relation between brother and sister. What then, for Hegel, is the nature of this familial relation such that it is uniquely able to be the 'active middle' (PhG/250/278), the site of passage, between the realms of human and divine law?

The definitive trait of this relation lies in the fact that, as members of the same family, brother and sister have a natural relation: 'they are,' as Hegel says, 'the same blood,' but in them, and in them alone, this blood 'has come to be at peace (*Ruhe*) and equilibrium (*Gleichgewicht*)' (PhG/247/274). There is here then, through the commonality of blood, a natural sibling bond. Yet it is precisely through their sexual difference that the basis of this relation, the blood itself, attains balance and peace. Non-reciprocity, a state of imbalance and instability, arises, Hegel affirms, when the relation of the sides to one another, their recognition, has its 'actuality' (PhG/246/273) outside the relation itself. In this sense, the recognition is not properly reciprocal or free and as such remains at the level of immediate desire. The bond of love between husband and wife, for instance, has its existence most properly in its children, and conversely the children have their being in their parents. Hence, each of these relations is, for Hegel, 'mixed with a natural relation and with feeling' (PhG/246–7/273). Here the blood remains in a state of perpetual tension and 'dissimilarity (*Ungleichheit*)' (PhG/247/274) since the moment of recognition is never a moment of mutual equality; recognition never attains here its completion within itself. Instead, the natural immediacy of feeling and emotion remains the basis of these relations and they are thereby embodiments of desire rather than true recognition. Both remain wholly indeterminate and abstract. Like these other relations, there is a natural bond between brother and sister, but here, uniquely, they exist with regard to one another as 'free individualities (*freie Individualität*)' (PhG/247/274), the realization of their reciprocal self-recognition takes place solely within the relation itself. Thus in the bond of brother and sister is found, Hegel concludes, 'the relationship in its unmixed form' (PhG/247/274). For a sister, then, the loss of a brother is 'irreplaceable' and her ethical duty towards him, his entombment, is the 'highest' (PhG/248/275).

The bond between brother and sister permits a decisive moment of mutual recognition, a recognition that enables the circle of *Sittlichkeit* to be closed. The 'equilibrium' of this blood-relation accomplishes the 'equilibrium' of the ethical sphere in general. Thus, this bond constitutes the 'limit (*Grenze*) at which the self-contained family breaks up and goes beyond itself' (PhG/248/275). The passage from divine to human law takes place here with the departure of the brother from the familial community. It is with regard to this specific moment that Derrida takes up the intertwined questions of difference, negation, and the movement of *Aufhebung* within Hegel's discussion of the family.

## Recognition, Quasi-Transcendentality, and the Determination of Difference: The Problematic of the Bond

The analysis carried out in *Glas* focuses upon the problematic nature of the bond between brother and sister. In particular, it attends to the very possibility of such a differential relation as this within the Hegelian system of science. Derrida begins by recalling that Hegel's own investigation of the structure of recognition had shown that truly mutual recognition is only possible given the confrontation of two self-consciousnesses such that each 'comes out of itself' (PhG/109/111). In this moment, each consciousness becomes other to itself in and through its confronting another consciousness. However, insofar as either consciousness attempts simply to eliminate or destroy this self-othering before the other, its own 'being-other (*Anderssein*)' (PhG/109/111), it falls back to the level of mere consumptive desire, engaging in a merely natural and self-defeating conflict. Here, no genuine recognition is possible. Yet if, in this very moment of confrontation, each consciousness sublates its being-other, returning thereby into itself, such that in so doing each 'lets the other be free (*entläßt also das andere wieder frei*)' (PhG/109/111), then the level of natural desire is transcended and genuinely free mutual self-recognition occurs. True recognition thus presupposes a moment of simple confrontation – a stage of immediate self-assertion that inherently gives rise to some form of conflict, taking the form perhaps even of a life and death struggle. But the mutual recognition of brother and sister arises precisely without this moment of initial encounter and pursuant conflict. Brother and sister, strictly speaking, do not depend upon one another for their being-for-self nor do they desire one another. They are, it would seem, Derrida says, 'two single consciousnesses that, in the Hegelian universe, relate to each other without entering into war' (G/208a/149a). Given the eidetic necessity of such confrontation, Derrida notes that 'one would be tempted to conclude that at bottom *there is no* brother/sister bond, there is no brother or sister' (G/208a/149a). In the midst of a relation uniquely at peace and in a state of equilibrium, devoid of assertion and conflict, the very conceivability of such a bond would seem in doubt. Hegel's own analysis appears to dictate as much. In this sense, the bond between brother and sister, a 'symmetrical relation that needs no reconciliation to appease itself' (G/210a/150a), appears as the 'unclassable' and 'absolute indigestible' (G/211a/151a) that the movement of 'pure essentialities,' the 'greater logic' of the Hegelian system, would seem to be unable to assimilate. This crucial and decisive bond is thus the 'inadmissible' (G/211a/151a), a relation excluded from the speculative genesis of *Geist*.

And yet, as our reading of the *Phenomenology*'s discussion of *Sittlichkeit* has shown, the bond between brother and sister is the fundamental union that accomplishes the very self-relation of *Geist* in its concrete immediacy. This union, though seemingly excluded by the system's own structural principles, is, at the same moment, absolutely necessary for the attainment of speculative closure within this finite sphere. At once both excluded and necessary, the familial bond between brother and sister may thus be said to provide the *a priori* condition enabling *Geist*, in the immediacy of *Sittlichkeit*, to achieve its being-with-itself (*Beisichselßstsein*). What then is the nature of this 'unique example' (G/210a/150a) within the Hegelian system? How is it possible that such a singularly impossible relation plays such a fundamental and decisive role in the constitution of the ethical sphere?

The scope of these questions is not simply limited to an interpretation of the *Phenomenology*'s discussion of *Sittlichkeit*. One must but recall the central motif of *Glas*' left-hand column: the family is at once a finite moment within the Hegelian system and a figure of this very system's totality. As such, the impossible yet necessary bond between brother and sister uncovered at this limit-passage reveals a problematic whose implications will not be able to be confined either to the realm of *Sittlichkeit* or to its treatment of the family. The relation between brother and sister represents a general structure endemic to the very nature of the Hegelian system. The constitution of *Geist*'s self-relation, its *parousia*, is always assured precisely by that which it excludes. This impossible yet necessary moment, constantly figured in each passage through which *Geist* constitutes itself, plays what Derrida refers to as an 'abyssal role' (G/211a/151a) within the Hegelian system. It calls into question and displaces the closure of this movement, its *telos*, at its very limit. This general structure is the 'quasi-transcendental' (G/226a/151a–162a) and it constitutes the non-totalizable and non-ontological 'space of possibility' (G/226a/162a), the irre-soluble remains, within which the attainment of *Geist*'s infinite self-relation, its *Beisichselßstsein*, is inscribed. Hence, the question concerning the nature of the bond between brother and sister lies at the very heart of the enigmas with which our inquiry began. The key to this problematic, as the *Phenomenology* makes quite evident, is to be found within the logic of difference structuring this relation. Thus, the nature of the brother/sister bond opens upon the fundamental issue of our study: the Hegelian teleological constriction of difference, the movement from abstract to determinate negation, the binding logic of *Aufhebung*.

The passage from the sphere of divine law to the sphere of human law takes place, we recall, with the brother's departure. Yet, in this moment of passage, the nature of the differential structure relating brother and sister is revealed for, as Hegel says, at this limit, 'the two sexes overcome their natural being' (PhG/248/275). This natural being, Hegel tells us, is manifested in the 'existence of a natural difference' (PhG/248/276): the immediate givenness of sexual differentiation. As we have noted, Hegel claims that the fundamental and intrinsic difference between the laws of universality and individuality within the ethical substance is embodied in a difference between sexually distinct self-consciousnesses, the natural difference between brother and sister. This difference is, Hegel maintains, originally given as a difference between the natural endowment of character, talent, and potentiality that each sex possesses as an embodied consciousness, a difference between their *'originally determinate nature'* (PhG/248/276).[29] Yet, as merely natural, the sexual difference between brother and sister remains, like the simple givenness of sexual difference in general, 'indeterminate' (PhG/248/276). Sexual difference is wholly external and abstract precisely in its naturality. Yet, the bond between brother and sister is, most importantly, permeated, by a 'contingent diversity (*Verschiedenheit*) of dispositions and capacities' (PhG/248/276) that moves beyond the merely external difference of man and woman in general. With the passage beyond the familial bond, this natural difference, this natural diversity, is overcome. The difference between brother and sister becomes 'the determinate opposition (*Gegensatz*) of the two sexes' (PhG/248/276). In this moment, natural and abstract sexual difference takes on 'the meaning of its ethical determination, its ethical destination (*ihrer sittlichen Bestimmung*)' (PhG/248/276).

Thus, at the limit of the familial bond, the passage from the divine to the human sphere is accomplished through what Derrida calls a 'dialectical process of sexual difference' (G/236a/168a): a movement from indeterminate and external sexual difference, through natural diversity, to sexual difference posited as a determinate and intrinsic ethical opposition. In this movement the natural givenness of sexual difference attains its proper destiny, its properly ethical *telos*, and thereby this difference is given its rightful place within the constitution of *Geist*'s infinite self-relation. As such, the nature of the bond between brother and sister is set out in a movement in which difference becomes determinate, in which it becomes sexual contradiction (*Widerspruch*). It is this determining movement that makes possible the unique recognitional structure between these siblings as well as the duplicitous nature, at once excluded and necessary, of their essential bond. Hence, in the movement from natural *Verschiedenheit* to ethical *Gegensatz*, the essential logic of *Aufhebung* is played out and the teleological constriction of difference within the Hegelian system is made evident. The transition from *Verschiedenheit* to *Gegensatz* is therefore the 'pure essentiality,' the 'formal aspect' (PhG/61/56) apparent only to the phenomenological We, which serves as the structural logic for this central passage. The self-relation of *Geist* is thus accomplished in and through this decisive transition.

Now Derrida notes that the opposition between difference in general and qualitative diversity is the 'hinge of the greater Logic' (G/234a/168a) around which this impossible site turns. He thus alludes to Hegel's important discussion of difference, diversity, and opposition in the *Science of Logic*. Curiously, Derrida has himself never sought publicly to analyse Hegel's own account of the transition here at issue in its most pure form.[30] And yet, a proper understanding of the unique process of sexual differentiation at work in the *Phenomenology* appears to require such a consideration. Moreover, recognition of the broader implications of this paradoxical bond for the Hegelian system in general depends upon understanding the precise way in which difference is here being put into the service of the *telos* of *Geist*'s infinite self-relation. This can only become clear given an adequate understanding of the transition from diversity to opposition.

A proper discussion of the texts at issue is beyond the limits of the present essay, but the relevant aspects of Hegel's account of the transition can be laid bare.

The transition from diversity to opposition is focused around the issue of the intrinsic nature of difference. According to Hegel, difference is understood as diversity when being, in its immediacy, presents itself as a manifold of self-contained and solely self-related objects, monads, that are wholly indifferent to one another. The senses in which the members of this manifold can be said to be similar or dissimilar would appear to arise then solely out of the reflective activity of comparison (*Vergleichen*), and these senses would be, as such, wholly extrinsic determinations of the immediacy they seek to describe. In this way, the 'determinate difference' (WL/268/419) of the diverse, as Hegel calls it, its 'similarity' (*Gleichheit*) and 'dissimilarity' (*Ungleichheit*) (WL/268/419), remains external to the immediate relation of each diverse object with itself. However, what Hegel's analysis shows is that this separation cannot be maintained. The very attempt to uphold it uncovers the truth that it is the unity of their similarities and dissimilarities that constitutes the immediacy of diverse things. In other words, the reflective activity of comparison is not extrinsic to the immediacy of being. Rather, it is the very inner determination of every diverse manifold and as such difference, and more specifically the fundamental difference between similarity and dissimilarity, that is properly said to be intrinsic to being. Understood in this manner, the concept of difference is no longer thought of as the indifference of diversity. It is instead the intrinsic determination of opposition. For Hegel then, the reflective constitution of being is always a matter of inherent opposition, and difference is thus properly understood as essential and immanent to the very givenness of things.

Given this account, we can now seek to understand just what these admittedly abstract reflections have to say about the bond between brother and sister.

## Recognition, the Structure of Remains, and the Enigmas: The Problem of the Third

The uniqueness of the bond between brother and sister presented itself as a problematic concerned with the structure of recognition. This structure is both made possible and accomplished in and through the movement from natural diversity to ethical opposition, the dialectical process of sexual difference. We have noted that it is at this familial limit that the passage between divine and human law takes place and the circular repetition of *Geist* is secured. It is this *telos* that orients the matter. However, as we have seen Derrida argue, the kind of mutual recognition between brother and sister necessary for this transition, a recognition devoid of confrontation, appeared excluded by the strictures of Hegel's own system. How then does the movement of sexual determination enable this seemingly impossible relation to carry out its central role?

The possibility of the assertion of the right of reciprocal recognition lies precisely within what for Hegel is the unique relation of sexually different siblings: natural diversity. The immediately given natures of these siblings already possess a kind of determination, the contingent diversity of their dispositions and capacities, and it is this determinateness that, as merely immediate, proves to be ultimately indeterminate with regard to the ethical realm. And yet, the natural existence of this difference is absolutely decisive for the emergence of the 'determinate opposition' (PhG/248/276) embodying the passage between human and divine law. The brother is for the sister, Hegel says, 'the peaceful similar being in general (*das ruhige gleiche Wesen überhaupt*)' (PhG/248/275). In this key phrase the definitive trait of the bond of brother and sister is uncovered: the conjoining of similarity (*Gleichheit*), dissimilarity (*Ungleichheit*), and peace (*Ruhe*).

Brother and sister are like one another insofar as they are both members of one and the same family, they share a common blood-origin. Yet there is in this bond, at the same time, a fundamental dissimilarity (*Ungleichheit*), the natural difference between the multitude of capacities and dispositions of male and female. Hence, the bond between brother and sister is a naturally given, immediately diverse relation. As merely natural beings, brother and sister are each, like self-contained monads, immediate unities possessing an infinite range of differences between them. Yet each remains wholly indifferent to these differences and thus to one another. The determinate difference of this bond, its similarity and dissimilarity, thus lies beyond its immediate givenness. In one respect then they are alike, while in another they are distinct.

The immediate givenness of this diverse relation, along with its extrinsic determinations, is the key to understanding how reciprocal recognition is able to arise within this sphere without confrontation or struggle. The immediate and natural givenness of siblings is already a multiplicity sustained by what at first appears as an extrinsic sphere of similarity, the family. The brother and sister bond is a differential relation that emerges and is sustained by this natural whole. As such, brother and sister are as profoundly distinct as sexually dissimilar. And yet they bear an extrinsic relation as members of the same family. Each sibling is thus already other than itself; each has always already come out of itself as a brother or as a sister, simply by virtue of its birth into this relation. Given that desire seeks always to eliminate this 'being-other,' the naturality of this moment paradoxically renders unnecessary the immediate confrontation of self-consciousnesses.

Due then to this natural diversity, Hegel tells us, the blood of brother and sister is not subject to the disparity and inequality permeating the other familial relations. It is instead uniquely at rest (*Ruhe*) because sexual desire is here not able to emerge within the *Gleichheit* of the family.[31] Likewise, as siblings, they do not receive from one another their immediate being-for-self. Instead, this comes, though in a wholly negative fashion, from their parents. The siblings' sexual difference is thus a difference, an alterity, that is sustained within the extrinsic similarity of the familial community. As fundamentally dissimilar siblings, however, the relation of brother and sister is able to allow the singularity (*Einzelnheit*) of both sides to remain uniquely distinct and irreducible, at equilibrium. No other sibling relation is capable of sustaining this simultaneity of similarity and dissimilarity, likeness and unlikeness. Hence, it is only in the familial relation of brother and sister that a genuine moment of reciprocal recognition is able to arise.

But the natural diversity of brother and sister enables recognition to emerge without confrontation only outside 'the horizon of war' (G/210a/150a), as Derrida says. However, it does not itself accomplish this central moment. In fact, mere diversity cannot accomplish this moment. It is rather in the move-ment from natural diversity to ethical opposition, from the multiplicity of differences between brother and sister to their speculative duality, that the affirmative recognition of each being as a free being-for-self by the other takes place.

The seemingly unrelated extrinsic determinations of the diverse brother and sister relation, their similarity as siblings and their distinctness as male and female, are – by means of what appears to be a merely subjective external comparison – related to one another. Each is what it is in and through the other. The family whole is a substantial similarity only insofar as it overcomes sexual difference in the love of husband and wife. While sexual difference is dissimilarity only insofar as it maintains precisely the distinction that gives rise, for Hegel, to conjugal desire. Through this attentiveness, each extrinsic moment is related to the bond itself as to a third and, in being thus related, the determinations are ultimately shown to be related to one another. Together they form a negative unity.

However, as we noted above, this negative unity is, for Hegel, nothing other than the self-relating reflection of diversity itself. The determinate difference of brother and sister is thus nothing other than the constituting movement between the family and sexual difference, their identity and their difference. These moments are genuinely opposed to one another within one reflective movement. The self-contained unities of the brother and the sister likewise are no longer a multiplicity but a negative duality, a 'determinate opposition' (PhG/248/276). They are at once intrinsically distinct and intrinsically related.

As opposed moments, each is already in contradiction with itself and thus with one another since each excludes its defining other from itself. Brother and sister thus form not just a negative unity, an intrinsic opposition, but more fundamentally a speculative contradiction. The very movement of *Geist* that posited these moments negates the sufficiency of both the brother and the sister and, in so doing, posits itself as an infinite self-relation. It is through this central moment, then, the 'union of man and woman' (PhG/250/278), that the stable transformation of human and divine law into one another, the *Aufhebung* of their implicit conflict, takes place. Here the opposed moments withdraw into the positive unity of justice, the equilibrium of human and divine law.[32] It is this that constitutes the true uniqueness of the bond between brother and sister and thus, held asunder in this unique speculative identity, brother and sister thereby transcend the level of mere desire and freely recognize one another as distinct consciousnesses: 'the individual self can here assert its right to recognize and to be recognized' (PhG/248/275). This then is why Hegel maintains that it is in the familial bond of brother and sister alone that recognition properly attains its completion within itself.

As an immediate diversity, the bond between brother and sister is excluded from the circular constitution of *Geist*, for this bond's determinateness lies outside *Geist*'s infinite self-relation. The intrinsic opposition of these siblings, however, is necessary for the *Aufhebung* of the conflict between divine and human law and thus the circular closure of the sphere of *Sittlichkeit*. Yet such a speculative duality cannot arise simply between a male and a female, within such an abstract difference. They must possess the natural diversity found solely within the bond of brother and sister. Hence diversity is at once necessary for the speculative genesis of *Geist* and excluded from this becoming because it harbors a fundamental separation between the movement of self-determination and its definitive moments: an externality seemingly beyond the self-relation of *Geist* itself. Thus, not only does the possibility of the mutual recognition of brother and sister arise out of the givenness of natural diversity, but so does its paradoxical nature as at once excluded and necessary.

With this analysis of the bond between brother and sister complete, our explication of the familial moment as presented in the *Phenomenology* is concluded. This specific moment, however, is but a figure for the general problematic that *Glas* has sought to uncover at the limit of the Hegelian system of onto-theology: the quasi-transcendental structure of the remains.

The duplicitous nature of the bond between brother and sister is, as we have noted, not confined to the sphere of *Geist*'s immediacy. It is instead a problematic endemic to the general movement of the dialectic as such. The constitution of the self-relation of *Geist*, its *Beisichselßstsein*, is always assured precisely by that which it excludes, the remains. This quasi-transcendental structure, a formulation reflecting the duplicitous nature of this moment, has now revealed itself at the most formal level. It is nothing other than difference thought of as diversity. As our examination of the bond between brother and sister makes clear, a diverse relationality, a natural multiplicity, constitutes the 'space of possibility' (G/226a/162a) within which *Geist* accomplishes its self-relation, its infinitely free repetition. Diversity then is the differential structure that permits the movement from abstract to determinate negation, the logic of *Aufhebung*, to take place. As the quasi-condition of this fundamental passage, Derrida argues, it functions as a non-ontological and non-totalizable differential 'matrix' (G/340a/244a) from which intrinsic speculative duality is drawn and within which the dialectic itself is inscribed. According to this analysis, then, *Geist*'s self-determining movement is always an 'economic restriction' (G/340a/244a) of this reserve of negativity. Its *telos* of circular relation must be rethought in terms of this quasi-transcendental structure.

Derrida thus maintains that, given the eidetic nature of diverse negativity, the logic of *Aufhebung* – a logic of absolute appropriation and exchange – 'can always be reread or rewritten as the logic of loss or of spending without reserve' (G/233a/167a), as absolute expropriation. The movement of the dialectic is always a matter of constricting diversity such that it forms a fundamental duality, a speculative contradiction. But in this constriction, there is always already a negativity that exceeds the resolving logic of contradiction: the diverse multiplicity of the remains. Diversity thus makes possible the identity of the absolute Idea and inscribes this identity within its ineluctable difference. It thereby fissures any speculative self-relation and constitutes the simultaneous movement of absolute presence and absolute alterity, the contamination of pure identity and pure difference. Derrida calls this contaminating negativity 'transcendental contra-band,' since it is both necessary and excluded from the constitutive movement of the dialectic, and concludes that it 'would be the (nondialectical) law of the (dialectical) stricture, of the bond, of the ligature, of the garrotte, of the *desmos* in general when it comes to clench tightly in order to make be' (G/341a/244a).

Diversity – marked within the logic of *Aufhebung* between abstract and determinate negation – uncovers the enigma of simultaneity, the quasi-transcendental remains, at the closure of the history of metaphysics. An infinitesimal and radical displacement of Hegelian speculation indeed appears to be carried out in this disclosure and it would seem possible then to isolate the precise point of rupture between the Derridean chain of infrastructures and Hegelian speculative logic. It is the category of diversity. Attentive to this moment at work in each and every juncture within the genesis of *Geist*, Derrida's work constantly engages in rereading 'the spiral chaining of the circle of circles' (G/341a/244a–245a) according to its inherent 'contra-band,' producing thereby a 'simulated repetition' of the very discourse that it seeks to call into question.

And yet such an assurance itself proves to be deeply enigmatic. If the remains are marked within Hegel's speculative logic by the category of diversity, then this differential condition is subject to the very analysis that Hegel's text carries out. A diverse multiplicity possesses no other determinateness than the movement between similarity and dissimilarity, its extrinsic aspects. The reflective self-movement constituting diversity is thus the movement between these aspects, now thought of as moments, and thereby difference is shown to be, of necessity, intrinsic opposition, speculative duality. The separation of the whole and its moments sustained in the moment of diversity collapses and a speculative duality arises.

In a crucial and revealing passage Derrida claims that:

> the contra-band is *not yet* dialectical contradiction. To be sure, the contra-band necessarily becomes that, but its not-yet is not-yet the teleological anticipation, which results in it never becoming dialectical contradiction. The contra-band *remains* (*reste*) something other than what, necessarily, it is to become.

(G/340a–341a/244a)

Yet, if the differential matrix constitutes a third to which identity and difference are related only externally, then how can it sustain this separation? How is this multiplicity not exhausted in the movement to intrinsic determination? Derrida has never articulated the impossibility of the movement from a given multiplicity to its intrinsic opposition. He has instead relied upon this very transition to reveal the space of possibility within which the dialectic moves. But if this space is the reflection-into-itself of the third, then in fact will not the very attempt to maintain its various aspects give way, as Hegel shows, to intrinsic opposition and, ultimately, to speculative contradiction? If so, the enigma of affinity remains perhaps the most troubling and inescapable matter for one concerned with Derrida's work. What may be called the 'problematic of the third' appears to inhabit his thought always threatening it from within with the possibility of being taken up in the genesis of *Geist*. The movement of contamination, the logic of simultaneous appropriation and expropriation, may thus be the very movement of *Aufhebung* and the infinitesimal displacement of Hegelian discourse may always already defer itself. *Différance* then may never be capable of being thought otherwise than as an intrinsic opposition and, as such, always already constrained by the *telos* of *Geist*'s *Beisichselßstsein*. The 'profound affinity' between deconstruction and speculative philosophy may finally prove inescapable and their relation irresoluble. Holding to this most problematic of enigmas, Derrida's famous pronouncement concerning Hegel's place within the history of metaphysics can begin to be read in a profoundly new fashion: 'the last philosopher of the book and the first thinker of writing' (DG/41/26).[33]

# 11

# Hegel, *Glas*, and the Broader Modernity

*Henry Sussman*

1. *Glas*'s bicolumnar architecture not only establishes a textual modality of reverberation, supplementarity, chiasmatic reversal, and constriction. In its persistent recurrence back to Hegel as synthesizer of a Western metaphysical mainstream, and to Genet as the poet of an amoral and homo-erotic counter-culture, whose text nonetheless interweaves many of the images and figures pivotal to the Hegelian enterprise, *Glas* may also be said to bracket two decisive, if not definitive limits to the broader Modernity. In no empirical way, *Glas* delimits a certain epoch in the history of Western culture(s) at the same time that it stages a tympanic modality of reversal and echoing evident in all textual articulation and elaboration. In this essay, I would like to explore and elaborate what *Glas*'s historical remark might be.

2. Here I would like to interject that one of the odd, rarely mentioned enterprises describing a certain commonality between the likes of Kant, Hegel, Nietzsche, Heidegger, and Derrida is their service as critics of Western idealism within a broader framework, one of whose offshoots is a perspective on 'Western' or 'World Civilization(s).' Whether ideologically *synthesizing* this tradition, as do (generally speaking) Kant and Hegel, or in asystematically and infrastructurally *resisting* the same entity, as do Nietzsche, Heidegger, and Derrida, these philosophers all devote considerable effort to surveying the damage and other impacts wrought by the fixation on idealistic operations and structures that characterizes the full gamut of Western disciplines and areas of political and social policy and administration over a long – but adjustable – span of 'history.' As a regular instructor of 'World Civilization' courses, perhaps I am commiserating in grandiose fashion by appropriating certain efforts on the

part of these epochal philosophers in the name of this endeavor. It is none-theless clear to me that Derrida, while he refers to Western 'metaphysics' or 'logocentrism'[1] far more often than he mentions idealism, is engaged in an ongoing damage report on the biases that have invaded Western societies and their colonies by virtue of this fixation on ideological protocols that may be demonstrated to pervade Western cultural artifacts and institutions.

The consummate performative irony of *Glas* is that *certain* of the metaphors that Hegel appropriates in *consolidating* a cluster of attitudes defining a secular, modern 'mainstream' of Western culture are *common* to the figures that Genet explores in elaborating the 'other,' sensational facet of the same tradition. Language, whether the language of poetic figures or logic, is expansive enough to entertain antipodal, radically differant polysemic significations of and sce-narios for *common* terms. *Glas*, in its typographic architecture and its motifs of splitting, reverberating, ringing, and castrating, to name a few, *performs* the relation between the ideology of Western culture(s) and its margins; the reflexive achievements of speculation and the mirror's tain;[2] the dialectical, organic, and consummate fate for the West that Hegel envisioned and that Genet's gay-criminal 'underworld subverted.'

*Glas*'s purview, the term of its 'validity,' is 'eternal' and it is not. We can surmise some vague Derridean 'universality' characterizing the tension between a general ideology at play in all cultures, times, etc., and its linguis-tically 'organized' undercurrent. We can hypostasize some ideologically struc-tured center to every culture, at whatever stage of technology, during whatever historical period, wherever located, and however exclusively oriented to idealism. And of all philosophers, Derrida most elaborately enumerates the remains that cannot be appropriated by this 'center,' even if this focal 'site' is itself, as in Chinese and Central Asian civilizations, differentiated and fragmen-ted. Yet supplementing this general, ongoing play between ideological machine and linguistic by-product, a play whose non-dialectical nature Derrida goes to great pains to reinforce, is the 'time-specific' drama of idealism in Hegel's philosophy and the particular cultural epoch it characterizes. Hegel imposes specifications upon Western cultures at the same time and in the same act that he does so upon organico-dialectical philosophical discourse. The brilliant, I am tempted to say 'comprehensive,' job of reconstructing and extrapolating Hege-lian ideology that Derrida performs in *Glas* includes, among its elements, Christian humanism as opposed to Judaic (and graphic) formalism and death; altruism as the single legitimate model of love and social interaction; and an altruism-based sacrifice of the familial, particular, and idiosyncratic in the interest of an overarching social good. These metaphysical attitudes more or less buttress Western ideologies from Hegel's late-Enlightenment moment until they go out of fashion, just before? during? the moment of Genet.

This is all by way of saying that there is an implicit architecture of history in *Glas*, a historiographic accompaniment to the knell by which ideology's appeal sounds its silent echo. And on this architectural blueprint, Hegel and Genet are (intertwined, reverberating) columns framing a certain (epistemological and cultural more than historical) epoch. And there is some utility in characterizing this epoch as the major span of the broader Modernity, which itself may be defined as the age in which subjectivity achieves an irremediable splitting and suspension between multiple and often conflicting obligations, and in which linguistic and poetic facility both epitomize and constitute the only available means of circumventing, suspending, this (losing) predicament. Projected into time, the architecture of *Glas* may be read as the historiographic map of an epoch – under certain of whose conditions and delusions we still labor, even in the endeavor of doing intellectual work. My aspiration for this essay is to explore the broader Modernity whose extremes *Glas* so innovatively and unforgettably delineates.

3. *Glas* is as broad as a linguistico-epistemological history of Modernity and as narrow as the vicissitudes of a wayward grapheme, a *gl* that may be associated with flowers, swords, classes, and the sound made when swallowing viscous fluids. Indeed, in Derrida's retelling of the history of Western thought, the adventures of a syllable are as consequential as matters get. The non-linear meanderings of a syllable replace established formats for history such as the History of Ideas and the stories of nations, World-Historical Individuals, and so on. Derrida designs *Glas* with an elision of subjectivity and the subjective history that is invoked in the explanation of so many cultural phenomena. Indeed, such a matter of intense subjective concern as sexual organs and imagery plays a major role in Derrida's reconstruction of modern ideology and its running subculture. There is a tendency in *Glas* for Derrida to *gl*ide between language- and subject-based models in his account of Hegel, Genet, and the ideological and cultural baggage they carry with them, to which we will turn our attention below. But for now it is sufficient to note that within the framework of the Derridean project, an enterprise of thinking culture at a remove from entrenched Western metaphysical assumptions regarding ideals, origins, purposes, identities, and the like, the trajectory of a single grapheme, a molecule if not an 'atom' of language, does better than a grandiloquent account

of an age, an epoch, a 'movement.' The syllable is a unit of singularity implicated countless times in a network of language that twists, doubles, reverts, and repeats upon itself endlessly.

4. *Glas* is Derrida's most architectural work. Its bicolumnar structure represents his most solid architecture. A distinctive stability and proportion are embodied in the equilibrium of its two typographic columns. The architectural structure formed by this blueprint is a house, a home, in the sense that the Freudian uncanny arises in the defamiliarization of the *heimlich*, the homey.

*Glas* is Derrida's most elaborate construction project. Architecture is crucial to both columns, and to the strained equilibrium with which they relate to each other. In addition, more so than in any other work, Derrida's reading of his 'subject matter,' Hegel and Genet, concentrates on a reconstruction of a tradition and a counter-culture out of key images, narrative and argumentative styles, and keywords. The deconstruction of *Glas* consists less in the disclosure and unleashing of a repressed counter-current in works' putative significations and cultural values than in the sustained dissonance between the two columns, each combining the constitutive elements of the same (Western metaphysical) tradition, but with a radically different nuance.

In *Glas*, Derrida pulls no unexpected rabbits out of hats. The bulk of the energy, interpretation, and rhetorical resources are devoted to a *constructive* effort, in one column the *assembly* of a major, Hegelian retrospective on Western values. On the other hand (or is that in the opposite column?), Derrida assembles no less constructively the underside of that same spiritualized if secular, teleological vision out of swatches of text appropriated from Jean Genet.

*Glas* is thus a construction project in two senses. To the degree that its argumentative plan emphasizes the sustained dissonance between the mainstream and the alienated undercurrent of modern Western values, and not so much the disclosure of repressed marginality (as is the case, say, in the readings of Rousseau in *Of Grammatology* and Heidegger in *Margins of Philosophy*), its construction project extends to both columns. But there is of course also the tendentious sense in which the left-hand column, as an amalgamation of the positivity of Western aspirations, at least as Hegel formulated them, is more 'constructive' than its counterpart on the right-hand side, which devotes so many resources to Genet's subversive reiteration of the same ideology.

*Glas* sustains a bicolumnar *Klang* or reverberation. The infrastructure of chiasmatic binary tension, no matter how dynamic, is crucial to its reading(s) and commentary. Yet each of the two architectural supports making this infrastructure possible is itself in an ongoing state of fragmentation and decomposition. I am referring here to Derrida's tendency to add splits (*coups*) to each column in the form of marginal additions, or in some cases spliced countertexts (e.g., Hegel's correspondence with his sister and her caretakers). *Glas*'s *Klang* echoes across the abyss in its typographical format, yet the architectural supports are in an ongoing condition of textual dissemination and dissolution. Cumulative, strategic fragmentation is thus as much an element in *Glas*'s construction as architectural planning.

5. Hegel, after the theological texts that Derrida also includes in his reconstruction project, demands, in a secular context, a human self-generation of knowledge, speculation, ethical values, and the cognitive faculties by which these achievements are produced. Human wonder, knowledge, sensibility, and institutions are to be exclusively human productions themselves. There is to prevail an organic dynamism, endowed with the qualities of life, in speculation itself and *between* the various faculties and stages involved in the generation and evolution of the human sensibility.

6. What are the Hegelian elements that Derrida recombines in his retrospective *assemblage* of post-Enlightenment Western ideology's high road? (Remembering that this gathering is too unconcerned with conclusiveness, *coverage*, symmetry, or design to qualify as modernist *bricolage*.)

The alliances of the conventional family and their imaginary (or speculative) correlatives; Christianity's sense of its urgent, particular mission, above all, in relation to a Judaism interpreted as legalistic, formalistic, and lacking in spontaneous altruism; the figure of Antigone as Western metaphysics' epitome and bad girl; the system's epiphenomena – including fetishism and the enigmatic figures of light, sound (*Klang*), and the gift – which derange it while serving as its uncanny, unforgettable talismans: these are the materials out of which Derrida fabricates and recreates post-Enlightenment Western culture's ideological high road. The left-hand column of *Glas* reconfigures this tradition and system in a manner that acknowledges the persistence and social utility of certain repressions brought about by systematic constraints and prohibitions at the same time – precisely in its modality of reconstruction – that it underscores and questions the arbitrariness of this repression, it points up the stress lines in the application of closure. The left-hand column debunks in an act of assembly, while it *constructs* the architecture of a system that can be 'experienced' only as confining by its in-dwellers, who are projected into a position shared by the implied residents in Piranesi's 'Prisons.'

It is commonly thought that Derrida points the way to some exit or escape from the prison of Western values so entrenched as to have become transparent, invisible. Yet Derrida's demonstration, in the left-hand column of *Glas*, is as much in the direction of affirming the inescapability of certain cornerstone Western values as it is in skeptically debunking them. The *assemblage* of *Glas*'s left-hand column should give pause to anyone wishing to accuse Derrida of facile escapism or megacynicism. Nowhere in the column is there the least expectation that religion can be eliminated, voice can be quelled into writing, phallocentrism transformed into the acceptance of a continuum of sexual possibilities. *Glas* thus constitutes Derrida's guarantee regarding the contrapuntal nature of deconstruction, its perdurance as sustained dissonance *within* the Western system and *between* its elements, rather than as a *definitive* dismantling or debunking.

7. Genet's philosophical poetry can be adequately appreciated *only* to the degree that it is read against the backdrop of the mainstream post-Enlightenment Western ideology whose terms it borrows, empties, subverts, and reconfigures. Derrida's reading of Genet's drama, fiction, essays, and poetry is the most bravura literary analysis of his that I have encountered; it alone comprises an ample response to detractors who claim that deconstruction is undoing even the most minimal allegiance to the literary pretexts for criticism. One possible explanation for the left-hand column is that it records the conceptual groundwork necessary before the Genet exegesis is possible. In preparation for my own appreciation for this wonderful and inspiring reading, I want to review a certain number of the left-hand column's discursive registers.

8. On the Hegelian side, discourse is held together by 'one thread' (*G*, 4a):[3] 'It is the law of the family: of Hegel's family, of the family in Hegel, of the concept family according to Hegel' (ibid.). If Derrida's most notable essays tend to be 'organized' by 'master' tropes: the *pharmakon* of 'Plato's Pharmacy,' the hymen of 'The Double Session,' or the sun and its heliotrope in 'White Metaphor,' then the choice of the family as the tissue connecting the Hegelian discourse of *Glas* is interesting to say the least. The family is a sociological and psycho-analytic unit as much as it may be translated into rhetorical and logical functions. Derrida's work on the family in *Glas* stands out because his other distinctive 'master' tropes – gifts, fabrics, membranes, crypts, and so on – display linguistic and logical operations and assumptions to the exclusion of

metaphysical 'attitude.' This avoidance of metaphysical assumptions regarding subjectivity, identity, and purpose, to name a few, is in keeping with an overall deconstructive design of rearticulating the traditions of Western philosophy and onto-theology from the perspective of the logical and linguistic processes that become constrained, limited, 'bent,' to the demands of idealism and ideology. As opposed to the *pharmakon*, the membrane, or the crypt, the family overflows with implications of a subjective, sociological, and teleological nature at the same time that, in Hegel's texts and elsewhere, it functions as a syllogism and semantic generator. The Derridean focus upon family matters in a critical 'reconstruction' of a major metaphysical position enables the left-hand column to freely pass *between* conceptual paradigms oriented, on the one hand, to language, and on the other to subjectivity. I suspect that this 'opening up' of the deconstructive purview in *Glas* to subject-oriented frameworks and mythology, as in Derrida's few early and more numerous later commentaries on Freud, occurs very much by design. A quasi-systematic deconstruction needs to address the distortion effects of ideology wherever found. The drawback to the family's pluralistic receptiveness to the metaphysics of identity and society as well as to the dynamics of representation and communication is the obscuration of the contrapuntal line of demarcation between language- and subjectivity-based models. In *Glas*, Derrida more than restores attention to this dynamic borderline in the ongoing tension and dance between the Hegel ('mainstream') and Genet ('marginal, textual, deviant') columns, but the intramural battles that prevail in the literary and philosophical professions have entered a remorseless repetition–compulsion on the basis of relative unclarity with regard to the essential differences between language- and subject-based paradigms, and the relative attitudes and 'results' that can be expected from them.

For all the family's relative breadth of nuances in comparison with other Derridean 'master' tropes, Derrida initially places its importance within a syllogism:

Now within *Sittlichkeit*, the third term and the moment of synthesis between right's formal objectivity and morality's abstract subjectivity, a syllogism in turn is developed.

Its first term is the family.
The second, civil or bourgeois society (*bürgerliche Gesellschaft*).
The third, the State or the constitution of the State (*Staatsverfassung*).

(*G*, 4a)

The Hegel column in *Glas* may well extrapolate in comprehensive fashion the metaphysical values prevailing during an epoch of Western culture not yet definitively terminated, but it remains true to Derrida's philosophico-linguistic field and style of intervention. He brings the family to our attention initially both *as* a syllogism and because of its characterization by and participation in dialectical process. The family plays a certain role in the emergence and reinforcement of the ethical (*Sittlichkeit*); the ethical is in turn a microcosm, a synecdochical insignia (or fetish) of the Hegelian mainstream of post-Enlightenment Western ideology in general.

> The family is a *party to* the system of the spirit: the family is both a part and the whole of the system.
>
> The whole system repeats itself in the family. *Geist* is always, in the very production of its essence, a kind of repetition. Coming to, after losing itself in nature and in its other, spirit constitutes itself as absolute spirit through the negative process of a syllogism whose three moments are *subjective spirit* (anthropology, phenomenology of spirit, psychology), *objective spirit* (right, morality, *Sittlichkeit*), and absolute spirit (art, religion, philosophy).
>
> (*G*, 20a)

9. There will never be any definitive escape from this system: at most there will be the playing, in the sense of a musical accompaniment, a *Klang*? of an ongoing counterpoint to the system's determinations and pretensions. There will never be a decisive victory by the knowing involutions of writing over the spiritual immanence of voice, by the barbarians over the citizens, by the margin over the mainstream. *Glas*, while most inventively, 'comprehensively' staging the play between modern Western ideology and its other(s), also most assuredly asserts the perdurance of the logocentric 'foreground.'

> Is it by chance that, in the paragraphs of the *Philosophy of Right* that present the concept *Sittlichkeit* . . . an almost proverbial or legendary citation appeals to the father and the son's education? It is a Remark following a paragraph. Education is also a constituting/deconstituting process of the family, an *Aufhebung* by which the family accomplishes itself, *raises itself* in destroying itself or falling (to the tomb) as family. As family: the *as*, the *comme*, the *as such* of the essentiality, of the essential property or propriety, since it raises only in crossing out, is itself the *as* only insofar as other than what it is; it phenomenalizes the phenomenalization it discovers. . . .

The father loses his son like that (*comme ça*): in gaining him, in educating him, in raising him, in involving him in the family circle, which comes down, in the logic of the *Aufhebung*, to helping him leave, to pushing him outside while completely retaining him. The father helps his son, takes him by the hand in order to destroy the family in accomplishing it within what dissolves it: first bourgeois or civil society (*bürgerliche Gesellschaft*), then the *State* that accomplishes *Sittlichkeit* in 'relieving the family and bourgeois society,' in magnifying them. . . .

The family is the first moment of this process.

(*G*, 13–14a)

Given what Derrida knows, and through him, what we know of Hegel, the family's dialectical position as a threshold between childhood and cultivation, between allegiance to the private and to the civil or public, comes as no surprise. There is an odd similarity between the father's double bearing to the son, the family's 'constituting/deconstituting' relation to itself and the Freudian 'fort-da' of fundamental human ambivalence (here I myself cross the threshold between the philosophical and the psychological). But there is no doubt here that Derrida and his readers have a vital stake in education, even where this function and institution harbor metaphysical twists and biases. Having backed ourselves into affiliations with education and its institutions, *we*, including Derrida, participate in the economy and metaphysics of voice and logocentrism, regardless of how decentering we would hope the effect of our pedagogy would be. The family, the state, education, public welfare and morality – these are some of the embarrassing, domestic contracts to which we subscribe all the more so by virtue of our compulsive thinking and writing. (Critics of gender and culture have been studying the contrast between this domesticity, its sublime other, and the values attached to them with the most productive results.)[4] Nowhere in his writing does Derrida more forthrightly address the potentially stultifying tangle of these ties, of course in the interest of his own philosophical thinking, than in the left-hand column of *Glas*.

10. The complex including the family, civil society, the Christian values that legitimize this society, the art deemed talismanic for it: in Derrida's reconstruction of this matrix, each element submits to the Hegelian schemata of dialectical progression, *Aufhebung*, and so on. Whether Derrida adresses the Christian sacrament of the eucharist or the systematic implications of

Sophocles' *Antigone*, he can demonstrate the torque and force, in the name of systematic, speculative philosophy, exerted by Hegel upon his 'material.'

Yet there is a moment, as I have suggested above, when even the left-hand, 'mainstream' column begins to fragment and crumble. This dissolution is an anticipation, in the logic and rhetoric of Hegel, of the systematic upheaval celebrated in the literature of Genet. For all the Hegelian high road's predictability as it extends from one complex of metaphysical values to another, a violence is contained by the Hegelian system that will lead to its loss of momentum and self-certainty. Derrida demonstrates how, through such figures as the gift and the resonation of *Klang* itself, the system harbors within itself the seeds and processes of its own dismantling. If the Genet column sketches out the realization of this implicit metaphysical violence or self-destruction, the *Klang*, the gift, and the treacheries of Hegelian architecture constitute a seed of the Genet column 'planted' in the Hegelian reconstruction itself. Although both columns of *Glas* never end, in the sense that the narrative of *Finnegans Wake* turns upon itself, it is in the elaboration of figures like resonation itself that the left-hand, 'mainstream' column comes as close as it does to any apotheosis or conclusion. The remainder of my comments on the Hegel column will be oriented to these 'pre-Genet' figures, but by way of a couple of 'way-stations' still within the established complex of metaphysical images and values.

11. One is struck by the splitting that pervades Derrida's reconstitution of Hegelian religion. Translated into Genet's underworld, the hits (*coups*), splits, separations, and gaps that Derrida observes to set the tone for Christianity will be sexualized into thrusts, penetrations, and climaxes. The purpose of Western onto-theology, according to Hegel, is to reconcile certain unavoidable and predetermined splits: in order for healing reunion to take place, a *pre*condition of radical conflict has to be endemic, systematic. 'The Hegelian reading of Christianity seems to describe a reconciliation, in order to say everything in two words: between faith and being, *Glauben* and *Sein*' (*G*, 91a).

Radical splitting, whether between textual columns or resonating antipodal value systems, becomes one of several pivotal infrastructures in *Glas*, distinct from dialectical opposition in its proliferation, displacement, and ultimate non-resolution. Coincidentally, the object-relations camp of a psychoanalytical overview that Derrida generally tries to circumvent selects the same radical splitting as a characterization of Western subjectivity during a Modernity with 'large' or 'small' bores, as long as the period from the Renaissance to the early twentieth century or as brief as 1800–1945. Perhaps there is a logic by which splitting could be so prominent both within the frameworks of Derrida's (generally) de-spiritualized reissue of Western philosophy *and* within the theory of the most 'psychodynamic' model of psychoanalysis.

The splits of Modernity resound at a major juncture in Derrida's recounting of Hegelian Christianity.

> The cleavage – which attains its absolute in absolute religion – is the need of/for philosophy. Philosophy is descended, as its own proper object, from Christianity of which it is the truth, from the Holy Family which it falls under (whose relief it is [*dont elle (est la) relève*]. 'The Need of Philosophy' . . . (that is the subtitle of a text nearly contemporaneous with *The Spirit of Christianity*) upsurges in the *between* [*entre*], the narrow gap [*écart*] of a split, a cleavage, a separation, a division in two. One divides itself into two, such is the distressing source of philosophy: '*Entzweiung ist der Quell des Bedürfnisses der Philosophie.*' Therefore reason proceeds to busy itself thinking the wound, to reduce the division, to return this side of the source, close by the infinite unity. . . . The progress of culture has led oppositions of the type spirit/matter, soul/body, faith/understanding, freedom/necessity, and all those deriving from these back toward the great couple reason/sensibility or intelligence/nature. . . . Now these oppositions are poised as such by the understanding that 'copies (*ahmt*)' reason. So this enigmatic relation, this rational *mimesis*, organizes the whole history of philosophy as the history of need, the history of reason's interest in relieving the two.
>
> (G, 95a)

In terms of *Glas*'s gestic treasury, and the rhetorical and logical implications of such acts, there is no more prevalent gesture in this book, in both columns, than cutting, splitting, cleaving, dividing, and so on. In terms of Derrida's ongoing philosophical project, this act underlines the *resolving function* that certain philosophical works and ideological institutions would implement, in accordance with their design. The role of philosophy, in terms of Derrida's ongoing critical endeavor, is both to point up the (infra)structure of division and the acts of repression performed in the name of its reconciliation. The above passage *names* reconciliation as the repressive act of philosophy in the name of advancing Western ideology even as it changes, evolves. The *primary* thrust of the Derridean demonstration is logical and rhetorical, treating the splits and cleavages that pervade philosophy as logical structures and rhetorical possibilities.

270

But Derrida's own rhetoric opens up a *secondary* field for the splits and wounds he chronicles, one that I would describe as both historiographical and psychoanalytical. Conditions of subjectivity, over the broader Modernity, in which linguistic facility and artistic intuition become transcendental values, appropriated to a few extraordinary men, are also characterized by multi-faceted splitting and ineradicable wounds. Whether by design or not, Derrida characterizes conditions of subjectivity over a period marked by a bewilder-ment of multiple jurisdictions and obligations demanding personal commit-ment. The 'wound' that reason keeps thinking in the above passage bears a striking similarity to the fundamental 'narcissistic wounds' at the core of a number of syndromes characterized by contemporary object-relations theorists as conditions of subjective fragmentation and the non-integration, the non-communication between fragments, affective states, and acts.[5] So the process of psychotherapy, as staged by object-relations theory, would yearn, like 'main-stream' Hegelian philosophy in the above passage, for the reconciliation ('integration'), of split-off moods, tempers, states.

Hegel defines a series of splits, of ones becoming twos (or more), as a pretext for modern, Hegelian philosophy. Philosophy, in turn, will resolve these disquieting discrepancies in fulfilling its mission. As Derrida is intensely aware, religion and art, on the philosophical side, play strategic roles in addressing this predicament of fragmentation, splitting, and systematic bad faith, which under certain conditions can be made good *only* through linguistic, artistic, and intellectual facility.

Even more than Hegel, Kant establishes the protocols by which the artist serves as a representative and medium for the transcendence of the systematic, radical splitting that pervades modern philosophy and subjectivity. The artist becomes a particularly critical figure in a post-Enlightenment world in which extrinsic theological and political institutions have undergone a severe reduc-tion in their stature and imputed legitimacy and efficacy. Careful reading of Kant's *Critique of Judgment* and its relation to its predecessors suggests that the Kantian artist is the priest in a secular religion of art to replace established creeds such as those analysed by Hegel in *The Philosophy of Right*, 'The Need of Philosophy,' and *The Spirit of Christianity*.[6] The Kantian artist is also, as Derrida would say, a term in a syllogism. The argument runs: if the artist can transmit certain elements of the universe's transcendental design to the human and empirical world by means of (atheological) intuitions and representational facilities, then it is possible to imagine a universe with transcendental and empirical strata conceived and designed in human terms. This project, as is

Hegel's, is in keeping with Enlightenment ideology: furnishing an account of knowledge and human conditions based on human abilities and faculties alone; also, endowing the human-generated systems of knowledge with human qualities, creating, in effect, human simulacra in a discursive medium, or, if you will, discursive robots.

Both the Kantian and Hegelian systems fall under the purview of this vast Enlightment project (or culture contract). Kant's design sacrifices human dynamism in the names of comprehensiveness and perspectival lucidity. A certain eighteenth-century heritage may show through in Kant's emphasis on *mapping*, but his work on the players in the process of human knowledge (including faculties, categories, intuitions, powers, and language), and the interplay between different *perspectives* and *levels* of understanding, is immaculate. Kant is content with observing the complicated interaction between faculties, powers, and so on, within the perspective provided by a single frame or dialectical cell (hence Derrida's focus on the Kantian notion of the frame in 'Parergon'). The Kantian framework, as Derrida would say, is structured by a single encompassing duality, the transcendental/empirical, perhaps a distant descendant of another duality, between soul and body.[7]

Hegel, on the other hand, leaves behind the precision and comprehensiveness afforded by a more spatial, stabilized purview, in the interest of infusing the framework of knowledge with the organicism and dynamism of its human sources. Consciousness, collective and individual, meanders along the course of its progressive development. Yet both Kantian and Hegelian systems require, at a certain point, the intervention of a meta-human (what Nietzsche would eventually call the *Übermensch*) to *embody* the humanness of human-based systems of authority, to bear this humanity into the world.

Elsewhere, I treat at length how the artist, the Kantian assurance of the continuity of Western metaphysics in a secular context, and the human interface with the transcendental, is formulated in the *Critique of Judgment*, in quasi-theological fashion, as the priest in a secular art religion.[8] Hegel's stages of thought and culture, incessantly displacing themselves, furnish no such focused figure for the over-human that epitomizes the human. As Derrida pieces together in *Glas*, Hegel fashions this meta-critical figure of human oversight out of multiple materials: Sophocles' character Antigone, and the stereotypical notion of the minister in 'The Unhappy Consciousness,' for example. But Hegel surely agrees with Kant that art is a crucial arena in which modern Western people can redeem and overcome the congenital splitting that conditions their very subjectivity. And he agrees with Kant that the arena (or workshop) of art is charged with theological values and scenarios, among which intuition, transcendence, mastery, and redemption play a major role.

> Art includes its own proper religion, which is only a stage in the spirit's liberation, and has its destination in 'true religion,' truth of the past art, of what art will have been. In the fine arts, the content of the idea was limited by the sensible immediacy and did not manifest itself in the universality of an infinite form. With *true* religion (the true, the Christian religion, that of the infinite God), the sensible, finite, and immediate intuition passes into the infinite of a knowing that, as infinite, no longer has any exteriority, thus knows itself, becomes present to itself. Presence (*Dasein*) that knows itself since it is infinite and has no outside, truth that announces itself to itself, resounds and reflects itself in its own proper element: the manifest, the revealed, *das Offenbaren*.
>
> (*G*, 212)

If Art *is* not exactly a religion for Hegel, as I believe it is for Kant, Art is a pretext and format for (Christian) religion, an even higher and more ultimate manifestation of Spirit. But Art *contains* 'its own proper religion' in the passage above. And the metaphysics of presence and immanence that Derrida teases out of Hegel's *situation* of Art is not at all far-removed from the intuition, a form of immediate knowledge, with which Kant distinguishes the artist as intermediate figure.

So Hegel too, even in his progressive, organicist *style,* anoints Art as a a successor to religion in a Modernity distinguished by its personal isolation, bipolarity of moral values, and overwhelming proliferation of conflicting moral imperatives and legal jurisdictions. Derrida's reading of Hegel in *Glas* performs a cultural diagnosis of modern subject conditions even while it emphasizes rhetorical and logical conditions of modern discourse.

12. The *dénouement* of the 'Hegel story' in *Glas* is of course the (Heideggerian) disclosure of the seismic instabilities underlying even so authoritative and sound an iteration of Western cant as Hegel's. The Hegel column of *Glas*, it turns out, is sitting in quicksand; it is in a state of its own perpetual dissolution and fragmentation. Even Hegel is subject to the fate of metaphysicians that Derrida has extrapolated with more philosophical rigor and lucidity than anyone else. The very language with which Hegel would cement an ideological mainstream of Western post-Enlightenment thought betrays him, 'whipsaws' him, undermines his politico-intellectual purpose and intent.

In Derrida's version of the horror story that can be inferred from the rapport between the empirical and the transcendental in Kant, the monster language of which the rationalistic and high-minded scientists were presumably in search is decisively victorious over its 'users.' The designs of Hegel, like those by any of the agents of the ideal to whose writings Derrida has directed his scrutiny (e.g. Plato, Rousseau, Freud) will be done in and frustrated by the very terminology that was their articulate medium.

(It is possible that deconstruction imputes enormous power and even brilliance to language in its resistant and destabilizing functions, even possible that language owes some of this magic to scenarios of secular, human-originated transcendence that evolved over the span of the broader Modernity, as articulated, among others, by Kant, Schlegel, Wordsworth, Hölderlin, the Shelleys, and Hoffmann. To see the parallelism between the nuclear power of language in deconstruction and certain *human*, subjective potentials that become liberated in Romantic discourse and literature is to begin to assemble some historical [or epistemological] context for deconstruction without in any way *containing* its discoveries.)

The Hegel column of *Glas*, then, does not 'end' without the disclosure of its architectural, conceptual, and rhetorical fissures. It is a credit to *Derrida's* brilliance that the very *terms* of instability in Hegel become the *terms* of insight and aesthetic creativity in Genet *and* the *modality* of resonation and sustained duplicity prevailing between Hegel and Genet, as between the 'inside' of metaphysics and its 'margin' in general. Before 'passing over' to the other column, to Genet's remarkable affirmative/antipodal contribution, I would like to pause over one or two of the key linguistic or rhetorical 'shifters' at the crux of the Hegel column's instability.

13.

Therefore without example, like God about which Hegel says that an example cannot be made, but because he, God, merges with the pure essence, pure essence is also without example. The all-burning — that has taken place once and nonetheless repeats itself ad infinitum diverges so well from all-essential generality that it resembles the pure difference of an absolute accident. Play and pure difference, those are the secret of an imperceptible all-burning, the torrent of fire that sets itself ablaze. Letting itself get carried away, pure difference is different from itself, therefore indifferent. . . . The light envelops itself in darkness even before becoming subject. In order to become subject, in effect the sun must go down [*décline*]. Subjectivity always produces itself in a movement of occidentalization. Now here the sun does not set – or else it sets immediately, does not know any going down, any route that leads back to self, any season, any season in the sense of cycle, just a pure season, in the sense of seminal effusion without return. This difference without subject, this play without labor, this example without essence devoid of self (*Selbst*), is also a sort of signifier without signified, the wasting of an adornment without the body proper, the total absence of property, propriety, truth, sense, a barely manifest unfolding of forms that straightway destroy themselves; is a One at once infinitely multiple and absolutely different, different from self, a One without self, the other without self that means (to say) nothing, whose language is absolutely empty, void, like an event that never comes about itself.

(*G*, 239a)

The Derridean discourse here circles around an exception – a miracle, if you will – transpiring within the language and imagery of natural religion: 'Now here the sun does not set.' Among the baggage and appurtenances of Western religion, and Hegel's organic, dialectical reformulation of its principles, is a careful attention to the metaphor of light as a spiritual emanation and presence. Light is not only a sure sign of Spirit's continuity and efficacy: it marks the propriety and timeliness of the divine natural order. Yet Derrida, having meticulously *assembled* the semiological and symbolic components of a Western metaphysics well beyond its Hegelian iteration, is in a singular position to note something wrong, out of whack in the Hegelian version. In the passage immediately above, Derrida teases out of Hegel a sun that refuses to set, a normally spiritual light that abrogates its function of marking the days and seasons with the coordinates of a natural and salutary order. Derrida 'immediately' notes, in terms of his own philosophical investigations, that a sun which does not set, a light that prevails over a single, indifferent season, deranges standard expectations with regard to difference. A light now eerily issues from the authoritative Hegelian late-Enlightenment reformulation of Western metaphysics that retracts the basic categories according to which the conceptual apparatus of that system operates. The system, at least in Hegel's hands, deranges its own most fundamental concepts and instruments, marks Derrida with regard to the deep-structural (or infrastructural) trope of sunlight. Hegel's acyclical sunlight also allows, notes Derrida, for the conception of a cosmos without a subject. Under the illumination of the non-compliant sun that peeps out just momentarily in the

275

Hegelian discourse, it becomes possible to imagine an articulation transpiring without the subject's will and intention, an articulation in purely linguistic terms, in the absence of subjectivity's sanction. Through the medium of the uncanny light that Hegel entertains, in other words, Derrida also intuits a plane of cultural articulation that is autonomous from the metaphysics of the subject. This derangement to the system for which Hegel allows, its uncannily continuous and difference-dissolving light, is 'always already' installed within it; the derangement is merely 'waiting' for the systematic torque to writing applied by Hegel (or any systematic 'thinker') to 'come out.'

'The difference and the play of the pure light, the panic and the pyromaniac dissemination, the all-burning offers itself as a holocaust to the for-(it)self, *gibt sich dem Fürsichsein zum Opfer* (G, 241a). In one of the most stunning of *Glas*'s polymorphous turns, Derrida envisions the holocaust, both historical and metaphorical, as an extension of the uncanny Hegelian 'blazing' (G, 242a). The holocaust, which encompasses its own economy of sacrifices and gifts, serves as yet another instance of an uncontainable violence *harbored within* the metaphysical mainstream.

A careful Derridean reading of its economic specificities brings us to yet another juncture at which the system provides for its own disintegration, where the bicolumnar architecture crumbles even on its left-hand (Hegelian) side.

The gift can only be a sacrifice, that is the axiom of speculative reason. Even if it upsurges 'before' philosophy and religion, the gift has for its destination or determination, for its *Bestimmung*, a return to self in philosophy, religion's truth. Always *already*, the gift opens the exchange, chains up, constructs its monuments, calculates on two registers the expenditures and receipts, the debit [*doit*], the must [*doit*], the goings out, the comings in, to how much it (*ça*) is raised and how much remains.

So the gift, the giving of the gift, the pure *cadeau*, does not let itself be thought by the dialectics to which, it, however, gives rise. . . .

If one can speak of the gift in the language [*langue*] of philosophy or the philosophy of religion, one *must say* that the holocaust, the pure gift, the pure *cadeau*, the cake [*gâteau*] of honey or fire hold on to themselves in giving themselves, are never doing anything but exchanging themselves according to the annulus. The gift for (it)self. The gift, *cadeau*, names what makes itself present.

*Cadeau* means chain.

(G, 243a)

Derrida has appreciated the treacheries of the gift since early in his work, whether in the context of Bataille's economic metaphors, or in assessing the role of the *pharmakon* in the Platonic patrimony of Western values. (*Pharmakon*, like the German *Gift*, encompasses a deadly as well as a generative facet.) In the above passage, the sacrificial aspect of the gift is chained to 'strange bedfellows': to cake (*gâteau*), for example. Indeed, the signifier *cadeau* also extends to the chaining of ring-like links in the process of metaphorical and conceptual association. *Gift* is not only an element in metaphysics' linguistic dismantling of its own authority: it describes the chaining process by which this dismantling takes place as well. The links of which chains are made are ring-shaped. Their annulation bespeaks a certain closure and contraction at the same time as the opening up or extension of associative *chains*. Like the fire by which the Hegelian natural religion 'burns up' the difference on which its own categorizations are based, the Hegelian gift predicates a constriction undermining and limiting the expansive claims asserted by the Hegelian dialectic. According to Rodolphe Gasché, this scenario of constriction constitutes one of *Glas*'s most significant contributions to the Derridean 'vocabulary' of infrastructures. Rings, tightening, and the enclosure of (pointed) objects also serve, in the world of Genet's counter-metaphysics, as major metaphors for homosexual activity. The restrictive economy also implicit in the Hegelian occasions for gifts thus provides an important hinge between the Hegelian annunciation of the system, in its modern emanation, and its postmodern emptying as 'registered' in the Genet column of *Glas*.

> The annular movement re-stricts the general economy (account taken and kept, that is, not taken or kept, of the loss) into a circulating economy. The contraction, the economic restriction forms the annulus of the selfsame, of the self-return, of reappropriation. The economy restricts itself; the sacrifice sacrifices itself. The (con)striction no longer lets itself be circumscribed [*cerner*] as an ontological category, or even, very simply, as a category, even were it a trans-category, a transcendental. The (con)striction — what is useful for thinking the ontological or the transcendental is then [*donc*] *also* in the position of transcendental trans-category, the transcendental transcendental. All the more because the (con)striction cannot produce the 'philosophical' effect it produces. There is no choosing here: each time a discourse *contra* the transcendental is held, a matrix — the (con)striction itself — constrains the discourse to

place the nontranscendental, the outside of the transcendental field, the excluded, in the structuring position.

(G, 244a)

Derrida thus traces the engendering of a constriction that qualifies and brackets the claims made by expansive conceptual systems of compelling in-built momentum. The system's purported sacrifice and generosity are marked and delimited ('barred,' in Lacanian parlance) by a constriction that relocates and redefines the transcendental. As was the case with the uncanny light of natural religion, the system is self-sufficient to engender the counter-movement contributing to its dissolution.

For all the acuity and persistence of Derrida's interrogation of the presence and immediacy attending the metaphysics of the voice, *Glas*, his most radical writing experiment to date, is surely his most sonorous and musical work. Sonority, *Klang*, joins the image of light and the movement of constriction marking the locus of a radical instability installed in the architectural nexus of Western metaphysics itself. The resonation of *Klang* penetrates every stratum and register of *Glas*. This persistent, destabilizing echo pervades not only the death knell that is one translation for the French 'glas': it characterizes the dissonance between the typographical columns of Hegelian and 'Genetic' discourse and the value systems these authors' texts bring into play. It furnishes a blueprint of the architectural stress prevailing not only between the columns of *Glas* but between the contrapuntal, constitutive, and perverse thrusts of metaphysics. Derrida may question the metaphysics of presence and voice severely, but the persistent after-image of *Glas* is a song, the acoustic image of *Klang*, hovering and ongoing dissonance.

> What is *Sprache* (*langue* or *langage*, speech or language)? An exteriorization that presents, it gives the there, the *Da-sein*, to the inner signification; but in order to move forward thus into presence, it must first let itself be filled, fulfilled, filled in, accomplished, inflated, curved [*galber*], *rounded* by the sense that penetrates it. It is the 'element (*Element*) in which the sense filling itself (*der erfüllende Sinn selbst*) is present (*vorhanden ist*).'
>
> This element is called voice: the spontaneous outside production of an inner sense filling with presence from then on the form of its emission. The spontaneity, the production of self by self gives voice. The sound, resounding ever since the blow [*coup*] struck from the outside, does not utter itself. The sound announces and represents the voice but also holds it back, too much on the outside or too much on the inside. . . .

The *Klang* of the stony block is *not yet* the voice that it *already* is: neither inside nor outside language, a mediation *or* an extended middle [*tiers*]. The deciphering of Memnon follows, in the *Aesthetics*, the reading of phallic columns.

(*G*, 253a)

The *Klang* issuing, droning from *Glas* marks the ultimate extension of Hegel's authoritative post-Enlightenment metaphysics, and it also spells out the rather severe limitations upon this self-sustaining, self-correcting system. The *Klang* is both 'too much on the outside' and 'too much on the inside.' The Hegel column terminates in a stalemate of architectural stress and dissonance.

14. We can say, then, of *Glas*'s bicolumnar architecture or its resonant counter-point, that the Hegel text situates a certain inwardness or interiority of Western idealism at a certain broad epoch in its 'history' and that the Genet counter-text traces out, assertively, the emptying or in-difference of the 'same' tradition. I have elsewhere posited one useful way of thinking the postmodern as a similar emptying, decontraction, and dispossession of a number of experiments associated with modernism (here narrowly defined as an aesthetic movement predominantly in Europe and the Americas roughly from 1890 to 1945).

The writing of Genet, and its remarkable reconstruction and interpretation by Derrida in *Glas*, may well play the tain of the mirror to Hegel's version of the high Western metaphysical road (or church). And to my mind, the modality of this playful but earnest engagement includes moves and attitudes inextricably associated with the postmodern (in the most productive terms in which its discussion may be couched). It would thus be possible to assert that the Genet column of *Glas* embraces the postmodern supplement, emptying, and in-difference to the (linguistic *and* subjective) conditions of a very broad Modernity that prevailed in the West at least from Shakespeare, Luther, Calvin, and Descartes through Romanticism and its defensive after-shocks. In terms of my own earlier work, then, Genet joins a group of postmodern writers including, among many others, the late Kafka and Joyce, Stein, Beckett, Blanchot, Barnes, Adorno, and Bernhard.[9] Whatever commonality may be extrapolated from these writers' script, I have argued, is distinguished at least in part by a certain monologic self-sustenance, a slowdown or blackout in the referential field and functions, and a pronounced *in*difference to exaggerated distinctions of identity and gender and to permutational games of structure that comprised, in *their* context, appropriate responses to the claims of Romantic and post-Romantic

279

theory. Derrida's generative reading of Genet establishes, among other things, that an in-different other to a historical or epistemological stage of *doxa* can consist of the *same* images (or material) of which the metaphysical base position is constructed. Derrida demonstrates as well in *Glas* that the *relationship* between the institutionalized Western base position, in this case, Modernity, and its other is characterized by supplementarity, the re-mark, chiasmatic duplicity, and constriction.

15. To indicate the *possible* (but never realized) *way out* of modern Western complacency, above all as formulated by Hegel, Genet would have to do a number of things. He would have to deflower its pieties; demolish its basis in a certain kind of (bourgeois, heterosexist, altruistic) *family*;[10] indicate a radical departure from its ideal-based morality, in which there is only a single 'right' alternative. According to the Derridean exegesis in *Glas*, Genet performs all these acts, and with a vengeance. A radical transvaluation of values, positioning Genet in an analogous (but historically different) situation to Nietszche's, is merely one, albeit striking, strategy by which Genet brings liberal Enlightenment ideology to its marginal, postmodern efflorescence.

Within this transfiguration, the religion of flowers, which in the Hegelian onto-theology resides at a certain (Indian) moment of mass or public spirituality (*G*, 2a, 240a, 246–7a), becomes, in Genet's underworld, a rhetorical and taxonomic system for queers (*G*, 13b, 17b, 31b, 35b, 47b, 57b, 187–8b); the bourgeois division of labor – predicating an entire metaphysics of sexual difference – by which the brother departs the family in public service while the sister (e.g. Antigone) defends the hearth and its 'natural' laws (*G*, 86a, 96a, 110–14a, 125–30a, 142–50a), becomes the in-difference of homosexual bondings, with their theatrical, 'assumed' roles (*G*, 25–7b, 38–40b, 74–6b, 82–6b, 103–6b, 128–42b); the prevalent Hegelian dynamic of *sublimated violence or instinct* (a close variation upon *Aufhebung*), by which consciousness advances itself and culture evolves, becomes, in a 'Genetic' environment, a highly explicit, demonstrative theater of perverse (from the perspective of conventional mores) sex acts, erections, ejaculations, impersonations, castrations, and the like (*G*, 2b, 11–12b, 17b, 21–5b, 47–57b, 77b, 86b, 108b, 111–14b, 118–28b, 132b, 136–42b, 149b, 167–73b, 202b, 210–16b, 223–9b). A Nietzschean transvaluation is involved in the *détour* from Hegelian conventionality to 'Genetic' perversity, but this act describes only one relation between the system and its manifold of supplemental values.

16. If the Hegelian *Phenomenology* would presume the self-generated rise of human (individual and collective) consciousness from 'sensible certitude' to cultural articulation, then the counter-system that Derrida so cleverly assembles from Genet's fiction and drama pursues a parallel *de*generation from an excessively rigid social code to the *inarticulate*, the glottal ejaculation, knell, or *glas* in which attempts at systematic articulation ultimately issue. The double columns of *Glas* are free-standing, but if any hinge or bridge links them, akin to the ultimate Proustian juncture betweeen the Guermantes and Méséglise Ways, it is the resonation between the Hegelian *Klang* and the 'Genetic' ejaculation.

Derrida marks a contrapuntal echoing within the pivotal trope of efflorescence itself:

> Thus the stamen, *l'étamine. Etamine* — the whore's rose, a verge's homage to Mary and taboo of the hymen rendered to the fag petal [*pétale*] — names not only the light material in which nuns are sometimes veiled, or through which precious liquids are filtered. But *étamine*, stamen, is also the male sex organ of plants: according to the *navette* [shuttle, rape] — that's the word — running between the textile code and the botanical code. Situated around the style and its stigma, stamens generally form a thin thread [*filet*], or filaments (*stamina*). Above the thin thread, a connective with four pollen sacs (microsporangia) that 'elaborate and disperse the pollen seeds': the (interring) anther. . . .
>
> The flower is hypogynous when the ovary dominates the rest [*reste*] of the flower. Sometimes the stamens are glued by their thin threads into one or more 'fraternities,' or else they become concrescent with petals (these are sometimes prolonged into spurs and carry nectariferous glands) or with the gynoecium: that's the case with orchids.
>
> (*G*, 250b)

Flowers not only figure in Hegel's comparative religious imagery and in Genet's homo-erotic underworld. In terms of their 'internal' metonymy linking spiritual innocence to sexual fecundity and arousal, they comprise a striking trope (as also noted in 'White Mythology') for Derrida's wider philosophical project. Flowers partake of indifferent, amoral sexuality at the same time that they are spiritualized into icons of chastity. Flower arrangements, as was noted by Proust as well as Genet, assume the form of textual webworks and interlacings. It is for this reason, in the passage cited immediately above, that Derrida devotes his attention to the interweavings of stamens and styles. The language of flowers, on both sides of the Hegel-Genet divide in *Glas*, is the textual script that is both the source and limit of ideals and other totalizing constructs. Tresses of flowers surround and qualify Western ideals in a manner analogous to the critique that deconstruction delivers to sanctioned Western ideal-based and ideal-oriented disciplines and intellectual procedures. The language of flowers exercises this role as an idealistic proto-writing on both sides of *Glas*'s bico-lumnar architecture. This may well be the only 'nature' attributable to flowers: they flourish on both sides of the Derridian guard-rail or fence.

*Glas* is Derrida's most explicitly sexual work at the same time that it is his most sonorous and musical. It is but a short step from the insemination of flowers to the fertilization on the periphery, if not at the 'heart,' of all sexual behavior. For all of Derrida's well-founded skepticism towards psychoanalysis and the metaphysics of the subject that it legitimates, the treatment of sexual symbolism in *Glas* uncannily assumes the tone of the sexual division of labor in classical psychoanalysis and its clinical and literary offshoots. This is to say that in both its columns, *Glas* conspicuously professes Western culture's biases in sexual ideology (heterosexuality and homophobia) and in symbolism as a point of departure and contrast *against* the counter-economies of writing and Genet's underworld. On the Genet side of things, then, the rhetoric of flowers *entrains* (in the French sense of the word) the classical Western heritage of sexual mores and its always persistent supplement.

Thus the flower (which equals castration, phallus, and so on) 'signifies' – again! – at least overlaps virginity in general, the vagina, the clitoris, 'feminine sexuality,' matrilinear genealogy, the mother's *seing*, that is, the Immaculate Conception. That is why flowers no longer have anything symbolic about them. 'They symbolized nothing.'

Demonstration. For castration to overlap virginity, for the phallus to be reversed into a vagina, for alleged opposites to be equivalent to each other and reflect each other, the flower has to be turned inside out like a glove, and its style like a sheath [*gaine*]. *The Maids* pass their time reflecting and replacing one sex with the other. Now they sink their entire 'ceremony' into the structure of the glove, the looking glass, and the flower. The onset is supported by the signifier 'glove.' *Glove* is stretched as a signifier of artifice. First words 'Those gloves! Those eternal gloves!'

. . . But these gloves are not only artificial and reversible signifiers, they are almost fake gloves, kitchen gloves, the 'dish-gloves' with which, at the close of the ceremony, the strangling of Madame is mimed, and which, in sum, circulate between places. . . . *The Maids* are gloves, the gloves of Madame. They are also called 'angels.' At once castrated and castrating (spiders or umbrella case), full and void of the phallus that Madame does not have. . . .

But between these pairs of gloves, flowers, only flowers, too many flowers. Their displacement is like the law, the metronome as well, nearly inaudible, the lateral cadence, dissimulated, of each gesture. . . .

In both cases, the gladiolus, *gladiolus*, little glaive, of the iris family (Provençal: *glaviol*; to the common gladiolus other therapeutic and nutritional powers have often been accorded; the gladiolus of the harvests used to pass for an aphrodisiac and emmenagogue).

(*G*, 47b–52b)

Flowers run roughshod over the sexual division of labor, the male and female stereotypes, that seem to define their place. Derrida remains most ambiguous in his neutralization of this sexual tradition, on the one hand, and, at the same time, his own appeal to it, in the footsteps of Hegel and Genet. This is in part because, as in the writing of *Glas*, he prefers to suspend, hold in reserve, the distinction between language-based models, in which flowers are signifiers caught in a network with other flowers and other signifiers, and subject-oriented models such as psychoanalysis, which sustain a process of identification through symbolism, whether of a sexual, socio-economic, ethnic, or other nature.

Flowers are thus characterized in two of their supplementary aspects in the above passage, whose typographical 'strange interlude' corresponds to the explicit design of *Glas*. Before the break, flowers neuter a systematic sexual division of labor that they both epitomize and predicate. After the gap, itself a sexual symbol, they join a network of signifiers, and their role consists in the variations of form and meaning that they assume in a non-rational, non-ideational cluster (*G*, 210b, 212b, 222b) of signifiers, whose principles of interrelation are linguistic rather than logical or metaphysical. Below the gap, it is of much greater consequence to flowers that they cluster around the letter 'g' and the combination 'gl' than that they contain, deface, or neutralize innocence. Through the careful reading of which *Glas* is a consummate example, a wreath of flowers, ultimately beginning and ending with the uncanny French signifier 'glas,' can be woven out of gladioli, gloves, swords (French: *glaives*), sheaths (*gaines*), and irises (*glaviols*). This chaining is not merely an exercise in ingenious etymologies. It is a concrete and precise demonstration of something fundamental to Derrida's philosophy, namely that the manifold accretion of language is just as legitimate a source to plumb the history and values of culture as canonical ideological statements. Surely the work of Nietzsche, especially as glossed by Heidegger, anticipated this position, but it took Derrida, and specifically the Derrida of certain demonstrations (the *floreligium* of *Glas* and 'Plato's Pharmacy' stand high on my list), to allegorize the accretion of nuances and values in a rigorously linguistic setting in an *explicit* and compelling manner.

In the supplemental economy and bicolumnar architecture of *Glas*, then, syllables with no meaning *in themselves* count for more than ideas and culturally mediated symbols. This is because their chaining out to like entities is *truly* cultural and sexual. Understanding the impasses of the Hegelian philosophy and its twentieth-century commentary/disfiguration by Genet hinges more on the pursuit of syllables and the gathering of clusters of meaning than on the 'history of ideas' or the 'anxiety of influence.' The book *Glas* is thus more a tribute to the sign and sound 'gl' than an appreciation or commentary on Hegel, Genet, or Western philosophy of the broader Modernity, although Derrida argues-by-performance that a more significant appreciation of these entities is to be reached through the pursuit of a sign and its affinities than through the extrapolation and paraphrase of concepts.[11] The letters and resonances of 'glas' help Derrida to articulate a philosophy of marks and remarks more than of concepts and their logical relations.

And as if all this galley-slaving had worn itself out with emitting (the word *emitting* strikes me as interesting but unsatisfying, it would also be necessary to say anointing, inducing, enjoining, smearing)

GL

I do not say either the signifier GL, or the phoneme GL, or the grapheme GL. Mark would be better, if the word were well understood, or if one's ears were open to it; not even mark then.

It is also imprudent to advance or set GL swinging in the masculine or feminine, to write or articulate it in capital letters. That has no identity, sex, gender, makes no sense, is neither a definite whole nor a part detached from a whole

gl remain(s) gl

falls (to the tomb) as must a pebble in the water – in not taking it even for an archigloss (since it is only a gloss morsel, but not yet a gloss, and therefore, an element detached from any gloss.

(*G*, 119b–120b)

In this fashion, Derrida identifies a thing, an object, that is as much the crux of a major work of philosophy as it is a meaningless grapheme and sound. Like a pebble in the water, it is a phenomenon of the nature of language: this is as close to phenomenality and to nature that Derrida chooses to venture. The most meaningful disclosure of the points of fixity in Hegel and the ideology and epoch he epitomizes are not simply the invocation of Genet's 'sacrilege' but the rigorous pursuit of the cluster of nuance and association surrounding a single rich and copulative fragment of writing.

I want to emphasize the thingly quality of the grapheme, GL. The above passage constitutes Derrida's principle frame for the language-thing which, more than the notion, accounts for the 'nature' of texts and culture. At two points in the passage, Derrida frames the GL-thing by centering it in the lines in which it appears. He amply attests to its ambiguous character: signifier, phenomenon, grapheme – exactly – it is not. Captioning it as a mark comes close to the point, but then veers away from the mark. The image Derrida selects, a pebble in the water, may be as apropos as any thing to describe the mark in this instance assuming the 'form' *GL*. A pebble is a thing of nature. A pebble interrupts, but also articulates, a continuous flow of water, an element whose transparent and relatively tasteless quality mimics the attributes by which certain transcendental entities and values in Western thought are identified, such as God or Being. As a concept-thing, the mark that Derrida sets in relief here, the mark of writing, would disrupt the seemingly natural and ongoing flow of Western systematicity in a fashion similar to the manner in which a mere thing, the pebble, would divert but heighten the flow of a stream.

The slippage of the grapheme GL describes a polymorphic dissemination that may be figured as sexual thrusts or shudders, the ejaculation of semen, or the evaporation or calcification of viscous liquids. Derrida takes it upon himself to explore exhaustively a non-linear cluster of meanings emerging from the grapheme GL. In the following extract, GL pursues a meandering path, passing from one semantic field to another with unpredictability, impunity, speed, and seeming arbitrariness (that is, the arbitrariness is 'always-already' installed in the language network itself). The GL-thing meanders from birds (the raptor) to bodies, from the ear to the throat, from physical and vocal fluidity to freezing and stammering, from warmth to cold, from the sperm to the foetus, and in the *genre* to which the passage belongs, from poetry to Teutonic philosophy. Merely for culture's discourse (and the university's) to embrace this stutter-stepping is tantamount to a revolution, an unmistakable sea change in the constitution and protocols of knowledge.

> the imperial flight of a raptor swoops down at one go [*d'un coup*] on your nape, the gluing, frozen [*glacé*], pissing cold name of an impassive Teutonic philosopher, with a notorious stammer, sometimes liquid and sometimes gutturotetanic, a swollen or cooing goiter, all that rings [*cloche*] in the tympanic channel or fossa, the spit or plaster on the soft palate [*voile du palais*], the orgasm of the glottis or the uvula, the clitoral glue, the cloaca of the abortion, the gasp of sperm, the rhythmed hiatus of an occlusion, the saccadanced spasm of an eructojaculation, the syncopated valve of tongue and lips, or a nail [*clou*] that falls in the silence of the milky say [*la voix lactée*] (I note, in parentheses, that, from the outset of this reading, I have not ceased to think, as if it were my principle object, about the milk trademarks Gloria and Gallia for the new-born, about everything that can happen to the porridge, to the mush of nurslings who are gluttinous, stuffed, or weaned from a cleft breast [*sein*], and now everything catches, is fixed, and falls in galalith).

(*G*, 120–1b)

The passage culminates, and a sexual analogy is unavoidable here, in a cum, a viscous suspension, a liquid glue, whose physical attributes act out the consistency of a linguistic medium in which meaning thickens, coalesces in its couplings and redundancies, but which remains to a significant degree fluid. Genet becomes the poet of the viscous density within the medium of language that for Derrida remains the only remotely legitimate source of knowledge and cultural authority. And the linguistic facility that Genet so powerfully demonstrates in his texts of course corresponds to the non-representational, playful, subversive, simultaneous, inherently ambiguous and inconsequential modality of language that Derrida associates with writing. The cum of writing spurts out on the Genet side of Derrida's bicolumnar writing project, in the environment tinged by the subversion and perversion of unapologetic homosexuality. This underworld may be, for a variety of reasons, conducive to the activity and culture of writing, but it is not, as the above passage indicates, entirely cut off from the biology and generation of sexual reproduction. The cum (*seing*) of writing, which, as in Proust's *Recherche,* embraces the economy of human reproduction, extends to mother's milk and neonates' pabulum.[12] To restore the medium of writing to its 'inherent' viscosity is to counter the tradition of ideation and systematicity figured in the sublime flight of the eagle (Hegel/ *aigle*, *GL*, 91a, 120–21b, 184a, 193–4b, 209a), and in the image of a brook's inevitable, transparent flow.[13] The ejaculation of this textual semen (in a sexual domain in which semen mostly, if not entirely, counts) describes, as well as any figure, the dance between the Genet column of *Glas* and its mainstream, Hegelian supplement.

In entirely liquid fashion, this textual glue or semen flows, above all, into itself. Yet it is but a short step from thick fluid to fluid membrane. Linguistic viscosity thus implicates the membranous qualities of texts, which can themselves be figured as fabrics, skins, and physiological membranes, such as the hymen.

> Sperm, saliva, glair, curdled drool, tears of milk, gel of vomit – all these heavy and white substances are going to glide into each other, be agglutinated, agglomerated, stretched out *(on)to the edge* of all the fixtures and pass through all the canals.
>
> The word '*glaviaux*' ['globs'] will not be uttered until later, after invisible assimilation and deglutition, after elaboration, agglutinated to '*glaïeul*' ['gladiolus'].
>
> But even before being presented in the text and blooming there right next to the flower, the word animates with its energetic and encircled absence the description of spit.
>
> (*G*, 139–140b)

> Like the wing of stamin (death), the membranous partition [*cloison*] that is called the soft palate, fixed by its upper edge to the limit of the vault, freely *floats*, at its lower edge, over the base of the tongue. Its two lateral edges (it has four sides) are called 'pillars.' In the middle of the floating edge, at the entrance to the throat, hangs the fleshy appendix of the uvula [*luette*], like a small grape. The text is spit out. It is like a discourse whose unities are molded in the manner of an excrement, an excretion.
>
> (*G*, 142b)

> And the spit with which the gliding mast would be smeared becomes, very quickly – the pen is dipped into a very liquid glue – some vaseline. And even, without forcing, a tube of mentholated vaseline.
>
> (*G*, 143b)

The elaboration continues. I have already begun to trace some of its intrinsic principles, which are akin to the activities incorporated into the above passage: gliding, floating, smearing, agglomerating, agglutinating. These are the activities of the 'soft' materials in the processes of proof and its assertion. *Glas* sets into relief an interface at which there is a material language for textual phenomena; at this threshold, viscous liquids and supple solids are continuous to each other. The counter-domain constituted by textual principles and activities is the kingdom in which softness and inconclusiveness, the passive partners and secret sharers in the enterprises of cultural production and knowledge generation, reign supreme. There is an abdication of power here, in the senses in which culture couches power in masculine, active, and logically consistent terms. The attention to limits and cuts in the passage below attests to the abdication that mainstream culture must undergo in order to acknowledge its foundation and substratum in Derridian writing.

gl tears the 'body,' 'sex,' 'voice' and 'writing' from the logic of consciousness and representation that guided these debates. While ever remaining a bit-effect (a death-effect) [*effet de mors*] among others, gl remarks in itself as well – whence the transcendental effect, always, of taking part – the angular slash [*coupure*] of the opposition, the differential schiz *and* the flowing [*coulant*] continuum of the couple, the distinction *and* the copulating unity (one example, of the arbitrary and the motivated). It is one of, only one but as a party to, the de-terminant sluices, open closed to a rereading of the *Cratylus*.

Socrates feigns to take part. For example: 'And perceiving that the tongue (*glōtta*) has a gliding movement (*olisthanei*) most in the pronunciation of l (*lambda*), he made the words (*ōnomase*) leia (level), *olisthanein* (glide) itself, *liparon* (sleek), *kollōdes* (glutinous), and the like to conform (*aphomoiōn*) to it. . . .'

So the enigma is of the sphingtor, of what will have let the sphigma pass. To squeeze (the text) so that it (*ça*) secretes, repress it with an antileptic (g), the liquid antagonism floods [*écoule*] the coming [*jouissance*]. No period after gl, a comma and yet, gl remains open, unstopped [*débouché*], ready for all concubinations, all collages. This is not an element; gl debouches toward what is called an element (an embouchure on the ocean [*la mer*], for example).

It is not a word – gl hoists the tongue but does not hold it and always lets the tongue fall back, does not belong to it — even less a name, and hardly a *pro-prénom*, a proper (before the first) name.

(*G*, 235–6b)

It is in no silly sense, then, that I can claim *Glas* as Derrida's tribute to a linguistic object so small that it is sub-syllabic. Following Derrida's hint, let us call this minute language-thing a mark. For the high road of Western culture truly to acknowledge its blindnesses, biases, and points of closure, it need only reorient itself to the smallest of things. In this, of course, lies the immense enterprise Derrida only begins — masterfully but inconclusively — to trace out in *Glas*.

17. Yet the performance of *Glas* is too intricate and persistent to allow us to take leave of it in this 'spirit' of textual ascendence. In what is perhaps Derrida's most masterful and fully realized performance of the disclosure and liberation of idea-oriented culture's linguistic substratum, he does not neglect to implicate himself in the process, to take responsibility for his role in the critique and its cultural reception. In the work in which it would be easiest for Derrida to conceal his interest in the process of cultural deconstruction, he marks his presence by attaching his name, by leaving the trace of his own signature. More precisely, he attaches his signature to his enterprise at a point where Genet assumes the same responsibility, where Genet, in the marvelous French tradition of the philosophy of writing, elaborated most fully by Blanchot in addition to Derrida, inscribes his own John Hancock:

> The emblem, the blazon open and close (noise and strict-ure of the valve) the jerky outpouring of a wound. The whole *Studio* works (over) this wound. 'There is no other origin for beauty than the wound — singular, different for everyone, hidden or visible — that every man keeps in himself. . . . The signature is a wound, and there is no other origin for the work of art. . . . Giacometti's art seems to me to wish to discover the secret wound of every being and even of every thing, so that the wound may illuminate them.' . . . The signature's hidden wound, the bleeding [*saignant*] cryptogram, is the morseling of Osiris. But the economy of the signature never interrupts its work. It finds in the remain(s) of infirmity a supplementary apotrope, a sort of reseda. As Stilitano bands erect a little more for being one-handed. As Querelle from squinting.
>
> (*G*, 184b)

To remark the cynical character of the paraph, one must see the photograph of the sculptor, full-face, at the beginning of the book (every trait falls [*tombe*] from it, as from a beaten dog); but above all the signature of [Genet's signature is reproduced at this point in *Glas*-HS] the other.

(*G*, 185b)

Ineffable and intricate though the involutions, dissimulations, and materials of writing may be, at a certain point, the true writer inscribes him/herself in the mess. Genet does so at the point of reporting on his visit to Alberto Giacometti's studio; also in locating himself within the 'little band' of queens and other perverts assembled in, among other texts, *Our Lady of the Flowers*. To the degree that the act of writing constitutes a return to the scene of a crime, the writerly writer, the writer who specifies his/her relation to the materials, exigencies, costs, and *jouissances* of writing – whether a Sterne, a Nietzsche, a Proust, a Genet, a Blanchot, or a Derrida – leaves a tangle of traces that will link him/her inextricably to the transgression. Genet's signatory tie to his acts of writerly composition may be the subculture of homosexuality: its practices, superstitions, and argot. For Derrida, it is not so far from this marginal subculture to the Jewishness that will constitute a major trace of his personal past that he will pin to the wider parameters of *Glas* as a trace of his having been there. As the scene of a babbling horde of North African Jews in mystified subservience to the Sefer Torah will indicate, his relation to this dimension of his personal tradition is not an unproblematical one. Yet Derrida has already discerned the outlines of a holocaust in the Hegelian dialectics of religion and the gift; and the enveloping *tissue* of the *talith* or Jewish prayer shawl serves him as an instance of what might be termed 'the textuality of everyday life,' in a culture supple and gentle enough to embrace, in some manner, its constituting textuality.

Our-Lady-of-the-Flowers thus will have prescribed the *glas* form. 'The great nocturnal occupation, admirably suited for enchanting the darkness, is tatooing. Thousands of thousands of little jabs [*coups*] with a fine needle prick the skin and draw blood, and figures that you would regard as most extravagant are flaunted in the most unexpected places. When the rabbi slowly unrolls the Torah, a mystery sends a shudder through the whole epidermis, as when one sees a colonist undressing. The grimacing of all that blue on a white skin imparts an obscure but potent glamor to the child who is covered with it, as a neutral [*indifférente*], pure column becomes sacred under the notches of the hieroglyphs. . . .'

In Algeria, in the middle of a mosque the colonists would have transformed into a synagogue, the Torah, brought forth from behind the curtains, is promenaded in the arms of a man or a child, and kissed or caressed by the faithful along the way. (The faithful, as you know, are enveloped in a veil. Some wear it all rolled up, like a cord, a sling, or an untied necktie around their neck. Others, more amply spread out on their shoulders and chest and trailing to the floor. Still others – and, at determined moments, everyone – on the head. Sometimes the veil is streaked in blue and white, and sometimes in black and white. Sometimes, though almost never, as if by chance or choice, it is pure white. The dead man is enveloped in his *taleth* – that is the name of the veil – after washing the body and closing all its orifices.)

The Torah wears a robe and a crown. Its two rollers are then parted [*écartés*] like two legs; the Torah is lifted to arm's length and the rabbi's scepter approximately followed the upright text. The bands in which it was wrapped had been previously undone and entrusted, generally, to a child. The child, comprehending nothing about all these signs full of sense, was to climb up into a gallery where the women, and old women especially, were and then to pass them the ragged bands. The old women rolled them up like crape bands for infants, and then the child brought them back to the Thebah.

Meanwhile, the body of the Torah was laid out on a table, and the men busied themselves.

(G, 240–1b)

The reading and ceremony of the Torah marks, although in no simple way, Derrida's stake and signature within the drama of repression, marginality, supplementarity, and textuality that coincides with his philosophical project. Yet he arrives at the Torah's idealism and innocence not by way of his own totalizing repression, his own economies in the name of intellectual lucidity, but at the end of a series that has included crime, incarceration, homosexual 'banding erect,' the Hegelian holocaust, and pasties (*postiche*, *GL*, 138–9b, 210b, 212b, 223b). The writer is a marked (wo)man, and Derrida makes himself no exception to this rule. Writing transpires in a multifaceted matrix of cultural conditions, including the writer's irreducible signature.

18. It is time to close our own brief introduction to the complexities and rewards of *Glas*, a word as well as a book, one that has resonated throughout its

dazzling project in unmistakably textual fashion. As a resonation and as a book, *Glas* frames the impulses and strategies characterizing both the broader Modernity and the postmodern enterprise of delimiting this Modernity's sway. The Modernity to which both Kant and Hegel are already responding arises in an uncanny, breathless sense of freedom and possibility and of the affinity between language and the claiming of these liberties. It is also pervaded, in a manner that Derrida has associated with logocentrism, with a dread at the very same open horizon of possibility. An entire battery of cultural and aesthetic defenses against this predicament is registered both in the Hegelian efforts at systematic philosophy and in the modern ideology that we have come to identify as 'Enlightenment,' 'emancipatory,' 'democratic,' 'self-determining,' and 'liberal.' *Glas* pursues the course of this Modernity, from the Hegelian projects of institutionalizing it to a 'Genetic' subculture whose obvious implications are its at least partial dismantling and derangement. Derrida's death knell or *glas* resonates over this epoch, framing an ambivalent architecture for intellectual achievement, and sounding the notes of a text-oriented counterpoint to the protocols of ideological intellectual operations.

# Notes

## Introduction: Hegel Before Derrida

1  Michel Foucault, 'The Discourse on Language,' in *The Archaeology of Knowledge* (New York: Pantheon, 1972), p. 235.
2  Jean-François Lyotard, *The Postmodern Explained*, trans. Don Barry *et al.* (Minneapolis: University of Minnesota Press, 1992), pp. 17–18.
3  Jean-François Lyotard, *The Postmodern Condition: A Report on Knowledge*, trans. Geoff Bennington and Brian Massumi (Minneapolis: University of Minnesota Press, 1984), pp. 33–4.
4  Ibid., p. 38.
5  As Marc Froment-Meurice notes in *Solitudes: From Rimbaud to Heidegger*, trans. Peter Walsh (Albany: SUNY Press, 1995): 'Yesterday Marx–Nietzsche–Freud, today Kant, who is making his return like an old diva who can never make up his mind to "bid the stage adieu"' (xxiv).
6  Bertand Russell, *A History of Western Philosophy* (New York: Simon & Schuster, 1972), p. 730.
7  See Karl Popper, *The Open Society and its Enemies* (Princeton: Princeton University Press, 1950), pp. 223–73. Popper discloses that it was the annexation of Austria in March of 1938 that galvanized him to write this study. The constant subtext of the study is accounting for fascism. And in this accounting Hegel surfaces as a prime suspect. As Popper sums up his assessment: 'Thus the formula of the fascist brew is in all countries the same: Hegel plus a dash of nineteenth-century materialism' (p. 256). He further describes Hegel in the following hyperbolic terms: 'Thus, liberalism, freedom and reason are, as usual, objects of Hegel's attack. The hysterical cries: We want our history! We want our destiny! We want our fight! We want our chains; resound through the edifice of Hegelianism, through this stronghold of the closed society and of the revolt against freedom' (p. 269). Hegel and Hegelianism thus define the closed society; as such, they are perhaps *the* enemy of the open society.
8  The situation is thus admittedly changing, but it is a gradual improvement that perhaps stands out because of the overall context of antipathy. As Rorty describes

the fate of Hegel: 'Before the appearance of M. H. Abrams' *The Mirror and the Lamp*, it often did not occur to students of English literature to read Hegel. During the same period, students of analytic philosophy were encouraged to keep their reading in literature well clear of their philosophical work and to avoid reading German philosophy between Kant and Frege. It was widely believed that reading Hegel rotted the brain.' *Essays on Heidegger and Others* (Cambridge: Cambridge University Press, 1991), p. 87. For an informative overview of the post-war reception of Hegel, see H. S. Harris, 'The Hegel Renaissance in the Anglo-Saxon World Since 1945,' *The Owl of Minerva*, vol. 15 (1983), pp. 77–106.

9 An indication of this lack of means of assessing Hegel and the continental tradition is surely the willingness of Quine to add his name to a letter to *The Times* of London denouncing Cambridge's move to award Derrida an honorary degree. This insulting document, which claims that Derrida is an 'embarrassment' capable only of 'tricks' and 'gimmicks,' is yet another sad indication of the suspicion Anglo-American philosophers bear towards Derrida. Interestingly, one of the major points of this letter is that Derrida is not a philosopher because he is read and taught 'almost entirely in fields outside philosophy.' Jacques Derrida, *Points* (Stanford: Stanford University Press, 1995), pp. 419–21.

10 Indicative of analytic philosophy's belief that it had dispelled the very errors that would lead to such metaphysical musings as Hegel's is Carnap's well-known essay 'The Elimination of Metaphysics Through Logical Analysis of Language' in *Logical Positivism*, A. J. Ayer (ed.) (Glencoe, Ill.: Free Press, 1959), pp. 60–81. Finding their inspiration in the later Wittgenstein, many analytic philosophers felt that what they derisively termed metaphysics was the result of a muddled and confused use of language.

11 J. N. Findlay, 'The Contemporary Relevance of Hegel,' *Hegel: A Collection of Critical Essays*, Alasdair MacIntyre (ed.) (Notre Dame: University of Notre Dame Press, 1976), pp. 1–2.

12 See the helpful essay by Peter Hylton, 'Hegel and Analytic Philosophy' in *The Cambridge Companion to Hegel*, Frederick Beiser (ed.) (Cambridge: Cambridge University Press, 1993), pp. 445–86, as well as his authoritative *Russell, Idealism and the Emergence of Analytic Philosophy* (Oxford: Oxford University Press, 1990).

13 G. E. Moore, 'The Refutation of Idealism,' *Philosophical Studies* (London: Routledge, 1922), pp. 1–30. See also A. J. Ayer's discussion of this essay in *Russell and Moore* (Cambridge, Mass.: Harvard University Press, 1971), pp. 143–55.

14 As Russell stated in an earlier study: 'The question of whether all propositions are reducible to the subject-predicate form is one of fundamental importance to all philosophy.' Bertrand Russell, *Philosophy of Leibniz* (London: George Allen & Unwin, 1937), p. 12.

15 See G. E. Moore, 'External and Internal Relations' in *Philosophical Studies* (London: Routledge, 1922), pp. 276–309. As Russell phrased it at a much later date: 'My reason for rejecting Hegel and monism in general is my belief that the dialectical argument against relations is wholly unsound. I think such a statement as "A is west of B" can be exactly true. You will find that Bradley's arguments on the subject

pre-suppose that every proposition must be of the subject-predicate form. I think this is the fundamental error of monism.' *The Autobiography of Bertrand Russell* (New York: Simon & Schuster, 1969), pp. 252–3.

16 As D. F. Pears reflects of Russell: 'His philosophical temperament combines in an unusual way the caution which is characteristic of British philosophy with the kind of speculation which, rather absurdly, we call "Continental." It is, of course, questionable whether the doctrines to which these two tendencies naturally lead can be combined.' *Bertrand Russell and the British Tradition in Philosophy* (New York: Random House, 1967), p. 269.

17 Bertrand Russell, *The Problems of Philosophy* (Oxford: Oxford University Press, 1959), pp. 47–8. Russell offers a more circumspect analysis of that table in *Our Knowledge of the External World* (New York: Mentor Books, 1960), pp. 64–5.

18 Indeed, the unknowing attempt on the part of many analytic philosophers to reach a Kantian resolution between the demands of rationalist truth and empiricism is quite remarkable. A sure indication of this strange state of affairs was the initial inability of the followers of Frege and Wittgenstein to understand or even perceive the Kantian background to these founders of the analytic tradition.

19 Amusingly, Russell took exception in a footnote to a similar suggestion by Alan Wood in the essay by Wood he included in *My Philosophical Development* (New York: Simon & Schuster, 1959): 'My final views are less Kantian than Alan Wood supposes. I will mention two points. First: though the external world is probably not quite like the world of perception, it is connected with the world of perception by correlations, which are impossible in a philosophy which regards time and space as subjective. Second: the principles of non-deductive inference which I advocate are not put forward as certain or *a priori*, but as scientific hypothesis' (p. 262). Note the qualifying 'final' in the first sentence.

20 For further exploration of the proximity of idealism and analytic philosophy, see David Lamb, *Language and Perception in Hegel and Wittgenstein* (New York: St Martin's Press, 1980).

21 As Sluga aptly notes: 'Because of this lack of historical interest, analytic philosophers themselves have tended to overestimate the discontinuity of their own philosophizing from that of the past and to underestimate the historical evolution of their own tradition.' *Gottlob Frege* (London: Routledge, 1980), p. 5. For further discussion of these issues, see pp. 1–7.

22 I am not claiming that Feyerabend is, by general consensus, the most representative figure of the philosophy of science. He has few outright followers. It is even hard to say that he had many students in the technical sense, given the paucity of dissertations he directed. I am arguing, rather, that Feyerabend is of strategic significance in that he draws out much that was implicit in the tradition within which he was trained.

23 'Consolations for the Specialist,' *Criticism and the Growth of Knowledge*, Imre Lakatos and Alan Musgrave (eds) (Cambridge: Cambridge University Press, 1970), p. 224.

24 As his autobiography attests, unlike Popper, Feyerabend was uninterested in

engaging in a debate with neo-Hegelianism. In fact, he seems unconcerned about its existence. See *Killing Time: The Autobiography of Paul Feyerabend* (Chicago: University of Chicago Press, 1995). My argument, however, is that the most vigorous forms of Hegelianism in the twentieth century have been thoroughly unconscious of the fact.

25 Richard Rorty, *Consequences of Pragmatism* (Minneapolis: University of Minnesota Press, 1982), p. 187.

26 Ibid., p. 148.

27 For a more detailed examination of this issue see Judith Butler, *Subjects of Desire* (New York: Columbia University Press, 1987); Mark Poster, *Existential Marxism In Postwar France: From Sartre to Althusser* (Princeton: Princeton University Press, 1975); and Michael S. Roth, *Knowing and History: Appropriations of Hegel in Twentieth Century France* (Ithaca: Cornell University Press, 1988). Also valuable is the well-documented introduction by John Heckman to Jean Hyppolite's *Genesis and Structure of Hegel's Phenomenology of Spirit*, trans. Samuel Cherniak and John Heckman (Evanston,Ill.: Northwestern University Press, 1974), pp. xv-xli.

28 Alexandre Koyré, 'Rapport sur l'état des études hégéliennes en France,' *Études d'histoire de la pensée philosophique* (Paris: Armand Colin, 1961), pp. 214–5. Unless otherwise noted, all translations are my own.

29 Georges Canguilhem, 'Hegel en France' *Revue d'histoire et de philosophie religieuses*, vol. 27 (1948), p. 284.

30 Mikel Dufrenne, 'Actualité de Hegel' *Esprit*, vol. 16 (1948), p. 396.

31 See Jean Wahl, 'Le rôle de A. Koyré dans le développement des études Hégéliennes en France,' *Hegel Studien* Beiheft 3 (1966), pp. 15–26.

32 Koyré, 'Rapport,' p. 205.

33 Dufrenne, p. 396.

34 Jean Hyppolite, *Figures de la pensée philosophique*, vol. 2 (Paris: Presses Universitaires de France, 1971), p. 974.

35 Canguilhem, 'Hegel en France,' p. 282.

36 For an overview, see Michael Kelly, 'The Post-war Hegel Revival in France: A Bibliographical Essay,' *Journal of European Studies*, vol. 12 (1983), pp. 199–216.

37 Henri Niel, 'L'interpretation de Hegel', *Critique*, vol. 3 (1947), pp. 426–37. 'A cette massive étude, il n'y a pas de conclusion personnelle. L'auteur se refuse à donner une vue d'ensemble de la pensée de Hegel. Il n'abandonne jamais l'explication fidèlement attaché au texte' (428).

38 For a concise and insightful overview of Kojève's reading of Hegel, see Patrick Riley, 'Introduction to the Reading of Alexandre Kojève,' *Political Theory*, vol. 9 (1981), pp. 5–48 and Tom Rockmore, *Heidegger and French Philosophy: Humanism, Antihumanism and Being* (London: Routledge, 1995), pp. 31–9. For a more detailed examination, see Dominique Auffret, *Alexandre Kojève: La philosophie, l'état, la fin de la histoire* (Paris: Grasset, 1990).

39 As Aimé Patri notes of the impact of these lectures: 'A partir de ce moment, on a respiré l'enseignement de Kojève avec l'air du temps.' 'Dialectique du maître et de l'esclave,' *Le contrat social*, vol. 5 (1961), p. 234.

40 Alexandre Kojève, *Introduction à la lecture de Hegel* (Paris: Gallimard, 1947). The English edition was edited by Allan Bloom. (*Introduction to the Reading of Hegel*, trans. James H. Nichols, Jr [Ithaca: Cornell University Press, 1980] – hereafter referred to parenthetically in the text.) Bloom severely truncated the text, excising much of interest to the student of Hegel. A substantial essay not included in Bloom's edition has been translated by Joseph J. Carpina – 'The Idea of Death in the Philosophy of Hegel,' *Interpretation*, vol. 3 (1973), pp. 114–56. This is part two of the appendix, pp. 529–75. This essay is of particular interest since it forms virtually the exclusive focus of Bataille's well-known essay, 'Hegel, Death and Sacrifice,' trans. Jonathan Strauss, *Yale French Studies*, vol. 78 (1990), pp. 9–28.

41 Alexandre Kojève, *Introduction à la lecture de Hegel*, p. 54.

42 As Kojève argues, work is the ultimate realization of the dominion of the master: 'It is this transformation of Nature in relation to a *non*material *idea* that is *Work* in the proper sense of the word: Work that creates a nonnatural, technical, humanized World adapted to the *human* Desire of a being that has *demonized* and realized its superiority to Nature by risking its life for the *non*biological end of Recognition' (42).

43 For further discussion, see Dennis J. Goldford, 'Kojève's Reading of Hegel,' *International Philosophical Quarterly*, vol. 22 (1982), pp. 275–94. As Goldford states: 'It is with the concept of work that Kojève constructs the immediate bridge between anthropogenetic desire and history' (284).

44 Alexandre Kojève, *Introduction à la lecture de Hegel*, p. 53.

45 Alexandre Kojève, 'The Idea of Death in the Philosophy of Hegel,' trans. Joseph J. Carpina, *Interpretation*, vol. 3 (1973), p. 123.

46 Ibid., p. 132.

47 Ibid., p. 129.

48 The intellectuals of the Communist Party in France knew quite well that the interest in Hegel was part of an attempt to challenge official Communist doctrine. Althusser, writing anonymously as 'La commission de critique du cercle des philosophes communistes' closes his analysis of this problem with the ringing words: 'Ce Grand Retour à Hegel n'est qu'un recours désespéré contre Marx, dans la forme spécifique que prend le révisionisme dans la crise finale de l'impérialisme: *un révisionisme de caractère fasciste.*' 'Le retour à Hegel: Dernier mot du révisionisme universitaire,' *La nouvelle critique* 20 (1950), p. 54. Althusser continued to struggle to demarcate a break in the work of Marx that would sanitize him of any influence from Hegel. See *For Marx*, trans. Ben Brewster (New York: Random House, 1970).

49 Kojève's impact was still acknowledged, in a positive sense, in 1968 – a decisive year for the thinkers to be considered. As Gilles Lapouge notes in the introduction to his 1968 interview with Kojève: 'Nul aujourd'hui ne se mettrait en route vers Hegel sans emprunter les boussoles de Kojève. Celui-ci occupe Hegel comme un territoire. Il y règne.' 'Entretien avec Kojève,' *Quinzaine Litteraire* July 1, 1968, p. 18.

50 As Sartre states: 'But if Hegel has forgotten himself, we can not forget Hegel. This

means that we are referred back to the *cogito*. In fact, if, as we have established, the being of my consciousness is strictly irreducible to knowledge, then I can not transcend my being toward a reciprocal and universal relation in which I could see my being and that of others as equivalent. On the contrary, I must establish myself in my being and posit the problem of the Other in terms of my being. In a word the sole point of departure is the interiority of the *cogito*.' Jean-Paul Sartre, *Being and Nothingness*, trans. Hazel Barnes (New York: Simon & Schuster, 1956), p. 329.

51 Hyppolite, *Figures*, vol. 2, 982.

52 Vincent Descombes, *Modern French Philosophy*, trans. L. Scott-Fox and J. M. Harding (Cambridge: Cambridge University Press, 1980), p. 13.

53 Ibid., p. 14.

54 See in particular 'Shattered Love' in *The Inoperative Community*, Peter Connor (ed.) (Minneapolis: University of Minnesota Press, 1991), pp. 82–109.

55 For a slightly different reading of Foucault – which elaborates on points only touched on here – see my 'Resisting Subjects: Habermas on the Subject of Foucault' in *Transitions in Continental Philosophy*, Arleen B. Dallery and Stephen H. Watson (eds) (Albany: State University of New York Press, 1994), pp. 43–56.

56 Kojève, *Introduction à la lecture*, p. 324.

57 Ibid., p. 413. Ellipses are Kojève's.

58 Ibid., p. 326.

59 Michel Foucault, *The Use of Pleasure*, trans. Robert Hurley (New York: Random House, 1985), p. 9.

60 Paul de Man, 'Sign and Symbol in Hegel's *Aesthetics*,' *Critical Inquiry*, vol. 8 (Summer 1982), p. 763.

61 Jacques Derrida, *Of Grammatology*, trans. Gayatri Spivak (Baltimore: Johns Hopkins University Press, 1974), p. 24.

62 Jacques Derrida, *Positions*, trans. Alan Bass (Chicago: University of Chicago Press, 1981), pp. 40–1.

63 Jacques Derrida, *Of Grammatology*, p. 26.

64 Jacques Derrida, *Positions*, p. 77.

65 See *Saving the Text: Literature/Derrida/Philosophy* (Baltimore: Johns Hopkins University Press, 1981). This remarkable study of Hartman's is not so much an explication *per se* of *Glas* as an indication of what criticism might look like once we come to terms with Derrida's reading of Hegel.

66 The fact that this investigation of the philosophical dimensions of Derrida's work is now underway in the United States is due to a great extent to the work of Rodolphe Gasché. See his *The Tain of the Mirror: Derrida and the Philosophy of Reflection* (Cambridge, Mass.: Harvard University Press, 1986) as well as his *Inventions of Difference: On Jacques Derrida* (Cambridge, Mass.: Harvard University Press, 1994). The prominence of the 'concept' of the quasi-transcendental in several of the essays in this volume testifies to his transformative effect upon the study of Derrida.

67 Indeed, what passes as theory in literary circles is often little more than a marketing ploy. We may be witnessing the birth of the culture industry industry. Yet, as

Adorno reminded us, it was always the destiny of the culture industry to seek to become transparent, to expose to a jaded public the mechanism of its own power – and thereby guarantee the futherance of its power. This reveals itself in the cheap cynicism of academics who write books exposing the political implications of aspects of popular culture (which will – because of this very fact – be widely discussed and reviewed in mainstream journalism) and the journalists, editors, and television reporters who present them to the public with feigned shock (and who would never bother reporting the teaching or research they keep urging academics to undertake). One cannot help wondering whether that shock of discovery – like that of Claude Rains's Capt. Renault when he shuts down Rick's Café because of gambling – is itself responding to a more sinister directive.

68 See the 'Preface' to the *Phenomenology of Spirit* and 'Outwork, prefacing' in *Dissemination*, trans. Barbara Johnson (Chicago: University of Chicago Press, 1981). See also Peter J. Burgard, 'Preface,' *Idioms of Uncertainty: Goethe and the Essay* (University Park: Penn State University Press, 1992), pp. 1–23.

## Chapter 1: Hegel at the Court of the Ashanti

1 G. W. F. Hegel, *Grundlinien der Philosophie des Rechts*, Werke 7, Frankfurt: Suhrkamp, 1970, secs. 340 and 341, p. 503; trans. by H. B. Nisbet, *Elements of the Philosophy of Right*, Cambridge, Cambridge University Press, 1991, pp. 371–2. Henceforth GPR and PR, respectively.

2 I have examined both the first edition of Hegel's lectures edited by Eduard Gans and the better known and widely reprinted revised edition undertaken by Karl Hegel in 1840. *Vorlesungen über die Philosophie der Geschichte*, Berlin: Duncker und Humblot, 1837, and *Vorlesungen über die Philosophie der Geschichte*, Werke 12, Frankfurt: Suhrkamp, 1970; trans. J. Sibree, *The Philosophy of History*, New York: Dover, 1956. However, the most extensive treatment of Africa can be found in what is also regarded as the superior edition: G. W. F. Hegel, *Vorlesungen über die Philosophie der Wetgeschichte*. Band 1: Die Vernunft in der Geschichte. Hrsg. J. Hoffmeister, fifth edition. Hamburg: Felix Meiner, 1955; trans. H. B. Nisbett, *Lectures on the Philosophy of World History*, Cambridge: Cambridge University Press, 1975. Henceforth VPW and LPW, respectively. I have sometimes departed from the Nisbett translation, noting the fact only when the change seemed particularly striking. Since the completion of my paper an edition of Hegel's lectures as delivered in 1822/23 has appeared, but Hegel did not deal with Africa on that occasion: *Vorlesungen über die Philosophie der Weltgeschichte*, Karl Heinz Ilting, Karl Brehmer and Hoo Nam Seelmann (eds), Hamburg: Felix Meiner, 1996. See already Heinz Kimmerle, 'Hegel und Afrika: Das Glas zerspringt,' *Hegel Studien* 28, 1993, pp. 307–8. Some of the arguments in my paper must be regarded as only provisional in the absence of a critical edition of Hegel's lectures on world history for the years in which he discussed Africa.

3 This paper is part of an ongoing research project in which I attempt to show that

the travel literature of the seventeenth and eighteenth centuries was transformed by academicians into a discourse of race that,when tied to the philosophy of history, was used to legitimate the violent and destructive character of nineteenth-century colonialism.

4 Duncan Forbes, Introduction, *Lectures on the Philosophy of World History*, p. xxii n.

5 W. H. Walsh, 'Principle and Prejudice in Hegel's Philosophy of History,' *Hegel's Political Philosophy*, Z. A. Pelczynski (ed.), Cambridge: Cambridge University Press, 1971, pp. 181–98.

6 It is not my intention here to focus on the charge that Hegel was a racist. I am more interested in the question of the pervasiveness of racist assumptions and the difficulty of eradicating them. However, it has to be said, contra Walsh, that, in the context of a discussion of the native peoples of South America as 'unintelligent (*geistlos*) and with little capacity for education (*Bildung*),' Hegel speaks of their *Inferiorität* in every respect including size (VPW 202; LPW 164). The argument of Bernard Bourgeois that Hegel is not a racist because he does not advocate strict biological predeterminism assumes that this is the only kind of racism with which one needs to be concerned. By the same token, Bourgeois uses the term 'humanism' as if it was obvious that humanism is always free of racism. *Études hégéliennes*, Paris: Presses Universitaires de France, 1992, pp. 246–8, 255 and 269.

7 It is worth bearing in mind that Hegel does try on occasion to give an objective basis to terms that would otherwise be simple cases of Eurocentrism. So, for example, he insists that in keeping the label 'the new world,' he is not simply continuing a name that arose because America and Australia came to be known to Europeans at a later stage of their history. 'The new world is not just relatively new, but absolutely so, by virtue of its wholly peculiar character in both physical and political respects' (VPW 199; LPW 162). For other accounts of this alleged 'physical immaturity' see Antonello Gerbi, *The Dispute of the New World*, trans. by Jeremy Moyle, Pittsburgh: University of Pittsburgh Press, 1973.

8 W. H. Walsh, 'Principles and Prejudice,' p. 185.

9 For example, Molefi Kete Asante, *Kemet, Afrocentricity and Knowledge*, Trenton, NJ: Africa World Press, 1990, p. 33. M. B. Ramose, 'Hegel and Universalism: An African Perspective,' *Dialogue and Humanism*, 1991, p. 82 and L. Keita, 'Two Philosophies of African History: Hegel and Diop,' *Presence Africaine*, 91, 1974, pp. 41–8. A European writer who also sees how easily Hegel might have been refuted had he not held to his division of Africa is Christian Neugebauer. See 'The Racism of Hegel and Kant,' *Sage Philosophy*, H. Odera Oruka, Leiden: E. J. Brill (eds), 1990, p. 261.

10 Peter Hodgson in the English edition of Hegel's *Lectures on the Philosophy of Religion* claimed that Hegel's treatment of the religions of the Eskimos, Africans, Mongols, Chinese, and American Indians 'evidences genuine phenomenological rigor.' 'Any tendencies that we might detect to trivialize or ridicule these religions are traceable not so much to Hegel as to his sources, which he quotes at length, often verbatim. Hegel is not free of the prejudices of his time toward people of color, but there is also reflected in his work an obvious fascination with Oriental and African religion

and culture.' *Lectures on the Philosophy of Religion. Vol. II. Determinate Religion*, (ed.) Peter C. Hodgson, Berkeley, University of California Press, 1987, p. 272 n. 108. Henceforth LPR II. One aim of the first part of my paper is to offer a tentative challenge to that assessment.

11 Shlomo Avinieri, *Hegel's Theory of the Modern State*, Cambridge: Cambridge University Press, 1974, p. 223.

12 Karl Ritter, *Die Erdkunde im Verhältnis zur Natur und zur Geschichte der Menschen oder allgemeine, vergleichende Geographie, Erster Theil, Erstes Buch. Afrika*, Berlin: Reimer, 1822. Ritter's importance for Hegel seems to be confined to the geographical discussion that preceded his discussion of 'Africa proper.' Although Ritter used almost all of the sources that Hegel used, and many more besides, his interests were very different from Hegel's. There is little overlap.

13 Gio. Antonio Cavazzi, *Istorica descrizione de' tre regni Congo, Matamba, Angola*, Bologna: 1687. Walter Jaeschke in his edition of Hegel's *Lectures on the Philosophy of Religion* has made an important contribution to our knowledge of Hegel's sources by identifying the specific passages on which Hegel drew. In the German edition of Hegel's *Lectures* the relevant passages from the German edition of Cavazzi are also cited. My knowledge of the German translation is limited to the extensive quotes provided by Jaeschke. J. A. Cavazzi, *Historische Beschreibung der in dem unteren occidentalischen Mohrenland ligenden drey Königreichen Congo, Matamba, und Angola*, trans. Fortunato Maldini, Munich: 1694 and G. W. F. Hegel, *Vorlesungen über die Philosophie der Religion* Teil 2b, hrsg. W. Jaeschke, Hamburg: Felix Meiner, 1985. Henceforth VPR II. Peter Hodgson's suggestion that Hegel may have read Cavazzi in the Italian original rather than in the German translation on the basis that the German translation of Cavazzi does not specify that the roots chewed by the Singhili were *Tabs-Wurzeln* is not borne out by comparison with the original Italian edition. *Lectures on the Philosophy of Religion*, vol. 2, p. 277 n. 118. It is also possible that Hegel, like Boulanger and Ritter before him, read not Cavazzi, but Labat, who produced a book in French that is described on the title page as 'translated from the Italian of Cavazzi augmented by many Portuguese accounts of better authors.' This description does not do justice to the liberties Labat took with Cavazzi's text. My own provisional research suggests that most if not all of the information drawn by Hegel from Cavazzi, both in the *Philosophy of History* and the *Philosophy of Religion*, can also be found in Labat. See J.-B. Labat, *Relation historique de l'Ethiopie Occidentale*, Paris: Charles-Jean-Baptiste-Delespine, 1732. However, there is no reference to 'tab-roots' in Labat, so I cannot claim to have resolved the question of which edition Hegel used. See further note 23 below.

14 T. E. Bowdich, *Mission from Cape Coast Castle to Ashantee*, London: John Murray, 1819. I have used the third edition (London: Frank Cass, 1966), which includes a photomechanical reprint of the first edition. A German translation by D. Leidenfrost was published as *Mission der English–Afrikanischen Compagnie von Cape Coast Castle nach Ashantee*, Weimar, 1820 (reprinted in two parts, Wien: Kaulfuss und Krammer, 1826). The fact that Hegel used the English original is suggested by the fact that when Hegel quotes from 'Mr. Hutchison's Diary' found in chapter 12, his

translation does not follow Leidenfrost's and yet is clearly a translation and not a paraphrase. Compare VPW 232; LPW 188 with Bowdich, *Mission* (1820), p. 534. This also makes it unlikely that Hegel was relying on a contemporary review of the German translation. However, the suggestion that Hegel read Bowdich in English is not sufficient to explain all the inaccuracies that emerged in the course of his retelling of it.

15 Charles des Brosses, *Du Culte des Dieux Fétiches ou parallèle de l'ancienne Religion de l'Egypte avec la religion actuelle de Nigritie*, Paris: Fayard, 1988. W. Bosman, *Nauwkeurige Deschryving van de Guinese Good-, Tand- en Slave- Kust*, Utrecht, 1704; trans. *A New and Accurate Description of the Coast of Guinea, Divided into the Gold, the Slave and the Ivory Coasts*, London: James Knapton, 1705.

16 G. W. F. Hegel, An die Königl. Bibliothek Berlin, 26 May 1824, No. 473, *Briefe von und an Hegel*, vol. III, Hamburg: Felix Meiner, 1969, p. 45. J. R. Tuckey, *Narrative of an Expedition to Explore the River Zaire*, London: John Murray, 1818.

17 Archibald Dalzel, *The History of Dahomey, an Inland Kingdom of Africa*, London: T. Spilsbury, 1783, pp. 12–13. Dalzel gives as his source for the story Robert Norris, but although Norris describes the scene in the same terms that are taken up by Dalzel and Hegel, there is no mention of parrot's eggs. Robert Norris, *Memoirs of the Reign of Bossa Ahadee, King of Dahomey, An Inland Country of Guiney*, London, W. Lowndes, 1789, pp. 11–12. Dalzel referred to the parrot's eggs, but it is only Hegel who specified that they were three in number. A. B. Ellis, writing in 1890, said that the custom of the parrot's eggs persisted until recent times 'if, indeed, it is yet altogether extinct.' *The Yoruba-Speaking Peoples of the Slave Coast of West Africa*, Chicago, Benin, 1964, p. 8n. Peter Morton-Williams has explained the background of the process as it arises out of a complex balance of power. The parrot's egg was the customary vessel for a suicide's poison. 'The Yoruba Kingdom of Oyo,' *West African Kingdoms in the Nineteenth Century*, Daryll Forde and P. M. Kaberry (eds), Oxford: Oxford University Press, 1976, pp. 53–4 and 67 n. 8.

18 James Bruce, *Travels to Discover the Source of the Nile*, 2nd edn, Edinburgh: Archibald Constable, 1805, vol. VI, pp. 372–3.

19 Herodotus Book II, ch. 33, Loeb Classical Library, trans. A. D. Godley, Cambridge, Mass.: Harvard University Press, 1975, pp. 312–15.

20 For example, William Bingley's *Travels in Africa from Modern Writers with Remarks and Observations*, London: John Sharpe, 1819. This volume includes the fact that the laws of Ashantee allow the king to have 3,333 wives (p. 284), the story of the parrot's eggs (p. 301) and much else used by Hegel, but, even though Bruce is one of his sources, the account of the king's executioner is not included.

21 Christian M. Neugebauer lists as Hegel's main source 'ignorance.' This seems appropriate enough given Hegel's own admissions (e.g. VPW 213 and 216; LPW 173 and 175), but does not justify the general tendency to fail to examine the information available to Hegel. 'The Racism of Hegel and Kant,' p. 262. Even a perceptive and relentless critic like Molefi Kete Asante is clearly hampered in his critique because he cannot be sure whether Hegel was culpably ignorant or simply

lacking in humility in the face of his ignorance. *Kemet, Afrocentricity and Knowledge*, pp. 32–3.

22 One might wonder about the fact that Hegel relied so heavily on Cavazzi, whose book was around 140 years old, when there were so many more recent works at his disposal. However, it is worth pointing out that Cavazzi's account, which was still being used by Emil Torday when he constructed his account of fetishism after years of anthropological research ('Le fétichisme, l'idolatrie et la sorcellerie des Bantou occidentaux,' *L'Anthropologie*, 39, 1929, pp. 431–54) is still regarded by Africanists as a useful source. I am grateful to John Thornton of Millesville University, the author of *Africa and Africans in the Making of the Atlantic World, 1400–1680* (Cambridge: Cambridge University Press, 1992), not only for sharing with me a draft of his introduction to a new edition and English translation of Cavazzi's manuscript that he is in the process of preparing, but also for offering me some most helpful comments on an earlier version of this paper.

23 The editors of the English edition of Hegel's *Lectures on the Philosophy of Religion* have drawn attention to Hegel's claim that Africans, citizens as well as prisoners, are killed in hundreds and thousands. *Vorlesungen über die Philosophie der Religion* vol. IIa, p. 201; trans. *Lectures on the Philosophy of Religion*, vol. 2, p. 297. They point out that Cavazzi said that the number of victims may be 'as high as a hundred.' In fact this is only according to the German translation. *Historische Beschreibung*, p. 145. However, the Italian original, like Labat's heavily altered version, specifies that in the case of the death of a prince or other eminent person the number of victims would be in 'the hundreds.' G. A. Cavazzi, *Istorica descrizione*, p. 123. J.-B. Labat, *Relation historique*, vol. 1, pp. 400–1. A more dramatic case of Hegel's misuse of Cavazzi can be found in his account of the woman who ruled over the Jagas (VPW 233; LPW 189). I have not yet been able to examine the sources of our knowledge of Ndumba Tembo, who is clearly meant here, but John Thornton has alerted me to the fact that, although Cavazzi gives a most unflattering portrait of her activities, some of the more gruesome anecdotes Hegel tells about her are not found in Cavazzi's text and that Hegel's description of 'a state of women' is unsupported by the account.

24 Bowdich was not just an ambitious young adventurer. He also had scholarly pretensions. He subsequently published *An Essay on the Superstitions, Customs, and Arts, Common to the Ancient Egyptians, Abyssinians and Ashantees*, Paris: J. Smith, 1821, which, had Hegel read it, might perhaps have led him to reconsider his attempt to separate Egypt from Africa.

25 See the discussion by W. E. F. Ward in his 'Introduction to Third Edition,' *Mission from Cape Coast Castle to Ashantee*, London: Frank Cass, 1966, pp. 44–7.

26 T. Bowdich, *Mission*, p. 254. See also p. 249.

27 Not surprisingly, Bowdich was closer to the truth than Hegel, but neither had it right. See R. S. Rattray, *Ashanti Law and Constitution*, New York: Negro University Press, 1969, pp. 107–9, and *Ashanti*, Oxford: Oxford University Press, 1923, p. 226. Also Ivor Wilks, *Forests of Gold*, Athens, Ohio University Press, 1993, pp. 147–50.

28 T. Bowdich, *Mission*, p. 420. Cf. VPW 232 and 271; LPW 188 and 220.

29 It is worth noting that both Bowdich and Joseph Dupuis, two of the main early reports giving knowledge of the Ashanti, both believed that it was possible to come to a working relationship with the Ashanti. It was the people with secondhand knowledge, including the Governor, Hope Smith, not to mention administrators in England, who believed, in part on the basis of their reports, that that would be impossible and that there was no point attempting to cultivate friendly relations. See W. E. F. Ward, Introduction to second edition, Joseph Dupuis, *Journal of a Residence in Ashantee*, London: Frank Cass, 1966, pp. 13–14.

30 Thomas Winterbottom, *An Account of the Native Africans in the Neighbourhood of Sierra Leone*, second edition, London: Frank Cass, 1969, vol. 1, pp. 166–7.

31 T. Bowdich, *Mission*, p. 300.

32 Ibid., p. 262.

33 Ibid., pp. 282–3.

34 However, if Hegel had indeed read Dalzel's *The History of Dahomey*, he would have been familiar with the speech of Adahoonzou, King of Dahomey, which included the comments: 'What hurts me most is, that some of your people have maliciously represented us in books, which never die, alleging, that we sell our wives and children, for the sake of procuring a few kegs of brandy. No; we are shamefully belied; and I hope you will contradict, from my mouth, the scandalous stories that have been propagated' (p. 219). Nevertheless, there are, as I shall note below, questions to be raised about the authenticity of this speech. Hegel's reference to a destitute man who had already sold his relatives comes from A. Cavazzi, *Istorica descrizione*, pp. 68–9 or J.-B. Labat, *Relation historique* I, p. 233.

35 T. Bowdich, *Mission*, pp. 289–90.

36 R. S. Rattray, *Religion and Art in Ashanti*, Oxford: Oxford University Press, 1927, p. 95n.

37 T. Bowdich, *Mission*, p. 288.

38 *Ibid.*, pp. 288–9.

39 A. Dalzel, *The History of Dahomey*, pp. 150–1. Describing earlier the death of the Viceroy of the Whydahs, Dalzel explained that his wives killed each other 'despairing to meet again with so indulgent a Lord' (p. 95). On the chaos caused by the death of a king, see also p. 67n.

40 *Ibid.*, p. 228.

41 For example, Richard Austin Freeman, *Travels and Life in Ashanti*, Westminster: Archibald Constable, 1898, pp. 442n and 474.

42 T. Bowdich, *Mission*, p. 241.

43 Ibid., p. 419.

44 T. B. Freeman, *Journal of Two Visits to the Kingdom of Ashanti*, London, 1843, pp. 164–5. Quoted in I. Wilks, *Asante in the Nineteenth Century*, Cambridge: Cambridge University Press, 1975, p. 594.

45 I. Wilks, *Asante in the Nineteenth Century*, pp. 594–5.

46 Quoted in I. Wilks, *Asante in the Nineteenth Century*, p. 594.

47 T. Bowdich, *Mission*, p. 33.

48 James' journal entry for 22 June 1817. Quoted by Edmund Collins, 'The Panic Element in Nineteenth-Century British Relations with Ashanti,' *Transactions of the Historical Society of Ghana*, vol. 5, no. 2, 1962, p. 122.

49 See, for example, William Snelgrave, *A New Account of Some Parts of Guinea*, London: P. Knapton, 1734, pp. 160–1: 'It is evident, that abundance of captives taken in War, would be inhumanly destroyed, was there not an Opportunity of disposing of them to the *Europeans*. So that at least many Lives are saved and great Numbers of useful Persons kept in being.'

50 Anthony Benezet, *Some Historical Account of Guinea* (1788), London, Frank Cass, 1968.

51 G. W. F. Hegel, *Enzyklopädie der philosophischen Wissenschaften III*, Werke 10, Frankfurt: Suhrkamp, 1970, §393, Zusatz, pp. 59–60; trans. M. J. Petry, *Hegel's Philosophy of Subjective Spirit*, vol. 2, Anthropology, Dordrecht: Reidel, 1978, pp. 53–5.

52 G. W. F. Hegel, *Enzyklopädie*, §394, Zusatz, p. 64; trans. *Hegel's Philosophy of Subjective Spirit*, vol. 2, p. 69.

53 This complicates the question of Hegel's racism and separates it from the most simple examples of racist ideology, but certainly does not decide the issue.

54 See also VPR II 181–2 and 443; LPR II 277–8 and 546. This was taken as the clearest indication that Africans knew nothing of natural causality (VPR II 441; LPR II 543). Hegel probably learned about this phenomenon from Cavazzi, *Istorica descrizione*, pp. 219–20; trans. *Historische Beschreibung*, p. 255 or from Labat's *Relation historique de l'Ethiopie occidentale* I, p. 266, but it was also emphasized by Bosman in his *A New and Accurate Description of the Coast of Guinea*, pp. 225–6.

55 For a history of the concept of fetish, see the essays of William Pietz. 'Bosman's Guinea: The Intercultural Roots of an Enlightenment of Discourse,' *Comparative Civilizations Review*, Fall 1982, pp. 1–22; 'The Problem of the Fetish,' Parts 1, 2, and 3a, *Res*, vol. 9, Spring 1985, pp. 5–17: vol. 13, Spring 1987, pp. 23–45: vol. 16, Autumn 1988, pp. 105–23; and 'Fetishism and Materialism' in *Fetishism as Cultural Discourse*, Emily Apter and William Pietz (eds), Ithaca: Cornell University Press, 1993, pp. 119–51. It is important to know something of this history given that the use of the term has led to such a total distortion of African beliefs. See, for example, R. Rattray, *Ashanti*, p. 91; and *Religion and Art in Ashanti*, p. 9.

56 Charles de Brosses, *Histoire des Navigations aux Terres Australes*, vol. 2, Paris: Durand, 1756, p. 377.

57 Charles de Brosses, *Du Culte des Dieux Fétiches*, pp. 11–13.

58 Ibid., p. 96.

59 Ibid., p. 14.

60 Charles de Brosses, *Histoire des Navigations aux Terres Australes*, vol. 2, pp. 372 and 380.

61 Charles de Brosses, *Historie des Navigations aux Terres Australes*, vol. 1, pp. 22–5 and 40–2, and vol. II, pp. 380 seq. See also M. V.-David, 'Le président de Brosses historien des religions et philosophe,' *Charles de Brosses 1777–1977*, J.-C. Gameta

(ed.), Geneva: Slatkine, 1981, pp. 123–40; and Alfonso M. Iacano, *Le fétichisme. Histoire d'un concept*, Paris: Presses Universitaires de France, 1992, pp. 39–46.

62 William Bosman, *A New and Accurate Description of the Coast of Guinea*, p. 367 and Charles de Brosses, *Du Culte des Dieux Fétiches*, p. 16.

63 W. Bosman, A New and Accurate Description of the Coast of Guinea, pp. 149 and 154–5.

64 Hegel's comments on this report are found in the *Lectures on the Philosophy of Religion* (VPR II 198; LPR II 294). The source is A. Cavazzi, *Istorica descrizione*, p. 223; *Historische Beschreibung*, pp. 258–9; or J.-B. Labat, *Relation historique*, vol. 2, pp. 218–9.

65 For example, Linnaeus, *Systema naturae*, reprint of the 1758 edition, London, Trustees of the British Museum, 1956, pp. 21–2. Quoted by Stephen T. Asma, 'Metaphors of Race,' *American Philosophical Quarterly*, 32, 1, 1995, p. 17.

66 I will not address Hegel's claim that 'the whole nature of Africa is such that there can be no such thing as a constitution' (VPW 228; LPW 185. See also *Philosophy of Right* §349). Reference to Rattray's *Ashanti Law and Constitution* would only be a first step, because Hegel had a technical sense of constitution, but it should also be noted that Bowdich already had a section on the 'Constitution and Laws' of the Ashanti.

67 A. Dalzel, *The History of Dahomey*, pp. 217–21. See Loren K. Waldman, 'An Unnoticed Aspect of Archibald Dalzel's *The History of Dahomey*,' *Journal of African History*, vol. 6, no. 2, 1965, pp. 185–92.

68 T. Bowdich, *Mission*, pp. 338–9. See also the reported conversation of Osei Bonsu in Joseph Dupuis, *Journal of a Residence in Ashantee*, pp. 162–3.

69 For a helpful review of the literature on African slavery that is particularly attentive to the distortions produced by European preconceptions, see Suzanne Miers and Igor Kopytoff, 'African Slavery as an Institution of Marginality' in Suzanne Miers and Igor Kopytoff (eds) *Slavery in Africa*, Madison: University of Wisconsin Press, 1977, pp. 3–81.

70 This is what underlies the apparent contradiction noticed by Jacques Derrida. *Glas*, Paris: Galilée, 1974, pp. 233–4; trans. John P. Leavey and Richard Rand, *Glas*, Lincoln: University of Nebraska Press, 1986, p. 208.

71 That the idea of slavery is different among Africans who lacked 'the love of rational freedom' was an important part of pro-slavery arguments. See Robert Norris, *A Short Account of the African Slave Trade*, Liverpool: Ann Smith's Navigation Shop, 1788, p. 8. Reprinted with minor changes in *Memoirs of the Reign of Bossa Ashadee*, p. 159.

72 A similar point is made by Michael Hoffheimer in an unpublished essay on slavery that makes an important contribution to the subject of Hegel's views on slavery, especially its role in American justifications of slavery.

73 G. W. F. Hegel, 'Philosophie des Rechts nach der Vorlesungensnachschrift K. G. v. Griesheims 1824/25,' *Vorlesungen über Rechtsphilosophie*, vol. 4, Karl-Heinz Ilting (ed.), Stuttgart-Bad Cannstatt: Frommann-Holzboog, 1974, p. 89; trans. Alan

S. Brudner, 'Prefatory Lectures on the Philosophy of Law,' *Clio*, vol. 8, 1, 1978, p. 68.

74 In 1860, on the eve of the Civil War, Mississippi Representative L. Q. C. Lamar read portions of Sibree's translation of Hegel's discussion of Africa into the record as part of his attempt to justify slavery in the United States. See Michael Hoffheimer, 'Does Hegel Justify Slavery?' *The Owl of Minerva*, vol. 25, no. 1, Fall 1993, pp. 118–9.

75 Tsenay Serequeberhan, 'The Idea of Colonialism in Hegel's Philosophy of Right,' *International Philosophical Quarterly*, 29, 115, 1989, pp. 311–12.

76 Hegel also insisted that it was 'the necessary fate (*Schicksal*) of Asian kingdoms, to be subjected to the Europeans' and that China would one day be obliged to this fate. G. W. F. Hegel, *Vorlesungen über die Philosophie der Geschichte*, Werke 12, Frankfurt: Suhrkamp, 1970, p. 179; trans. J. Sibree, *The Philosophy of History*, New York: Dover, 1956, pp. 142–3.

77 Steven B. Smith, 'Hegel on Slavery and Domination,' *Review of Metaphysics* 46, 1992, pp. 111–2.

78 There is an immediate sense in which Africa is said to be an 'unhistorical continent:' 'it does not exhibit movement or development' (VPW 234; LPH 190). That sense also applies quite clearly to China and India, whose status at the beginning of history I intend to discuss elsewhere. It should also be emphasized that there are other exclusions apart from Africa. Siberia, for example, is ruled out from having its own shape of world history (VPW 235; LPH 191), and it is clear that Native Americans also lacked the conditions that made history possible (VPW 202–3; LPH 165).

79 Nisbett's translation is misleading when he has Hegel say that Africa must be mentioned 'before we cross the threshold of world history itself.' Hegel locates the discussion on the threshold (*an der Schwelle der Weltgeschichte*).

80 T. Bowdich, *Mission*, p. 264. The passage is omitted from both editions of the German translation.

81 Imperfect in part because the Ashanti were said to lack the ability to compute time: Bowdich, *Mission*, p. 179.

82 W. E. B. Du Bois, *Writings*, New York: Library of America, 1986, pp. 815–26.

83 Hegel, *Enzyklopädie*, §394, Zusatz, p. 60; trans. *Hegel's Philosophy of Subjective Spirit*, vol. 2, pp. 53–5. Darrel Moellendorf understands this passage as somehow running contrary to Hegel's racist view that Blacks allow themselves to be sold as slaves without reflecting on whether it is right or wrong. In general, Moellendorf tries to show Hegel to be ambivalent in his racism. However, it seems that Moellendorf's analysis is guided by an attempt to make the discussion of race a grid for Hegel's philosophy of history, instead of recognizing that it is Hegel's philosophy of history that determines his account of race. Hence Hegel is not a biological racist. 'Racism and Rationality in Hegel's Philosophy of Subjective Spirit,' *History of Political Thought* 13, 2, 1992, p. 247.

84 This dichotomy appears to have been a motif of European descriptions of Africans. See, for example, Archibald Dalzel, *The History of Dahomey*, Introduction, p. xix:

'The general character of the Dahomans is marked by a mixture of ferocity and politeness.' See also S. Gilman, 'Hegel, Schopenhauer and Nietzsche see the Black,' *Hegel Studien* 10, 1981, p. 165.

85 James A. Snead, 'Repetition as a Figure of Black Culture,' *Out There: Marginalization and Contemporary Culture*, Russell Ferguson, Martha Gever, Trinh T. Minh-ha and Cornel West (eds), Cambridge, Mass.: MIT Press, 1990, p. 215. Snead surprises his reader by finding some truth in certain select aspects of Hegel's characterization, albeit by reversing the valuation placed on it.

86 H. S. Harris, 'Hegel's Phenomenology of Religion,' *Thought and Faith in the Philosophy of Hegel*, J. Walker (ed.), Dordrecht: Kluwer, 1991, pp. 100–1.

87 I offer this example following my participation in a conference organized by Peter Kemp in March 1995 in Copenhagen on the occasion of the United Nations World Summit for Social Development in which I tried to show that current ideas of social development are not free of the colonialist legacy.

## Chapter 2: Of Spirit(s) and Will(s)

I am grateful to both the Alexander von Humboldt Foundation and the University of California, Irvine, Research Committee, for granting me fellowships that made the research for this essay possible. I also wish to thank Ken Reinhard, UCLA, for his careful reading of a draft of this essay.

1 Jacques Derrida, *Of Spirit: Heidegger and the Question*. trans. by Geoffrey Bennington and Rachel Bowlby (Chicago: University of Chicago Press, 1991). Originally *De l'esprit* (1987). See the volume of essays edited by David Wood, *Of Derrida, Heidegger, and Spirit* (Evanston, Ill.: Northwestern University Press, 1993).

2 On Hegel, see pp. 7 and 117; 15 and 118; and 99 and 136. On Schelling, pp. 78 and 102. I shall be analysing these passages in greater detail below.

3 On the un-thought, see *Of Spirit*, p. 13: 'Needless to say, these unthoughts may well be mine and mine alone. And what would be more serious, more drily serious, they may well *give* nothing. 'The more original a thought,' says Heidegger, 'the richer its Un-thought becomes. The Unthought is the highest gift (*Geschenk*) that a thought can give."' And also note 5, p. 117, where Derrida quotes Heidegger (against himself): 'What is unthought in a thinker's thought is not a lack inherent in his thought. What is *un*-thought is there in each case only as the un-*thought*.'

4 After all, at the heart of the concept of ghost is the uncanny *return* of the dead, hence in French as Derrida reminds us, *revenant* ('I shall speak of ghost [*revenant*], of flame, and of ashes' – the first sentence in *Of Spirit*).

5 In *Glas*, consider p. 23i: 'The concept wins against matter that can hold its own against the concept only by relieving itself, only by denying itself in raising itself [*s'élevant*] to spirit. The concept also wins against death: by erecting even up to the tomb. The burial place raises itself. Let us not approach too quickly Hegel's burial place, about which we will have to concern ourselves later.' *Glas*, translated by John

P. Leavey, Jr and Richard Rand (Lincoln: University of Nebraska Press, 1990), orig. 1974. Page references are all to the 'left column' and an 'i' after the number refers to an insert in the column. For an alternative rumination on the crypt, see Nicolas Abraham and Maria Torok, *The Wolf Man's Magic Word: A Cryptonymy*, trans. by Nicholas Rand (Minneapolis, University of Minnesota Press, 1986). Also Laurence A. Rickels, *Aberrations of Mourning: Writing on German Crypts* (Detroit: Wayne State University Press, 1988).

6  Were this a paper on Nietzsche, I would focus on the connection of his 'Will to Power' and the *Nachlaß*, his literary remains, the site of considerable squabbling over a reading of the will. And indeed, Nietzsche's ghost and remains spook through this essay.

7  On 'foreclosure,' see *Of Spirit*, where he says of spirit, using terms that have a particular weight for my analysis: 'Is it not remarkable that this theme, spirit, occupying . . . a major and obvious place in this line of thought, should have been disinherited [*forclos d'héritage*]?' (p. 3).

8  See Bill Martin, *Matrix and Line: Derrida and the Possibilities of Postmodern Social Theory* (Albany: State University of New York Press, 1992). He explicitly deals with the Spirit/Letter dualism as the one basic to the Enlightenment and hence also to Derrida's critique (pp.6–8). Martin's thought-provoking discussion suffers, however, by being likewise captured in this opposition and its deconstruction. He never examines the will, or Hegel's treatment of it in the *Philosophy of Right*, even though he claims we 'must deal with otherness in a post-Hegelian way' (p. 52). This is a perfect example of how a postmodern political theory could be enhanced by a thorough treatment of the will of idealism.

9  We shall see that this is practically a Homeric epithet. It occurs as well in his debate with Gadamer, where Derrida picks up on Gadamer's call for a 'good will' at the heart of hermeneutics and uses this to criticize him for remaining caught in a 'metaphysics of subjectivity.' See Diane P. Michelfelder and Richard Palmer (eds) *Dialogue and Deconstruction: The Gadamer–Derrida Encounter* (Albany: State University of New York Press, 1989). This volume contains numerous readings of this debate, but none pursues the central issue around which deconstruction and hermeneutics elliptically revolve, the will.

10  'If the thinking of *Geist* . . . is neither thematic nor athematic and if its modality thus requires another category, then it is not only inscribed in contexts with a high political content. . . . It perhaps decides as to the very meaning of the political as such. In any case it would situate the place of such a decision, if it were possible' (*Of Spirit*, p. 6). See also below on the politics of and in *Glas*.

11  Hegel writes in §4: 'The basis [*Boden*] of right is the *realm of spirit* (*das Geistige*) and its precise location and point of departure is the *will*, which is free.' I will cite according to paragraph (§), and indicate if the reference is from an addition or a note (the latter only in the German edition). G. F. W. Hegel, *Grundlinien der Philosophie des Rechts oder Naturrecht und Staatswissenschaft im Grundrisse* (Mit Hegels eigenhändigen Notizen und den mündlichen Zusätzen). Frankfurt am Main: Suhrkamp, 1989. With minor variations (and the notes), English translations are taken

from *Elements of the Philosophy of Right*, translated by H. B. Nisbet (Cambridge: Cambridge University Press, 1991). References to Hegel's *Enzyklopädie der Wissenschaften* will follow the same format.

12 I will not be able to deal in depth with Heidegger in this essay. Derrida, however, refers on numerous occasions to his use of will (esp. in Chapter V). I agree in large measure with Hannah Arendt's argument that the *Kehre* occurs thanks (unfortunately?) to Heidegger's rejection of the will as a major category, a turn that occurs through his reading of Schelling and Nietzsche on the will. It is Heidegger, then, who identifies will and metaphysics. See Hannah Arendt, *Das Wollen* . . . p. 50f. – One place to locate a discussion of Heidegger, as Derrida hints, is in the analysis of *Entschlossenheit*. Consider also the short dialogue, *Zur Erörterung der Gelassenheit*, with its culmination in a notion of 'Wollen-nicht-Wollen.' Also, clearly the lectures on Nietzsche contain numerous passages with brilliant analyses of the will. Richard Wolin, *The Politics of Being: The Political Thought of Martin Heidegger* (New York: Columbia University Press, 1990) provides an interesting reading of *Entschlossenheit* in terms of philosophical and political theories of decisionism and voluntarism (esp. pp. 37–53).

13 See, e.g. *Glas*, where Derrida points out that the privileging of the last two moments of *Sittlichkeit* (civil society and the state) over the family as *the* sites of the political is open to question (p. 16).

14 Jacques Derrida, *Speech and Phenomenon and Other Essays on Husserl's Theory of Signs*, trans. by David B. Allison (Evanston, Ill.: Northwestern University Press, 1973).

15 On Derrida's spatial metaphors of inclusion and exclusion, boundaries and limits, esp. their inadequacy for approaching Hegel critically, see my 'U-Topian Hegel: Dialectic and Its Other in Poststructuralism,' (*The German Quarterly*, Spring 1987, pp. 237–61).

16 For reasons of space I must bracket out a reading of Husserl here, i.e. whether Derrida inherits from Husserl this reduction of will to *Geistigkeit* or imposes it on him.

17 In 'Otobiographies: The Teaching of Nietzsche and the Politics of the Proper Name' we see how Derrida tends on the other hand to discuss 'last wills' not in terms of the will but, as opposed to Spirit, in terms of the *name*: 'Only the name can inherit, and this is why the name, to be distinguished from the bearer, is always and a priori a dead man's name, a name of death' (p. 7). In Jacques Derrida, *The Ear of the Other*, trans. by Avital Ronell (Lincoln: University of Nebraska Press, 1988).

18 In this regard, see the theological reading of Hegel by Alan M. Olson, *Hegel and the Spirit: Philosophy as Pneumatology* (Princeton: Princeton University Press, 1992).

19 Another way of getting at Derrida's strategy is to consider the triangulations of concepts he develops (involving three languages): '*Spirit/soul/life, pneuma/psyché/ zoé* or *bios, spiritus/anima/vita, Geist/Seele/Leben* – these are the triangles and squares in which we imprudently pretend to recognize stable semantic determinations, and then to circumscribe or skirt round the abyss of what we ingenuously call translation. Later we shall wonder what the opening of these angles might mean'

(p. 74). That is, Derrida takes these conceptual relations and destablizes them. But I wonder what is involved in his leaving out the concept of will? After all, is there not there too a problem of 'translation' (esp. for someone like Heidegger), since Greek philosophy did not have a corresponding concept? Does will not actually have a place in many of these triangles and squares at the same time?

20 As we shall see, however, freedom for Hegel is actually to be associated with the will.

21 Consider the problematic and highly reductive reference to 'the epoch of Cartesian–Hegelian subjectivity' (p. 55). Now, to use Derrida's own game, this *could* perhaps be in quotes as a citation of a kind of periodization within Heideggerian *Seinsgeschichte*. But it is not in quotes and, I think, tells us also about Derrida's unnuanced notion of subjectivity.

22 Another of the major phantoms of Derrida's *opus* is Nietzsche and Heidegger's *Nietzsche*. I am working on a study of the Derrida–Gadamer debate over the 'will to interpretation,' a study that will deal with the reception of Heidegger and Nietzsche.

23 In this, Derrida is in good company. Virtually no work exists on Heidegger and Schelling. As for the politics, does one not have to look with extreme care at lectures presented in 1936 in Germany, by a man of Heidegger's stature and leanings, on the essence of human freedom? F. W. J. Schelling, *Philosophische Untersuchungen über das Wesen der menschlichen Freiheit und die damit zusammenhängenden Gegenstände* (1809). Frankfurt: Suhrkamp, 1990. Also translated by James Gutmann as *Philosophical Inquiries into the Nature of Human Freedom* (Open Court: LaSalle, Ill., 1992). Translations in the body of my essay are my own, although I also give the page numbers of the English edition.

24 And thus in his essay on Trakl, Heidegger refers to *Geist*, according to Derrida, 'in formulations which here again often recall Schelling' (p. 107).

25 Indeed, he cites two passages, one from the Trakl essay and the other from the Schelling lectures in which evil arises out of *Geist* in the first case ('Evil is *geistlich*.') and out of a form of the will in the latter ('The ground of evil thus resides in the primordial will [*Urwillen*] of the primary base') (p. 104).

26 'Idealism is the soul of philosophy; realism its/her body. Only the two together make a living totality. The latter can never provide philosophy's principle, but it must be the basis and means by which the former becomes reality, takes on flesh and blood. If a philosophy lack this foundation, which is usually a sign that its ideal principle was weak and ineffective from the start, then it loses itself in those systems that consist of abstract concepts of a-se-ity, modifications, etc. which stand in stark contrast to the vital force and fullness of reality' (German, p. 51; English p. 30f) – We see here, and will see below on Hegel, that the body/soul dichotomy is central to idealism and the idealist concept of the will. But we need to be wary of therefore assuming that it remains a 'metaphysical' dualism.

27 Referred to in Jacques Lacan, *The Four Fundamental Concepts of Psycho-Analysis* (translated by Alan Sheridan. Norton: New York, 1981), p. 29, as 'pre-ontological.' See also the translator's notes (p. 281), where it is pointed out that Lacan himself

proposed the neologism 'want-to-be' as a way of translating 'manque-à-être.' The place of the will (wanting) in Lacan also traverses his work, from the Seminar on ethics (VIII), through 'Kant avec Sade,' to the *vel* (the doubly bound choice, whose 'v' is often associated with that of *volonté*). – See also Manfred Frank's association of Lacan and Schelling, *Der unendliche Mangel an Sein* (Frankfurt am Main: Suhrkamp, 1980). – See also Kunio Kozu, *Das Bedürfnis der Philosophie. Ein Überblick über die Entwicklung des Begriffkomplexes 'Bedürfnis,' 'Trieb,' 'Streben' und 'Begierde' bei Hegel*. *Hegel-Studien*, Beiheft 30 (Bonn: Bouvier Verlag, 1988). He pursues the recurrent thought in Hegel's oeuvre of the fundamental need-lack-impulse-drive behind philosophy itself.

28 The notion of 'resource' here will echo in an interesting way with Hegel's discussion on the way a 'last will' passes on the 'resources' of a family.

29 Consider p. 108: 'To read Hegel from the inside, the problematic of *Sittlichkeit*, and then, in that of the family, can henceforth be unfolded only in a philosophy of spirit.' Derrida turns to the Jena lectures and claims that this is 'confirmed, if such can be said, fifteen years later, in the *Philosophy of Right*.' But is Derrida not missing a point here about the will? And since this follows a passage (p. 107) in which Derrida gives his version of a hermeneutic for Hegel (how he 'must' be read), one must wonder in turn if Derrida is not imposing a philosophy of Spirit too much onto Hegel, as if that is all *he* wants to see.

30 That Derrida is interested in the architectonics, see p. 4f. He summarizes the three stages of the *PdR*: abstract right (the insistence on general principles), morality (appeal to individual conscience), and *Sittlichkeit* (ethical community in which the individual and general are interrelated). And then the three stages of *Sittlichkeit*: family (the first, 'natural' community), civil or bourgeois society (the fragmentation into atomized individuals with rights), and the State (where individuals make the general laws governing them). I should state here explicitly that Hegel's actual 'syllogisms' and tripartite structures may be largely untenable in their *content*, but we can still embrace their dialectical logic. For example, we do not need (and hopefully would not) see the family as the first, 'natural' stage of *Sittlichkeit* that gives way to an 'abstract' one, even though we might accept a notion of *Sittlichkeit* that *in principle* must be both natural and rational.

31 Derrida writes: The interpretation of the 'familial moment . . . directly engages the whole Hegelian determination of right on one side, of politics on the other' (p. 4). And again, p. 16: Although most 'political' analyses of Hegel focus on civil society and the state, Derrida would (legitimately) question the privileging of such overtly 'political' forms over the family (and its deconstruction) in getting to the political core of Hegel.

32 On the notion of a '(de)parting point' in the specific instance of marriage, see *Glas*, 192f. Again, Derrida does not deal with *the* point of departure of the entire *Philosophy of Right*.

33 Here he follows Hegel, who refers to *Antigone* in §166 of the *Philosophy of Right* and from there back to his own *Phenomenology of Spirit*. Note, however, that in

the *PdR* Hegel is *not* using *Antigone* as an example of the breakup of the family but of 'familial piety' (*Pietät*).

34  I skip over Derrida's reading of Hegel on *Antigone* not because it is not insightful but because I want to get to what Derrida is skipping over by reading *it* as the discussion of the 'collapse of the family' rather than the section following this in the *Philosophy of Right* on last wills, testaments, and inheritance. Were *Glas* 'about' the *Phenomenology of Spirit*, then the focus on *Antigone* as the site of the transition from the Greek *Sittlichkeit* to the Roman 'state of law' (*Rechtszustand*) would be more appropriate. But since Derrida is explicitly dealing with the *Philosophy of Right* and the transition there from the family to civil society, his exclusive attention to *Antigone* over Hegel's own discussion of the decline of the family is questionable.

35  He continues: 'Inheritance is essentially a taking proper possession of [literally: a "stepping into," *Eintreten*] what *in themselves* are common resources – an acquistion [again: *Eintreten*] which, in the case of more distant relationships and with increasing self-sufficiency (*verselbständigende Zerstreuung*) of civil society, becomes more inde-terminate as the disposition of (comm)unity declines and as every marriage leads to the renunciation of previous family relationships and the establishment of a new and self-sufficient family' (§178).

36  Frederick Neuhouser, *Fichte's Theory of Subjectivity* (Cambridge: Cambridge UP, 1990) provides an interesting historical analysis of some of the crucial arguments around the relationship between *Wille* and *Willkür* in the late eighteenth century (esp. Kant, Reinhold, Fichte). See esp. pp. 144–56. Reinhold argued that each act, to the extent that it is free, involves a free choice (*Willkür*) that is essentially groundless, undetermined. Kant, on the other hand, argued that free acts are determined by 'subjective grounds' that are maxims we choose on the basis of more general principles, which, in turn, we choose to follow because of our 'disposition' (*Gesinnung*). Needless to say, even Neuhouser points out that 'since Kant provides no alternative explanation of the self-groundedness of this original choice, we can only conceive of it negatively, as spontaneous and ultimately arbitrary' (152).

Near the end of the discussion, Neuhouser formulates the peculiar relationship between the arbitrariness inherent in our choices and our sense of the reasons for willed actions in a way I would endorse: 'While it is true that such an espousal of norms [behind making a choice] might be regarded as "ungrounded" in a strict sense of the term, it is also more than merely "blind"' (163).

To my knowledge, no account of the changes in meaning of *Willkür* (esp. in the years of idealism) has been written. It is also one of those German terms that is impossible to translate, since it ranges from arbitrariness (in a strongly negative sense) to free choice (in a strongly positive sense).

37  Here one could make a link to Hegel's earlier writings on the Last Supper, and hence again to Derrida's reading in *Glas*. After all, one of the main issues for Hegel is what it meant for Christ to pass on his 'testament' to the apostles (the problematic substitution at the heart of Christianity – a 'circle' of friends takes the place of the 'natural' family). See Derrida's analysis of Hegel's hermeneutic of Christ's last words as an 'act of friendship' (p. 66) which at the same time 'makes

them sons' (pp. 88 and 92). See also Werner Hamacher, *pleroma: Zu Genesis und Struktur einer dialektischen Hermeneutik bei Hegel* (introduction to Hegel, *Der Geist des Christentums*, Frankfurt: Ullstein, 1978). Also my *The Spirit and Its Letter: Traces of Rhetoric in Hegel's Philosophy of* Bildung (Ithaca: Cornell, 1988), pp. 134–7.

38  Hegel writes, referring to an earlier discussion: 'The principle that the members of the family become self-sufficient and rightful persons (see §177) allows something of this arbitrariness and differentiation (*Willkür und Unterscheidung*) to arise within the family circle among the natural heirs; but it must occur only on a very limited scale if the basic relationship is not to be damaged' (§180). See also the *Vorrede* (p. 12) for the attack on *Willkür* that would pass itself off as philosophy. Interestingly, this is linked to rhetoric. Thus, we could venture a massive analogy traversing Hegel's (and Derrida's?) work – *Willkür*: Will: rhetoric: philosophy.

39  'To make this arbitrariness the main principle of inheritance within the family was, however, part of that harsh and unethical aspect of Roman law. . . .' (§180).

40  He points out that this practice rests on an 'arbitrariness that, in and of itself, has no right to be recognized' (§180). Hegel does seem to have the interests of the girls in mind here (see the second subsection, 'ß' [beta] in the second note to §180).

41  'Love, the ethical moment in marriage, is, as love, a feeling (*Empfindung*) for actual individuals in the present, not for an abstraction' (§180).

42  I know of no work pointing to *King Lear* as the subtext of this passage, but the references to England are numerous and the description of Roman law applies well to Lear: 'This was associated with the terrible instability of the main institutions [of the state], and with a frantic activity of legislation (*Gesetzgeben*) designed to counteract the outbreak of evils which resulted from it. The unethical consequences which this right of arbitrariness in testamentary dispositions had among the Romans are familiar enough from history.' And also the following: 'The simple direct arbitrariness of the deceased cannot be made the principle of the *right to make a will* (*Recht, zu testieren*), especially if it is opposed to the substantial right of the family; for the love and veneration of the family for its former member are primarily the only guarantee that his arbitrary will will be respected after his death' (§180). In this regard, it would be interesting to consider Hegel's other discussions of *Lear*, i.e. in the concluding section of the *Aesthetics*, where it is mentioned as an example of a tragedy in which an individual imposes a particular subjectivity as universal. The tragedy arises out of the 'decisive tenaciousness' (*entschiedene Festhalten*) and the 'strength of will' (*Stärke ihres Willens*) of the heroes.

43  One of the most poignant and biting arguments has to do with the way those who would embrace a pure subjectivity end up 'longing for an objective condition in which the human being gladly debases himself to servitude and total subjection simply in order to escape the torment of vacuity and negativity,' like the Romantics who converted to Catholicism (Addition, §141). This also prefigures in a remarkable way the famous conclusion of Nietzsche's *Genealogy of Morals*: 'Man would rather will nothing than not will at all.' And, of course, the first section on 'abstract law' culminates in the all too true argument that the insistence on an absolute right leads to crime (which is the flipping over into the purely subjective).

44  On Hegel's concept of dialectical demonstration (*Beweisen*), see the end of §141 and *Glas*, p. 11. Schelling also provides some fascinating cases of (the need for) dialectical thinking in the *Philosophical Inquiries* (German, p. 38f; English, pp. 12–14).

45  Derrida refers to this section and argument (p. 12f) but without providing any analysis or taking a stance. Rather, he trivializes it by implying that for the subject to recognize itself in the *sittliche Welt* is to give itself over to 'its right, its police, its prisons, its penal colonies.' This evades the *issue* of Hegel's argument.

46  Clifford Geertz, *The Interpretation of Cultures* (New York: Basic Books, 1973), p. 5. When he then goes on to say that the analysis of culture is 'an interpretive [science] in search of meaning,' we can understand the 'meaning' or *vouloir dire* in terms of this dialectical will. See also p. 10: 'Culture, this acted document, thus is public, like a burlesqued wink or a mock sheep raid. Though ideational, it does not exist in someone's head; though unphysical, it is not an occult entity. The interminable, because unterminable, debate within anthropology as to whether culture is "subjective" or "objective," together with the mutual exchange of intellectual insults ("idealist!"–"materialist!"; "mentalist!"–"behaviorist!"; "impressionist!"–"positivist!") which accompanies it, is wholly misconceived. Once human behavior is seen as (most of the time; there *are* true twitches) symbolic action – action which, like phonation in speech, pigment in painting, line in writing, or sonance in music, signifies – the question as to whether culture is patterned conduct or frame of mind, or even the two somehow mixed together, loses sense.' This responds both to the Husserl presented by Derrida and to Derrida's critique in a way that is strongly Hegelian.

47  Consider the anthropological notion of 'cultural sensitivity,' for example. To belong to a (sub)culture is to experience the world in those categories which are not 'held' as beliefs but are in fact more radically 'subjective.' I am clearly giving a kind of Heideggerian reading here. (The *Zeugnis* in Hegel could be related to the *Zeug* in Heidegger.) But note the difference. *Sittliche Substanz* is linked to the *will*, not to *Being*, and therefore I would be arguing against an 'ontological' reading and for a phenomenology or even a genealogy (of will).

48  Vittorio Hösle (a neo-Hegelian) points out that therefore this is the location of a significant tension in Hegel's thought that does *not* fully work out the intersubjective. That is, he sees the later Hegel incorrectly prioritizing *Intelligenz* and theoretical philosophy, a position that contradicts both his earlier writings and his emphasis on the objectivity of the spirit. Despite our difference in approach, I would conceive of the will as the place for engaging an 'intersubjective' reading of Hegel. See his *Hegel's System*, vol. 2, pp. 390–5.

49  This notion of 'being in accordance with its concept' is not a particularly metaphysical belief. Think of the way we use concepts in real life, e.g. what you expect of the engine in your car: to be in accordance with its concept it must be functioning; that does not mean that it always works, but when it does not, you try to get it fixed to be in accordance with the concept. It is only a 'true' engine when it works. Thus, while the will is often limited to a 'metaphysics of

subjectivity,' that is not to say we should leave it at that, since its 'truth' breaks the bounds of the subject.

50 That Kant introduced this more radical notion of the will could be considered his major achievement in the history of philosophy, although the problem afterwards, as Schelling implied, was how to think through the contradictory determinations dialectically. Kant did not. See also Adorno, *Negative Dialektik* (Frankfurt: Suhrkamp, 1982), esp. the chapter on 'Freiheit. Zur Metakritik der praktischen Vernunft' (pp. 210–95) with its incredible analyses of a 'dialectical determination of will (*dialektische Bestimmung des Willens*).'

51 In the notes to §142: 'The *unity* (will as in itself universal) – that I – [in] thinking – i.e. as a universal – want the universal – and I am this wanting of the universal – in the empirical. . . .'

52 This is one of the main points of Joseph C. Flay's essay, 'Hegel, Derrida, and Bataille's Laughter' and is extended by Judith Butler in her reponse. In *Hegel and his Critics: Philosophy in the Aftermath of Hegel*, William Desmond (ed.) (Albany: State University of New York Press, 1989), esp. pp. 168f and 175.

53 Think of Freud's *Drei Abhandlungen zur Sexualtheorie* (1905), according to which the psychical order of human beings is 'determined' paradoxically by the indeterminacy of the means, objects, and goals of satisfaction of the drives.

54 The translation of the *Philosophy of Right* points out the play on connotations that Hegel is making here between the sense of 'closing off' contained in *beschließen* and 'opening oneself' contained in *sich entschließen*. Here one could bring in Heideggerian *Entschlossenheit*: the openness to a decision and the necessity of some decision need to be thought together. For this reason, an individual's most particular 'decisiveness' is co-constituted by the responsiveness to a 'call' of *Dasein* (itself neither objective nor subjective). *Sein und Zeit* (Tübingen: Max Niemeyer, 1986), esp. §§54–60.

55 See §13: 'By resolving (*Beschließen*), the will posits itself as the will of a specific individual and as a will which distinguishes itself from everything else.' And in the Addition: 'A will which resolves on nothing is not an actual will. . . .' See also Neuhouser's discussion of Fichte, Tugendhat, and Taylor for an understanding of 'self-determination' such that 'in reflecting upon one's true nature, one allegedly constitutes that nature' (p. 156). In choosing between different values, he argues, one is also making them (since a value is a hierarchical ordering that determines and is determined by the choice). Moreover, one does not just make the choice on the basis of 'who one is' since 'who one is' emerges from the choices one makes (pp. 156–66).

56 In Hegelian terms: *Willkür* is the certainty (*Gewißheit*) of freedom, the will is its truth (*Wahrheit*); i.e. there would be no freedom without [the certainty of] this contradiction, but to be free, the individual needs to grasp [its truth]. But as we know from the entire movement of the *PdG*, truth is not *different from* certainty, and hence this contradiction fully inheres in the will. See also the *Encyclopedia*, §413, Addition.

57 Recall that for Lacan, the subject is also always 'inmixed' with the Other. See his

lecture at the famous Johns Hopkins conference, 'Of Structure as an Inmixing of an Otherness Prerequisite to Any Subject Whatever,' in *The Structuralist Controversy: The Languages of Criticism and the Sciences of Man*, by Richard Macksey and Eugenio Donato (eds) (Baltimore: The Johns Hopkins University Press, 1970), pp. 186–95.

58 This is the logic of the lack/supplement according to Hegel: 'One may ask here why it has this deficiency. If that which is deficient does not at the same time stand above its deficiency, then its deficiency does not exist for it.' That is, the lack (or wanting) is always already superseding itself insofar as it is 'found wanting.' Here again we have in terms of the will a version of a Lacanian dialectic *avant la lettre*.

59 Hegel writes: 'A will which . . . only wants the abstract universal wants *nothing* and is therefore not a will at all' (Addition to §6). Nietzsche's clearest formulation of the rejection of both such a 'free will' and its inversion, an 'unfree will' in the sense of a world caught in mechanistic cause-and-effect, can be found in *Jenseits von Gut und Böse*, §21.

60 Addition to §7: 'The will which limits itself exclusively to a *this* is the will of the stubborn person (*der Eigensinnige*) who considers himself unfree unless he has *this* will. But the will is not tied to something limited; on the contrary, it must proceed further, for the nature of the will is not this one-sidedness and restriction. Freedom is to will something determinate, yet to be with oneself (*bei sich*) in this determinacy and to return once more to the universal.'

One could perhaps use these conceptions of the free will to read back a fundamental tension into the concept of Spirit as well. In the definitions of Spirit in the opening paragraphs of the third volume of Hegel's *Encyclopedia* (esp. §382), one can see a similar simultaneity of the Spirit as 'freedom from' and 'production of' Otherness.

61 See Stephen Houlgate, *Hegel, Nietzsche and the Criticism of Metaphysics* (Cambridge: Cambridge University Press, 1986). He argues that Hegel's arguments against metaphysics are ultimately more critical than Nietzsche's. And while I would disagree with him on that score (and would place more emphasis on the will in each thinker), I would tend to agree with the general point that *both* reject the basic forms of metaphysics (of subjectivity, the will, etc.). I think the Hegel–Nietzsche connection needs to be more fully developed in terms of their alternative conceptions of will.

## Chapter 3: The Surprise of the Event

1 TN: The multiple meanings of the French '*arriver*' – chief among which are 'to happen,' 'to arrive' and 'to succeed' – cannot be entirely conveyed in a one-word translation into English. '*Arriver*' refers both to the approach to and the reaching of a destination: it means both to be coming to a point and to reach that point. The French '*arrivée*' means arrival or coming, but Nancy plays throughout with the past participle form of the verb.

2 TN: All quotes from Hegel taken from A.V. Miller, trans., *Science of Logic* (New York: Humanities Press, 1976), p. 588. The translation has occasionally been modified (e.g. 'concept' instead of 'Notion' is used for '*Begriff*') in order to bring it closer to the French translation used by Nancy.

3 TN: The form employed by Nancy in the expression '*qu'il arrive*' can move between the present 'that it happens' and the subjunctive 'that it happen' – a particularly suggestive form since the subjunctive is also the Biblical imperative, as in 'let there be light.' That the past tense is formed with the verb '*être*' (to be) furnishes ample occasion for suggestive plays on 'is' come/'is' happened. '*Arriver*' is usually translated as 'to happen'; where not, the French is indicated parenthetically.

4 That is only if one understands the *to ti èn einai* as subordinated or identical to the *upokeimenon* – instead of separating one from the other, as Rudolf Boehm has proposed. Such a disjunction may be understood as the disjunction of being-event and being-ground.

5 TN: The expression employed here by Nancy – *qu'il y ait* – involves the subjunctive of the French expression 'il y a' or 'there is,' which is also the tense used for the imperative: let there be as in the opening passage of Genesis. Here Nancy's argument hinges upon a play on two French expressions for 'there is': '*il est*' and '*il y a.*' The former employs the third person conjugation of the verb '*être*' (to be), whereas the latter involves the third person conjugation of the verb '*avoir*' (to have) and the adverb '*y*' indicative of place.

6 Here the principal of the *disputatio* with Badiou is the 'event of being' rather than the decoupling of being and event.

7 TN: The idiom '*à même*' used here by Nancy, as Brian Holmes points out in his translator's notes to 'Identity and Trembling,' works with the *an* of the German *an sich*: 'Usually translated 'in itself,' this term means literally 'at itself,' with an having the force of Latin *ad* in 'adjacent'. No single English phrase can convey this sense – the semantic domain overlaps with English 'just at,' 'right with,' 'in the very,' and even just 'in,' in the baggy sense not of 'within,' carrying its ghost of some nesting transcendence, but of 'inseparable from, yet not identical to.' The term conveys the emphasis on exteriority, on the naked givenness of the existent to what cannot safely be encased within itself, of such terms as the exposition of objects, or their exscription. A moving gloss is given by the author himself, in a letter written while suffering a rejection after a heart transplant: 'To what extent is this heart, which the rest of my body tries to reject, *à même* my body?' (396 n 12).

8 In French: E. Kant, *Critique de la raison pure*, trans. A. Tremesaygues and B. Pacaud (Paris: Presses Universitaires de France, 1986), p. 182.

9 We thus have here a question of 'originary temporality,' the major concept of *Sein und Zeit*. Is such a concept nevertheless itself subject to that of the time of presence (*already* present and homogeneous to itself), or is it an exception? This is the most important stake in a debate doubtless internal to Heidegger, and in the open between Derrida and Heidegger, indeed between Derrida and himself. (Compare 'Ousia et grammé' and *Donner le temps*, p. 6). But perhaps we must think that it is

presence which precedes itself – which pres-ents itself – heterogeneous to itself, and that this is where lies the event (of Being).

10  TN: The French word '*survenue*,' or 'unexpected occurrence,' has been translated as 'coming-up' where Nancy uses '*sur-venue*' in order to preserve the play on '*venue*' or '*coming*.' See also chapter 11, 'Freedom and Destiny: Surprise, Tragedy, Generosity' in *The Experience of Freedom*, trans. Bridget McDonald (Palo Alto: Stanford University Press, 1994).

11  Even and above all if it 'arises [*relève*] from what-is-not-being-as-being' (Badiou, *L'être et l'événement*, p. 211), since 'not-being-as-being' is the condition of Being, or, to be more precise, the *existing* condition of Being. On this (essential) minimum, there would be without doubt an accord between all the compelling wagers of the *diputatio* – unless one did not exactly commence in the manner of announcing this minimum.

12  On this see JLN, *Le sens du monde*.

13  TN: The French '*saut*,' subsequently translated as leap, is also the nominal form of '*sauter*,' which means 'to jump,' 'to leap,' 'to spring,' but also 'to blow up' or 'explode.' '*Au saut du lit*,' meaning 'just after getting up from bed,' is here being played on.

14  *The Fundamental Concepts of Metaphysics*, p. 501 ff.

15  TN: The work of Parmenides of Elea exists only in fragments, much of it in the work of other writers such as Sextus Empiricus and Simplicius. Parmenides describes a journey on a chariot that involves passage through a gateway to which the goddess Justice (*Diké*) holds the key. The goddess instructs the traveler in the ways of error and truth: 'it is'; 'it exists and must exist.' The ambiguity of the 'it' has stirred much speculation and controversy.

16  TN: Beethoven wrote over the manuscript of the finale of this quartet – the last before his death – '*Der schwer gefasste Entschluss*.' Over the opening *grave* theme, he wrote '*Muss es sein?*' Over the *allegro* theme he wrote '*Es muss sein*.' As Beethoven wrote in October of 1826 to Moritz Schlesinger: 'Here, my dear friend, is my last quartet. It will be the last; and indeed it has given me much trouble. For I could not bring myself to compose the last movement. But as your letters were remind-ing me of it, in the end I decided to compose it. And that is the reason why I have written the motto: The decision taken with difficulty – Must it be? – It must be, it must be.' *The Letters of Beethoven*, Emily Andrews (ed.) (New York: Norton, 1961), pp. 1,318–19.

## Chapter 4: (The End of Art with the Mask)

1  Hegel, *Phänomenologie des Geistes*, Gerhard Göhler (ed.) (Berlin: Ullstein Verlag, 1973). A volume in Ullstein's 'Materialen' series, this edition reprints the first edition of 1807. Page numbers are here and hereafter indicated in the text. The second number refers to the English translation by J. B. Baillie, *The Phenomenology*

*of Mind* (New York: Harper & Row, 1967). The translation has been slightly modified.

2  In the same line in which he speaks of the 'forgetfulness' and the 'disappearance of the reality and action of the powers of the substance,' Hegel writes of the 'essence' into which these conflicting powers retreat: 'this [essence] consists in the undisturbed calm of the whole within itself, the immovable unity of Fate, the quiescent existence (and hence the inactivity and lack of vitality) of the family and government . . . and the return of their spiritual life and activity into Zeus simply and solely' (408–9/743).

3  That Hegel here and in other passages of the *Phenomenology* plays with the terms 'mask' and 'person' is of course unthinkable without the terminological speculations bound up in the philosophical tradition with the determination of what 'nature,' 'person,' 'substance' and 'subsistence' are, and particularly the speculation of Boethius' *Contra Eutychen* in the discussion of the difficult transition from Greek to Latin and further to Christian terminology. Boethius writes: 'persona est definitio: "naturae rationabilis individua substantia."' *Persona*, this individual substance of a rational nature, is regarded by Boethius as the translation of the Greek *hypostasis*. However, he must concede that *persona* is also the translation of another Greek concept, namely *prosopon*. 'The Greeks,' he writes, 'call these masks (personas) *prosopon*, because they are set upon the face (in facie, pros optus) and conceal the appearance to the eyes' (*Contra Euthychen* III, 3–25). The tension in the concept of person, which is produced through its double determination as hypostasis and mask, as substance and that which conceals or brings to light, is resolved for Boethius in that 'person' even as 'mask' is nothing other than 'individual substance,' for, according to his argument, through these masks (*personis inductis*) in tragedy and comedy the actors represent (*repraesentabant*) individuals (Boethius, *The Theological Tractates* [Cambridge, Mass.: Harvard University Press, 1973], pp. 84–8). The best philological presentation of the *prosopon* in Greek antiquity is in Françoise Frontisi-Ducroux, *Du masque au visage* (Paris: Flammarion, 1995), esp. pp. 19–38. On *persona* in Romantic and Christian terminology cf. Siegmund Schlossmann, *Persona und prosopon im Recht und im christlichen Dogma* (Leipzig, 1906). For the attempt at a 'social history of the category' of person, cf. Marcel Mauss, 'Eine Kategorie des menschlichen Geistes: Der Begriff der Person und des "Ich"' (1938) in M. M., *Soziologie und Anthropologie*, vol. II (Frankfurt/M.: Ullstein Verlag, 1978), pp. 221–52.

The modern split between person and mask is already completed when Hobbes introduces the distinction in *De homine* between 'artificial man' and 'true' or 'natural man': 'What the Greeks called *prosopon* the Latins sometimes call man's *facies* (face) or *os* (countenance), and sometimes his *persona* (mask): *facies* if they wished to indicate the true man, *persona* if an artificial one, such as comedy and tragedy were accustomed to have in the theatre' (Thomas Hobbes, *Man and Citizen* [Indianapolis: Hackett, 1991], p. 83; cf. *Leviathan*, ch. xvi: 'Of Persons, authors, and things personated'). Kant, for whom 'person' no longer stands as objective substance nor as technical product, sees 'person' in the recurring phrase 'humanity in our person,' as the true representative of freedom, a 'factum of reason' to which no empirical appearance can correspond, but which grounds every possibility of empirical experience and praxis. To the question 'what origin is there worthy of thee' the answer for him can only be 'personality, i.e. the freedom and independence from the mechanism of nature' (KpV, A 155) [My translation, K. B.]. Hegel's theory of comic self-consciousness as a play with the mask and the person can be read as a continuation of Kant's philosophy of person and freedom. For Hegel it is no longer a question of the self-positing of the moral law but of the confirmation of the thetic force, even in the sublation of the substantial self.

4 As such, it is fundamentally different from that play and spectator, which Walter Benjamin in an excursus in his book on the *Trauerspiel* indicates as the culmination of Baroque theater. He writes of Hamlet: 'The secret of his person is contained within the playful, but for that very reason firmly circumscribed, passage through all the stages in this complex of intentions, just as the secret of his fate is contained in an action which, according to this, his way of looking at things, is perfectly homogenous. For the *Trauerspiel,* Hamlet alone is a spectator by the grace of God; but he cannot find satisfaction in what he sees enacted, only in his own fate.' In what Benjamin calls 'the silver-glance of self-awareness,' Hamlet turns his glance to his own observation, he turns his glance and turns to his glance itself and hence to the intentional form under which the world must appear as mournful. But in his silver-glance – in his sidelong glance – precisely this form, the intentionality of the subject, is dissolved and lets the 'mournful images transform themselves into a blessed existence' (Walter Benjamin, *Gesammelte Schriften*, I: 1, pp. 334–5) [The English translation, here slightly modified, is from *The Origins of German Tragic Drama*, trans. John Osborne, (London: NLB, 1977), pp. 157–8]. However different the playful self-observation of the person in the English tragedy and the Hegelian play with the comic persona may be, both have to do with the analysis and dissolution of the subject and with its foundation in a movement or a topography that cannot be reduced to the subject, substantial or intentional. Benjamin is concerned with a similar gesture in his Kafka essay of 1934, where he writes of the 'Nature Theater of Oklahoma' in Kafka's *America*: 'all that is expected of the applicants is the ability to play themselves. It is no longer within the realm of possibility that they could, if necessary, be what they claim to be. With their roles these people look for a position in the Nature Theater just as Pirandello's six characters sought an author. For all of them this place is the last refuge, which does not preclude it from being their salvation' (Ibid., vol. II 2, pp. 422–3) [The English translation is from Walter Benjamin, *Illuminations*, trans. Harry Zohn (New York: Schocken, 1969), pp. 124–5]. Whoever plays himself, in Benjamin's account, can for precisely this reason not *be* himself – and has precisely therefore evaded the fixation onto a self and, perhaps, been saved from it. Kafka's Nature Theater does not present a comedy, but very much like in Hegel's theory of comedy, it is about the possibility of – and if not the salvation, then the dissolution of – the self and its ab-solution.

5 With the same sense of *Leichtsinn*, Hegel writes at the beginning of the chapter on 'Art-Religion': 'The complete fulfillment of the moral life in free self-consciousness,

and the destiny of the moral world, are therefore that individuality which has entered into itself; the condition is one of absolute levity on the part of the moral spirit; it has dissipated and resolved into itself all the firmly established distinctions constituting its own stability, and the separate spheres of its own articulated organization, and, being perfectly sure of itself, has attained to boundless cheerfulness of heart and the freest enjoyment of itself' (389; 710–11).

6 G. W. F. Hegel, *Vorlesungen über die Ästhetik*, vol. III in *Werke*, vol. 15, ed. Moldenhauser/Michel (Frankfurt/M.: Suhrkamp, 1970), p. 572. [My translation, K. B.]

7 Ibid., p. 573.

8 Ibid., p. 553.

9 Ibid., p. 572.

10 Ibid., p. 528.

11 *Vorlesungen über die Ästhetik*, vol. I, p. 97.

12 G. W. F. Hegel, *Grundlinien der Philosophie des Rechts*, Helmut Reichelt (ed.) (Frankfurt/Berlin/Vienna: Ullstein Verlag, 1972), p. 140 (§140).

13 Friedrich Schlegel, *Kritische Ausgabe*, vol. I (Paderborn: Schöningh) p. 30. [My translation, K. B.]

14 *Athenäum*, vol. 2 (Rowohlt Taschenbuch), p. 243. [My translation, K. B.]

15 On Schlegel, cf. my study 'Position Exposed' in W. H. *Premises* (Cambridge, Mass.: Harvard University Press, 1997).

16 Adorno's theory of art draws, with the greatest candor and least reserve, one of the consequences of the liberation – that is, the indetermination – of the end. The pertinent text I refer to here is the short essay from 1967 'Is Art Lighthearted?' which discusses, among other things, the possibility of comedy in modernity: 'A withering away of the alternative between lightheartedness and seriousness, between the tragic and the comic, almost between life and death, is becoming evident in contemporary art. With this, art negates its whole past, doubtless because the familiar alternative expresses a situation divided between the happiness of survival and the catastrophe that forms the medium for that survival. . . . Art that is beyond lightheartedness and seriousness may be as much a figure of reconciliation as a figure of horror. . . . The art that moves ahead into the unknown, the only art now possible, is neither lighthearted nor serious; the third possibility, however, is cloaked in obscurity, as though embedded in a void the figures of which are traced by advanced works of art' (*Noten zur Literatur IV*, Frankfurt/M.: Suhrkamp, 1981, pp. 605 ff.). [The English translation is from *Notes to Literature*, trans. Shierry Weber Nicholsen (New York: Columbia University Press, 1992), p. 253.]

17 The only commentator whom the connection between comedy and Christianity has not entirely escaped is likely Alexandre Kojève. As capricious and distorting as many of his interpretations turn out, particularly his attempts at actualization, his attention to the construction of the system allows him to observe the transition between the end of art-religion and revealed religion. At the same time, his presentation of their relation is symptomatically lax: 'It is the same actual life

which reflects itself in the comedy that has given birth to Christianity: "bourgeois" life. Comedy, which has shown the possibility of secular life, sublates itself as comedy; what remains is bourgeois man, who takes himself seriously and lives the life that was presented to him in the comedy: it is the Christian bourgeois man who does Christian theology' (*Introduction à la lecture de Hegel*, Paris: Gallimard, 1968, p. 255). [My translation, K. B.]

## Chapter 5: Eating My God

1 Much of the menu that follows here is borrowed – but then who owns a recipe? – from Werner Hamacher's work on this same essay and related texts. See 'pleroma: Zu Genesis und Struktur einer dialektischen Hermeneutik bei Hegel' in *Der Geist des Christentums* (Frankfurt am Main: Ullstein, 1978). A translation of this text is due to be published by Stanford University Press.

2 Another alternative approach to this essay is suggested by Walter Kaufmann: 'The essay has little originality or importance. . . . While Schelling, as Hegel was to put it later, carried on his education public, issuing book after book, sometimes several in one year, Hegel filed this latest attempt in a desk drawer, where it belonged.' *Hegel: A Reinterpretation* (Notre Dame: University of Notre Dame Press, 1978), p. 38.

3 Gisela Schüler, 'Zur Chronologie von Hegels Jugendschriften,' *Hegel Studien* 2 (1963), p. 149.

4 H. S. Harris, *Hegel's Development: Towards the Sunlight 1770–1801* (Oxford: Oxford University Press, 1972), pp. 330–1. Harris differs from Schüler in arguing that the essay does not even begin where is should begin. The proper beginning, Harris argues, is the fragment beginning *Abraham in Chaldäa geboren hatte schon*.

5 Or perhaps it is the essay in the strictest sense. For further consideration of the essay as anti-genre, see Theodor Adorno, 'Der Essay als Form,' *Noten zur Literatur* (Frankfurt am Main: Suhrkamp Verlag, 1981), pp. 9–33 and Geoffrey Hartman, *Minor Prophecies: The Literary Essay in the Culture Wars* (Cambridge, Mass.: Harvard University Press, 1991).

6 In a different context Carol Jacobs addresses the same issues in 'Allegories of Reading Paul de Man,' *Reading de Man Reading*, Lindsay Waters and Wlad Godzich (eds) (Minneapolis: University of Minnesota Press, 1989), pp. 105–20.

7 Yet the question remains: how does one read Hegel? As Adorno reminds us, one of the persistent questions Hegel in turn forces upon us is: what is reading *überhaupt*? See *Drei Studien zu Hegel* in *Gesammelte Schriften*, vol. 5 (Frankfurt am Main: Suhrkamp Verlag, 1975). See in particular 'Skoteinos oder Wie zu lesen sei,' pp. 326–75.

8 As Gerard Lebrun notes: 'Souvent, dans l'intention d'accuser l'inspiration théologique du Système hégèlien ou les préoccupations religieuses qui y demeureraient vivantes, on a minimisé la violence antichrétienne des écrits de jeunesse.' *La patience du Concept* (Paris: Gallimard, 1972), p. 23.

9 Hegel, *Early Theological Writings*, trans. T. M. Knox (Chicago: University of Chicago

Press, 1948), p. 185. Hereafter referred to in the text as K. *Hegel's Theologische Jugendschriften*, Herman Nohl (ed.) (Tübingen: Mohr [Paul Siebeck], 1907), p. 245–6. Hereafter referred to in the text as N.

10 Bernard Bourgeois notes in *Hegel à Francfort ou Judaïsme–Christianisme–Hegelianisme* (Paris: Vrin, 1970): 'Bref, la moralité n'est que l'intériorisation de la relation maître-servitude. L'universel kantien, c'est le maître intérieur; Kant, c'est bien encore Abraham' (p. 60).

11 This note is not included in Knox's translation. The translation here is my own.

12 I employ '(im)part' to draw on the resonances of Jean-Luc Nancy's use of the term 'partage,' usually translated as 'sharing.' See Michael Holland's discussion of this term in a footnote to his translation of Nancy's 'Of Divine Places' in Jean-Luc Nancy, *The Inoperative Community*, Peter Connor (ed.) (Minneapolis: University of Minnesota Press, 1991), pp. 168–9.

13 Knox's translation is indeed more elegant and more logical: 'love him as the man whom thou art.' Yet it smooths over the philosophically significant slippage in grammar. This slippage does not escape Derrida: 'Love has no other: love your neighbor as yourself does not imply that you must love your neighbor as much as you. Self-love is 'a word without sense (*ein Wort ohne Sinn*).' Love your neighbor as one (*als einen*) who is you or 'that you is (*der du ist*).' The difference between the two statements is difficult to determine. If self-love had no sense, what would it mean (to say) to love the other as one that you is? Or who is you? One can love the other only as an other, but in love there is no longer alterity, only *Vereinigung*. Here the value of neighbor (*Nächsten*) foils this opposition of the I to the You as other.' *Glas*, trans. John P. Leavey, Jr and Richard Rand (Lincoln: University of Nebraska Press, 1986), p. 64. (p. 76)

14 As Werner Hamacher notes in *pleroma*: 'Im Mahl sind die Teile das Ganze. Jeder einzelne Bissen vom Brot *ist* das Brot, ist Christus und ist die Gemeinschaft der Esser. Jeder einzelne Schluck vom Wein ist der Wein, das Leben Christi, die Versammlung der Trinkenden. . . . Aber: Jeder einzelne Biß vom Brot *ißt* das Brot, *ißt* Christus und *ißt* die Gemeinschaft der Esser' (p. 121).

15 As Bernard Bourgeois notes: 'La communauté chrétienne tout entière est tournée vers l'amour intérieur de ses membres, mais elle est incapable de s'unir en vue d'un autre but, d'un autre objectif, qui serait effectivement pour elle un *ob-jet*, quelque chose d'*autre* que sa propre indétermination, c'est-à-dire une œuvre déterminée' (p. 81).

16 As Bourgeois acutely remarks: 'L'amour est la première manifestation de l'*universel concret* – identité de l'identité et de la différence – dans la réflexion hégélienne, l'anticipation de ce qui sera désigné plus tard comme l'*esprit*' (p. 64).

17 Ironically, it could be argued that communion itself is part of the failure to achieve community. As Monika K. Hellwig notes in her article on the eucharist in *The Encyclopedia of Religion*: 'It is paradoxical that the Eucharist is the sacrament of unity for Christians yet is a sign and cause of disunity among denominations. In general denominations exclude others from their eucharistic table, usually on account of

theological differences' (*The Encyclopedia of Religion*, Mircea Eliade (ed.) vol. 5 [New York: Macmillan, 1987], p. 186).

18 A recent instance of this ambition is William Gibson's *Agrippa: A Book of the Dead*, a brief narrative on disk that destroyed itself as one read it. I had merely read about this narrative – that is, until I came across a copy of the text of this narrative while browsing through the Internet and was able to download it. In ways (perhaps) beyond what Gibson intended, *Agrippa* is indeed a book of the dead, as all books are, for the signifier will endure, persist beyond, and haunt every reading.

19 In *pleroma,* Werner Hamacher links this process of reading to melancholy: 'Alles Lesen ist traurig, weil es die Erfahrung der Unvereinbarkeit des Leichnams der Schrift, in dem der Gedanke zur äußerlichen Form erstarrt ist, und seiner subjektiven Verlebendigung im Verstehen durchzuarbeiten hat. Lesen ist die Arbeit der Trauer über den Verslust dieser von Objektivierung. Subjektivität, den der Akt der Lektüre selber bewirkt. Es ist deshalb potentiell Unendlich, Melancholie, weil es selber den Riß wiederholt, des es zu schließen sich müht' ('pleroma,' pp. 123–4).

## Chapter 6: The Remnants of Philosophy: Psychoanalysis After *Glas*

1 Sarah Kofman, 'Ça cloche,' a talk on *Glas* delivered in 1980 at the Colloque de Cérisy – 'Les Fins de l'homme' and later published in *Les Fins de l'homme: à partir du travail de Jacques Derrida*, p. 113 – all translations from the French, unless otherwise indicated, are my own. The remark quoted above was made during the discussion following her talk and applies, in particular, to the concept of fetishism, which for Kofman is the principal element linking Derrida's Hegel and Derrida's Freud.

2 Derrida's willingness to embrace the label 'critical' to characterize deconstruction and at the same time his reservations with respect to it are evident in a passage from an interview in which he describes his own procedure in *Glas*: '[Deconstruction] can have, it has had critical and even scientific powers. It retains these powers within certain limits. It is even essentially *critical* (but deconstruction is not a critical operation, critique is its object; deconstruction always bears, at one moment or another, on the confidence in critical or critical–theoretical authority, that is to say in an authority that decides and in the ultimate possibility of decidability; deconstruction is deconstruction of dogmatic critique)' ('Ja, ou le faux-bond,' *Points de suspension* [Paris: Galilée, 1992], p. 60).

3 In the discussion following Kofman's talk, Derrida made the following remark: 'Can the passage from *Glas* on Freud's concept of fetishism play the role of a central lever and can the generalization of fetishism constitute the key to the text? In the first place, there are in *Glas* not one but *two* analyses of the text on fetishism, in the two columns – a "duplicity" which counts. In the second place, my concern was not to privilege any point in passing. I thus resist the gesture of making it into the key to the text. Because one could do the same thing, for example, with the Hegelian theory of fetishism, etc.' Kofman responded: 'Generalized fetishism is not a transcendental key for me either. But many things become clear when one rereads

*Glas* on the basis of this premise. And it does not seem to me that one could do the same work in terms of Hegelian fetishism, without having already, as you have, read Hegel in terms of Freud.' To which Derrida responded: 'It's a fact and, empirically, I could not have written [*Glas*] without knowing a bit of Freud' (p. 113).

4 Jacques Derrida, *Glas* (Paris: Galilée, 1974), pp. 130, 113e. Translations from the French edition of *Glas* are my own. Each quotation from *Glas* is followed by two page references, the first to the French edition and the second to the corresponding passage in the English translation (the reference to the English translation is followed by an 'e'): Jacques Derrida, *Glas*, trans. John P. Leavey, Jr. and Richard Rand (Lincoln: University of Nebraska Press, 1986). Unless otherwise noted, quotations are from the Hegel column.

5 In making her assumptions about fear and the role it supposedly plays in fetishism Kofman also assumes a great deal concerning the character of infantile narcissism. In a manner that recalls Freud's texts on female sexuality, she takes it for granted that infantile narcissism is fundamentally libidinal and thereby turns her back on the problem of primary masochism and the role it could potentially play in a scene such as the one she describes.

6 Sigmund Freud, 'Some Psychological Consequences of the Anatomical Difference Between the Sexes,' XIX, p. 257.

7 For a fuller discussion of the relationship between Freud's attempt to theorize repression and his interpretation of femininity, see Chapter 4 of my *Interrupted Dialectic: Philosophy, Psychoanalysis, and Their Tragic Other* (Baltimore: Johns Hopkins University Press, 1992), pp. 97–132.

8 In *Eperons: les Styles de Nietzsche* (Paris: Flammarion, 1978) Derrida discusses the term 'the feminine' in the following passage, which fuses his own perspective and style with that of Nietzsche: 'That which in truth cannot be grasped is *feminine*, a term that one should not hasten to translate by 'femininity,' the 'femininity of the woman,' 'feminine sexuality' or other essentialist fetishes that are precisely what one thinks are being grasped when one settles for the foolishness of the dogmatic philosopher, the impotent artist, or the inexperienced seducer. . . . Let's not even say the feminine. [Let's say rather] the 'feminine operation' (p. 43).

It should be noted, however, that elsewhere Derrida has indicated a willingness to embrace several apparently divergent paths to the question of 'the feminine.' He has done this, moreover, in language that stresses the importance not so much of identifying the appropriate terms for raising this question but rather of maintaining a critical perspective that can itself embrace several different terms, even of the most traditional type: 'In brief, you see, like the unconscious – the unconscious that I am – I do not want to give up anything.

1. Neither what has been just said *about* sexual difference (2+n, beyond phallogocentrism, beyond oppositional dialectics, beyond psychoanalytic philosophy when it repeats that phallocentrism).

2. Nor a re-elaboration of what is "psychoanalytic" – in other words, no looking back in this respect.

3. Nor an attentive opening (by contrast to what is happening in the "world" of

psychoanalysis) onto all new forms of knowledge about the "body," about "biology," without considering as "closed" the so-called "anatomical" case' ('voice ii. . . ,' *Boundary Two*, v. XII, n. 2 (Winter 1984), pp. 89–91. Translation modified).

9   Jacques Derrida, 'Freud and the Scene of Writing,' p. 197.

10  'In order to avoid empiricism first of all and by all means, Kant had to confine his transcendental discourse to a world of constituted ideal objects whose correlate was therefore itself a constituted subject. This protohistory [of the constituted subject], whose notion is made contradictory but at the same time necessary by all of Kantian philosophy, becomes a theme [in its own right] for Husserl' (Jacques Derrida, 'Introduction,' in Edmund Husserl, *L'Origine de la géométrie*, p. 25.

11  Of course, this passage from *Glas* represents a decidedly different position from that taken in the 'Introduction' with respect to the status of Husserl. In the earlier essay, Derrida stressed the critical value of Husserl's work from the *Krisis* on, and contrasted Husserl with Kant, while in the passage from *Glas* quoted here, Derrida stresses the affinity between Husserl and Kant.

12  See, for example, *L'Origine de la géométrie*, p. 25.

13  G. W. F. Hegel, *Phenomenology of Spirit*, p. 275.

14  G. W. F. Hegel, *Philosophy of Right*, p. 115.

15  In a spirit similar to that in which Derrida brings forward the numerous Hegelian terms that overlap with or are related to Hegel's concept of restriction, it is important to note that the central Freudian concept of repression overlaps similarly with a number of related concepts, none of which can be wholly reduced to any other. In their *Vocabulaire de la psychanalyse* (Paris: Presses Universitaires de France, 1967), Jean Laplanche and J.-B. Pontalis stress the relative elasticity of this central Freudian term, which at times seems to be limited to meaning one form of a more general process of 'defense,' and at other times seems itself to provide the general model for all of the defensive mechanisms: 'The part is then taken for the whole' (p. 392). They go on to note Freud's differentiation, under the umbrella of a single concept of repression, of three distinct, albeit related, processes: a primary repression, a repression proper, and the return of the repressed. Additionally, they note that repression concerns psychic representations of the drives, but does not concern affect, which is instead 'suppressed.' André Green's *Le Discours vivant* (Paris: Presses Universitaires de France, 1973) suggests that he might dispute this latter assertion, or at least find it somewhat simplistic, since he notes that according to Freud affect is also turned into its opposite and even that it escapes dream-censorship or repression (pp. 48–50). But Green would doubtlessly agree with Laplanche and Pontalis that the case of affect nonetheless necessitates an additional refinement – and complication – of the notion of repression. Taken together, these various refinements clearly call for a more systematic and detailed discussion. Nonetheless, even the most cursory consideration of them in their diversity suggests that the concept of repression is not exemplified in its purity in any single instance of repression, even a 'primary' one. This is why the notion of repression is ultimately indissociable from a dynamic and open or undetermined model of the psyche, in which repression and 'what is repressed' are indistinguishable.

16 Derrida makes a similar affirmation in a more succinct form when he writes: 'Prohibition and repression are thus thinkable. . .as effects of sublation. The *Aufhebung* would thus dominate the process [of repression]' (pp. 224–5, 200e–1e).

17 Jacques Lacan, 'Aggressivity in Psychoanalysis,' p. 21.

18 The ambiguous alterity which describes Antigone's relation to the transcendental system in *Glas* is also conveyed through Derrida's use of the image of the crypt, of which he writes elsewhere: 'Whatever one writes on them, the parietal surfaces of the crypt do not simply separate an interior depth [*for intérieur*] from an exterior depth [*for extérieur*]. They make the interior depth an outside included in the interior of the inside' ('Fors,' *Cryptonymie: Le Verbier de l'homme aux loups* (Paris: Aubier Flammarion, 1976) p. 13.

19 Jacques Derrida, 'Le Facteur de la vérité,' p. 481.

20 'The letter – place of the signifier – is found in the place where Dupin and the psychoanalyst expect to find it: on the immense body of the woman, between the "legs" of the fireplace. Such is its proper place, the terminus of its circular itinerary. . . . This determination of the proper, of the law of the proper, of *economy*, therefore leads back to castration as truth, to the figure of the woman as the figure of castration *and* of truth' ('Le Facteur,' pp. 440–1).

21 In the passage in question, the expression 'to take on' ('prendre en charge') clearly has two senses: both 'to challenge' and also 'to assume or accept for oneself.'

22 For a fuller discussion of the manner in which Hegelian philosophy and Freudian psychoanalysis are shaped by their interpretations of tragedy, see the Introduction and Chapters II, III, and IV of my *Interrupted Dialectic: Philosophy, Psychoanalysis, and Their Tragic Other.*

## Works Cited in Text

Derrida, Jacques. 'Le Facteur de la vérité,' *The Post Card*, trans. Alan Bass. Chicago: University of Chicago Press, 1987.

———— 'Freud and the Scene of Writing,' *Writing and Difference*, trans. Alan Bass. Chicago: University of Chicago Press, 1978.

———— *Glas*. Paris: Galilée, 1974.

———— 'Introduction,' in Edmund Husserl, *L'Origine de la géométrie*. Paris: Presses Universitaires de France, 1962.

———— 'To Speculate – on "Freud",' *The Post Card*, trans. Alan Bass. Chicago: University of Chicago Press, 1987.

Freud, Sigmund. *The Standard Edition of the Complete Psychological Works of Sigmund Freud*, trans. James Strachey. London: Hogarth Press, 1953.

———— *Civilization and Its Discontents*, v. XXI.

———— *The Interpretation of Dreams*, v. IV, V.

———— 'Some Psychological Consequences of the Anatomical Distinction Between the Sexes,' v. XIX.

Hegel, G. W. F. *Phenomenology of Spirit*, trans. A. V. Miller. Oxford: Oxford University Press, 1977.

———— *Philosophy of Right*, trans. T. M. Knox. Oxford: Oxford University Press, 1977.

Lacan, Jacques. 'Aggressivity in Psychoanalysis,' *Ecrits: A Selection*, trans. Alan Sheridan. New York: Norton, 1977.

Laplanche, Jean and Pontalis, J.-B. *Vocabulaire de la psychanalyse*. Paris: Presses Universitaires de France, 1967.

Kofman, Sarah. 'Ça cloche,' *Les Fins de l'homme: à partir du travail de Jacques Derrida*. Paris: Galilée, 1981.

## Chapter 7: Hegel/Marx: Consciousness and Life

1  Marginal note by Marx in: Karl Marx and Frederick Engels, *The German Ideology*, vol. 5 of *Collected Works* (New York: International Publishers, 1976), p. 91. The German can be found in Karl Marx, *Die Frühschriften,* (ed.) Siegfried Landshut (Stuttgart: Alfred Kröner, 1971), p. 411.

2  *The German Ideology*, p. 37. *Die Frühschriften*, p. 349.

3  *The German Ideology*, p. 41. *Die Frühschriften*, pp. 353–4.

4  For the distinction between simple and overdetermined contradiction, our reference is, of course, Louis Althusser, 'Contradiction and Overdetermination,' in *For Marx* (New York: Vintage, 1970), pp. 87–128.

5  *The German Ideology*, p. 36. *Die Frühschriften*, p.348.

6  *The German Ideology*, p. 43–4. *Die Frühschriften*, pp. 353–7.

7  *The German Ideology*, p. 45. *Die Frühschriften*, p. 358.

8  An extended reading of the fourth Thesis on Feuerbach – which is itself something of a 'rhetorical reading' of Feuerbach – would be necessary here. For some indications on how ideology is to be read as self-undoing trope, see our 'Ending Up / Taking Back (with two postscripts on Paul de Man's historical materialism),' in *Critical Encounters: Reference and Responsibility in Deconstructive Writing*, Cathy Caruth and Deborah Esch (eds) (New Brunswick: Rutgers University Press, 1994), and my 'Introduction' in Paul de Man, *Aesthetics, Rhetoric, Ideology*, Andrzej Warminski (ed.) (Minneapolis: University of Minnesota Press, 1996).

9  For an attempt at an 'allegorical reading' of what one could call Hegel's 'ideology of consciousness' in the *Phenomenology of Spirit*, see below. Althusser's famous statement that 'ideology represents the imaginary relationship of individuals to their real conditions of existence' could be read as very much consistent with our account of it as an 'allegorical' language. That is, ideology 'represents' all right, but what it represents (in distorted form or otherwise) is *not* the real conditions, but rather the *imaginary relation to* those real conditions. This is why an operation of demystification can uncover only the *imaginary* relations and *not* the real conditions. A second operation is necessary to read not what ideology *represents* but what it actually *means*. Cf. Louis Althusser, 'Ideology and Ideological State

Apparatuses,' in *Lenin and Philosophy*, trans. Ben Brewster (New York and London: New Left Books, 1971).

10 That is, one of the 'ingredients' that went into producing 'Marx' (again, *as* Marx) would be missing. Cf. Louis Althusser, 'Marx's Relation to Hegel,' in *Montesquieu, Rousseau, Marx, Politics and History*, trans. Ben Brewster (London: Verso, 1982), p. 170: 'Which means very schematically that Marx (*Capital*) is the product of the work of Hegel (German Philosophy) on English Political Economy + French Socialism, in other words, the *Hegelian dialectic* on: *Labour theory of value* (R) + *the class struggle* (FS).'

11 'Science of the Experience of Consciousness' is, of course, one of the titles of the book that came to be called *The Phenomenology of Spirit*. On the question of the titles (and the title-pages) – a question that, when read, not only renders the *Phenomenology*'s place within Hegel's system most uncanny but also threatens to destabilize that system's coherence – see: Otto Pöggeler, 'Zur Deutung der Phänomenologie des Geistes,' in *Hegels Idee einer Phänomenologie des Geistes* (Freiburg/Munich: Karl Alber, 1973), and our 'Parentheses: Hegel by Heidegger,' in *Readings in Interpretation* (Minneapolis: University of Minnesota Press, 1987).

12 One example would be Richard Norman in his otherwise very helpful and extremely clear *Hegel's Phenomenology, A Philosophical Introduction* (London: Chatto & Windus for Sussex University Press, 1976), p. 46: 'The section on 'Self-certainty' is extremely unrewarding, and since I find large parts of it unintelligible I shall say little about it. The one important point to be gleaned from it is the claim that in order to be conscious of one's own existence one must experience *desire*. . . . The experience of desire, however, does not constitute self-consciousness in the full sense. Why is this? In 'Self-certainty' Hegel offers a preliminary explanation, but the whole question is dealt with much more satisfactorily in the 'Master and Slave' section, to which we may now gratefully turn.'

13 See the end of the 'Introduction' to *Phenomenology of Spirit*, trans. A. V. Miller (Oxford: Oxford University Press, 1977), p. 56: 'Thus in the movement of consciousness there occurs a moment of *being-in-itself* or *being-for-us* which is not present to the consciousness comprehended in the experience itself. The *content*, however, of what presents itself to us does exist *for it*; we comprehend only the formal aspect of that content, or its pure origination. *For it*, what has thus arisen exists only as an object; *for us*, it appears at the same time as movement and a process of becoming.' The German is, as always, more precise. See G. W. F. Hegel, *Phänomenologie des Geistes*, ed. Johannes Hoffmeister (Hamburg: Felix Meiner, 1952), p. 74: 'Es kommt dadurch in seine Bewegung ein Moment des *Ansich- oder Fürunsseins*, welches nicht für das Bewußtsein, das in der Erfahrung selbst begriffen ist, sich darstellt; der *Inhalt* aber dessen, was uns entsteht, ist *für es*, und wir begreifen nur das Formelle desselben oder sein reines Entstehen; *für es* ist dies Entstandene nur als Gegenstand, *für uns* zugleich als Bewegung und Werden.'

14 See Alexandre Kojève, *Introduction à la lecture de Hegel* (Paris: Galimard, 1947) and Jean Hyppolite, 'The Concept of Existence in the Hegelian Phenomenology,' in

*Studies on Marx and Hegel*, (ed. and trans. by John O' Neill) ( New York: Harper & Row, 1973).

15  That the testing of (various figures of) apparent knowing is also always a test of the object of that knowing is stated with all possible clarity in the thirteenth paragraph (#85 in Miller's numbering) of the 'Introduction' to the *Phenomenology* (p. 54): 'But, in fact, in the alteration of the knowledge, the object itself alters for it too, for the knowledge that was present was essentially a knowledge of the object: as the knowledge changes, so too does the object, for it essentially belonged to this knowledge. . . . Since consciousness thus finds that its knowledge does not correspond to its object, the object itself does not stand the test; in other words, the criterion for testing is altered when that for which it was to have been the criterion fails to pass the test; and the testing is not only a testing of what we know, but also a testing of the criterion of what knowledge is.' The dialectic of sense-certainty is always the clearest example: sense-certainty thinks its object is particular and that it knows this object immediately, but it turns out that its object is universal and it knows this object mediatedly. In short, sense-certainty is *not* sense-certainty but rather a form of knowing that knows its object as universal and mediated: i.e., 'perception' (*Wahrnehmung*), which now becomes the new figure of apparent knowing whose truth is to be tested.

16  *Phenomenology of Spirit*, p. 108; *Phänomenologie des Geistes*, pp. 137–8.

17  *Phenomenology of Spirit*, p. 109 (my translation); *Phänomenologie des Geistes*, p. 138.

18  The commentators who do not just skip over life's pointing in our passage and valiantly try to re-mediate the relation between life and consciousness (into a determinately negative relation) can do so only by having recourse, in one way or another, to self-consciousness, when the burden of this passage is precisely to demonstrate how it is that self-consciousness (*as* self-consciousness) is possible! One intelligent example would be that of Johannes Heinrichs in *Die Logik der 'Phänomenologie des Geistes'* (Bonn: Bouvier, 1974), p. 176: 'Wieso verweist das Leben auf die fürsichseiende, sich wissende Einheit? Der Übergang ist nicht ein solcher der Bewußtseinserfahrung, sondern ein solcher für uns. Selbst der Phänomenologie scheint hier aufgefordert, die Sache logisch zu nehmen, d.h. von der bloß ansichseienden substantiellen Einheit als Möglichkeit (Leben) zur fürsichseienden Einheit überzugehen, die das SelbstBewußtsein ist: als die sich selbst wissende und somit wissend-wirkliche Gattung seiner selbst.' Although to say that the transition takes place not for consciousness but rather for us is an ingenious solution, its questionable character becomes apparent when we remember *who* the 'we' of the *Phenomenology* is. If we follow the rigor of Hegel's logic (in the 'Introduction') to its end, it turns out that the 'we' of the phenomenological presentation – who observe the progression of consciousness through the various figures of apparent knowing and who put themselves in by leaving themselves out – are not some vague 'philosophical observers' or 'phenomenologists' but none other than self-consciousness! This is so because the single indispensable determination of the 'we' is 'our' being those who give up the position of consciousness in relation to the consciousness 'we' are observing when we realize that 'our' relation to it is a

relation *internal to* consciousness. In other words, 'we' are the negation *of* consciousness, consciousness's *self*-negation, i.e. *self*-consciousness. But the positing of this 'formal' self-consciousness has to be verified in turn when consciousness's essence and truth turn out to be self-consciousness, and this is precisely the burden of the dialectic of life and desire. In any event, a painstaking reading of the 'Introduction' is necessary to demonstrate this, and I will do so in another essay. It should be noted, however, that many interpretations of the *Phenomenology* fall short of Hegel's rigor and precision because their understanding of the 'we' is far too vague. For a helpful survey of various (insufficient) interpretations of the 'we,' see Kenley Royce Dove, 'Hegel's Phenomenological Method,' *The Review of Metaphysics* 23 (1970), 615–41.

19 Putting this disjunction in terms of 'reference' and 'phenomenalism' is intentional, for I want to mark explicitly the close relation between our reading here and Paul de Man's 'definition' of ideology in 'The Resistance to Theory' as the confusion 'of reference with phenomenalism.' See *The Resistance to Theory* (Minneapolis: University of Minnesota Press, 1986), p. 11. Indeed, the reading can be taken as just a commentary on or an elaboration of de Man's hints in this essay and in the short but packed and very difficult reading of sense-certainty in 'Hypogram and Inscription,' also in *The Resistance to Theory*, pp. 41–2: 'Consciousness ("here" and "now") is not "false and misleading" because of language; consciousness *is* language, and nothing else, because it is false and misleading. And it is false and misleading because it determines by showing (*montrer* or *démontrer, deiknumi*) or pointing (*Zeigen* or *Aufzeigen*), that is to say in a manner that implies the generality of the phenomenon as cognition (which makes the pointing possible) in the loss of the immediacy and the particularity of sensory perception (which makes the pointing necessary): consciousness is linguistic because it is deictic. Language appears explicitly for the first time in Hegel's chapter in the figure of a *speaking* consciousness. . . . The figure of a speaking consciousness is made plausible by the deictic function that it names.' For an extended reading of de Man on ideology, see my Introduction to de Man's *Aesthetic Ideology* (Minneapolis: University of Minnesota Press, 1996). For a precise understanding of the 'proper sense,' see de Man's footnote on the tripartite structure of metaphor in 'Reading (Proust),' *Allegories of Reading* (New Haven: Yale University Press, 1979), p. 65: 'When Homer calls Achilles a lion, the literal meaning of the figure signifies an animal of a yellowish brown color, living in Africa, having a mane, etc. The figural meaning signifies Achilles and the proper meaning the attribute of courage or strength that Achilles and the lion have in common and can therefore exchange.'

20 See Georges Bataille, 'Hegel, la mort et le sacrifice,' *Deucalion* 5 (October 1955), pp. 32–3: 'Pour que l'homme à la fin se révèle à lui-même il devrait mourir, mail il lui faudrait le faire en vivant – en se regardant cesser d'être. En d'autres termes, la mort elle-même devrait devenir conscience (de soi), au moment même où elle anéantit l'être conscient. C'est en un sens ce qui a lieu (qui est du moins sur le point d'avoir lieu, ou qui a lieu d'une manière fugitive, insaisissable), au moyen d'un subterfuge. Dans le sacrifice, le sacrifiant s'identifie à l'animal frappé de mort.

Ainsi meurt-il en se voyant mourir, et même en quelque sorte, par sa propre volonté, de coeur avec l'arme du sacrifice. Mais c'est une comédie!'

21 Cf. Paul de Man, *The Resistance to Theory*, p. 11: 'It would be unfortunate, for example, to confuse the materiality of the signifier with the materiality of what it signifies. This may seem obvious enough on the level of light and sound, but it is less so with regard to the more general phenomenality of space, time or especially of the self; no one in his right mind will try to grow grapes by the luminosity of the word "day," but it is very difficult not to conceive the pattern of one's past and future existence as in accordance with temporal and spatial schemes that belong to fictional narratives and not to the world. This does not mean that fictional narratives are not part of the world and of reality; their impact upon the world may well be all too strong for comfort. What we call ideology is precisely the confusion of linguistic with natural reality, of reference with phenomenalism.'

22 For Heidegger on *eidos* and the *Idea*, see his *Nietzsche, Volume I: The Will to Power as Art*, trans. David Farrell Krell (New York: Harper & Row, 1979), pp. 171–199.

23 Paul de Man, 'Genesis and Genealogy (Nietzsche),' in *Allegories of Reading*, p. 102.

24 On catachresis and its (self-)mutilations, see my 'Prefatory Postscript: Interpretation and Reading,' in *Readings in Interpretation: Hölderlin, Hegel, Heidegger* (Minneapolis: University of Minnesota Press. 1987), pp. liii–lxi.

25 The most famous successfully 'Hegelian' re-mediation of self-consciousness as desire and self-consciousness as self-consciousness – by means of a 'desire of desire,' i.e. by means of a rigorously 'Hegelian' negation of negation – would, of course, be that of Kojève. The ironies attendant upon this interpretation are many: in being more Hegelian than Hegel and 'succeeding' where Hegel 'failed,' Kojève winds up being closer to 'Hegel' than 'Hegel' is to 'Marx.' Ironically (but consistently and predictably) enough, Kojève's anthropologization of phenomenology – i.e. his identification of man and self-consciousness – ends up with neither man nor self-consciousness. That is, he ends up with the thesis of the end of man in either animal (or the automaton) or god, an utter falling apart of life and consciousness. By mediating life and consciousness – by phenomenologizing 'man' and anthropologizing 'consciousness' – successfully, Kojève ends up with an utter abstract 'materialism' (not unlike Feuerbach's) that immediately turns over into an equally abstract 'idealism.' End of man, end of history. (The moral being: real materialists do not mediate.) But a long, careful exposition of Kojève would be necessary to demonstrate this. In the end, Kojève may be the ultimate romantic ironist; and a comparison with the end of Kleist's *Marionettentheater* would be most appropriate: recall that the last chapter of the history of the world ends up with the marionette (no consciousness) or the god (infinite consciousness). See not only his *Introduction to the Reading of Hegel* but also his correspondence with Leo Strauss published in Leo Strauss, *On Tyranny*, Victor Gourevitch and Michael S. Roth (eds) (New York: The Free Press, 1991), p. 255: 'Besides, "not human" can mean "animal" (or, better – automaton) as well as "God." In the final state there naturally are no more "human beings" in our sense of an *historical* human being. The "healthy" automata are "satisfied" (sports, art, eroticism, etc.), and the

"sick" ones get locked up. As for those who are not satisfied with their "purpose-less activity" (art, etc.), they are the philosophers (who can attain wisdom if they "contemplate" enough). By doing so they become "gods." The tyrant becomes an administrator, a cog in the "machine" fashioned by automata for automata.'

26 Cf. Hegel's distinction here between that which would be death for 'natural life' and that which would be the 'death' of consciousness: 'Whatever is confined within the limits of a natural life cannot by its own efforts go beyond its immediate existence; but it is driven beyond it by something else, and this uprooting entails its death. Consciousness, however, is explicitly the *Notion* of itself. Hence it is something that goes beyond limits, and since these limits are its own, it is something that goes beyond itself. . . . Thus consciousness suffers this violence at its own hands: it spoils its own limited satisfaction' (*Phenomenology*, p. 51). The German is, as always, more precise: 'Was auf ein natürliches Leben beschränkt ist, vermag durch sich selbst nicht über sein unmittelbares Dasein hinauszugehen; aber es wird durch ein anderes darüber hinausgetrieben, und dies Hinausgerissen werden ist sein Tod. Das Bewußtsein aber ist für sich selbst sein *Begriff*, dadurch unmittelbar das Hinausgehen über das Beschränkte und, da ihm dies Beschränkte angehört, über sich selbst. . .Das Bewußtsein leidet also diese Gewalt, sich die beschränkte Befriedigung zu verderben, von ihm selbst' (*Phänomenologie*, p. 69). In a sense, at this moment of decision (i.e. cutting apart), Hegel here sets himself the task of transforming the sheer exteriority of death into a 'death' proper to consciousness: in short, he has to transform death into consciousness. This is the 'decision' that catches up to him in 'The truth of self-certainty' and needs to be verified. It is no wonder that it 'fails,' for the sheer exteriority, otherness, of death can be transformed into the *self*-limiting of life only thanks to an impossible, aberrant trope.

27 See Louis Althusser, 'On Marx and Freud,' *Rethinking Maxism* 4:1 (Spring 1991), pp. 24–5: 'In the category of the self-conscious subject, bourgeois ideology *represents* to individuals what they *must be* in order for them to accept their own submission to bourgeois ideology . . . *consciousness* is *necessary* for the individual who is endowed with it to realise within "himself" the unity required by bourgeois ideology, so that every subject will conform to its own ideological and political requirement, that of unity, in brief, so that *the conflictual violence of the class struggle will be lived by its agents as a superior and "spiritual" form of unity.*'

28 On the first sentence of the 'Einleitung' to the *Phenomology*, see my 'Parentheses: Hegel by Heidegger,' in *Readings in Interpretation: Hölderlin, Hegel, Heidegger*.

29 That our reading should, in a sense, collapse the *first* figure of self-consciousness (i.e. desire) and the last figure of self-consciousness (i.e. the unhappy conscious-ness) is no accident, for the disarticulation of the dialectic of life and consciousness would indeed mean that self-consciousness gets stuck here, as though in a stutter or a 'syncope' that can only repeat allegories of its self-erosion, the impossibilty of constituting itself as self-consciousness.

30 On this 'after-life,' see Jacques Derrida, *Les Spectres de Marx* (Paris: Flammarion,

1993). My essay was written before Derrida's text and hence could not profit from it.

31 Jacques Derrida, *Positions*, trans. Alan Bass (Chicago: University of Chicago Press, 1981), pp. 62–4, 77–8.

32 For Derrida's 'definition' of deconstruction as 'what happens,' see the 1984 interview 'Deconstruction in America: An Interview with Jacques Derrida,' *Critical Exchange* 17 (Winter 1985), 1–33.

## Chapter 8: A Commentary Upon Derrida's Reading of Hegel in *Glas*

1 Prefatory Note (1995): The following text, my earliest published piece on a philosophical topic, was commissioned to appear in a special issue of the *Bulletin of the Hegel Society of Great Britain*, on the topic, 'Hegel and Deconstruction' (No. 18, 1988, pp. 4–32). The essay was therefore aimed at a sophisticated but slightly sceptical audience of Hegel specialists, and my governing intention was to try and show, as carefully and rigorously as possible, the philosophical and scholarly seriousness of Derrida's reading of Hegel in contradistinction to certain, more playful, accounts of *Glas*. The text formed part of a much longer commentary on *Glas*, which I had the intention – long abandoned – of publishing separately as a small book. A reworked remnant of this commentary appeared under the title 'Writing the Revolution: The Politics of Truth in Genet's *Prisoner of Love*' (*Radical Philosophy*, No. 56, 1990, pp. 25–34). It is hoped that other parts of this manuscript – which deal in greater detail with the methodology of *Glas*, giving a reading of the Genet column and trying to establish a context for Derrida's reading by comparing *Glas* with Sartre's Hegelian–Kojèvian reading of Genet in *Saint Genet* – will appear in a forthcoming collection of essays to be published by Verso. The following text is here reprinted with very few modifications, although such slight revisions should not lead the reader to imagine that I am entirely sanguine about certain of my rather baroque formulations and somewhat naïve general pronouncements.

2 Maurice Blanchot, *L'écriture du désastre* (Paris: Gallimard, 1980) pp. 79–80.

3 All references to *Glas* are to the translation except where the original context is significant or where I have substantially altered the translation; in these cases, I also refer to the two-volume French paperback edition (see abbreviations). Following the practice of Derrida's translators, 'Page references to *Glas* are given in the following form: 000bi. First the page number of the translation is indicated, after which is placed an *a* to indicate the left column or a *b* to indicate the right column. If the reference is to the inserts or tattoos in the column, the *a* or *b* is followed by an *i* to indicate the insert' (GL13). I would like to thank Jay Bernstein, Peter Dews and John Llewelyn for their comments on a draft of this essay.

4 Paris: Vrin, 1970.

5 The conception of matter as that which remains outside of itself and outside the horizon of essence and the thinking of Being (Gtr22–3ai) is highly significant for

Derrida, which raises the question as to what extent a deconstructive reading could be understood as a materialist reading.

6 Derrida's relation to Jewish philosophy, theology and tradition is discussed, albeit with a rather limited and non-philosophical understanding of Derrida's work, by Susan Handelman in 'Reb Derrida's Scripture', in *The Slayers of Moses. The Emergence of Rabbinic Interpretation in Modern Literary Theory* (Albany: State University of New York Press, 1982), pp. 163–178. An expanded version of the same argument appears in *Displacement. Derrida and After*, edited by Mark Krupnick (Bloomington: Indiana University Press, 1983), pp. 98–129. It is the latter article that is discussed by Habermas in a long footnote of the *Philosophical Discourse of Modernity* (Cambridge: Polity Press, 1987) pp. 406–7, and in which Habermas finds support for his interpretation of Derrida. Habermas' thesis is that

> . . . even Derrida does not extricate himself from the constraints of the paradigm of the philosophy of the subject. . . . Derrida passes beyond Heidegger's inverted foundationalism, but remains in its path. As a result, the temporalised *Ursprungsphilosophie* takes on clearer contours. The remembrance of the messianism of Jewish mysticism and of the abandoned but well circumscribed place once assumed by the God of the Old Testament preserves Derrida, so to speak, from the political–moral insensitivity and the aesthetic tastelessness of a New Paganism spiced up with Hölderlin.
>
> (pp. 166–7)

Habermas' claim is that the deconstruction of the (Christian) metaphysics of presence is ultimately the attempt to renew a specifically Judaic relation to God. Regardless of the truth of Habermas' argument, which might be truer than he imagines, and whose crude reductionism is sadly only fuelled by Handelman's analysis, my question is: why should the accusation of Judaism be an accusation? What is the possible force of Habermas' argument?

7 For an interesting feminist reading of these passages, see Genevieve Lloyd's 'Hegel: the feminine nether world' in *The Man of Reason* (London: Methuen, 1984), pp. 80–5.

8 Cf. Freud, 'Mourning and Melancholia,' in *On Metapsychology. The Theory of Psychoanalysis* (Harmondsworth: Penguin Books, 1984), pp. 251–68.

9 Phaedrus, 247a Metaphysics, 983a.

10 Cf. *Critique of Practical Reason*, translated by Lewis White Beck (Indianapolis: Bobbs-Merrill, 1956), pp. 126–30.

11 *La voix et la phénomène* (Paris: P.U.F. 1967), p. 114.

12 I owe this formulation to conversations with Jay Bernstein.

13 Mention of Zoroaster is suggestive here and alerts the reader to the two references to Nietzsche's *Also Sprach Zarathustra* (Leipzig: Alfred Kröner Verlag, 1930. Translated by R. J. Hollingdale [Harmondsworth: Penguin Books, 1961]) that occur during the discussion of Genet (Gtr102bi & 262b). At the close of the Genet column, Derrida cites six lines from 'Before Sunrise' ('*Vor Sonnenaufgang*' p. 180–1/tr. pp. 184–5), where Zarathustra speaks to the sky, 'You abyss of light! (*Du*

*Lichtabgrund!*)' and of the god that came to him before the sun (*'Vor der Sonne'*). Zarathustra speaks of the friendship between himself and the god of light, in which they have both 'the sun in common' (*'die Sonne ist uns gemeinsam'*) and 'the vast and boundless Yes-' (*'das ungeheure unbegrenzte Ja-'*). The parallels between, on the one hand, Zarathustra and the God of Light and, on the other, Derrida and Genet are clear, even if their precise implications are not. Pulling a remark out of context, one might suggest that in *Glas*, 'you have here at your disposal, as if in contraband, everything necessary for an almost complete, literally literal (*littéralement littérale*) reading of *Zarathustra*. You can verify.'

(Gtr102bi/G143bi ).

14 Cf. Heidegger, 'Der Rückgang in den Grund der Metaphysik,' in *Was is Metaphysik?* (Frankfurt: Vittorio Klostermann, 1969), pp. 19–20. Translated by Walter Kaufmann as 'The Way Back into the Ground of Metaphysics' in *Existentialism from Dostoevsky to Sartre* (New York: Meridian, 1975), pp. 275–6. Further page references given in the text.

15 Cf. Gtr11–12ai, 20a, 22–3ai, 57a; and references to onto-theo-logy (33a), the history of Being (94a), and an earlier important reference to *Zeit und Sein* (167a), which occurs, significantly enough, during the discussion of *Antigone*.

16 But what holocaust is Derrida discussing here? Is it the Greco-Christian ecclesiastical notion of *to holocauston*, a burnt offering, or the *Shoah*, or indeed both at once? If Derrida is referring to the *Shoah* with the word holocaust, then – and here one need only allude to debates current within Holocaust studies – would this not unwittingly constitute a Hellenization or Christianization of the *Shoah*, its assimilation into the language of Greek metaphysics? The deliberateness of Derrida's translation of *Opfer* by *holocauste* leads one to conclude that he is discussing the *Shoah* in terms of the gift and the sacrifice. But is this a felicitous language in which to discuss the *Shoah*? And, perversely, what of Heidegger's intervention in this context? What of Heidegger's much discussed silence or near silence on the Holocaust? And what of Derrida's use of the notion of *es gibt Sein* to open up the non-metaphysical thought of the gift or holocaust in Hegel? To what extent can and does Heidegger think the Holocaust?

17 On the issue of an ethics of sacrifice with reference to the 'Heidegger affair' see Emmanuel Levinas's 'Mourir Pour' in *Heidegger. Questions Ouvertes* (Paris: Editions Osiris, 1988), pp. 254–64.

18 Cf. Heidegger, 'Das Wesen der Sprache,' in *Unterwegs zur Sprache* (Pfullingen: Neske, 1959), pp. 159–61. Translated by Peter D. Hertz as 'The Nature of Language' in *On the Way to Language* (New York: Harper & Row, 1971), pp. 57–9.

## Chapter 9: On Derrida's Hegel Interpretation

1 TN: First published as 'Über Derridas Hegeldeutung' in *Philosophie und Poesie: Otto Pöggeler zum 60. Geburtstag.* Annemarie Gethmann-Siefert (ed.) (Stuttgart: Fromman-Holzboog Verlag, 1988), pp. 415–32. Translated and published by permission of the author and the publisher.

2 Jacques Derrida, *Writing and Difference*, trans. Alan Bass (Chicago: University of Chicago Press, 1978), p. 296.

3 See Jacques Derrida, *The Post Card*, trans. Alan Bass (Chicago: University of Chicago Press, 1987).

4 TN: Kimmerle uses the German 'Rest' the virtual homophone for the French 'reste,' which is the word and concept – as employed by Derrida in *Glas* – that Kimmerle addresses here. To maintain this allusion in English, I have adopted 'remain(s),' the rendition used by John P. Leavey, Jr and Richard Rand in the English translation of *Glas*.

5 Jacques Derrida, *Parages* (Paris: Galilée, 1986), p. 9.

6 See Jacques Derrida, *Schibboleth: Pour Paul Celan* (Paris: Galilée, 1986).

7 See 'From Restricted to General Economy: A Hegelianism Without Reserve,' in *Writing and Difference*, trans. Alan Bass (Chicago: University of Chicago Press, 1978), pp. 251–77.

8 See Bataille, 'Hegel, Death and Sacrifice,' trans. Jonathan Strauss, *Yale French Studies* 78(1990), pp. 9–28.

9 See *Phänomenologie des Geistes*, Johannes Hoffmeister (ed.) (Hamburg: Meiner, 1952), pp. 464–72. 401–09.

10 Bataille, pp. 20–3.

11 Ibid., pp. 23–5.

12 Ibid., p. 24.

13 Hegel, *Enzyclopädie*, Friedhelm Nicolin and Otto Pöggeler (eds) (Hamburg: Meiner, 1959), p. 463. (§577).

14 Theodor W. Adorno, *Negative Dialektik* (Frankfurt: Suhrhamp, 1966), pp. 31–5; pp. 311–13.

15 Bataille, p. 20–1.

16 'Hegel, Death and Sacrifice,' p. 40 f.

17 Bataille, *La part maudite* (Paris: Editions de Minuit, 1965), pp. 110–15. See also Marcel Mauss, *Die Gabe: Form und Funktion des Austausches in archaischen Gesellschaften* (Frankfurt: Suhrkamp, 1990), p. 77–119.

18 TN: 'Completion' translates the German 'Abarbeitung.' It is important to note that this word also means the wearing down, the working off of a material such as wood or stone. Thus nature's completion should be understood as part of a process of paring down what is 'inessential.'

19 See Hegel, *Grundlinien der Philosophie des Rechts*, Johannes Hoffmeister (ed.) (Hamburg: Meiner, 1967), p. 150 (§161).

20 *Glas*, p. 61.

21 I am indebted to Hans Christian Lucas for drawing my attention to this matter.

22 *Glas*, p. 45.

23 Hegel, *Jenaer Systementwürfe I*, Klaus Düsing and Heinz Kimmerle (eds) (Hamburg: Meiner, 1985), p. 228.

24 Hegel, *System der Sittlichkeit*, Georg Lasson (ed.) (Hamburg: Meiner, 1967), p. 17.

25 *Glas*, p. 145.

26 *Phenomenologie*, pp. 339–40. 228.

27 See *Glas*, p. 133.
28 *Phänomenologie*, p. 526. See also p. 548, 457, 478.
29 See Karl Rosenkranz, *Hegels Leben* (Berlin, 1944), p. 139.
30 See Hegel, *Enzyklopädie*, pp. 447–577 (§§547–77).
31 *Glas*, p. 221.
32 See *Glas*, p. 228 left column; *Phenomenology*, pp. 558, 486–7.
33 *Glas*, p. 262.

## Chapter 10: Hegelian Dialectic and the Quasi-Transcendental in *Glas*

1 References to the works of Derrida and Hegel are included in the text according to the following scheme of abbreviation. Citations include the pagination of the original followed by that of the English translation, separated by a slash (/). While the standard translations have generally been followed, revisions have been made.

### *Jacques Derrida*

D  *La dissémination* (Paris, 1972).
   *Dissemination*, trans. Barbara Johnson (Chicago, 1981).
ED *L'écriture et la différence* (Paris, 1967).
   *Writing and Difference*, trans. Alan Bass (Chicago, 1978).
G  *Glas* (2 vols) (Paris, 1981).
   *Glas*, trans. John P. Leavey, Jr and Richard Rand (Lincoln, Neb., 1986).
   [Note: I have used the Denoël two-volume edition of this work. *Glas* was originally published in one volume by Galilée in 1974. Its columns are indicated by 'a' for the left-hand and 'b' for the right.]
DG *De la grammatologie* (Paris, 1967).
   *Of Grammatology*, trans. Gayatri Chakravorty Spivak (Baltimore, 1974).
M  *Marges de la philosophie* (Paris, 1972).
   *Margins of Philosophy*, trans. Alan Bass (Chicago, 1982).
P  *Positions* (Paris, 1972).
   *Positions*, trans. Alan Bass (Chicago, 1981).

### *G. W. F. Hegel*

GW  *Gesammelte Werke. Kritische Ausgabe*, (ed.) Deutsche Forschungsgemeinschaft im Verbindung mit Rheinisch-Westflischen Akademie der Wissenschaften (Hamburg, 1968–).
    [Note: cited by abbreviation followed by volume number.]
PhG *Phänomenologie des Geistes*, Wolfgang Bonsiepen and Reinhard Heede (eds) (Hamburg, 1980), GW 9.

*Phenomenology of Spirit*, trans. A. V. Miller (Oxford, 1977).

WL *Wissenschaft der Logik, Erster Band: Die Objective Logik (1812/1813)*, Friedrich Hogemann and Walter Jaeschke (eds) (Hamburg, 1978), GW 11.
*Science of Logic*, trans. A. V. Miller (Atlantic Highlands, NJ, 1969).

2  The concept of clôture in Derrida may be said to encompass both of the enigmas that I will attempt to explore in this essay. On this important notion see Simon Critchley, 'The Problem of Closure in Derrida (Part One),' *Journal of the British Society for Phenomenology* 23 (1992): 3–19; and 'The Problem of Closure in Derrida (Part Two),' *Journal of the British Society for Phenomenology* 23 (1992): 127–45.

3  This description of the Hegelian system is, of course, taken from Heidegger's 'Die onto-theologische Verfassung der Metaphysik,' in his *Identität und Differenz* (Stuttgart, 1957); 'The Onto-theo-logical Constitution of Metaphysics,' trans. Joan Stambaugh in *Identity and Difference* (New York, 1969). This essay, along with 'Hegels Begriff der Erfahrung,' in his *Holzwege* (Frankfurt, 1950); *Hegel's Concept of Experience*, trans. by J. Glenn Gray (New York, 1970), provide the foundational questions concerning Hegel that Derrida pursues during the period we are here examining, 1967 through 1974.

4  For this formulation of the central intention of philosophy see 'Tympan' (M/i/x).

5  Several commentators have taken up this general question. See in particular: Rodolphe Gasché, *The Tain of the Mirror: Derrida and the Philosophy of Reflection* (Cambridge, Mass., 1986), chapters 2, 3, and 9, as well as his *Inventions of Difference: On Jacques Derrida* (Cambridge, Mass., 1994), chapters 5 and 7; Manfred Frank, *What is Neo-Structuralism?*, trans. Sabine Wilke and Richard Gray (Minneapolis, 1989), lecture 17; Gabriella Baptist and Hans-Christian Lucas, 'Wem schlägt die Stunde in Derridas Glas? Zur Hegelrezeption und -kritik Jacques Derridas,' *Hegel-Studien* 23 (1988): 139–79; Heinz Kimmerle, 'Über Derridas Hegeldeutung,' *Philosophie und Poesie: Otto Pöggeler zum 60. Geburtstag. Band I*, Annemarie Gethmann-Siefert (ed.) (Stuttgart-Bad Cannstatt, 1988); and John H. Smith, 'U-Topian Hegel: Dialectic and Its Other in Poststructuralism,' *The German Quarterly* (Spring, 1987): 237–61.

6  The structure of *reste* has continued to be a sustained theme throughout Derrida's work. Among numerous texts, see 'Tympan' (M/i-xxv), 'Signature, Event, Context' (M/365–93/307–30), *Limited Inc.*, Gerald Graff (ed.) (Evanston, Ill., 1988), *Cinders*, trans. Ned Lukacher (Lincoln, Neb., 1991), and, more recently, *Given Time: I. Counterfeit Money*, trans. Peggy Kamuf (Chicago, 1992).

7  Derrida develops this concept of identity in terms of the general structure of the remark. On this structure and its relation to Hegel's 'positive infinite' see Rodolphe Gasché's important essay, 'Nontotalization without Spuriousness: Hegel and Derrida on the Infinite,' *Journal of the British Society for Phenomenology* 17 (1986): 289–307; rpt. as 'Structural Infinity' in his *Inventions of Difference*, 129–49.

8  In his piece on Bataille's reading of Hegel, Derrida states that 'Hegel, through *precipitation*, blinded himself to that which he had laid bare under the *rubric of negativity*' (ED/381/259). The constriction of negativity, the constriction of

difference, could thus be said to constitute the 'blind spot (*tache aveugle*) of Hegelianism' (ED/380/259).

Gasché has attempted to set forth the minimal traits of the infrastructure at issue here, which he calls 're-strict-ure.' See his *Inventions of Difference*, 195–8.

9 The best general guide to *Glas*' Hegel column is Simon Critchley's 'A Commentary Upon Derrida's Reading of Hegel in *Glas*,' *Bulletin of the Hegel Society of Great Britain* 18 (1988): 6–35. See also Geoffrey Bennington's helpful discussion of several of this column's crucial passages in his 'Derridabase' in *Jacques Derrida* (Chicago, 1993), 267–316.

10 Derrida proposed a thesis on Hegel's semiology in 1967. It was carried out under the supervision of Jean Hyppolite. Part of this work was presented in Hyppolite's 1968 seminar on Hegel's *Logic* at the Collège de France. It was first published, under the title 'The Pit and the Pyramid: Introduction to Hegel's Semiology,' in the proceedings of this seminar, *Hegel et la pensée moderne* (Paris, 1971), 27–83, and was subsequently revised and published under the same title in 1972 in M/79–127/69–108.

11 For the announcement of 'a work in preparation on Hegel's family and on sexual difference in the dialectical speculative economy,' see M/89n/77n. The 1967 version of 'The Pit and the Pyramid' did not contain this interesting footnote.

Derrida presented *Glas* as a six-month seminar in Berlin in 1973–74.

12 This passage from external difference to speculative contradiction forms the central matter of concern of Jean Hyppolite's *Logique et existence* (Paris, 1952), 135–63. On this matter also see Gilles Deleuze's important review of this work published in *Revue philosophique de la France et de l'étranger* 144 (1954): 457–60.

The importance of Hyppolite's work for the development of Derrida's own thought cannot be overstated. For a discussion of its influence upon Derrida see Leonard Lawlor, *The Basic Problem of Phenomenology: A Study of Derrida's Interpretation of Husserl* (forthcoming).

13 Derrida quotes this decisive passage twice: at P/60n6/101n13 and at D/12n5/6n8.

On the concept of speculative contradiciton see Franz Grégoire, *Études Hégéliennes: Les points capitaux du système* (Louvain, 1958), 51–139.

14 For Hegel's critique of what he calls 'absolute difference' see WL/265–7/417–18.

15 This passage appears in a footnote added to the 1967 republication of 'Violence and Metaphysics: An Essay on the Thought of Emmanuel Levinas' in ED. For the original see *Revue de métaphysique et de morale* 69 nos. 3–4 (1964): 322–45, 425–73, esp. p. 470.

16 For this critique of pure difference, pure alterity, in Derrida see his readings of Levinas, Artaud, and Bataille. Perhaps the first sign of Derrida's recognition of this problematic occurs in the 1966 publication of one of the pieces on Artaud, 'Le théâtre de le cruauté et la représentation,' *Critique* 22 no. 230 (1966): 595–618. There Derrida speaks, again in a footnote, of the necessity of 'conceiving difference as original impurity, that is to say as difference in the finite economy of the same'

(ED/366n/333n20). Derrida changed '*différence*' in the 1966 version to '*différance*' for the 1967 republication of the text in ED (ED/366n/333n20).

17 Derrida discusses the necessity of distinguishing *différance* from the movement of *Aufhebung* and thus from speculative contradiction at D/12n5/6n8.

18 Hyppolite takes this sentence as the basis for his own discussion of Hegelian *Logos*; see *Logique et existence*, first part. In so doing, he follows the lead of G. R. G. Mure's *A Study of Hegel's Logic* (Oxford, 1950), 1–27. For a helpful guide to the secondary literature that has grown up around this issue see John McCumber, *The Company of Words: Hegel, Language, and Systematic Philosophy* (Evanston, Ill, 1993), esp. chapters 7 and 10.

19 The Bataillean figures of laughter and sacrifice are invoked in 'From Restricted to General Economy: A Hegelianism without Reserve' (ED/369–407/251–77), while the figure of the heliotrope appears in 'White Mythology: Metaphor in the Text of Philosophy' (M/247–324/207–71).

   The hymen, fan, and mime of Mallarmé appear in 'Double Session' (D/197–318/172–286) and the non-teleological machine comes from 'The Pit and the Pyramid.'

20 For Derrida's considerations of the problematic intertwining of discourse and *Aufhebung*, see ED/371/252–3, M/101–27/88–108, and M/308–24/258–71.

21 There is a constant play throughout *Glas'* columns based upon the assonance of the noun, *la partie* (part), and the verb, *partir* (to leave or depart). This play would allow a substantial connection to be developed between the Hegel and Genet columns around the function of the family and the flower as structures of what Derrida calls 'transcendental excrescence' (G/20b/15b); a structure disclosed through the phrases: 'the flower is (de)part(ed) (*le fleur est partie*)' (*Ibid.*), and 'how can a part take part, be party to? (*comment une partie peut-elle être prenante?*)' (*Ibid.*).

   On the function of flowers in the Genet column see Claudette Sartiliot, 'Herbarium, Verbarium: The Discourse of Flowers,' *Diacritics* (1988): 68–81. On this column's important relation to Sartre, see Christina M. Howells, 'Derrida and Sartre: Hegel's Death Knell,' in *Derrida and Deconstruction*, Hugh Silverman (ed.) (New York, 1989), 169–81.

22 Every interpretation of the *Phenomenology*, in so far as one must always in some sense isolate the moment under investigation from the encompassing movement, faces the necessary danger of reading the *Phenomenology* merely at the level of mundane description rather than as itself already the Science of the 'movement of pure essences' (PhG/28/20). It is a risk that confronts each reading of the *Phenomenology* in so far as every interpretation of this text engages in the necessary violence of extraction; as Derrida says, one indeed always enters this text 'with one blow (*d'un coup*)' (G/198/141).

23 Hegel tells us that action forces a differentiation between ethical substance and the individual insofar as substance is taken to be the *telos* of consciousness's activities. Action forces not only the moments of substance and individuality apart but likewise divides substance and consciousness within themselves; consciousness

distinguishes between its merely abstract 'individualized reality' (PhG/240/266) and its true essence as universal self-consciousness, while the ethical substance articulates itself in the tragic conflict of human and divine law. Experiencing this conflict, this 'contradiction' (PhG/241/266) of powers, self-consciousness undergoes the 'mutual destruction' (PhG/241/266) of these objectivities and thus, in and through its own going under, self-consciousness attains its truth and realizes its essential work of mediation in the universality of legal personhood. With the emergence of legal status then, the undoing of the intrinsic unity of *Sittlichkeit* is begun and *Geist* enters into self-alienation.

24 The relation of divine and human law within the sphere of *Sittlichkeit*, and more importantly the familial moment itself, are commonly interpreted in light of Hegel's theory of Greek tragedy, in particular his reading of Sophocles' *Antigone*. The present study does not wish to deny the fruitfulness of this approach, but it does seek to remain faithful to the *Phenomenology*'s own analyses, which make no reference here to this play.

On these issues and the subsequent influence of Hegel's reading see Martin Donougho, 'The Woman in White: On the Reception of Hegel's *Antigone*,' *The Owl of Minerva* 21 (1989): 65–89.

25 Hegel also refers to death as the proper lord of human beings in the discussion of lordship and bondage and in the analysis of the Unhappy Consciousness. For a discussion of these passages as well as other crucial texts see Alexandre Kojève, 'L'idée de la mort dans la philosophie de Hegel,' Appendix II of his important commentary *Introduction à la lecture de Hegel* (Paris: Gallimard, 1947), 527–73; 'The Idea of Death in the Philosophy of Hegel,' trans. Joseph J. Carpino, *Interpretation: A Journal of Political Philosophy* 3 (1973): 114–56.

26 *Bewährung* means both authentication in the sense of proving to be true and suspension in terms of legal probation. This term thus encompasses the double movement of *Aufhebung*, canceling while preserving.

27 For an excellent study of the family as presented in the *Phenomenology* see Wilfried Goosens, 'Ethical Life and Family in the *Phenomenology of Spirit*,' in *Hegel on Ethical Life, Religion, and Philosophy*, A. Wylleman (ed.) (Dordrecht, 1989), 163–94.

28 For an important study of the concept of *Anerkennung* in Hegel's thought see Robert R. Williams, *Recognition: Fichte and Hegel on the Other* (Albany, NY, 1992), esp. chapters 7–8. The discussion that follows has benefited greatly from Williams' work.

29 Hegel discusses the concept of an 'originally determinate nature' at PhG/216–19/237–41.

30 The relevant passages are however the focus of Hyppolite's important discussion of what he sees as Hegel's overcoming of the metaphysical tradition; see his *Logique et existence*, 135–63.

31 It should be noted that Hegel's discourse on the 'incest taboo' runs as a continuous thread throughout the entire course of his development, from Jena to Berlin. The analysis of the family bond in terms of *Gleichheit* informs the discussions througout.

For examples of this see Hegel's discussions of the family in his lectures on *Rechtsphilosophie* as recorded by his students: *Vorlesungen über Naturrecht und*

*Staatswissenschaft. Heidelberg 1817/1818 mit Nachträgen aus der Vorlesungen 1818/19*, C. Becker *et al.* (eds) (Hamburg, 1983); *Vorlesungen über Rechtsphilosophie. 1818–1831*, Karl-Heinz Ilting (ed.) (Stuttgart, 1974); and *Philosophie des Rechts. Die Vorlesung von 1819/20 in einer Nachschrift*, Dieter Henrich (ed.) (Frankfurt, 1983).

32 The actual performance of an action within the public realm, of course, explicitly posits the contradiction of human and divine law and self-consciousness undergoes the withdrawal of this conflict into the ground of legal right. But this withdrawal is already prepared by the withdrawal into the speculative unity of human and divine law, what Hegel terms justice, carried out in and through the union of brother and sister.

33 I want to thank John Caputo, Leonard Lawlor, and John Protevi for their comments on earlier versions of this essay.

## Chapter 11: Hegel, *Glas*, and the Broader Modernity

1 For example, see Jacques Derrida, *Writing and Difference*, trans. Alan Bass (Chicago: University of Chicago Press, 1978), 92–109, 134–53, 251–77; also *Of Grammatology*, trans. Gayatri Chakravorty Spivak (Baltimore: Johns Hopkins University Press, 1976), 6–26, 44–54, 144–64, 270–95.

2 My reference here is of course to Rodolphe Gasché's seminal study (a tongue-in-cheek predication with regard to *Glas*), *The Tain of the Mirror: Derrida and the Philosophy of Reflection* (Cambridge, Mass.: Harvard University Press, 1986). It is in this study that Gasché elaborates the infrastructures that become prominent features in Derrida's critical rethinking of key metaphysical and ontological dimensions of Western philosophy. Infrastructures are tropes that manage to evade form and formalism; philosophical constructs that never overcome the local flavor of their contexts while marking something compelling with regard to broader issues of language and representation. The supplementarity prevailing between the Hegel and Genet columns of *Glas*; the marking and remarking of ideational processes; the constriction that is both a moment of systematic closure and an aspect of textual-sexual dissemination: these are infrastructures of the sort explicitly or implicitly set into play by Gasché in *The Tain of the Mirror*. On the notion of infrastructures see 144, 147, 149, 152, 155–7, 172–5. Gasché has written brilliantly about *Glas* in 'Strictly Bonded,' in *Inventions of Difference* (Cambridge, Mass.: Harvard University Press, 1994), 171–98). Gasché suggested the infrastructural possibilities for the movement of constriction in *Glas* to me in private conversation.

3 Jacques Derrida, *Glas*, trans. John P. Leavey, Jr and Richard Rand (Lincoln: University of Nebraska Press, 1986), henceforth abbreviated '*G*.' This excellent translation includes many features for helping the reader, including the incorporation, generally between brackets, of pivotal terms in the 'original' French. In extended extracts to which I refer, I retain *the translators'* incorporations of French terms. At the end of citations, I indicate whether material derives from the left-hand, 'Hegel' column, 'a,' or its 'Genet' counterpart, 'b.'

4 I think, among others, of Nancy Armstrong's splendid recent work.

5 As will be evident below, Derrida is himself aware of the writerly implications of wounds experienced on a subjective plane but figured as cuts, scars, and so on. He addresses this issue in reading Genet's commentary upon *L'Atelier d'Alberto Giacometti* (*G*, 184–5b). I elaborate on the critical and aesthetic implications of the 'narcissistic wound' explored by object-relations psychoanalysts, such as Heinz Kohut, in *Psyche and Text: The Sublime and the Grandiose in Literature, Psychoanalysis, and Culture* (Albany: SUNY Press, 1993), 72–3, 77, 87, 180, 189–90, 194, 201, 204.

6 I begin this investigation in *Psyche and Text*, *op. cit.*, 27–43, and elaborate upon it in my forthcoming *The Aesthetic Contract: Statutes of Art and Intellectual Work in the Broader Modernity* (Stanford: Stanford University Press, 1997).

7 See Jacques Derrida, 'Parergon,' in *The Truth in Painting*, trans. Geoff Bennington and Ian McLeod (Chicago: University of Chicago Press, 1987), 17–147.

8 This above all in *The Aesthetic Contract*, *op. cit.*

9 See Henry Sussman, *Afterimages of Modernity* (Baltimore: Johns Hopkins University Press, 1990), 161–205.

10 See *Glas*, *op. cit.*, 20a, 33–4a, 36a, 52a, 76a, 97a, 162–70a, 175–6a, 187–8a, 202–3a.

11 If I am right here, that certain of Derrida's texts can be better described as tributes to sub-syllabic snips of letters than as elaborations of texts and their relation to concepts or ideas, then the rhetoric of infrastructures, as exemplified by Rodolphe Gasché, traces this ambiguity. To a certain degree, the rhetoric of infrastructures, like that of structures before it, cannot totally escape the aporia according to which consequential accounts, even of the dismantling of systems and systematicity, lapse into the ideational procedures they critique. The authoritative discourse of structures, as elaborated and exemplified by Lévi-Strauss, Barthes, and Foucault, attempted to have things both ways; played at an ambiguity in the notion of structures between their formal and substantive aspects. The discourse of infrastructures is analogously placed between a *metacritique* that would allegorically incorporate the performance of its design, and a *critique* simply adding to the available polemical thrusts within the critical literature.

12 I have characterized the complex economy by which the genetics and legitimacy of pregnancy and homosexuality are intertwined in Proust's *Recherche* in 'The Pregnant Invert,' in *The Hegelian Aftermath: Readings in Hegel, Kierkegaard, Freud, Proust, and James* (Baltimore: Johns Hopkins University Press, 1982), 221–30.

13 A figural example of the concentration that can be embodied within textual 'objects' is the cone of Jorge Luis Borges's 'Tlön, Uqbar, Orbis Tertius,' a tiny metallic thing so heavy and concentrated that a full-grown man can barely lift it. See Borges, *Ficciones* (New York: Grove Press, 1962), 33. I discuss it in *Afterimages of Modernity*, *op. cit.*, 143–48.

# Select Bibliography

Bahti, Timothy. (1992) *Allegories of History: Literary Historiography After Hegel*. Baltimore: Johns Hopkins University Press.

—— (1981) 'The Indifferent Reader: The Peformance of Hegel's Introduction to the *Phenomenology*.' *Diacritics* 11.2: 68–82.

Baptist, Gabriella and Hans-Christian Lucas. (1988) 'Wem Schlägt die Stunde in Derrida's *Glas*: Zur Hegelrezeption und -kritik Jacques Derridas.' *Hegel-Studien* 23: 139–179.

Bataille, Georges. (1990) 'Hegel, Death and Sacrifice,' trans. Jonathan Strauss, *Yale French Studies* 78: 9–28.

Bennington, Geoffrey. (1992) 'The Frontier: Between Kant and Hegel.' *Enlightenments: Encounters Between Critical Theory and Contemporary French Thought*, Harry Kunneman and Hent de Vries (eds) Kampen, the Netherlands: Kok Pharus, 45–60.

Berezdivin, Ruben. (1978) 'Gloves: Inside-Out,' *Research in Phenomenology*. 8: 111–126.

Briel, Holger. (1992) 'Derridas Hyperkarte: *Glas*.' *Weimarer Beiträge* 38: 485–505.

Butler, Judith. (1987) *Subjects of Desire: Hegelian Reflections on Twentieth-Century France*, New York: Columbia University Press.

Chase, Cynthia. (1983) 'Getting Versed: Reading Hegel with Baudelaire.' *Studies in Romanticism* 22.2: 241–266.

Chaffin, Deborah. (1989) 'Hegel, Derrida, and the Sign.' *Derrida and Deconstruction*, Hugh Silverman (ed.). New York: Routledge, 77–91.

Clark, Timothy. (1985) 'Hegel in Suspense – Derrida/Hegel and the Question of Prefaces.' *Philosophy* 29: 122–134.

Corn, Tony. (1985) 'La Negativité sans emploi: Derrida, Bataille, Hegel' *Romanic Review* 76.1: 65–75.

Cornell, Drucilla. (1992) *The Philosophy of the Limit*. New York: Routledge.

Cresap, Steven. (1985) 'Hegel as Deconstructor.' *CLIO* 14.4: 407–422.

Cutrofello, Andrew. (1991) 'A Critique Derrida's Hegel Deconstruction: Speech, Phonetic Writing, and Hieroglyphic Script in Logic, Law, Art' *Clio* 20: 123–137.

De Man, Paul. (1982) 'Sign and Symbol in Hegel's Aesthetics.' *Critical Inquiry* 8.4: 761–775.

—— (1983) 'Hegel on the Sublime.' *Displacement: Derrida and After*, Mark Krupnick (ed.) Bloomington: Indiana University Press.

Derrida, Jacques. (1986) 'The Age of Hegel,' trans. Susan Winnet. *Demarcating the Disciplines: Philosophy, Literature, Art*, Samuel Weber (ed.) Minneapolis: University of Minnesota Press, 3–35.

—— (1978) 'From Restricted to General Economy: A Hegelianism Without Reserve' *Writing and Difference*. Trans. Alan Bass, Chicago: University of Chicago Press.

—— (1986) *Glas*. Trans. John P. Leavey, Jr., and Richard Rand. Lincoln: University of Nebraska Press.

—— (1982) 'The Pit and the Pyramid: Introduction to Hegel's Semiology.' *Margins of Philosophy*. Trans. Alan Bass. Chicago: University of Chicago Press, 69–108.

—— (1981) *Positions*. Trans. Alan Bass. Chicago: University of Chicago Press.

—— (1986) 'Proverb: 'He that would pun . . . ' In John P. Leavey, Jr., *Glassary*. Lincoln: University of Nebraska Press, 17–20.

Desmond, William. (1986) *Art and the Absolute: A Study of Hegel's Aesthetics*. Albany: SUNY Press.

—— (1985) 'Hegel, Dialectic, and Deconstruction.' *Philosophy and Rhetoric* 18.4: 244–263.

Donougho, Martin. (1982) 'The Semiotics of Hegel.' *Clio* 11.4: 415–430.

Gasché, Rodolphe. (1994) *Inventions of Difference: On Jacques Derrida*. Cambridge: Harvard University Press.

—— (1986) 'Non-Totalization Without Spuriousness: Hegel and Derrida On the Infinite.' *Journal of the British Society for Phenomenology* 17: 289–307.

—— (1986) *The Tain of the Mirror: Derrida and the Philosophy of Reflection*. Cambridge: Harvard University Press.

Gearhart, Suzanne. (1986) 'The Dialectic and Its Other: Hegel and Diderot.' *MLN* 101: 1042–1066.

Goldford, Dennis J. (1982) 'Kojève's Reading of Hegel.' *International Philosophical Quarterly* 22: 275–294.

Hamacher, Werner. (1978) 'pleroma: Zu Genesis und Struktur einer dialektischen. Hermeneutik bei Hegel.' *Der Geist des Christentums*. Frankfurt am Main: Ullstein. (Translation forthcoming from Stanford University Press.)

—— (1981) 'The Reader's Supper: A Piece of Hegel.' Trans. Timothy Bahti. *Diacritics* 11: 52–67.

Hartman, Geoffrey. (1981) *Saving the Text: Literature, Derrida, Philosophy*. Baltimore: Johns Hopkins University Press.

Harvey, Irene E. (1982) 'The Linguistic Basis of Truth for Hegel.' *Man and World* 15: 285–297.

Heckman, John. (1974) 'Introduction.' In Jean Hyppolite, *Genesis and Structure of Hegel's Phenomenology*, trans. Samuel Cherniak and John Heckman. Evanston: Northwestern University Press, xv-xli.

Heidegger, Martin. (1980) 'A Heidegger Seminar on Hegel's *Differenzschrift*' *Southwest Journal of Philosophy* 11: 9–45.

—— (1990) 'Colloqium über Dialektik.' *Hegel-Studien* 25: 9–23.

Hofstadter, Albert. (1975) 'Ownness and Identity: Rethinking Hegel' *Review of Metaphysics* 28: 681–697.

Howells, Christina. (1989) 'Derrida and Sartre: Hegel's Death Knell' *Derrida and Deconstruction*. Hugh Silverman (ed.). New York: Routledge, 169–181.

Janicaud, Dominique. (1976) 'Recent French Hegel Scholarship' *Owl of Minerva* 7: 1–4.

Jamme, Christoph. (1988) "Allegory of Disjunction: 'Zur dekonstruktivistischen Lektüre Hegels und Hölderlins in Amerika.'" *Hegel-Studien* 23: 181–204.

Kelly, Michael. (1986) 'Hegel in France Today: A Bibliographical Essay' *Journal of European Studies* 64: 249–270.

—— (1983) 'The Post-war Hegel Revival in France: A Bibliographical Essay' *Journal of European Studies* 13: 199–216.

Kimmerle, Heinz. (1981) 'Umkehrung, Dekonstruktion, Pragmatisierung' *Zeitschrift für Philosophische Forschung* 35: 417–424.

Kolb, David. (1987) *The Critique of Pure Modernity: Hegel, Heidegger, and After*. Chicago: University of Chicago Press.

Krell, David Farrell. (1981) 'Results.' *Monist* 64: 467–480.

Leavey, John P., Jr. (1982) 'Jacques Derrida's *Glas*: A Translated Selection and Some Comments on an Absent Colossus' *Clio* 11: 327–337.

—— (1986) Glassary. Lincoln: University of Nebraska Press.

Llewelyn, John. (1987) 'A Point of Almost Absolute Proximity to Hegel' *Deconstruction and Philosophy: The Texts of Jacques Derrida*. John Sallis (ed.). Chicago: University of Chicago Press.

—— (1985) 'Thresholds.' *Derrida and differance*. Robert Bernasconi and David Wood (eds). Evanston: Northwestern University Press.

Marsh, James. (1990) 'The Play of Difference/Differance in Hegel and Derrida' *The Owl of Minerva* 21: 145–153.

Nancy, Jean-Luc. (1973) *La remarque spéculative*. Paris: Galilée.

—— (1993) 'The Jurisdiction of the Hegelian Monarch' *The Birth to Presence*. Trans. Mary Ann and Peter Caws. Stanford: Stanford University Press.

Newmark, Kevin. (1983) 'Between Hegel and Kierkegaard: The Space of Translation' *Genre* 16.4: 373–387.

Plotnitsky, Arkady. (1993) *In the Shadow of Hegel: Complementarity, History and the Unconscious*. Gainsville: University of Florida Press.

—— (1986) 'The Historical Unconscious: In the Shadow of Hegel' in Gary Saul Morrison, (ed.) *Literature and History: Theoretical Problems and Russian Case Studies*. Palo Alto: Stanford University Press, 157–175.

Pöggeler, Otto. (1970) 'Hegel und die Anfänge der Nihilismus-Diskussion' *Man World* 3: 163–199.

—— (1974) 'Philosophy in the Wake of Hölderlin.' *Man World*. 7: 158–176.

Poster, Mark. (1975) *Existential Marxism In Postwar France: From Sartre to Althusser*. Princeton: Princeton University Press.

Riley, Patrick. (1981) 'Introduction to the Reading of Alexandre Kojève' *Political Theory* 9: 5–48.

Roth, Michael S. (1988) *Knowing and History: Appropriations of Hegel in Twentieth-Century France*. Ithaca: Cornell University Press.

Rühle, Volker. (1993) 'Spekulation und Dekonstruktion: Die Darstellbarkeit von Negativität im Blick auf Hegel und Derrida' *Philosophisches Jahrbuch* 100 22–38.

Sallis, John. (1987) 'Ending(s) – Imagination, Presentation, Spirit' *Spacings – Of Reason and Imagination in Texts of Kant, Fichte, Hegel*. Chicago: University of Chicago Press, 132–158.

Sartilot, Claudette. (1989) 'Telepathy and Writing in Jacques Derrida's *Glas*' *Paragraph* 12: 214–228.

Schmidt, Dennis. (1982) 'Between Hegel and Heidegger.' *Man World* 15: 17–32.

—— (1988) *The Ubiquity of the Finite: Hegel, Heidegger, and the Entitlements of Philosophy* Cambridge: MIT Press.

Smith, John H. (1987) 'U-Topian Hegel: Dialectics and Its Other in Poststructuralism' *The German Quarterly* 60.2: 237–261.

Stambaugh, Joan. (1974) 'Time and Dialectic in Hegel and Heidegger' *Research in Phenomenology*. 4: 87–97.

Smith, Christopher P. (1971) 'Heidegger's Critique of Absolute Knowledge' *The New Scholasticism* 45: 56–86.

Stoekl, Allan. (1988) 'Hegel's Return.' *Stanford French Review*. 12.1: 119–128.

Sussman, Henry. (1982) *The Hegelian Aftermath*. Baltimore: Johns Hopkins University Press.

—— (1982) 'The Metaphor in Hegel's *Phenomenology of Mind*' *CLIO* 11.4: 361–386.

Taylor, Mark. (1986) 'Introduction: System . . . Structure . . . Difference . . . Other' *Deconstruction in Context: Literature and Philosophy*. Mark Taylor (ed.). Chicago: University of Chicago Press.

Warminski, Andrzej. (1987) *Readings in Interpretation: Hölderlin, Hegel, Heidegger*. Minneapolis: University of Minnesota Press.

# Index

Absolute 5, 9, 223

Absolute Knowledge 158, 213, 215–17, 220, 222, 224; and Christianity 205

Absolute Religion 215

Adorno 229, 230–1, 322n

Africa 28–9; and cannibalism 56; and colonialism 59, 62–3; and Egypt 43; and fetishism 53–4, 144; and human sacrifice 49–50; and Kant 51; and religion 52–3; and *Sinnlichkeit* 52, 56; and slavery 55–8; and travel literature 44–5; and world history 41–51; as unhistorical 42, 60–1; division of by Hegel 43; Hegel's treatment of 42, 50

Althusser 192, 297n, 329n

America, and slavery 56

Analytic philosophy, affinity with idealism 8–13; and empiricism 8

Antigone 32, 75–6, 78, 161, 166, 207, 221, 235; and femininity 168; and psychoanalysis 165; and *Sittlichkeit* 209–10; as bad girl 263; as critic of phallocentrism 148; as figure of the process of repression/idealization 165–6; contrasted to *Oedipus Rex* 169; death of 210; Derrida's exclusive attention to 313n

anti-Hegelianism 21–2

Aristotle 93, 96, 122

art, and irony 106; end of 105, 107, 120–4, 126–7, 129

art-religion 105, 107–8, 125, 127, 129

Ashanti 28, 41, 45; and cannibalism 46; and funeral customs 47–8; and human sacrifice 49–50

*Aufhebung* 31–2, 228, 231, 240, 242, 247, 259; affinity to *différance* 239; and Bataille 229–30; and *différance* 26, 239; and family 244; and Last Supper 140; and phallocentrism 149; and repression 154, 156–9; and restriction 156; and structuralism 27; and Trinity 237; and truth 84; as tainted with false sense of harmony 88; structure of 235

Avinieri, Shlomo 44

Barthes, Roland 21–2

Bataille, Georges 22, 34, 185, 227, 277; interpretation of Hegel 228; on *Aufhebung* 229–30

Beethoven, Ludwig van 104

being, event of 95

Benjamin, Walter 321n

Bernasconi, Robert 28–9

Bourgeois, Bernard 198, 300n

Bowdich, T. E. 44–5, 49–50, 60, 304n; on cannibalism 46–7; on funeral customs 47–8

351

brother and sister bond 248, 257; and
mutual recognition 250, 254–5; and
recognition 208; and sexual difference
254–5; and *Sittlichkeit* 249; as asexual
162; as speculative contradiction 256

Canguilhem, Georges 13–14
cannibalism 46–7, 56
Carnap, Rudolf 294n
castration 167–8, 282
Christ, and Dionysus 222; *see* Jesus
Christianity 133–5, 137, 141–4; and
absolute knowledge 205
colonialism, Hegel's understanding of 59,
62–3
communion, as reading 143
concept, law of 136; logic of 92
consciousness, abstract 128; and action
110; and language 109; as comic 122,
126; as ideology 189; of loss 113;
transition to self-consciousness 176
constriction 277–8
contra-band 258–259
Critchley, Simon 33–34, 36
cum, and writing 286

Dahomey 304n
deconstruction, and avoidance of will 29,
64; and ethics 33–4; contrapuntal
nature of 265; enabled by Hegel 27;
future of 191, 193; Hegel's importance
to 26
Deleuze, Gilles 99
de Man, Paul 25, 186; and ideology 322n
Derrida, Jacques, and Africa 28–9; and
Antigone 166, 207–10; and equation of
*Geist* and will 67; and femininity 326n;
and flowers 281–3; and Gadamer
309n; and Kant 214; and marriage
212; and politics of will 70; and
pyschoanalysis 154; and repression
150; and Schelling 70, 72–3; and
signature 289, 291; and subjectivity
70; Hegel's transcendental will in 64;

on Antigone as critic of phallocentrism
148; on castration 167–8; on fetish as
model of repression 167; on *Geist* 65;
on Hegel's flower religion 218; *works*:
*Feu la cendre* 216; *Of Grammatology*
26–7; *Of Spirit* 64, 67–8; *Positions* 26;
*The Other Heading* 28; *The Post Card*
227; see *Glas*
desire 16, 177, 248, 250, and slave 17
*différance* 240, and *Aufhebung* 26, 239; and
negation 242; constriction of 251
difference, as diversity 253, 257
discourse 18; as suicide of man 19, 22
Dufrenne, Mikel 13–14

ethics, and deconstruction 33–4; and
Kant 133–4; of singular 211, 221
event 219, 221; and being 95; and leap
101; as happening 97; of time 99;
surprise of 96–7, 102

family, and *Aufhebung* 244; and filiation
202; and *Geist* 244; and labor 234; and
phallocentrism 163; and repression
159; and *Sittlichkeit* 75, 199, 201–2;
and transition to civil society 77; and
Trinity 235; as master trope 265; as
problematic hinge in Hegel 200;
centrality to *Glas* 75; dissolution of 74,
77–80, 268; syllogistic structure of
199
femininity, and mourning 207, 235
fetish 50
fetishism 150, 153; and *Glas* 325–6n;
African 50, 54; Freudian 149; sources
on African 44–5, 53
Feuerbach, Ludwig 114, 172, 212–13
Feyerabend, Paul 10–11; 295n; 295–6n
Findlay, Joseph 6
Forbes, Duncan 42
Foucault, Michel 15, 22–5; on
Hegelianism 2–3
France, anti-Hegelianism in 21–2;
reception of Hegel 13–26

Frege, Gottlob 8, 295n
Freud, Sigmund, and castration 151, 153; and penis envy 151–3; and repression 151–2; 154; relation to Hegel 153; *works: Interpretation of Dreams* 151–2; *Civilization and Its Discontents* 160–3

Gadamer, H. G. 309n
Gasché, Rodolphe 277, 344n, 345n; influence of 298n
Gearhart, Suzanne 31–2
Geertz, Clifford 83, 315n
*Geist* 68, 251, 257–9; and death 84; and family 244; and will 73; as consciousness apart 174; as law 246–7; Derrida on 65; ghost in 73; Heidegger and 68–9; self-relation of 250, 252–3
Genet 207, 222, 223, 263, 265, 269, 274, 277, 280, 282, 285, 289; and anti-Semitism 204; and flowers 234; and postmodernism 279; and Sartre 204, 212; *works: Funeral Rites* 211; *Our Lady of the Flowers* 290
*Geschichte*, as happening 94
Gibson, William 325n
gift 218, 220–1, 277
*Glas* 26–8, 31, 33, 35–6, 278; and affirmation of Western values 265; and fetishism 325–6n; and *Finnegans Wake* 269; and Heidegger 219; and modernity 35–6; and Proust 281, 286; and psychoanalysis 170; and repression 150, 159; and sexual ideology 282; and the history of western culture 260; architecture of 263, 284; as psychoanalysis 147; radical splitting in 269–70; typography of 27, 33
Goethe 234
grapheme 262, 284–5

Habermas, Jürgen 336n
Hamacher, Werner 30–1
Harris, H. S. 63, 132

Hartman, Geoffrey 27, 298n
Hegel, G. W. F., and Anglo-American philosophy 6–7, 9; and art 272; and Ashanti 41 45–7; and Christ 128; and Christianity 202–3, 205; and christo-ontology 129; and comedy 106, 114, 117; and death 121; and division of Africa 43; and end of art 105, 107; and epic 107; and flower religion 222; and Heidegger 318–19n; and history 93; and irony 105–6, 118–19, 123; and Judaism 134, 202–3; and justification of slavery 58, 307n; and Kant 155; and Mary Magdalene 141–2; and Marx 171; and Marxism 20, 25; and metaphor of light 275; and modernity 93; and Nietzsche 21; and phallocentrism 149, 206; and postmodernism 2–3; and repression 153–4; and role of art 273; and Romantics 123; and self-consciousness 20; and task of deconstruction 26; and testaments, 80–1; and tragedy 109; and will 64, 84, 88–9, 271; as divided against himself 191; as materialist 187; as phallocentric 161; as philosopher of the will 88; assessment of Christianity 142; critique of Kant 213, 223; importance to deconstruction 26–7; on clitoris 206; on colonialism in Africa 59; on family as *Aufhebung* 155, 205; on incest taboo 343n; on Jews 203; on Last Supper 137; on Schlegel 123–4; on *Sinnlichkeit* of Africans 59; on slavery 55; on the Dahomey 47; on transition from family to civil society 74; racism of 300n, 305n, 307n; reception in England and U.S. 5–13; reception in France 13–26; relation to Freud 153; use of Bowdich 46–7; use of sources on Africa 43–5, 50; *works: Encyclopedia* 20–1; 51, 69, 213, 229, 236; *Lectures on Aesthetics* 121–2, 222; *Lectures on the Philosophy of History* 28,

53, 58, 92; *Lectures on the Philosophy of Religion* 45, 53–4, 213, 217; *Lectures on the Philosophy of World History* 41–2, 50–1, 53, 55, 63, 201; *Phenomenology of Spirit* 20, 24, 30, 83, 105, 114, 129, 176, 180, 183, 188, 190, 207, 216, 223, 228, 231, 235, 244–5, 257; *Philosophy of Nature* 157, 206, 222; *Philosophy of Right* 34, 55, 58–9, 62–3, 65, 67, 74, 76, 82–3, 199, 212, 234; *Science of Logic* 30, 91–2, 238, 242, 245; *The Spirit of Christianity* 31, 131, 132, 202, 233, 271

Heidegger, Martin 218, 310n; and Derrida 318–19n; and *Geist* 64, 67–9; and *Glas* 219–20; and Schelling 71, 311n

Hesse, Mary 10

holocaust 221–2, 276, 290–1, 337n

Holy Family 205

Hösle, Vittorio 315n

Husserl, Edmund 66, 154

Idealism, and analytic philosophy 8–13

irony 105, 118–19; and art 166; and Schlegel 123; as ethical discourse 211

Jesus 31, 237; and love 135; and Trinity 236; as love 139–40; as signifier 141; death of 140–1; separates self from society 134; see Christ

Kafka, Franz 37

Kant, Immanuel 13, 92, 97, 273, 274, 292, 313n, 316n; and Africa 51; and Derrida 214; and ethics 133–4; and Judaism 133; and phallocentrism 206–7; and postmodernism 4, and role of artist 271, 272; as Jew 213

Kantianism, as Judaism 213

Kimmerle, Heinz 33, 34

*King Lear* 80, 314n

*Klang* 263–4, 267, 269, 278, 279, 281

Kofman, Sarah 148, 154, 168; and

fetishism 146, 325–6n; and infantile narcissism 326n; deconstructs fetishism 153

Kojève, Alexandre 14–25; and anti-Hegelianism 21; and comedy 322–3n; and discourse 18; and Foucault 23–4; as romantic idealist 333n; on desire 16, 297n; on master/slave 15–17, 25, 229; on recognition 16; on the sign 18; on wise man 24

Koyré, Alexandre 13–14

Kuhn, Thomas 10

labor, of family 234; of slave 17; of spirit 235

Lacan, Jacques 278, 311–12n, 316–7n; on castration 168; on connection between repression and death drive 164; on the phallus 187

language, of action 110, 113; violation of 137

Laplanche, Jean 158

Last Supper 137; and *Aufhebung* 140; and love 138, 233; and reading 143; and signifiers 139

Lenin, V. I. 19

*Lichtwesen* 216–17, 220

life, as object of self consciousness 181; as self-negating 181–2

logocentrism 261

love, and family 249; and Jesus 135, 137; and *Last Supper* 138; as communal 139, 142; as spirit 142; command of 137; spiritualization of 233

Lukács, Georg 19

Magdalene, Mary 141–2, 233

Mallarmé, Stéphane 243

Marx, Karl 17, 114; and labor 232; critique of Feuerbach 172, 212; relation to Hegel 171, 173; *works*: *Economic and Philosophical Manuscripts* 176, 212; *The German Ideology* 171–2, 174

master/slave 17, 20, 22–4
Mauss, Marcel 231
modernity 260, 262, 270–1, 273, 279, 284, 292; and *Glas* 35; Lyotard's understanding of 4–5
Moore 7–8

Nancy, Jean-Luc 22, 29–30
negation, teleological constriction of 243
negativity, and surprise of event 102; positivity of 100
Nietzsche, Friedrich 21, 87, 223, 280, 284, 309n, 317n, 336n

*Oedipus Rex* 166; contrasted to *Antigone* 169
onto-theology 26, 218
ordinary language philosophy 9

Parmenides 104
*parousia* 26, 215, 241, 251
phallocentrism 148, 163, 207
Pontalis, J. B. 158
Popper, Karl 6; on Hegel 293n
post-Enlightenment 264
postmodernism 12; and Genet 279; and Hegel 2, 3, 25; and Kant 4
*prosopon* 115, 116, 124, 320n
psychoanalysis, 147, 149, 153–4, 165; and Antigone 165

Quine, W. V. O. 8, 294n

recognition 16, 248, 250; and *Sittlichkeit* 249
remains, marked by diversity 258
repression, and *Aufhebung* 156–9; and death drive 164; and dialectics 156–7; and dream work 152; and fetish 168; and idealization 168; and *Sittlichkeit* 212; differentiation of 327n; relation to desire 160; utility of 264
Rorty, Richard 10, 11–12; and

postmodernism 12; and reception of Hegel 293–4n
Russell, Bertrand 6–9; and Kant 294n; and monism 294–5n; external relations 7; theory of description 7–8

Sartre, Jean-Paul 20–1; and Genet, 204, 212, 297–8n
Schelling F. W. J. 139, 234; and Derrida 70, 72–3; and Heidegger 71, 311n; and will 71
schematism 102–3
Schlegel, Friedrich, and irony 123
self, as mask 114–16
self-consciousness 20; and death 120; and forgetting 113; and otherness 180; as comic 117–18; as death 185; as desire 178–9; performative action of 111
semen 286; as textual glue 287
sense-certainty 216
sexual difference 252
*Sittlichkeit* 21, 34, 223; and Antigone 209–10; and brother/sister bond 249; and death 163; and exclusion of woman 161; and family 75, 199, 201–2; and homosexuality 207; and recognition 249; and repression 212; and will 78, 82–4; as constellation of will 65; emergence of 206
slavery 28, 55–8, 306n; Hegel's justification of 58
Smith, John H. 29
spirit, and Antigone 210; as filiation 202; dependent upon exclusions 201; labor of 232, 235; wanting of 71, 89; see *Geist*
structuralism 21, 27
Sussman, Henry 2, 35–6

teleology 243
Thompson, Kevin 33, 35–6
time, and event 98; annulment of 237; emptiness of 98–9
tragedy 110, 314n

Trinity, and *Aufhebung* 237; and Jesus 236

Wahl, Jean 13–14
Warminski, Andrzej 32–3, 36
will, and *Geist* 73; and non-dualistic

politics 70; and Schelling 71; and
*Sittlichkeit* 78, 82–4; and politics 65;
and *Willkür* 86; as action 85, 87; as
order and arbitrariness 81; as wanting
89; lack of purity of 85